# THE COURTS AND EDUCATION

# THE COURTS AND EDUCATION

## The Seventy-seventh Yearbook of the National Society for the Study of Education

### PART I

*Edited by*

CLIFFORD P. HOOKER

*Editor for the Society*

KENNETH J. REHAGE

19 | NSSE | 78

*Distributed by* THE UNIVERSITY OF CHICAGO PRESS • CHICAGO, ILLINOIS

## The National Society for the Study of Education

The purposes of the Society are to carry on investigations of educational problems and to publish the results of these investigations as a means of promoting informed discussion of important educational issues.

The two volumes of the seventy-seventh yearbook (Part I: *The Courts and Education* and Part II: *Education and the Brain*) continue the well-established tradition, now in its seventy-eighth year, of serious effort to provide scholarly and readable materials for those interested in the thoughtful study of educational matters. The yearbook series is planned to include at least one volume each year of general interest to all educators, while the second volume tends to be somewhat more specialized.

A complete list of the Society's past publications, including the yearbooks and the recently inaugurated series of paperbacks on Contemporary Educational Issues, will be found in the back pages of this volume.

It is the responsibility of the Board of Directors of the Society to select the subjects to be treated in the yearbooks, to appoint committees whose personnel are expected to insure consideration of all significant points of view, to provide for necessary expenses in connection with the preparation of the yearbooks, to publish and distribute the committees' reports, and to arrange for their discussion at the annual meeting. The editor for the Society is responsible for preparing the submitted manuscripts for publication in accordance with the principles and regulations approved by the Board of Directors.

Neither the Board of Directors, nor the Society's editor, nor the Society is responsible for the conclusions reached or the opinions expressed by the Society's yearbook committees.

All persons sharing an interest in the Society's purposes are invited to join. Regular members receive both volumes of the current yearbook. Those taking out the "comprehensive" membership receive the yearbook volumes and the volumes in the current series of paperbacks. Inquiries regarding membership may be addressed to the Secretary, NSSE, 5835 Kimbark Avenue, Chicago, Illinois 60637.

Library of Congress Catalog Number: 77-15768

*Published 1978 by*

THE NATIONAL SOCIETY FOR THE STUDY OF EDUCATION

5835 Kimbark Avenue, Chicago, Illinois 60637

Copyright, 1978, by KENNETH J. REHAGE, Secretary

First Printing, 9,000 Copies

*Printed in the United States of America*

# Officers of the Society
## 1977-78
*(Term of office expires March 1 of the year indicated.)*

N. L. GAGE

(1979)
*Stanford University*
*Stanford, California*


JACOB W. GETZELS

(1978)
*University of Chicago, Chicago, Illinois*


JOHN I. GOODLAD

(1980)
*University of California, Los Angeles, California*


A. HARRY PASSOW

(1978)
*Teachers College, Columbia University, New York, New York*


KENNETH J. REHAGE

*(Ex-officio)*
*University of Chicago, Chicago, Illinois*


HAROLD G. SHANE

(1979)
*Indiana University*
*Bloomington, Indiana*


RALPH W. TYLER

(1980)
*Director Emeritus, Center for Advanced Study in the Behavioral Sciences*
*Stanford, California*

## Secretary-Treasurer
KENNETH J. REHAGE
*5835 Kimbark Avenue, Chicago, Illinois 60637*

v

# Contributors to the Yearbook

CLIFFORD P. HOOKER

(Editor)
Professor of Educational Administration
University of Minnesota
St. Paul, Minnesota


DAVID A. ABEL

Director of Programs and Training
Coro Foundation
Los Angeles, California


ALAN ABESON

Associate Director, State and Local Governmental Relations
Council for Exceptional Children
Reston, Virginia


LINDSAY A. CONNER

Law Student, Harvard University
Cambridge, Massachusetts


LUVERN L. CUNNINGHAM

Professor of Educational Administration
The Ohio State University
Columbus, Ohio


DONALD A. ERICKSON

Director, Center for Research on Private Education
University of San Francisco
San Francisco, California


KELLY FRELS

Attorney, Houston Independent School District
Houston, Texas


WILLIAM M. GORDON

Professor of Education
Miami University
Oxford, Ohio

CONTRIBUTORS

### H. C. HUDGINS, JR.

*Professor of Educational Administration*
*Temple University*
*Philadelphia, Pennsylvania*

### LARRY W. HUGHES

*Professor of Education*
*Chairman, Department of Administration and Supervision*
*University of Houston*
*Houston, Texas*

### ROBERT A. KOENIG

*Adjunct Professor, University of Minnesota*
*Minister, First United Presbyterian Church*
*Chippewa Falls, Wisconsin*

### DAVID C. LONG

*Director, School Finance Reform Project*
*Lawyer's Committee for Civil Rights under Law*
*Washington, D.C.*

### RALPH D. MAWDSLEY

*Attorney*
*Adjunct Professor, University of Minnesota*
*Minneapolis, Minnesota*

### MARION A. MC GHEHEY

*Executive Secretary, National Organization on Legal Problems of Education*
*Executive Director, Kansas Association of School Boards*
*Topeka, Kansas*

### VIRGINIA DAVIS NORDIN

*Professor of Law and Higher Education*
*University of Wisconsin*
*Madison, Wisconsin*

### RAPHAEL O. NYSTRAND

*Professor of Education*
*Chairperson, Academic Faculty of Educational Administration*
*The Ohio State University*
*Columbus, Ohio*

ANN RYAN ROBERTSON

*Attorney*
*Tenneco, Incorporated*
*Houston, Texas*

W. FREDERICK STAUB

*Professor of Education*
*The Ohio State University*
*Columbus, Ohio*

JEFFREY J. ZETTEL

*Educational Specialist, Federal Governmental Relations*
*Council for Exceptional Children*
*Reston, Virginia*

# Foreword

The Board of Directors of the National Society for the Study of Education first considered a volume on the law and education in 1973. Authorization for the preparation of the volume was given in 1974. Discussions of the role and function of the courts with respect to education, especially regarding educational policy, were then on the increase. The desegregation of northern and western school districts escalated the visibility of the courts as policy makers. So did the litigation regarding equity in school finance, testing, corporal punishment, privacy, censorship, collective bargaining, compulsory attendance, and nonpublic schools.

The issues of educational policy confronting the judicial system arose in some instances out of deeply embedded philosophical differences. The courts were being called upon for clarification and resolution. The use of public funds for nonpublic schools was one example. The determination of who can and who cannot attend schools and colleges was another. Affirmative action, Title IX of the Elementary and Secondary Education Act, and Public Law 94-142 emerged from executive and legislative sources and each stimulated a new flow of judicial attention. In fact, a new dependency seemed to be emerging. At local, state, and federal levels, the functioning of executive and legislative branches appeared to be less and less able to respond to challenges to the traditional expectations for educational management and governance. The local, state, and federal courts were processing more and more actions ranging from injunctions against work stoppages and strikes to school desegregation cases anchored in the Fourteenth Amendment. The costs of litigation were rising, the sluggishness of judicial processes was disturbing, the impact of decisions was far-reaching, the conventional processes of educational policy development were threatened.

It was a recognition of this climate and context that led the NSSE board to approve this volume and led also to the choice of Clifford Hooker as the editor. Professor Hooker has had extensive experience as a teacher, an educational administrator, and a professor of educational administration. At the University of Minnesota he has worked intensively in the areas of educational finance and school law. In recent years, he has been called upon by many federal courts as an expert witness in school desegregation cases. He is one of the few persons who blends teaching and administrative experience in the public schools with academic interests in education and law. His knowledge of constitutional principles and judicial issues as well as his understanding of teaching and learning, of educational systems, and of administration are reflected in the preparation of the yearbook.

The society intended this yearbook to reflect especially the interests of teachers, administrators, and other professionals as well as school board members and other citizens. Thus it is written with the needs of people in the field in mind, respecting simultaneously the concerns of academicians from law and education.

Experience of the last two decades has brought into focus tensions between and among the legislative, executive, and judicial divisions of local, state, and federal governments. The power of the presidency and the importance of the Congress have been topics of traditional as well as contemporary concern. So it is with governors and legislatures, as well as with school superintendents and boards of education. Increasingly, the judiciary is assuming a prominence not only in adjudication but also in policy (traditionally the province of the Congress, legislatures, and boards of education) and in administration (traditionally the province of presidents, governors, and school superintendents.)

The freedom of school officials to establish and sustain neighborhood schools and to administer pupil assignments has been affected by the courts in dozens of school districts. As a consequence school board members and administrators often harbor deep resentments toward the courts. The judicial system is both the symbol and the object of growing discontent. The increasing incidence of court resolutions of what in the past were administrative problems reflects negatively upon the performance of administrators. Similarly, the modification, substitution, or assertion of new educational policy by the courts at local, state, and federal levels rankles policy makers.

Desegregation and school finance cases are among the most

upsetting to school board members and administrators. As indicated earlier, who, where, and under what conditions persons attend school, as well as the specification of educational programs and levels of financial support, have been the responsibilities of legislatures, state and local boards of education, and school administrators. Invoking principles of equity and justice, a legion of challengers have questioned legislatively produced policies and the administration of them. In most school desegregation cases local school districts (and more recently at least one state) have been found liable for establishing and perpetuating segregated schools. Such circumstances are not expected to increase the affection of one division of government for another.

The widely held beliefs regarding local control of education complicate attempts to fix responsibility between and among divisions of government. Those beliefs add a vertical dimension to a horizontal problem. Local control for some has become a right or a privilege to be defended vigorously. For others, it provides a convenient opportunity to redirect an argument or avoid responsibility. The unending references to local control in the media and discussions of educational authority among the professionals and laymen give credence to the assumption that there is local control and dulls the realization that in each of the fifty states education is a state responsibility. The states in their wisdom have chosen to create school districts and provide for school boards or for other forms of trusteeship. But none of the states has given over control of schooling to local jurisdictions. Responsibility remains with the state, for example, for determining how schools are to be financed and for ensuring that compliance with the federal constitution is achieved.

At this writing, levels and divisions of government in the state of Ohio are wrestling with the horizontal and vertical dimensions of authority over and responsibility for public schooling. Two federal district judges, in separate suits, found the Ohio State Board of Education and the Ohio State Superintendent liable for school segregation along with two local school districts, Cleveland and Columbus. In each city the findings of liability and the remedies proposed were appealed. Meanwhile, an intense struggle is taking shape.

The questions of responsibility and control were occasioned

initially in the findings of shared liability for segregated schooling. Subsequently, the two districts involved raised the question of whether the state of Ohio was to pay for school buses and other clearly defined costs of desegregating the schools of these two large districts. In responding to the findings of the federal court that the state was liable, the Ohio State Board of Education agreed to pay for approximately 80 percent of the costs of pupil transportation to achieve desegregation. The issue then came before the State Controlling Board in the form of a request for funds needed to meet the state's liabilities.

The State Controlling Board has not yet acted but media reports indicate a reluctance among its members to authorize such monies. Their argument is that the Ohio legislature must first approve the use of state monies for transportation to desegregate the schools. Key leaders in the legislature are saying that the costs of such transportation ought to be the responsibility of local districts, not the state.

In a separate but related action the same federal court in Cleveland has intervened and ordered the poverty stricken (but still segregated) Cleveland Public Schools to remain open despite the absence of operating monies to do so. Adding still another dimension, an Ohio state court ordered the Cleveland Public Schools to repay loans from private lending institutions on time rather than create a deficit.

The tensions at governmental interfaces are sufficiently severe that some formal attention may be required to reduce those frictions. More importantly, ways must be found to restore the courts to essentially adjudication and to reduce the appearance or the fact of administering and developing policy for the schools. The problem is more a matter of achieving responsible performance of the traditional functions of each governmental division than one of changing or clarifying executive, legislative, and judicial responsibilities (although that would be helpful). Equity and justice are matters of enormous social, political, and economic significance. Legislators and administrators have the freedom to exercise initiatives in this regard. Failure to take initiatives or to behave consistently with constitutional principle and mandate leads the aggrieved directly to the courts. While most courts are reluctant to enter policy and/or administrative domains, they are nonetheless confronted not only with determinations of liability or innocence, but also with effecting remedies on behalf of plaintiffs when the defendant public officials are found liable. Administrators and policy makers often sow the seeds of their own loss of control through inactivity or recalcitrance.

The number of school desegregation cases and their protracted nature allow for close inspection of the relationships between school systems and the courts. Observing the behavior of school systems and the courts at their interface leads to several conclusions.

First, each is substantially ignorant of the other. School officials by and large are not well informed about the roles and functions of the judiciary, its processes, its professionals, or its politics. They are not well acquainted with the law or the legal canons of the American Bar Association. The rules of the bar are not the law, but often have the consequence of law. Similarly, federal and state judges, their staffs, and other resource people traditionally available to the courts know little about the workings of school systems or their governance and management. Each one's knowledge of the other is hardly beyond the eighth-grade civics level. Errors are made by school systems and by courts simply because of inadequate information and understanding. It takes months, even years, for shared knowledge and understanding to develop to the point where serious problems can be avoided.

Second, common understanding is inhibited by the language and traditions of two sets of professionals, the legal-judicials and the educators. Legal-judicial professionals approach the settling of issues essentially through patterns of adversarial thought and practice. Educators approach the settling of issues in a less rational, more confused manner and style. The legal-judicials have a vast information system that is organized and easily accessed to assist them with their responsibilities. The educators draw upon a multitude of information systems, none of which is as well organized or disciplined as that available to the legal-judicials.

Litigation provokes interactions between these two groups. Their traditions and practices do not blend well. In fact, one is alien to the other. Furthermore, their statuses are not equivalent, which leads to deference on some occasions and to suspicions and even hostilities on others.

Third, legally trained minds dominate the proceeding, which can lead to further complications. School districts develop a critical dependency upon their legal counsel, especially in the prosecution of litigation on desegregation and school finance. The outcomes of each have severe implications for children and youth, including their life chances and opportunities. The school district lawyers become for the most part the single conduit of formal association between school systems and the courts. Those lawyers carry the joint burdens of legal and educational arguments. Yet they are trained to carry only one half of that burden. The schools and the courts rely on one single, formal umbilical linkage, one trans-lation of the educational meanings of decisions pending before the courts. Legal traditions and procedures discourage the develop-ment of other linkages and other representations of the educational effects of litigation to the courts. Thus school systems hang upon a single, legal-judicial professional thread. School officials as de-fendants or plaintiffs must rely on the skills of their counsel to incorporate the districts' interests through legal brief or the or-ganization and development of testimony. The courts may employ educators as experts to help with interpretations of information or plans produced by local districts. And occasionally special masters are selected, some of whom have been professional educators, to act as a bridge between the courts and the schools. Nevertheless, an imbalance in understanding results. Courts can render decisions that are constitutionally sound but educationally disastrous. That consequence is often unnecessary. Remedies can be achieved that are sound constitutionally and educationally.

The dependency described above manifests itself in other ways. School board members and superintendents, untrained and unfamiliar with the language and practice of legal-judicial profes-sionals, turn to the lawyers increasingly for advice about matters occasioned by but essentially peripheral to litigation in process. For example, counsel for school districts are sometimes asked by school officials to comment at public meetings of school boards on the relationship between cases in process, for example, desegre-gation cases, and their effects upon local elections to approve increases in millage rates. Attorneys usually decline to comment as counsel but offer observations "as citizens." Such requests occur frequently, formally and informally, and tend to confuse the legal counsel function. Some school district attorneys appear to take on the responsibilities of boardmanship. They acquire behaviors that are similar to those of board members. Counsel often are seated at the tables where school boards conduct their meetings. Their physical location at the meeting table contributes to public confusion and misunderstanding about their roles. Holding seats at the table makes it difficult to distinguish their role as counsel providing legal services from formal board membership. Not infrequently, school counsel exert influence in areas beyond the immediate issue for which a legal opinion is needed. They can become board members without the attendant responsibilities. Similarly, the "representation privileges" of school district attorneys are embedded in shades of grey. How far can school district lawyers go in representing their clients, especially on legal issues of extensive policy significance, without explicit clearance or approval on the part of school boards?

The relationships between the courts and school systems and the rules, functions, and responsibilities of those who preside over that interface warrant inspection on the part of school officials and representatives of the courts.

School officials are ill prepared for fulfilling their responsibilities in litigation. School board members, unless they are lawyers, have limited knowledge of the judicial system. Most board members become acquainted with the scope and particulars of their individual legal obligations as board members (let alone those of the school district) after they are appointed or elected, not before. Thus their encounters with complex issues of desegregation and/or finance become frustrating, sometimes unnerving. School administrators have a better knowledge of school law than most board members but, as noted before, they are not well acquainted with the judicial system nor the processes that are embedded there. Furthermore their formal training has not prepared them for participation in those processes. They learn on the job how to work with school district attorneys, how to prepare materials for the court, and how to give testimony at hearings and trial proceedings. They discover, for example, the incredible pressure of producing school desegregation plans within short periods of time and within social-political climates that more often than not are hostile to such activity. They assume advocacy postures at personal and professional peril and some appear to take on the protective colorations of the prevailing sentiments in their midst.

Those who are responsible for preparing and licensing administrators and teachers should take note of these circumstances and modify preparation and licensure consistent with the needs for change.

The costs of litigation are growing consistent with the number and range of school cases before the courts. School districts have been the defendants traditionally and have availed themselves of appellate options. Given the slowness of the court system and cases that involve a series of appeals and remands, the ultimate determinations may require many years. School districts with increasing frequency have filed legal actions of their own, becoming plaintiffs themselves to seeking recourse through the courts. The result is a large-scale increase in legal costs. Costs for ordinary every-day legal services are substantial but the bill for a protracted public school desegregation case or a higher education admissions case (for example, *Regents of the University of California, Petitioner* v. *Allan Bakke*) are very high. Furthermore there is little or no prospect for relief in reducing either the number of cases or the price tags for legal services.

Even more costly to the public education enterprise, in dollars as well as in educational effects, is the impact that litigation in process has on school systems. The presence of litigation can be measured in several ways. There are dollar costs in the preparation of trial materials by administrators, for example. Plans to remedy school desegregation require thousands of man hours, including those provided as a rule by outside experts, and production costs. As a consequence of diverting personnel from their normal responsibilities, routine tasks are less well attended, contributing to deterioration in the day-to-day performance of the school system. Similarly, school board members are distracted from other policy needs of systems especially where the emotional content of litigation is high.

The full assessment of the impact of cases in progress must include the meaning of indecision or suspended decision for students, teachers, parents, administrators, board members, and the community. Again school desegregation and school finance cases are good examples. The uncertainty about the content of the decisions themselves and the indefiniteness as to when they will appear produce an unfortunate result. Teacher morale suffers; parent antagonisms and misunderstandings occur; little or no planning takes place or is possible. Pupils are the unwitting victims of such circumstances over and over again. In states where major decisions involving finance and/or collective bargaining and/or school desegregation are in suspension simultaneously, erosions of institutional performance and public confidence are potentially catastrophic.

There seems little likelihood that the prominence of the courts in the life of the schools will diminish. There is no foreseeable termination of court involvement in school desegregation, for example. Nor has the church-state question been laid to rest. Add to those key issues the continuing question of equity in the financing of public education, affirmative action, censorship, privacy, corporal punishment, compulsory education, and the likely elevation of the "right to an education" to the constitutional level. Such matters will continue to involve the courts in their clarification and ultimate determination for decades.

It is the hope of the authors, the editor, and the Society that this timely volume on the courts and education will elevate the understanding of basic issues and will both provoke and inform discussions of those issues.

LUVERN L. CUNNINGHAM
*December, 1977*

*Acknowledgments*

The Society is indebted to Professor Hooker for providing the leadership in the development of this volume, and to the several authors for their respective contributions. We also wish to acknowledge the assistance of Professor Herman G. Richey, formerly Secretary-Treasurer and Editor of the Society, who has prepared the "List of Cases Cited" that appears at the end of the volume, as well as the index. As with the Society's other publications, this volume could not have appeared without an enormous amount of work on the part of those who have contributed to it.

KENNETH J. REHAGE
Editor for the Society

# Table of Contents

# CHAPTER I

# The Law and Education in Historical Perspective

ROBERT A. KOENIG

## Historical Origins of Governmental Interest in Education

Throughout our two hundred year history as a nation, government in one form or another has expressed its interest in education. Indeed, this interest emerged long before the founding of the United States and predates the American Revolution by more than a hundred years. In 1647, the General Court of the Colony of Massachusetts Bay passed the "Old Deluder Satan Act." Section two of that act provided that when any town increased to one hundred families or households a grammar school would be established with a master capable of preparing young people for university level study.[1] The Colony of Massachusetts Bay was not unique in its concern for education; other colonies also gave unrestricted aid through land grants and appropriations of money. Both practices were later adopted by the Continental Congress and the Congress of the United States.

The land grant was the most common means employed to support education at all levels during the colonial period, with colleges faring well under this practice. Orfield writes:

Prior to 1787, the time when the question of federal land grants for the support of universities came up for serious consideration in Congress, eight of the original thirteen states had made use of public land for the maintenance of institutions of learning of college rank. In a ninth, New Jersey, the only land grant of this kind had come from a local community. Two other states, North Carolina and New York, adopted the policy within the next three years. Delaware and Rhode Island had no college until the next century.[2]

1. Edgar W. Knight and Clifton L. Hall, *Readings in American Educational History* (New York: Appleton-Century-Crofts, 1951), pp. 62-63.
2. Matthias N. Orfield, *Federal Land Grants to the States with Special Reference to Minnesota*, Bulletin of the University of Minnesota, no. 2 (Minneapolis, Minn.: University of Minnesota, 1915), p. 21.

Of the many colleges that benefited from land grants, high on the list is Dartmouth College. Dartmouth was the outgrowth of Moor's Indian Charity School, established by the Reverend Eleazar Wheelock. Its purpose was to educate and Christianize the Indians to do missionary work among their own people.[3] In 1769, a charter was granted, and Dartmouth College was officially established in Hanover, New Hampshire. The response to the new college in land grants was impressive. In 1890, Blackmar provided this account:

The inhabitants of Hanover presented the college with twelve hundred acres of valuable land; the State of New Hampshire endowed it with about seventy-eight thousand acres more, in several successive grants, the most important of which was made in January, 1789, when the Legislature gave a tract of four thousand two hundred acres located above Stewartstown. . . . One of the most remarkable grants on record is that made by the Legislature of Vermont in 1785-86. . . . The Legislature granted the college the entire township of Wheelock—one-half for the school and one-half for the college. It was this grant which led Daniel Webster to remark that "the State of Vermont is a principal donor to Dartmouth College."[4]

The colonial practice of providing land grants for the support of education established a ready precedent later to be used by the Continental Congress, the Congress of the Confederation, and in time, the Congress of the United States of America. Land grants were thus the original means used to provide federal aid to education.

The first measure enacted by the federal government in support of education came when the Continental Congress passed the Ordinance of 1785, which disposed of lands in the western territory and reserved Section Sixteen of each congressional township for the support of schools.[5] The ordinance provided that "there shall be reserved the lot N [sic] 16, of every township, for the main-

3. Ibid., p. 20.

4. Frank W. Blackmar, *The History of Federal and State Aid to Higher Education in the United States*, Bureau of Education, Circular of Information no. 1, ed. Herbert B. Adams (Washington, D.C.: U.S. Government Printing Office, 1890), p. 52.

5. Truman M. Pierce, *Federal, State, and Local Government in Education* (New York: Center for Applied Research in Education, 1964), p. 24.

tenance of public schools, within the said township. . . ."[6] Two years later, the same Congress passed the Northwest Ordinance, which some have hailed as "the Bill of Rights for Education"[7] or "the charter of public education."[8] In any event, this ordinance did represent the first policy statement made by Congress with respect to education. Its third article reads: "Religion, morality, and knowledge being necessary to good government and the happiness of mankind, schools and the means of education shall forever be encouraged."[9] Although the Ordinance of 1787 made no provisions for land grants to schools, that same year the Continental Congress passed another ordinance that reiterated the provisions of the Ordinance of 1785. Section Sixteen was to be reserved for public schools and one additional congressional township was set aside for an institution of higher education.[10] Interestingly enough, some scholars and legal experts have argued that the Ordinances of 1785 and 1787 allowed "sectarian institutions to use the land for the establishment of schools."[11] Similar views are held by Blum[12] and by Stokes.[13] Stokes in particular asserts that all levels in the educational process were equally eligible for land grants from the federal government until 1860.[14]

On April 30, 1789, the Articles of Confederation were superceded by the Constitution of the United States. While the new

6. U.S., *Journals of the Continental Congress, 1774-1789*, vol. 28, p. 378.

7. Lee M. Thurston and William H. Roe, *State School Administration* (New York: Harper and Brothers, 1957), pp. 324-25.

8. Arthur B. Moehlman, *School Administration*, 2d ed. (Boston: Houghton Mifflin Co. 1951), p. 24.

9. U.S., *Statutes at Large*, vol. 1, p. 50.

10. Fletcher Harper Swift, *A History of Public Permanent Common School Funds in the United States, 1795-1905* (New York: Henry Holt and Co., 1911), p. 47.

11. David H. Baris, Legislative Attorney, Library of Congress, in a letter to the Honorable Hubert H. Humphrey, January 12, 1972.

12. Virgil C. Blum, S.J., *Freedom in Education: Federal Aid for all Children* (Garden City, N.Y.: Doubleday and Co., 1965), p. 102.

13. Anson Phelps Stokes, *Church and State in the United States* (New York: Harper and Row, 1950), vol. 1, p. 481.

14. Ibid.

document clearly vested in the Congress of the United States the power to control and dispose of the national domain, it was not until 1802, when Ohio was admitted to the Union, that the Congress reiterated the principle of conveying land grants to the states for educational purposes. The Ohio Enabling Act of 1802 established the practice of granting Section Sixteen of each township to the residents for the use of schools. The act stipulated that "the Section, number sixteen, in every township, and where such section has been sold, granted or disposed of, other lands equivalent thereto, and most contiguous to the same, shall be granted to the inhabitants of such township, for the use of schools."[15] As new states were admitted to the Union, they also received land grants for schools. The exceptions to the act of 1802 were the thirteen original states and the new states carved from them, namely, Maine, Vermont, and West Virginia. Kentucky received no land grants since it was admitted to the Union before the legislation was enacted. Texas did not qualify since it owned its own land at the time of annexation and the states of Alaska and Hawaii also failed to benefit.[16] In all, thirty of the fifty states received land grants for public schools totaling 80,385,964 acres or over 125,568 square miles.[17] Lu reports that if the land given to other educational institutions were included the figures would be more than doubled and would equal an area larger than the state of Texas.[18] Moreover, the endowment generated from these land grants was estimated at $1 billion in 1956 for the schools in the states involved.[19]

Passage of the first Morrill Act of 1862, sometimes referred to as the Land Grant Act, extended federal aid to higher education. This act assisted the states in establishing colleges whose primary mission was teaching "such branches of learning as are related

15. U.S., *Statutes at Large*, vol. 2, p. 175.

16. Pierce, *Federal, State, and Local Government in Education*, p. 25.

17. Hsien Lu, *Federal Role in Education* (New York: American Press, 1965), p. 33.

18. "The total is 175,313,000 acres (273,000 square miles), an area larger than the state of Texas, nine-tenths as large as Turkey, twice as large as Germany as a whole." Ibid., p. 41, footnote 19.

19. Lu, *Federal Role in Education*, p. 33.

to agriculture and the mechanic arts." [20] Under its provisions, public lands were apportioned to the several states in an amount equal to 30,000 acres of public land for each member in both houses of Congress according to the representation to which the states were respectively entitled under the apportionment and census of 1860.[21]

The first Morrill Act also stipulated that states with insufficient federal land were to receive their equivalent value in the form of land script.[22] It further provided that all moneys derived from the sale of land given to the states were to become a perpetual fund, with the income used to support at least one college of agriculture and mechanic arts.[23] Twenty-three states embraced the provisions of the first Morrill Act and established colleges of agriculture and mechanic arts.[24] Several private institutions benefited from the Land Grant Act of 1862. The Massachusetts Institute of Technology, Yale, Cornell, and Brown universities all received federal aid under the act.[25]

While the land grant was the most common form of aid during the colonial period as well as later, monetary support of education can also be traced back to colonial times. The General Court of the Massachusetts Bay Colony not only passed the Old Deluder Satan Act; it also voted £400 for the establishment of a "public school or college."[26] Initially, the school was referred to as a "seminary," a "college," and the "School of the Prophets."[27] In time, it became known as Harvard College. The second college in the English colonies in America was the College of William and Mary. Chartered by the crown in 1693, "this college had

20. Pierce, *Federal, State, and Local Government in Education*, p. 28.

21. Paul R. Mort, *Federal Support for Public Education* (New York: Bureau of Publications, Teachers College, Columbia University, 1936), p. 48.

22. Pierce, *Federal, State, and Local Government in Education*, p. 28.

23. Lu, *Federal Role in Education*, p. 44.

24. Ibid., p. 45.

25. Robert A. Koenig, "An Analysis of Federal Legislation and Selected Court Cases Relating to Financing Nonpublic Education in the United States" (Ph. D. diss., University of Minnesota, 1973), pp. 364-68.

26. Alvin W. Johnson and Frank H. Yost, *Separation of Church and State in the United States* (New York: Greenwood Press, 1934), p. 19.

27. Ibid.

received government aid, but not in the form of land grants."[28] In 1701, Yale became the third collegiate institution in the colonies. From the outset, Connecticut was benevolent toward its first college, making an annual grant of £100, which was doubled in 1735, tripled in 1741, and increased still further over the years.[29]

Some of the first federal moneys were awarded to Dartmouth College. In 1776, the Continental Congress authorized congressional aid in the amount of $500 for each Indian youth enrolled in the college.[30] In 1752, the College of New Jersey moved to Princeton, whose name it eventually assumed. The Reverend Doctor John Witherspoon, the college president and the only clergyman to sign the Declaration of Independence, requested congressional aid for the College of New Jersey. The Continental Congress responded in 1781 by granting £137 to help defray the educational expenses of three Indian youths from the Delaware Nation attending Princeton College.[31]

The amounts of money received by public and private education from the various levels of government—from village to the Continental Congress—serve to confirm the historic interest of government in education. After the ratification of the federal Constitution, the Congress of the United States frequently used appropriations of money as a means of supporting American education. As early as 1870, Congress appropriated $25,000 for Wilberforce University, an African Methodist Episcopal college in Ohio.[32] At the time of the original grant, Wilberforce included a theology school.[33] From its inception to the present, Howard University has received a direct grant from the federal government annually.[34]

---

28. Orfield, *Federal Land Grants to the States*, p. 20.

29. Blackmar, *History of Federal and State Aid to Higher Education*, p. 109.

30. Richard J. Gabel, *Public Funds for Church and Private Schools* (Washington, D.C.: Catholic University of America Press, 1937), p. 177.

31. Ibid.

32. U.S., *Statutes at Large*, vol. 16, p. 315.

33. Gabel, *Public Funds for Church and Private Schools*, p. 518.

34. For a detailed accounting of congressional appropriations to Howard University for the period of 1879-1970, see Koenig, "An Analysis of Federal Legislation," pp. 713-17.

Howard University received its first federal grant in 1879 in the amount of $10,000. Since then, congressional appropriations have continued and increased.

In 1887, Congress passed the Hatch Act.[35] This act appropriated $15,000 for the establishment of agricultural experiment stations in connection with those land grant colleges established under the first Morrill Act and represented the first federal legislation providing annual recurring cash grants to states cooperating in federal-state educational programs.[36] Over the years, Congress has greatly expanded the benefits first extended under the Hatch Act. In 1890, the Congress passed a second Morrill Act, which provided an initial annual appropriation of $15,000 to each state or territory for the support of colleges of agriculture and mechanic arts.[37] The amount of this appropriation has also increased substantially over the years.

The passage of the Morrill Acts had a profound and lasting effect on American education. The land grant policy of the federal government benefited common schools as well as colleges, and such aid was conferred to both with no strings attached. Expenditure of funds was left to the discretion of the receiver. The Morrill Acts, while illustrative of the interest of the federal government in education, also demonstrate the intent of the federal government to impose controls on education through defining curriculum and establishing conditions for funding. Under the first Morrill Act, grants were made only to those institutions engaged in special kinds of education. Through a grant system, the federal government was able to define curriculum in institutions of higher education. The second Morrill Act went a step further by setting the conditions for receiving federal moneys and by vesting certain discretionary powers for withholding such funds in the hands of the Secretary of the Interior.

Federal aid to and interest in education have expanded dramatically since the days of the early land grants and first grants of money. A search of the congressional acts from 1789 through 1970

35. U.S., *Statutes at Large*, vol. 24, p. 440.

36. Lu, *Federal Role in Education*, p. 49.

37. U.S., *Statutes at Large*, vol. 26, p. 417.

shows that Congress provided direct federal aid to all levels of education, although the mode of distribution sometimes changed as did those receiving the aid.[38] From the beginning, Congress has awarded the largest portion of federal aid to collegiate-type institutions of higher education; elementary, secondary, and post-secondary education have received significant benefits but to a far lesser degree. Traditionally, Congress has also used institutions rather than individuals as the vehicle for conveying federal aid. During the period of 1900-1943, Congress began to make appropriations for education to assist particular segments of American society. Specific groups were identified to receive federal aid such as the children of deceased servicemen, the disabled, students, and defense workers. Some moneys were given directly to students through such programs as the National Youth Administration, but this method for distributing aid received limited usage. Grants in money and contracts were the most widely used forms for conveying federal aid to education between 1900 and 1970. Then, some interesting shifts in congressional aid occurred during the period of 1944-1964 when the Congress designed massive programs for federal aid in the fields of science, health, and education. This was also the period when programs for institutional research and student loans were launched. Science, health, and education programs continued to receive the bulk of federal aid between 1965 and 1970, with education emerging the most prosperous. In this period programs were enacted dealing with the training of personnel working directly with specific segments of groups in American society. Congress seemed to have developed a moral sensitivity as well as an educational awareness of societal needs during this period. Federal government has always been interested in and supportive of American education from pre-Constitutional times to the present.

## Basic Legal Tenets Undergirding American Education

The federal partnership in American education has already been documented. From the Ordinance of 1787 through the Morrill Acts and the massive program legislation enacted following World

38. For a detailed discussion of the findings see Koenig, "An Analysis of Federal Legislation," pp. 673-84.

War II to the present, the federal government has shown itself to be a willing partner and an active advocate in using education to help meet the needs of our society. This is a historic position since Congress has never admitted a territory seeking admission to the Union unless it made provisions in its constitution for an educational system.[39] Even though the federal government enacted legislation before the adoption of the U.S. Constitution, its role with respect to education has been the subject of continued debate. The Constitution makes no explicit reference to education. This does not mean, however, that education is beyond the purview of the federal government or is the exclusive function of the states. Early justification in legal theory for the intrusion of the federal government into education was based on the interpretation given to the general welfare clause of the Constitution. Section eight of Article One reads: "The Congress shall have Power To lay and collect Taxes, Duties, Imposts and Excises, to pay the Debts and provide for the common Defence and general Welfare of the United States. . . ."[40] Debate ensued between James Madison and Alexander Hamilton on how the clause should be interpreted. Although Congress had spent millions of dollars that could never have been justified without the clause, the Supreme Court did not rule on an interpretation of it until 1936, when it ruled favorably on the constitutionality of the Social Security Act. For the first time the Court recognized a legislative act using tax dollars as a legitimate exercise of authority under the general welfare clause. This has led experts in the field of school law to conclude that the same rationale could be applied to education and that Congress can support education under the general welfare clause but cannot use such support to set educational policy for the several states, although the effect is often to induce the states to cooperate with the federal government to meet pressing social needs.[41]

Spurlock has written that it is important to "keep in mind

39. Dawson Hales, *Federal Control of Public Education*, (New York: Bureau of Publications, Columbia University, 1954), p. 55.

40. U.S. Constitution, Article 1, sec. 8.

41. Newton Edwards, *The Courts and the Public Schools*, 3d ed. (Chicago: University of Chicago Press, 1971), pp. 4-5.

the legal theory that schools are primarily for the protection of the state through their basic function of providing an informed and competent citizenry."[42] Historically, Americans have felt that their welfare as a nation was tied to an efficient and effective educational system. Dating back to the Old Deluder Satan Act, which provided for instruction in such basic skills as reading and writing, the interest was in promoting the general welfare of the Massachusetts Bay Colony rather than advancing the well-being of children. The ability to read and write were tools needed to insure the religious and political survival of the colony. Only as individuals acquired such skills could they be expected to assume their rightful religious and civic responsibilities. Moreover, anyone who could read and write would more than likely be self-supporting.[43] Later, the free public school movement would be built on the premise of promoting the general welfare.[44]

The foundations of the public school movement were firmly laid in the period from 1820 to 1865 with the establishment of public common schools and public teacher training institutions.[45] The intent was to educate all children with public tax dollars.[46] In practice, the outcome was quite different. Until compulsory education laws were enacted, even common schools tended to benefit a select clientele. This was particularly true in the case of the first public high schools.[47] And while few colleges were founded with the national interest primarily in view, higher education and the federal government have a good record of working together for the general welfare and national security of the nation.[48] Then as now, education was seen as essential to economic

42. Clark Spurlock, *Education and the Supreme Court* (Urbana, Ill.: University of Illinois Press, 1955), p. 7.

43. Richard Pratte, *The Public School Movement: A Critical Study* (New York: David McKay Co., 1973), p. 40.

44. Ibid., p. 50.

45. Ibid., p. 49.

46. Stephen R. Goldstein, *Law and Public Education* (Indianapolis, Ind.: Bobbs-Merrill Co., 1974), p. 8.

47. Pratte, *The Public School Movement*, p. 54.

48. Logan Wilson, "The Federal Government and Higher Education," in *Education and Public Policy*, ed. Seymour E. Harris (Berkeley, Calif.: McCutchan Publishing Corp., 1965), pp. 59-61.

growth and the advancement of the general welfare of our society. In our history as a nation, we have had several periods of national emergency caused by national disaster or foreign crisis. In such situations, the Congress of the United States has never hesitated to act. Undoubtedly, much of the legislation enacted during these periods would have been viewed as an exercise of authority under the general welfare and national defense clauses of the Constitution. For example, it seems likely that many enactments passed during the Great Depression of the 1930s, such as the Civilian Conservation Corps (CCC), the Federal Emergency Relief Administration (FERA), the Works Progress Administration (WPA), the National Youth Administration (NYA), and the School Lunch Program, would have been sustained under the general welfare clause if their constitutionality had been challenged. Similarly, it is reasonable to conclude that acts establishing the United States military academies, the Army War College and other special service schools, the National Defense Act of 1916 (ROTC) and the Naval Reserve Officers Training Corps (NROTC), the Lanham Act of 1941, which provided funds for construction, operation, and maintenance of school buildings in communities where war activities had created an undue financial burden, and other legislation would have been found constitutional under the national defense clause. Indeed, congressional programs enacted since World War II clearly reflect an interest in issues related to the general welfare and national security of the United States.

It should be evident by now that the general welfare and national defense clauses could be summoned in defense of much congressional legislation involving education should the need ever arise, but this has not been the case. Therefore, the Supreme Court and other federal courts have become interested in education for other reasons and on other grounds, which raises several related topics.

The function of the courts is to interpret the law. But how and what kinds of law must the court consider? While it is the task of the court system to interpret the law, the courts do not operate in a vacuum. As with legislative enactments, court decisions must also take into consideration the issues and temper of the times. Interpreting the law requires more than passing judgment on the constitutionality of an act or determining whether a given performance does or does not comply with the law. The court must have a keen sensitivity to the generation being served. In its interpretation of the law, the court must weigh constitutional provisions, legislative enactments, common law, as well as rules and regulations operative in existing society. Many principles governing schools are founded on common law or that law which emerges from case decisions rather than statutory or constitutional law. The basic law of the land, however, is the Constitution of the United States. All other enacted law must stand under the Constitution, and when there is disagreement, the Constitution prevails.

Although the courts have no authority to initiate action, courts have profoundly affected American education. From 1789 through 1900, the U.S. Supreme Court had spoken only nine times in cases pertaining to education.[49] Since the beginning of the twentieth century, the Court has been much busier with education cases. Appeals from lower state and federal courts have provided a variety of opportunities for the Court to speak on educationally related issues and problems.

Since neither the federal Constitution nor its amendments explicitly mention education, education is never directly at issue before the Supreme Court. In theory, the sections of the Constitution that may affect education are Article I, sections 8 and 10, and the First, Fifth, Tenth, and Fourteenth Amendments.[50] In practice, the Supreme Court has heard cases affecting education under the First and Fifth Amendments, which deal with civil rights; under the Fourteenth Amendment, which guarantees each citizen due process and equal protection under the law; and under Article I, section 8, which provides for the general welfare of American citizenry. The Court has also heard cases involving the constitutional powers and functions of the states and federal government.[51] However, the sections of the Constitution which come before the courts for interpretation most frequently are those protecting the inherent rights of individuals under Article I, section 10, and the First, Fifth, and Fourteenth Amendments.[52]

49. Spurlock, *Education and the Supreme Court*, p. 3.

50. Ibid., p. 14.

51. Pierce, *Federal, State, and Local Government in Education*, pp. 73-74.

52. E. Edmund Reutter, Jr. and Robert R. Hamilton, *The Law of Public Education*, 2d ed. (Mineola, N.Y.: Foundation Press, 1976), p. 2.

Early in our history as a nation our forebears recognized the necessity of preserving contractual agreements without possible later modification or abrogation by the laws of the states. The first education case to reach the Supreme Court of the United States involved the charter of Dartmouth College.[53] In 1816, the legislature of New Hampshire passed an act to alter the charter granted by the English crown in 1769 to Dartmouth College. The act was sustained by the New Hampshire Supreme Court. The decision was promptly appealed to the Supreme Court of the United States, which held that the charter was a contract between the state and the corporation of the college and that the state legislature could not alter or revoke the charter without the consent of those to whom it had been granted. The Dartmouth College Case clearly established that a college charter is a contract that the state cannot alter at will. It also settled the basic question of whether or not a state can exercise a specified power over education without violating the federal Constitution.

Article I, section 10, reads in part that "no State shall . . . pass any . . . law impairing the obligation of contracts." This provision can be invoked any time a state legislature attempts to change teacher tenure or retirement laws perceived to be deleterious by those teachers who acquired their status under previous legislation. At the present time, there is much legal debate as to whether or not teacher tenure and retirement laws do indeed create a contractual agreement between teachers and the state which a subsequent legislature cannot abridge even should the best interests of education and society seem to demand it. If such teacher tenure and retirement laws are held to be valid contracts, any changes in them will clearly violate Article I, section 10, of the U.S. Constitution.

The first ten amendments to the federal Constitution are called the Bill of Rights. They were adopted to insure certain basic individual freedom and rights. Cases arising under the Bill of Rights frequently allege that such constitutional guarantees as freedom of religion, nonestablishment of religion, freedom of speech, or freedom of the press have been violated. In a substantial number of

53. *Trustees of Dartmouth College v. Woodward*, 4 Wheaton (U.S.) 518 (1819).

cases involving education and the federal Constitution, it is alleged that fundamental religious and civil rights have been denied.

The First Amendment was particularly formulated to guarantee our basic individual freedoms and rights. The clause, "Congress shall make no law respecting an establishment of religion or prohibiting the free exercise thereof" has profoundly influenced education in the United States. The list of U.S. Supreme Court cases involving either the "establishment" or "free exercise" clause lengthens each year. An annual survey conducted by the American Jewish Congress found that forty-seven church-state and religious liberty cases are currently pending before state and federal courts.[54] Prior to the adoption of the Fourteenth Amendment, the religion clause was limited to the Congress. Later the Supreme Court ruled that the Fourteenth Amendment makes the First Amendment applicable to the states as well.[55] The religion clause of the First Amendment is invoked in those school cases involving the use of public funds for the support of nonpublic education and also in those cases in which public school regulations or procedures are found objectionable because of religious conviction.

In recent years, the freedom of speech clause of the First Amendment has been involved in education cases concerned with the civil rights of students and teachers. There has also been increased interest on the part of educators in their rights of assembly and petition as they seek to influence educational policies and practices through employee organizations.

Fifth Amendment consciousness seemingly erupted during the early 1950s through the Army-McCarthy hearings. The provisions of the amendment guarantee citizens of the United States certain protections should they be accused of committing a crime. The amendment also contains a clause prohibiting the taking of private property for public use without just compensation—a clause that should have special meaning for every state or local school board planning to purchase property for school sites. This amendment is also pertinent to those cases involving educators who may be ac-

54. "Dockets Heavy with Religion," *A. D. 1976* (December 1976-January 1977): 54.

55. *Everson v. Board of Education of the Township of Ewing*, 330 U.S. 1 (1947) and *Cantwell v. Connecticut*, 310 U.S. 296 (1940).

cused of belonging to subversive organizations or of illegal use of school funds or property.

The two clauses of the Fourteenth Amendment dealing with "due process" and "equal protection" are most applicable to education cases. Both have been invoked in cases concerned with the administration of public schools.

Since the Supreme Court has ruled that the Fourteenth Amendment makes the provisions of the First Amendment applicable to the states, it is mandatory that the provisions imposed by both amendments be considered with the provisions of the particular state constitution when determining the validity of a state enactment or a local school board regulation.

The Fourteenth Amendment has had a far-reaching effect on school law. Under its provisions, the courts have made decisions involving flag salutes, the right to attend private schools, rights of parents and students, racial segregation, school desegregation, teacher dismissal, uses of school funds, and student discipline.

## The Question of Governance in American Public Education

The absence of any mention of education in the federal Constitution has interested many students of American education. Lieberman[56] and Pratte[57] explain the omission by saying that the Founding Fathers feared the potentialities for dictatorship in a federal school system. They also assert that the idea of free public schools had not occurred to those early planners.[58] Pratte further speculates that establishing a federal school system would have produced such controversy as to jeopardize the ratification of the federal Constitution itself.[59] Others have taken the view that the literal absence was not an absence at all because the Constitution had implied power for education and the few schools in existence hardly warranted direction from the Constitution.[60]

56. Myron Lieberman, *The Future of Public Education* (Chicago: University of Chicago Press, 1960), p. 39.

57. Pratte, *The Public School Movement*, p. 42.

58. Ibid.

59. Ibid.

60. Lu, *Federal Role in Education*, p. 263.

From the outset, education was largely controlled by the home, the church, and local communities—an educational pattern transplanted by the early settlers from England.[61] With the advent of industrialization and the rise of democracy, parental and local control began to wane.[62] Soon it was perceived that the education and future opportunities of a child could not be left to the whims of parents or of a local community.[63] By the nineteenth century, education was viewed as the prerogative of the states.[64] This, of course, raises the question: Under what rubric does education become an exclusive function of the states? Some have argued that the Founding Fathers intended education to be a federal responsibility as evidenced by the level of federal involvement and support of education over the years.[65] Others have made a similar case by saying that education has never been nor should it ever become an exclusive function of the states; it is a national function to be implemented by all levels of government.[66] Still, the prevailing view is that education is a function of the states.

The Tenth Amendment of the federal Constitution provides the basis in legal theory for making education a function of the states. It reads: "The powers not delegated to the United States by the Constitution, nor prohibited by it to the States, are reserved to the states respectively, or to the people." While the amendment does not specifically direct the states to assume the responsibility for providing education, its effect has been no less. Each state constitution has provided for the establishment of a statewide school system. In some cases, state constitutions define in detail the structure for organizing and maintaining a system of public education; in others, the state constitutions merely accept such responsibility and delegate authority for its implementation to the state legislature.[67] Both the United States Supreme Court and the state courts

61. Goldstein, *Law and Public Education*, p. 7.

62. Hales, *Federal Control of Public Education*, p. 38.

63. Lieberman, *The Future of Public Education*, p. 35.

64. Hales, *Federal Control of Public Education*, p. 48.

65. Mort, *Federal Support for Public Education*, p. 47.

66. Lu, *Federal Role in Education*, p. 266.

67. Pierce, *Federal, State, and Local Government in Education*, p. 43.

have consistently ruled that education is a function of the states.[68]

State constitutions usually empower state legislatures to maintain and support a statewide system of education. The actual powers delegated to state legislatures vary according to the provisions of the individual state constitutions. In general, the courts have consistently held that the state legislatures have plenary power over the public schools of their respective states.[69] They must act, however, in conformity with the provisions of both the federal and state constitution involved as interpreted by the courts. State legislatures are also restricted by federal enactments and higher court decisions. For example, the U. S. Supreme Court limits and affects state legislatures each time it interprets the federal Constitution, a state constitution, federal or state statutes, acts of local boards of education, or acts of state officials involving education.[70] In brief, no legislation or rule-making at any level within a state can be in conflict with higher authority.[71]

Notwithstanding those limits imposed on state legislatures already mentioned, there is no contesting the influence of a state legislature in shaping educational policy and practice. A state legislature is more flexible than a state constitution in responding to public will. It is far easier to enact a law than to amend a constitution. Hence, there is no greater source of law affecting education than the enactments of state legislatures, which stand as law until ruled unconstitutional by our court system. It has been suggested that the simplest synonym for "control" is "influencing."[72] State legislatures control or influence educational policy by the kinds of schools established, the systems devised for their support, the administrative procedures and curricula approved, and by the professional qualifications set for educators. There is no doubt that the establishment, maintenance, and governance of public education resides with state legislatures.

68. Hales, *Federal Control of Public Education*, p. 49.

69. Reutter and Hamilton, *The Law of Public Education*, p. 7.

70. Spurlock, *Education and the Supreme Court*, p. 7.

71. Reutter and Hamilton, *The Law of Public Education*, p. 7.

72. Lu, *Federal Role in Education*, p. 14.

The matter of state and local control of education as related to school districts and officials is an identifiable concern of many people. Local control of education was an established fact in the colonial period.[73] Today local school districts exist but perform as creatures of the states. Although they are legal entities, they have no inherent rights, serving at the pleasure of the state legislature, which may increase or restrict their authority, change their judicatory area, or abolish them altogether.[74]

In education, there are three kinds of governmental control: (a) statutory, (b) judicial, and (c) administrative. Administrative control attempts to build a bridge between those state and local authorities responsible for implementing state educational policy. Since the legislature of a state is "the constitutionally established custodian of the legislative power, [it] may not delegate its legislative powers to any other tribunal, agency, or official." [75] On the other hand, the legislature may, if it so chooses, delegate authority to certain administrative boards and agencies created specifically to help perform duties that it assigns.[76] To assist in the tasks of organizing and administering a statewide educational policy, the legislature often vests its authority in the state board of education and its commissioner, in state departments of education, as well as in local school boards and their administrators. Local school districts have only those powers explicitly granted to them and no others. Those powers include "(a) those expressly granted by statute, (b) those fairly and necessarily implied in the powers expressly granted, and (c) those essential to the accomplishment of the objects of the corporation." [77] Local school districts cannot levy taxes for school purposes unless that power has been granted or implied in order to accomplish some assignment that requires the power to tax. Nor can a school district issue bonds without authority from the state legislature.

All states have created local boards of education to assist in

73. Pratte, *The Public School Movement*, p. 42.

74. Hales, *Federal Control of Public Education*, p. 48.

75. Edwards, *The Courts and the Public Schools*, p. 30.

76. Ibid.

77. Ibid., p. 146.

carrying out state educational policy. Since the state controls education, local school officials represent the state and perform as its
agents.[78] All local school officers are officers of the state.[79] Education is a state institution and not a local one. Therefore, governance
or control of state school systems rests with state legislatures and
not with local boards of education.[80] The single exception to this
statement are the local rights guaranteed under the federal and state
constitutions. A state legislature also must stand under the provisions of these two documents, and it is possible for a legislature to
violate one and not the other.

## Legal Tenets Surrounding Nonpublic Education

Governmental involvement in nonpublic education is long and
impressive. In colonial America, education was clearly the child of
the church. Earlier it was pointed out that the Continental Congress
provided funds for educating American Indian youth at both Dartmouth and the College of New Jersey (now Princeton). This particular example of aid provides insight both into the problems confronting a government with a nonexistent public school system and
into the magnitude of government support given to sectarian education.

For over two centuries, Indian education was left to the
churches, with both Roman Catholic and Protestant clergy serving
as pioneer educators. During that time, treaties were made between
the Indian and the white man in which the govenment promised
to educate and establish schools for the Indians. But the government had no delivery system for providing such education. In
order to meet the crisis, government developed an elaborate contract school system, which flourished until 1900 when it was
terminated.[81] Under this system, the federal government appropriated public moneys to sectarian groups engaged in Indian education. House and Senate Documents for the period from 1824 to

78. Pierce, *Federal, State, and Local Government in Education*, p. 84.

79. Edwards, *The Courts and the Public Schools*, p. 29.

80. Pierce, *Federal, State, and Local Government in Education*, p. 83.

81. U.S., *Statutes at Large*, vol. 30, p. 79.

1901 confirm the level of support.[82] For example, in 1891, $910,836 was paid to sectarian groups providing Indian education.[83]

Prior to the Civil War, there were 180 denominational colleges.[84] Many of these institutions received direct federal aid in the form of land grants.[85] Private institutions of higher learning such as Yale, the Massachusetts Institute of Technology, Cornell, and Brown also benefited under the first Morrill Act of 1862. Between 1865 and 1871, immediately following the Civil War, the federal government paid the greater part of $5 million to schools run by religious groups teaching young people secular subjects.[86]

According to Lu, "since 1876 Congress has insisted that the schools be free from sectarian control." [87] Such a statement admits to at least two facts: (a) that sectarian control of the schools did exist and (b) that such a demand did not apply to sectarian Indian education.

Throughout our two hundred years as a nation, federal aid has been provided to all levels of nonpublic education as demonstrated by the acts passed by Congress.[88] Over that period, Congress has given the largest portion of federal aid to collegiate type institutions, although elementary, secondary, and postsecondary education have also benefited significantly.[89]

Since the federal government has been supportive of nonpublic

---

82. For a detailed analysis of federal support of sectarian Indian education, see Koenig, "An Analysis of Federal Legislation," pp. 285-341 and Appendices C-D, pp. 690-712.

83. Ibid., p. 336.

84. Donald Tewksbury, *The Founding of American Colleges and Universities before the Civil War* (New York: Bureau of Publications, Teachers College, Columbia University, 1932), p. 90.

85. Koenig, "An Analysis of Federal Legislation," p. 364.

86. Blum, *Freedom in Education*, p. 102.

87. Lu, *Federal Role in Education*, p. 33.

88. See Koenig, "An Analysis of Federal Legislation," pp. 342-685, for an analysis of legislative enactments.

89. Nonpublic education receives aid under the Federal Surplus Property Act, the National School Lunch Program, the National Defense Education Act of 1958, the G. I. Bill, the Higher Education Facilities Act of 1963, the Economic Opportunity Act of 1964, and the Elementary and Secondary Education Act of 1965, to cite a few examples of federal aid.

education, what then is the legal basis under which church-state-education cases can be heard? Such cases find their way into the federal court system under the establishment and free exercise clauses of the First Amendment and under the due process and equal protection clauses of the Fourteenth Amendment.

Because many people came to America for religious reasons it is no surprise to find the establishment and free exercise clauses incorporated in the First Amendment. The interpretation and application of these clauses pertaining to religion, however, have been no easy judicial assignments. A case involving the free exercise clause reached the Supreme Court for the first time in 1878. In *Reynolds* v. *United States* the Court held that an individual was free to believe what he wanted, but his actions were subject to the laws of the state and the moral standards of the community.[90] A more recent decision by the Court seems to have abandoned the "belief-action" rule. In *Wisconsin* v. *Yoder* the Court ruled that an individual may exercise freedom of religion unless the state establishes that it has a compelling interest in the case justifying infringement of the individual's free exercise of his religion.[91] In 1970, the Supreme Court said that the establishment clause was intended to provide protection against "sponsorship, financial support, and active involvement of the sovereign in religious activity."[92] This means that the public schools must be nonsectarian, that the federal government cannot support church-related schools, that public schools cannot promote a particular religion, and that the federal gvernment must avoid "excessive entanglement" in policing the activities of church-related schools. In the absence of precisely stated constitutional prohibitions with respect to the establishment and free exercise clauses, the Court has had a continuing struggle to interpret and apply the religion clauses of the First Amendment to church-state education cases.

The challenge has been no less formidable under the due process and equal protection clauses of the Fourteenth Amendment. It was not until 1940 that the religion clauses of the First Amend-

90. *Reynolds* v. *United States*, 98 U.S. 145 (1878).

91. *Wisconsin* v. *Yoder*, 406 U.S. 205 (1972).

92. *Walz* v. *Tax Commission*, 397 U.S. 664, 668 (1970).

ment were made applicable to the states under the provisions of the Fourteenth Amendment.[93] At that time, the Supreme Court held that the Fourteenth Amendment clause providing that "no state shall make or enforce any law which shall abridge the privileges and immunities of citizens of the United States" makes the First Amendment applicable to the states. Therefore, citizens have the same religious rights under state governments as they do under the federal government.[94] Previously, the First Amendment religion prohibitions had applied only to Congress.

Practically all states have religion clauses similar to those of the First Amendment. State courts will entertain petitions alleging violations of both state and federal constitutions. On the other hand, federal courts will assume jurisdiction of only those cases in which there has been an alleged violation of some right guaranteed by the federal Constitution.[95] It is under these regulations and procedures that church-state education cases find their way into the state and federal court systems.

It has been argued that the establishment clause of the First Amendment creates a "wall of separation" between church and state,[96] but it is not always clear what the wall separates.

There are several thorny issues confronting the courts in dealing with education and the religion clauses of the First Amendment. One of the basic problems involves the religion clauses themselves. According to Howe, the principle that Congress shall adopt no law respecting an establishment of religion and the rule that Congress shall adopt no law abridging religious liberty are incompatible.[97] The confrontation occurs when government seeks to protect religious liberty and in so doing finds itself giving aid to religion. Howe asks the question: "Can we have a rule that forbids Govern-

93. Reutter and Hamilton, *The Law of Public Education*, p. 13.

94. Ibid.

95. Edwards, *The Courts and the Public Schools*, p. 50.

96. For a detailed discussion of the historical context surrounding the establishment clause, including the origins of the "wall" metaphor, see Koenig, "An Analysis of Federal Legislation," pp. 38-99.

97. Mark DeWolfe Howe, "Political and Religious Issues of Federal Aid," in *Education and Public Policy*, ed. Harris, p. 43.

ment to give any aid to religion and, at the same time, requires it to defend religious liberty?" [98]

Another problem involves the question of indirect aid. In a school, moneys spent for secular educational purposes release other moneys for religious purposes. There is the question of loans versus grants or scholarships. Since both represent potential forms of indirect aid to church-related institutions, what then is the constitutional difference between the two forms of aid? Under the establishment clause, is the issue preferential treatment of religion or no aid to religion? It has been argued that the granting of aid to secular private schools while denying aid to sectarian private schools performing the same kinds of educational functions smacks of preferential treatment for secular private schools. Moreover, since sectarian and private schools antedate American public schools and continue to provide valuable public services, should they be considered part of the American educational system and therefore receive aid from the federal government?

It has been only recently that an individual taxpayer has had standing in the federal court system to challenge congressional expenditures in purported violation of the federal Constitution. In 1968, the U. S. Supreme Court ruled that taxpayers would be permitted to sue in federal courts to challenge the constitutionality of congressional acts using federal funds in alleged violation of the establishment clause.[99] Under the provisions of the establishment clause, the federal and state governments are prohibited from spending moneys collected by taxation in support of sectarian educational institutions. Since the *Flast* decision in 1968, church-state education cases involving the establishment clause have reached the Supreme Court with increasing frequency.[100] The Court, however, has also

---

98. Ibid.

99. *Flast v. Cohen*, 392 U.S. 83 (1968).

100. The following cases deal with the First Amendment establishment clause: *Everson v. Board of Education*, 330 U.S. 1 (1947); *McCollum v. Board of Education*, 333 U.S. 203 (1948); *Zorach v. Clauson*, 343 U.S. 306 (1952); *Engel v. Vitale*, 370 U.S. 421 (1962); *Abington School District v. Schempp*, 374 U.S. 203 (1963); *Board of Education v. Allen*, 392 U.S. 236 (1968), *Lemon v. Kurtzman*, 403 U.S. 602 (1971); *Earley v. DiCenso*, 403 U.S. 602 (1971); *Tilton v. Richardson*, 403 U.S. 672 (1971); *Sloan v. Lemon*, 93 S. Ct. 2982 (1973); *Levitt v. Committee for Public Education and Religious*

heard cases involving religion and education under the free exercise clause of the First Amendment[101] and the due process[102] and equal protection[103] clauses of the Fourteenth Amendment, although equal protection cases are somewhat of a rarity.

In deciding the constitutionality of acts involving education and the establishment clause, the Court has developed several legal tests. The first test emerged in the 1947 *Everson* case, in which the provision of transportation for parochial school students at public expense was held to be constitutional. At that time, Mr. Justice Black established the "no-aid" test, writing as follows:

The "establishment of religion" clause of the First Amendment means at least this. Neither a State nor the Federal Government can set up a church. Neither can pass laws which aid one religion, aid all religions, or prefer one religion over another. Neither can force nor influence a person to go to or remain away from church against his will or force him to profess a belief or disbelief in any religion. No person can be punished for entertaining or professing religious beliefs or disbeliefs, for church attendance or nonattendance. No tax in any amount, large or small, can be levied to support any religious activities or institutions, whatever they may be called, or whatever form they may adopt to teach or practice religion. Neither a State nor the Federal Government can, openly or secretly, participate in the affairs of any religious organizations or groups and vice versa. In the words of Jefferson, the clause against establishment of religion by law was intended to erect "a wall of separation between church and state."[104]

---

Liberty, 93 S. Ct. 2814 (1973); *Committee for Public Education and Religious Liberty v. Nyquist*, 413 U.S. 756 (1973); *Hunt v. McNair*, 413 U.S. 734 (1973); *Meek v. Pittenger*, 421 U.S. 349 (1975); *Roemer et al. v. Board of Public Works of Maryland et al.*, S. Ct. No. 74-730 (June 21, 1976).

101. The following cases deal with the First Amendment free exercise clause: *Quick Bear v. Leupp*, 210 U.S. 50 (1908); *Minersville School District v. Gobitis*, 310 U.S. 586 (1940); *West Virginia State Board of Education v. Barnette*, 319 U.S. 624 (1943); *Zorach v. Clauson*, 343 U.S. 306 (1952); *Lemon v. Kurtzman*, 403 U.S. 602 (1971); *Earley v. DiCenso*, 403 U.S. 602 (1971); *Wisconsin v. Yoder*, 406 U.S. 205 (1972).

102. The following cases deal with the Fourteenth Amendment due process clause: *Quick Bear v. Leupp*, 210 U.S. 50 (1908); *Meyer v. Nebraska*, 262 U.S. 390 (1923); *Pierce v. Society of Sisters*, 268 U.S. 510 (1925); *Cochran v. Louisiana State Board of Education*, 281 U.S. 370 (1930); *Everson v. Board of Education*, 330 U.S. 1 (1947).

103. The following case deals with the Fourteenth Amendment equal protection clause: *Luetkemeyer v. Kaufmann*, 364 F. Supp. 376 (W. D. Mo. 1973), Aff'd 419 U.S. 888 (1974).

104. *Everson v. Board of Education*, 330 U.S. 1 (1947).

According to the no-aid test, government was to remain neutral among religions as well as maintaining neutrality in matters of religion and nonreligion. Government was also to avoid involvement in religious affairs. The no-aid test as stated by Justice Black was quoted fully by the Supreme Court in three of its decisions prior to 1963. It has not been so quoted by the Court since, although individual phrases have been cited.[105]

In the 1963 *Schempp* Bible reading case the Supreme Court announced a new test to be applied in establishment cases. The Court said:

The test may be stated as follows: what are the purpose and primary effect of the enactment? If either is the advancement or inhibition of religion, then the enactment exceeds the scope of legislative power as circumscribed by the Constitution. That is to say that to withstand the strictures of the Establishment Clause there must be a secular legislative purpose and primary effect that neither advances nor inhibits religion.[106]

The "purpose and effect" test was applied in 1968 in *Board of Education* v. *Allen*, which upheld a state law loaning textbooks for use in parochial schools.[107]

The decision in *Walz*, a 1970 case involving tax exemption of church property, expanded the purpose and effect test to add a third criterion. To be found constitutional, a statute must not foster "an excessive government entanglement with religion."[108] The "entanglement" test in reality became the third part of the "purpose and effect" test established in *Schempp*. A year later the Court invoked the three-part test in handing down its first decision involving federal aid to church-related colleges in *Tilton* v. *Richardson*,[109] which challenged the inclusion of sectarian colleges in the Higher Education Facilities Act of 1963. It has subsequently been applied in *Hunt* v. *McNair*[110] and *Roemer* v. *Board of Public Works of Maryland*.[111]

105. Leo Pfeffer, *God, Caesar, and the Constitution* (Boston, Mass.: Beacon Press, 1975), p. 37.

106. *Abington School District v. Schempp*, 374 U.S. 203 (1963).

107. *Board of Education v. Allen*, 392 U.S. 236 (1968).

108. *Walz v. Tax Commission*, 397 U.S. 664, 668 (1970).

109. *Tilton v. Richardson*, 403 U.S. 672 (1971).

110. *Hunt v. McNair*, 413 U.S. 734 (1973).

111. *Roemer et al. v. Board of Public Works of Maryland et al.*, S. Ct. No. 74-730 (June 21, 1976).

At the present time, the Supreme Court of the United States is applying the three-part test in judging the constitutionality of laws involving the establishment clause and sectarian education. Such acts must not (a) have as their purpose the advancement or inhibition of religion, (b) have the principal effect of advancing or inhibiting religion, or (c) result in excessive government entanglement with religion. The majority of cases appealed to the Supreme Court have been heard under the establishment clause of the First Amendment.

# CHAPTER II

# The Courts as Educational Policy Makers

RAPHAEL O. NYSTRAND AND W. FREDERICK STAUB

Our purpose in this chapter is to consider the manner and extent to which the courts shape educational policy.[1] One thesis popular with many educators is that the courts are usurping the policy-making roles of professional educators and board of education members. We shall challenge this thesis and argue instead that judicial participation in educational matters has been essentially a conservative process that endeavors to support state and local school officials insofar as their actions are consistent with constitutional guarantees. The issue, however, is as complicated as the society in which it exists and the evidence is mixed. Our definition of policy is that of an authoritative decision that guides future decisions.[2] Given this definition, the courts have clearly impacted behavior. Our effort in this chapter will be to describe the nature of this impact and to establish that it has been directed primarily toward providing legitimacy for and compliance with constitutional provisions and/or enactments of legislative bodies.

## Court Action as a Challenge to the
## Local Control Ideology

More than twenty years ago, Gross authored a book entitled

1. In preparing this paper we were aided by discussion with and by the critical review of many persons, including John and Suzanne Burkholder, Luvern L. Cunningham, Jacob E. Davis, II, Eric Gilbertson, Michael Olivas, Nancy Pitner, and Thomas Staub.

2. This definition is similar to that used in Roald F. Campbell and Tim L. Mazzoni, Jr., *State Policy Making for Public Schools* (Berkeley, Calif.: McCutchan Publishing Corp., 1976). See also Roald F. Campbell et al., *The Organization and Control of American Schools*, 3d edition (Columbus, Ohio: Charles E. Merrill Publishing Co., 1975).

*Who Runs Our Schools?*[3] Since then, so many scholars have given attention to various aspects of this question that they have created a subdiscipline on the politics of education.[4] The issue has generated a considerable scholarly interest and it is also of great practical and ideological significance. Its practical importance stems from the widely held assumption that schools as institutions affect the distribution of rewards and resources in society. That is to say, those who work for, or contract with, schools are directly rewarded and those who attend and graduate from schools are prepared to earn a living in later life. Thus some persons are interested in knowing who makes decisions about schools in the hope of influencing such decisions in their own behalf. Ideologically, the issue is important, for in American culture it is believed that educational decisions should not be rendered in favor of special interests but should represent the general will of local school constituents.

Historically, the ideology of local control has been and continues to be a potent force in school politics. According to this view, policy for local schools is and should be made by a local board of lay citizens who represent the general will of the community. These policy directives are carried out, in turn, by school administrators, and the line between lay policy formulation and professional implementation is mutually noted and respected. In reality, of course, local discretion has long been circumscribed by federal and state laws, college entrance requirements, accreditation associations, and other factors.[5] Moreover, the policy making-administration dichotomy is an artificial one. Administrators have long influenced the shaping of policy; and teachers, particularly as they have become organized, are increasingly effective in this regard.

To the extent that it has ever been present, the ideal of local

3. Neal Gross, *Who Runs Our Schools?* (New York: John Wiley and Sons, 1958).

4. An annotated biliography is found in G. S. Harman, *The Politics of Education: A Bibliographic Guide* (St. Lucia, Queensland, Australia: University of Queensland Press, 1974). See also Paul E. Petersen, "The Politics of American Education," in *Review of Research in Education*, ed. Fred N. Kerlinger and John B. Carroll (Itasca, Ill.: Peacock Publishers, 1974) and *The Politics of Education*, Seventy-sixth Yearbook of the National Society for the Study of Education, Part II, ed. Jay D. Scribner (Chicago: University of Chicago Press, 1977).

5. See Roald F. Campbell, "The Folklore of Local School Control," *School Review* 62 (Spring 1959): 1-16.

lay control has been increasingly challenged during the past two decades. The making of school policy has become more complex as boards of education have been called upon to deal with organized teachers, civil rights advocates, militant interest groups, and a wide range of state and federal officials who administer legislation which, while sometimes offering additional money for programs, also imposes requirements for record keeping and rule compliance. A frequent response by school officials has been to criticize the activities of such outsiders as a threat to established and cherished patterns of local control. The effect of such rhetoric is often to rally citizen support for the current regime and opposition to whatever "outsider" threatens.

Over the past twenty years, the courts have been characterized increasingly as outsiders who threaten the norm of local school control. This tendency has been most apparent in the prolonged controversies surrounding court-ordered school desegregation and has been given credence by the often politically motivated pronouncements of governors, congressmen, and presidents. However,

TABLE 1

ESTIMATED NUMBER OF STATE AND FEDERAL COURT CASES THAT HAVE AFFECTED THE ORGANIZATION, ADMINISTRATION, AND PROGRAMS OF THE SCHOOLS, 1789-1971

| PERIODS | TOTAL CASES | STATE COURT CASES | FEDERAL COURT CASES |
|---|---|---|---|
| 1789-1896[a] | 3,096 | 3,046 | 50 |
| 1897-1906 | 2,304 | 2,289 | 15 |
| 1907-1916 | 3,060 | 3,038 | 22 |
| 1917-1926 | 4,464 | 4,420 | 44 |
| 1927-1936 | 6,324 | 6,257 | 67 |
| 1937-1946 | 5,544 | 5,456 | 88 |
| 1947-1956 | 7,203 | 7,091 | 112 |
| 1957-1966 | 4,420 | 3,691 | 729 |
| 1967-1971[b] | 3,510 | 2,237 | 1,273 |
| Totals | 39,925 | 37,125 | 2,800[c] |

[a] One hundred and seven-year period.
[b] Five-year period (incomplete because 1971 cases were still being reported).
[c] Includes cases decided by the lower federal courts and the Supreme Court of the United States.

SOURCES: *The American Digest System* (Century Edition, and 1st, 2d, 3d, 4th, 5th, 6th, and 7th Decennial Editions), and *General Digest* (Fourth Series), 1658-1971; *The Federal Cases*, 30 vols., 1789-1880; *United States Supreme Court Digest*, vol. 12 and Pocket Part, 1754-1971; *Federal Digest*, vol. 57 and Pocket Part, 1754-1960; *Modern Federal Practice Digest*, vol. 44 and Pocket Part, 1939-1971; Clark Spurlock, *Education and the Supreme Court* (Urbana, Ill.: University of Illinois Press, 1955); and *Official Reports of the Supreme Court of the United States*, 1789-1971.

Reprinted by permission of the publisher from John C. Hogan, *The Schools, the Courts, and the Public Interest* (Lexington, Mass.: Lexington Books, D. C. Heath and Co., 1974), p. 7.

the growing complexity of the policy process in education and the litigious tendencies of diverse school clients have also led in other matters to court decisions that have limited the discretionary authority of school officials.

As table 1 indicates, the courts have long been involved with education. Hogan characterizes this relationship as evolving through several stages.[6] The first, which he terms a period of "judicial laissez faire," was from 1789 to about 1850 and was marked by relatively little judicial activity. He describes the following century as an era of "state control," during which few education cases entered the federal system and "a body of case law developed at the state level which permitted, if not actually sanctioned, educational policies and practices that failed to meet federal constitutional standards and requirements." The fourth and fifth stages, according to Hogan, began concurrently about 1950, extend to the present, and are marked by reformation of educational policies and practices to meet minimal constitutional requirements and by court supervision to ensure that judicial decisions are implemented. Finally, Hogan asserts that the 1973 decision of the Supreme Court in *San Antonio Independent School District* v. *Rodriguez*[7] signaled the start of a new era of "strict construction" in which the courts will curb their recent activist tendencies.

The most significant trend reflected in table 1 is the sizable increase in federal cases since 1956. This trend represents a shift from earlier times when almost all federal cases involved tests of the constitutionality of state statutes. More recently local school policies and practices have also been challenged in federal courts. Fundamental to this shift was the recognition by the Supreme Court in *Brown* v. *Board of Education of Topeka* that "education is perhaps the most important function of state and local governments."[8] Es-

6. John C. Hogan, *The Schools, the Courts, and the Public Interest* (Lexington, Mass.: Lexington Books, D. C. Heath and Co., 1974), pp. 5–6.

7. *San Antonio Independent School District v. Rodriguez*, 411 U.S. 1 (1973).

8. *Brown v. Board of Education of Topeka*, 347 U.S. 483, 493 (1954). See also Thomas A. Shannon, "The New Tactics Used by Plaintiffs in Imposing Their Views on, or Enforcing Their Rights against Public School Boards—A Commentary," *Journal of Law and Education* 2 (January 1973): 77–87.

sential from a procedural point of view was the willingness of the
Court to extend the equal protection and due process provisions
of the Fourteenth Amendment to students. Prior to 1956, most
challenges to school policies and practices were heard in state courts
where the standard presumption and result was that locally established policies would be upheld unless plaintiffs could prove them
to be arbitrary, capricious, or unreasonable.[9] The extension of
Fourteenth Amendment protections to students in relation to
school policies has substantially eroded the formerly prevalent
doctrine of *in loco parentis* and has expanded the policy-making
concerns of school officials.

The Fourteenth Amendment states in part that:

No state shall make or enforce any law which shall abridge the privileges
or immunities of citizens of the United States; nor shall any State deprive
any person of life, liberty, or property, without due process of law; nor
deny to any person within its jurisdiction the equal protection of the
laws.

Adopted in 1868 primarily as a measure to safeguard the rights
of newly freed slaves, this Amendment has had widespread application to guarantee the rights of individuals.[10] It ensures that the
rights and privileges accorded by the federal Constitution and laws
are available to citizens of all states, including, for example, the
rights of free speech and religion guaranteed by the First Amendment. Although very complex in their application, the essence of
the due process and equal protection clauses in the Fourteenth
Amendment is that all states (or agents thereof, such as school districts) must treat all their constituents equally and fairly.

The courts have distinguished between two kinds of due process,
substantive and procedural, and have held that state action to be
constitutional must provide for both. Substantive due process refers
to the nature of legislation. As explained by Reutter and Hamilton,
"A law must have a purpose within the power of government to

9. See, for example, *Pugsley v. Sellmeyer*, 158 Ark. 247, 250 S.W. 538
(1923).

10. Implications of the Fourteenth Amendment for education are discussed
in Michael W. La Morte, "The Fourteenth Amendment: Its Significance for
Public School Educators," *Educational Administration Quarterly* 10 (Autumn
1974): 1-19.

pursue and it must be clearly and rationally related to the accomplishment of that purpose."[11] For example, in *White v. Davis*[12] a district court held that police surveillance in a classroom was a violation of substantive due process rights.

Procedural due process refers to the process employed by the board of education or some other authoritative body, or their empowered employees, before taking action that would deprive any person of a right or interest protected under the Constitution. For example, the U. S. Supreme Court held that it was a violation of procedural due process to dismiss students for presumed misconduct without first providing them notice and an opportunity for a hearing.[13] On the other hand, the Court did not regard it as a violation of procedural due process when the contract of a nontenured teacher was not renewed, and when that teacher was not afforded a statement of reasons and an opportunity for a hearing.[14]

The equal protection clause assures that in the absence of a legitimate state interest no state may discriminate against any particular class or citizen. The best-known application of this clause is in *Brown*, where the Supreme Court held that the dual school systems of southern states discriminated against black children.[15] The concept has also been applied in other areas, however, such as in rulings that scores on the Graduate Record Examination cannot be used as a basis for employing or dismissing teachers,[16] and that female students cannot be barred from interscholastic athletic competition.[17]

While it is not possible to review the full range of cases in which the Fourteenth Amendment has provided a basis for court

11. E. Edmund Reutter, Jr., and Robert R. Hamilton, *The Law of Public Education*, 2d ed. (Mineola, N.Y.: Foundation Press, 1976), p. 5.

12. *White v. Davis*, 533 P. 3d 222 (1975).

13. *Goss v. Lopez*, 419 U.S. 565 (1975).

14. *Board of Regents v. Roth*, 408 U.S. 564 (1972).

15. *Brown v. Board of Education of Topeka*, 347 U.S. 483 (1954).

16. *Armstead v. Starkville Municipal Separate School District*, 461 F. 2d 276 (5th Cir. 1972).

17. *Brenden v. Independent School District, 742*, 342 F. Supp. 1224 (Minn. 1972).

decisions regarding schooling, five decisions of the U. S. Supreme Court seem particularly noteworthy in their implications for school policy makers. These cases are *Brown* v. *Board of Education*,[18] *Tinker* v. *Des Moines Independent School District*,[19] *San Antonio Independent School District* v. *Rodriguez*,[20] *Goss* v. *Lopez*,[21] and *Wood* v. *Strickland*.[22]

It is doubtful that any decision has prompted more court action than *Brown*. By overturning the "separate but equal" doctrine, which had permitted the existence of dual school systems, and by holding that the courts should retain jurisdiction of cases until desegregation is achieved,[23] the Court gave rise to a line of litigation for which an immediate end is not yet in sight.[24] Implementation of subsequent decisions has required particular school districts to take such specific acts as redistricting attendance areas, reassigning faculty to achieve racial balance among schools, rejecting certain potential school building sites in favor of others, and busing children away from their neighborhood schools.

By speaking to First Amendment rights through the Fourteenth Amendment, *Tinker* opened the federal courts to cases dealing with student discipline and behavior. Prior to this decision, virtually all such cases were heard in state courts on statute and common law grounds and were generally decided in favor of school officials.[25] These decisions typically affirmed the policy-making prerogatives

18. *Brown v. Board of Education of Topeka*, 347 U.S. 483 (1954) and 349 U.S. 294 (1955).

19. *Tinker v. Des Moines Independent School District*, 393 U.S. 503 (1969).

20. *San Antonio Independent School District v. Rodriguez*, 411 U.S. 1 (1973).

21. *Goss v. Lopez*, 419 U.S. 565 (1975).

22. *Wood v. Strickland*, 420 U.S. 308 (1975).

23. *Brown v. Board of Education of Topeka*, 349 U.S. 294, 301 (1955).

24. For a review of this litigation see Frank T. Read, "Judicial Evolution of the Law of School Integration," *Law and Contemporary Problems* 39 (Winter 1975): 1-49.

25. Richard L. Berkman, "Students in Court: Free Speech and the Functions of Schooling in America," *Harvard Educational Review* 40 (November 1970): 567, cited in David L. Kirp and Mark G. Yudof, *Educational Policy and the Law* (Berkeley, Calif.: McCutchan Publishing Corp., 1974), p. 137.

of local boards of education and the right of school officials to act *in loco parentis* and exercise discretion so long as their action was not arbitrary, unreasonable, or capricious. The rationale in some of these cases also argued that because students attended school as a privilege granted by the state rather than as a "right," the state could attach whatever conditions it pleased to this privilege.[26]

Tinker was a fifteen-year-old high school student who, along with his sister and a friend, wore a black armband to school in protest of the Vietnam War. Because they refused to remove the armbands upon request, the three were suspended in accord with a school regulation. They subsequently filed a suit seeking an injunction restraining the board of education and school administrators from enforcing this disciplinary action. They also sought nominal damages. The federal district court dismissed their complaint on the grounds that the school action was reasonable in order to prevent "a disturbance of school discipline."[27] On review, the Supreme Court disagreed, holding that:

(U)ndifferentiated fear or apprehension of disturbance is not enough to overcome the right to freedom of expression. . . . In order for the state in the person of school officials to justify prohibition of a particular expression of opinion, it must be able to show that its action was caused by something more than a desire to avoid the discomfort and unpleasantness that always accompany an unpopular viewpoint. Certainly where there is no finding and no showing that engaging in the forbidden conduct would materially and substantially interfere with the requirements of appropriate discipline in the operation of the school, the prohibition cannot be sustained.[28]

In delivering the majority opinion of the Court, Mr. Justice Fortas went on to speak more generally about the rights of students:

School officials do not possess absolute authority over their students. Students in school as well as out of school are "persons" under our Constitution. They are possessed of fundamental rights which the state must respect, just as they themselves must respect their obligations to the state. . . . They may not be confined to the expression of those sentiments that are officially approved. In the absence of a specific show-

26. Kirp and Yudof, *Educational Policy and the Law*, pp. 137-38.

27. *Tinker v. Des Moines Independent School District*, 258 F. Supp. 971, 973 (1966).

28. *Tinker v. Des Moines Independent School District*, 393 U.S. 503, 508-9 (1969).

ing of constitutionally valid reasons to regulate their speech, students are entitled to freedom of expression of their views. . . .[29]

The opinion in *Tinker* foreshadowed a large number of cases filed in federal courts pertaining to the regulation of student behavior. Among them have been cases relating to rules for student dress and hair styles, censorship of student newspapers and other publications, and disciplinary actions accorded student protestors who wear buttons, picket, petition, speak, sit in the halls, or otherwise demonstrate on behalf of a cause or issue. The implication of *Tinker* was not only to encourage the filing of such suits by aggrieved students and their parents but to shift the emphasis of court action from the plaintiffs' need to show that official actions were unreasonable or arbitrary to the need of school officials to show that such actions were warranted. In order to defend such a case successfully, school authorities must show that their restraint of student expression was justified by the likelihood of substantial disruption in the event it was not regulated. Here the facts of each particular case become important and the lower federal courts appear to employ somewhat different standards in determining what constitutes potential disruption,[30] as is perhaps demonstrated most clearly in the disagreement among these courts regarding the constitutionality of dress and hair regulations.[31]

In a very different kind of case, the Supreme Court spoke directly to the "right to education" issue. During the 1960s a series of cases challenged the constitutionality of state school finance programs that relied heavily upon local property taxes as a source of revenue. The rationale for these cases was that because relatively poor school districts could tax themselves heavily and still not achieve the same level of expenditure as wealthy districts, which expend equal or less effort on such programs, the state was not extending equal protection to taxpayers in the poorer districts.[32]

29. Ibid., p. 511.

30. La Morte, "The Fourteenth Amendment," p. 8 ff. See also *Guzick v. Drebus*, 431 F. 2d 594 (6th Cir., 1970), cert. denied 401 U.S. 948 (1971) and *Hernandez v. School District Number One*, 315 F. Supp. 389 (Colo. 1970).

31. This disagreement is discussed in *Massie v. Henry*, 455 F. 2d 779 (4th Cir., 1972).

32. Arthur E. Wise, *Rich Schools, Poor Schools* (Chicago: University of Chicago Press, 1969).

This issue reached the Supreme Court in *Rodriguez*.[33] The Court struck down this type of challenge to the Texas foundation program for financing schools, holding that education, while important, is not a "fundamental" right:

Education, of course, is not among the rights afforded explicit protection under our federal Constitution. Nor do we find any basis for saying it is implicitly so protected.[34]

Elaborating the position that it would be inappropriate for the Court to intervene in this matter, Mr. Justice Powell suggested where that responsibility would best lie:

(T)his Court's action today is not to be viewed as placing its judicial imprimatur on the status quo. The need is apparent for reform in tax systems which may well have relied too long and too heavily on the local property tax. And certainly innovative thinking as to public education, its methods and its funding, is necessary to assure both a higher level of quality and greater uniformity of opportunity. These matters merit the continued attention of the scholars who already have contributed much by their challenges. But the ultimate solutions must come from the lawmakers and from the democratic pressures of those who elect them.[35]

Given state laws establishing a public school system, education is a property right of students and is protected by the due process clause. This principle was established in *Goss*.[36] At issue in this case was a state law empowering a principal to suspend a student for misconduct for a period of up to ten days provided that the student's parents were notified and given reasons within twenty-four hours and provided that the opportunity existed to appeal this

33. *San Antonio Independent School District v. Rodriguez*, 411 U.S. 1 (1973).

34. Ibid., p. 35. When a fundamental right is at issue the Court employs a test of strict scrutiny that requires the state to justify the need for the classification which the law imposes. This procedure is discussed in *Rodriguez*. Also, see La Morte, "The Fourteenth Amendment," p. 11.

35. *San Antonio Independent School District v. Rodriguez*, 411 U.S. 1, 58-59 (1973).

36. *Goss v. Lopez*, 419 U.S. 565 (1975). Note, however, that the minority opinion held that the same source (that is, Ohio Statutes) that establishes the right to free education can also define the conditions attendant to that right.

action at the next meeting of the board of education. In striking down this law, the Court held:

(T)he total exclusion from the educational process for more than a trivial period, and certainly if the suspension is for ten days, is a serious event in the life of the suspended child. Neither the property interest in educational benefits temporarily denied nor the liberty interest in reputation, which is also implicated, is so unsubstantial that suspensions may constitutionally be imposed by any procedure the school chooses, no matter how arbitrary.[37]

Minimal due process in such situations, said the Court, would require "that the student be given oral or written notice of the charges against him and, if he denies them, an explanation of the evidence the authorities have and an opportunity to present his side of the story." [38] The Court also spoke to the possibility that in suspensions involving more than ten days or "unusual situations . . . involving only a short suspension, something more than the rudimentary procedures will be required." [39] The impact of *Goss* has been to require at least one state (Ohio) to change its law regarding suspensions and to modify the disciplinary practices of at least some administrators. Such modifications range from following the letter of the law as set forth in the decision to substituting "in-school suspensions" for the more traditional type of suspension.

The final case involving the Fourteenth Amendment to be discussed here is *Wood*.[40] Its significance is that it speaks directly to the question of liability and penalities for school officials (under the provision of Section 1983, Title 42, of the U. S. Code) who deny students the kinds of rights spoken to in the aforementioned decisions. The facts of the case involved three tenth-grade girls who were suspended from school for three months for allegedly "spiking the punch" at an extracurricular event. The girls and their parents sued school officials for monetary damages, claiming violation of their procedural due process rights. Ruling in favor of the girls, the Supreme Court employed what many school officials regard as far-reaching language:

37. Ibid., p. 576.
38. Ibid., p. 581.
39. Ibid., p. 584.
40. *Wood v. Strickland*, 420 U.S. 308 (1975).

(A) school board member who has voluntarily undertaken the task of supervising the operation of the school and the activities of the students, must be held to a standard of conduct based not only on permissible intentions, but also on knowledge of the basic unquestioned constitutional rights of his charges. . . . In the specific context of school discipline, we hold that a school board member is not immune from liability for damages . . . if he knew or reasonably should have known that the action he took within his sphere of official responsibility would violate the constitutional rights of the student affected, or if he took the action with the malicious intention to cause deprivation of constitutional rights or other injury to the student. That is not to say that the school board members are "charged with predicting the future course of constitutional law." . . . A compensatory award will be appropriate only if the school board member has acted with such an impermissible motivation or with such disregard of the student's clearly established constitutional rights that his action cannot reasonably be characterized as being in good faith.[41]

Not surprisingly, school people have expressed concern about the growing activity of the courts in the educational sector. Some resent the increased time they must spend in court, in consulting legal counsel, and in maintaining the records necessary in the event they are called into court. Others worry that the absence of immunity explained in *Wood* may either jeopardize them personally or encourage them and their colleagues to be unduly concerned about legalisms in their day-to-day activities. Still others express concern that the courts are replacing local authorities as policy makers. Some even believe that the courts have taken not only desirable but necessary power from school officials. For example, the reaction of one principal to the *Tinker* decision was to say, "You know, if I cannot make a regulation limiting the length of my student's hair, I don't believe I have the authority and the power to prevent fornication in the hallways of my school." [42]

## Judicial Respect for Local Control

As Johnston observed about the principal whose objection to *Tinker* was noted above, the position confuses necessary power

41. Ibid., p. 322.

42. Cited in Dan L. Johnston, "The First Amendment and Education—A Plea for Peaceful Coexistence," *Villanova Law Review* 17 (June 1972): 1027.

with absolute power.[43] There is no question that decisions such as *Tinker*, *Goss*, and *Wood* have limited the prerogatives that some administrators and board of education members have exercised in the past. Less clear is both the need for and legitimacy of such actions. Rather than taking legitimate power from administrators in such situations, the courts are calling attention to past abuses which, so long as they were unquestioned, were accepted as standard administrative practice.[44] The recurring message of the courts to school officials as explained by Johnston is that their latitude in decision making is bounded by the Constitution:

(T)heir [school officials] power is not absolute and is not nearly so broad as that which parents may exercise over their children because public officials are creatures of a Constitution that creates a limited government. Before they make a decision that interferes or invades or alters the decisions of a citizen, no matter how young that citizen is, they must be able to justify it.[45]

The courts have spoken often and with consistency regarding their role in shaping educational policy beyond assuring compliance with the Constitution. The point was made directly by the Supreme Court in *Epperson* v. *Arkansas*:

By and large, public education in our nation is committed to the control of state and local authorities. Courts do not and cannot intervene in the resolution of conflicts which arise in the daily operation of school systems and which do directly and sharply implicate basic constitutional values. On the other hand, "The vigilant protection of constitutional freedoms is nowhere more vital than in the community of American Schools." *Shelton* v. *Tucker*, 364 U.S. 479, 487.[46]

In a more recent case, the Court upheld the right of a Wisconsin board of education to dismiss teachers who went on strike because of inability to reach a negotiated collective bargaining agreement with the board. The teachers claimed that because the board had been the party with whom they negotiated, the board lacked neces-

43. Ibid.

44. This point is suggested by M. Chester Nolte, "How Fast is the Power of Superintendents Slipping Away?" *American School Board Journal* 161 (September 1974): 43-44.

45. Johnston, "The First Amendment and Education," p. 1026.

46. *Epperson v. Arkansas*, 393 U.S. 97, 104 (1968).

sary impartiality to "exercise discipline over the striking teachers and that the due process clause of the Fourteenth Amendment required an independent, unbiased decision maker." [47] The Court disagreed and affirmed the policy-making responsibility of state and local officials:

State law vests the governmental, or policy-making, function exclusively in the School Board and the State has two interests in keeping it there. First, the board is the body with the overall responsibility for the governance of the school district; it must cope with the myriad day-to-day problems of a modern public school system including the severe consequences of a teachers strike; by virtue of electing them the constituents have declared the board members qualified to deal with these problems, and they are accountable to the voters for the manner in which they perform. Second, the state legislature has given to the Board the power to employ and dismiss teachers, as a part of the balance it has struck in the area of municipal labor relations; altering those statutory powers as a matter of federal due process clearly changes that balance. Permitting the Board to make the decision at issue here preserves its control over school district affairs, leaves the balance of power in labor relations where the state legislature struck it, and assures that the decision whether to dismiss the teachers will be made by the body responsible for that decision under state law.[48]

While the principle of judicial abstinence from nonconstitutional policy questions is clearly established, its implementation is often controversial. For example, in his dissent to Goss, Mr. Justice Powell criticized the majority opinion, saying "however one may define the entitlement to education provided by Ohio law, I would conclude that a deprivation of not more than ten days suspension from school, imposed as a routine disciplinary measure, does not assume constitutional dimensions." [49] On the other hand, in dissenting from the majority opinion in Milliken v. Bradley, Mr. Justice Marshall referred to the majority's refusal to uphold a metropolitan remedy for school desegregation in Detroit as "emasculation of our constitutional guarantee of equal protection of the laws." [50]

47. *Hortonville Joint School District No. 1* v. *Hortonville Education Association*, 462 U.S. 482 (1976), cited in Tom Shannon, "New Standards in School District Employer-Employee Relations Established by the U.S. Supreme Court," *School Administrator* 33 (July-August 1976): 6.

48. Ibid., pp. 6-7.

49. *Goss v. Lopez*, 419 U.S. 565, 587 (1975).

50. *Milliken v. Bradley*, 418 U.S. 717, 782 (1974).

The majority opinion in *Milliken* also gave prominent voice to the local control ideology. Chief Justice Burger, writing for the majority (albeit 5–4), states rather sweepingly:

No single tradition in public education is more deeply rooted than local control over the operation of schools; local autonomy has long been thought essential both to the maintenance of community concern and support for public schools and to quality of the educational process. . . . Thus, in *San Antonio School District* v. *Rodriguez*, 411 U.S. 1, 50, we observed that local control over the educational process affords citizens an opportunity to participate in decision making, permits the structuring of school programs to fit local needs, and encourages "experimentation, innovation and a healthy competition for educational excellence." [51]

Lest it be inferred that carte blanche is conferred under a sanctified local control rubric, the Chief Justice raised the possibility that justiciability might be in the picture, as well:

The metropolitan remedy would require, in effect, consolidation of fifty-four independent school districts historically administered as separate units into a vast new super–school district. Entirely apart from the logistical and other serious problems attending large-scale transportation of students, the consolidation would give rise to an array of other problems in financing and operating this new school system. . . .

(I)t is obvious from the scope of the interdistrict remedy itself that absent a complete restructuring of the laws of Michigan relating to school districts the District Court will become first, a de facto "legislative authority" to resolve these complex questions, and then the "school superintendent" for the entire area. This is a task which few, if any, judges are qualified to perform and one which would deprive the people of control of schools through their elected representatives.[52]

He then followed with a statement that seems almost a pro forma warning but which also suggests the basis for any continued court involvement:

Of course, no state law is above the Constitution. School district lines and the present laws with respect to local control are not sacrosanct and if they conflict with the Fourteenth Amendment federal courts have a duty to prescribe appropriate remedies.[53]

51. Ibid., p. 742.
52. Ibid., pp. 743-44.
53. Ibid.

The point to be stressed is that despite their growing participation in education-related cases, the courts have continued to be mindful of local policy-making prerogatives. Court involvement has come primarily at the behest of those who feel that the educational system has not operated in a manner consistent with constitutional ideals.[54] As suggested above, the courts have been hesitant to substitute their judgment for that of educators and have not done so in the absence of constitutional violation. Moreover, when the courts have found inequities, they often have given local policymakers the first opportunity to remedy them. For example, the Supreme Court suggested that the Texas legislature reconsider its state foundation program for financing schools even though they decreed the program constitutional.[55] More telling has been the general practice of the federal courts in desegregation cases. Consistent with the holding in *Brown II*,[56] the Supreme Court and circuit courts have relied on the respective district courts to implement desegregation plans. The district courts, in turn, have called upon local officials to submit plans that meet constitutional requirements. Only when persuaded that the proposals of local officials are unsatisfactory do the courts seek plans and remedies from outsiders.

## Judicial Processes and Resources in Cases Involving Education

The basic functions of the courts are to reconcile facts in dispute and to interpret laws as they apply to these facts. In interpreting the law, courts rely heavily upon decisions rendered in similar cases in the past. This emphasis on precedent lends a certain degree of predictability to the evolution of case law and to the chances of either party in an impending law suit. On the other hand, the facts in most cases generally differ in some respects from those previously litigated. Moreover, the courts are often called upon to adjudicate cases in which different rights (for example, property and education) are at issue. Some parties argue that as

54. Don J. Young, " 'Interesting Times' for School Administrators," *NOLPE School Law Journal* 4 (1974): 178-84.

55. *San Antonio Independent School District v. Rodriguez*, 411 U.S. 1 (1973).

56. *Brown v. Board of Education of Topeka*, 349 U.S. 294 (1955).

courts decide such cases they have the effect of making laws rather than interpreting or discovering them in past precedents.

Our perspective is that the judicial system is essentially a conservative one. A partial explanation for this is that local and state judges are often elected or otherwise selected in ways that encourage them to reflect local values and preferences. Thus, it is not uncommon for definitions of justice to vary from one locale to another.[57] Of course, the appellate system is an important safeguard in this respect, as is the fact that case precedents at appellate levels are binding upon lower courts in their jurisdictions.

Another conservative feature of the process is the use of *obiter dictum* by judges. In particular, federal decisions involving constitutional rights often include in their written opinions strong expressions of feeling which, although not essential to deciding and therefore not binding in the instant case, may well be harbingers of things to come. The oft-repeated words from *Brown* are illustrative:

> Today, education is perhaps the most important function of state and local governments. . . . In these days, it is doubtful that any child may reasonably be expected to succeed in life if he is denied the opportunity of an education. Such an opportunity, where the state has undertaken to provide it, is a right which must be made available to all on equal terms.[58]

That statement was a warning by the Court in 1954, years before *Goss*, *Wood*, and the many cases involving the rights of the exceptional child in the public schools. Had we the perceptiveness to hear and to work proactively in 1954, we could have avoided countless problems and quite staggering amounts of resources spent in dealing with them reactively.

The most controversial activity of the courts from a policy-making perspective is the process of judicial review. Established by Supreme Court Chief Justice John Marshall in 1803 when he declared a part of the Judiciary Act of 1789 unconstitutional, the process has remained at the crux of our judicial system. Morris has spoken to the importance of judicial review as follows:

57. Henry J. Schmandt, *Courts in the American Political System* (Belmont, Calif.: Dickenson Publishing Co., 1968), p. 14.

58. *Brown v. Board of Education of Topeka*, 347 U.S. 483 (1954).

Judicial review—that is, the power of American courts to set aside national and state legislation as unconstitutional—is one of the outstanding contributions of the United States to the science and art of government. Fundamentally, judicial review really accomplishes three things, each of which is vitally important. First, although the Supreme Court may say only that a law is "not constitutional," the public tends to believe that the court places a stamp of legitimacy upon any law or practice that successfully passes its muster. Secondly, courts serve as a check on the otherwise unbridled power of the other branches of government whenever they seek to trespass onto territory forbidden by the Constitution as it is interpreted by the Supreme Court. Thirdly, by fearlessly upholding a humane interpretation of our Constitution, the Supreme Court preserves, and requires the other branches of government to observe our great constitutional idea of human dignity which otherwise might be forgotten.[59]

Obviously, this process of judicial review is a power that requires the most careful stewardship. Accordingly, the Court has imposed the following conditions upon itself as it performs this crucial function.

1. The Court will not pass upon the constitutionality of legislation in a friendly nonadversary proceeding, declining because to decide such questions is legitimate only in the last resort, and as a necessity in the determination of real, earnest, and vital controversy between individuals.
2. The Court will not anticipate a question of constitutional law in advance of the necessity of deciding it. . . . It is not the habit of the Court to decide questions of a constitutional nature unless absolutely necessary to a decision of the case.
3. The Court will not formulate a rule of constitutional law broader than is required by the precise facts to which it is to be applied.
4. The Court will not pass upon a constitutional question although properly presented by the record, if there is also present some other ground upon which the case may be disposed of.
5. The Court will not pass upon the validity of a statute upon complaint of one who fails to show that he is injured by its operation.
6. The Court will not pass upon the constitutionality of a statute at the instance of one who has availed himself of its benefits.[60]

The Fourteenth Amendment cases discussed above are examples

59. Arval A. Morris, *The Constitution and American Education* (St. Paul, Minn.: West Publishing Co., 1974), pp. 59-60.

60. *Ashwander v. Tennessee Valley Authority*, 297 U.S. 288, 346-48 (1936), quoted in Edward C. Bolmeier, *Landmark Supreme Court Decisions on Educational Issues* (Charlottesville, Va.: Michie Co., 1973), p. 5.

of the application of judicial review by the U.S. Supreme Court. While the process is fundamental to our governmental system of checks and balances, it is also one that the courts recognize must be employed prudently.

Like legislators and executives, judges must often seek information beyond their areas of expertness in order to deal wisely with the problems before them.[61] Professional associations are usually not litigants in cases involving education although they are becoming increasingly active particularly at the state level. Associations are interested in judicial outcomes and in most cases wish to help shape the court's decision. Having attorneys on their staffs, or on retainer, those associations can and do develop *amicus curiae* briefs, upon permission of the court, that call issues to the attention of the court, provide data thought to be relevant to the case, and offer positions for the consideration of the judges.

In like manner, educators as individuals or as members of their associations can do the research, develop the requisite skills, and explicate well-thought-out positions about the issues that are being litigated at particular times. By so doing, they can serve as fact finders and expert witnesses increasingly needed as cases take on specialized matters of appreciable complexity.[62]

From time to time, the courts will appoint experts or masters to advise them in dealing with the technicalities of complex problems. For example, the U. S. district courts have frequently relied upon such experts to design school desegregation plans. Such experts have been influential in leading the courts to expand desegregation orders to include curricular and other program modifications.[63] The scope of some such orders is often cited as evidence that the

61. See J. Braxton Graver, Jr., "The Impact of Social Science Evidence on the Judge: A Personal Comment," *Law and Contemporary Problems* 39 (Winter 1975): 150-56.

62. Luvern L. Cunningham, "Influence of the Courts: Judicial Mandates and Educational Policy," a presentation to the National Symposium on Critical Issues in Educational Policy, Chicago, Ill., October 29, 1976.

63. See, for example, Robert A. Dentler, "Improving Public Education: The Boston School Desegregation Case," *The Advocate* 7 (Fall 1975): 3-8. For a revised and updated version of this article, see Robert A. Dentler, "Educational Implications of Desegregation in Boston," in *The Future of Big-City Schools*, ed. Daniel U. Levine and Robert J. Havighurst (Berkeley, Calif.: McCutchan Publishing Corp., 1977), ch. 11.

courts have usurped local prerogatives. The counterargument is that they are issued only after local officials failed to take the initiative to bring local policies into compliance with constitutional requirements.

One means of settling disputes out of court in the face of litigation is the consent decree, developed jointly by parties involved in problems that are being litigated or quite often are enroute toward the courts. The decrees are approved by the court, whose judges are often quite willing and pleased to have commonly agreed upon approaches to the solution of problems tried. By negotiating a settlement of their concerns, prospective litigants can head off lengthy and costly court activities and retain more control over the decision than if they relied upon the court for a decision.

In addition, other advantages seem to be evident. The solution to be tried must be acceptable to the judge, who is mindful of its appropriateness relative to the legal ramifications concerned. The feasibility of the solution can also be field tested; thus, experience can be gained relative to the implementability of the solution. The data can be useful to legislators, judges, and disputants in similar problem situations. More appropriate laws can be drafted and sharper decisions can be made by judges about adjudicability. Governmental agencies can become more insightful about the impact of rules, regulations, and standards; and parties to disputes can learn more about good-faith efforts to solve problems short of litigation.

One of the better-known examples of a consent decree, is that which was developed in 1972 between the Commonwealth of Pennsylvania and the Pennsylvania Association for Retarded Children.[64] This decree greatly extended educational opportunities for handicapped children in Pennsylvania. Experiences there have informed those who drafted subsequent legislation relative to the educational rights of exceptional children.

It is sometimes a problem for the courts to effect compliance with their orders, particularly in complex cases involving fundamental changes in societal structures. Some courts have acted

64. *Pennsylvania Association for Retarded Children v. Commonwealth of Pennsylvania*, 333 F. Supp. 1257 (ED Pa. 1971), 343 F. Supp. 279 (ED Pa. 1972).

dramatically in this regard. For example, the New Jersey Supreme Court forced the state education system to shut down for a brief period until the legislature enacted a new program for school finance.[65] Another well-publicized action was that of placing South High School in Boston in receivership because of problems in achieving desegregation there.[66]

A less drastic and more promising means of achieving compliance has been the appointment of local monitoring commissions by the courts. For example, Judge Robert E. DeMascio created such a commission as part of the desegregative effort necessitated by the decision of the U.S. Supreme Court in *Milliken*.[67] Judge DeMascio required that the Michigan State Superintendent of Public Instruction develop and file with the court a proposed monitoring plan. The resulting monitoring commission, with fifty-five members, is responsible to the court and includes several educators at the K-12 and higher educational levels to provide support services and advisory assistance. The commission has had the discretionary authority to recruit monitors in each of the schools who are responsible for fact finding, information gathering, observation, and the evaluation and reporting of information. The commission is to report its findings to the court. While the use of the commission assists the court with its oversight function, it also provides a basis for expanded citizen participation in the judicial process.

## The Impact of Court Decisions

The ultimate test of the judiciary as policy makers is that of determining whether or not the decisions rendered by the courts change the behavior of those to whom they are directed. Despite events such as those in New Jersey and Boston mentioned above, there is considerable evidence that court decisions do not always bring about change. The fact that the nation has experienced more than twenty years of "all deliberate speed" and continues to be embroiled in litigation regarding school desegregation is a widely

65. *Robinson v. Cahill*, 358 A. 2d 457 (1976).

66. For a discussion of events in Boston, see Charles W. Case, "Highlights of Desegregation in Boston," in *Citizen Guide to Desegregation* (Cleveland, Ohio: Citizens' Council for Ohio Schools, 1976), pp. 20-27.

67. *Milliken v. Bradley*, 418 U.S. 717 (1974).

noted example of this phenomenon. The record with regard to school prayers and Bible reading is similar. La Morte and Dorminy found that ten years after the decision in *Abington School District v. Schempp*,[68] which declared prayers and Bible reading unconstitutional, three states continued to require Bible reading, four authorized it, and two authorized prayer in the local schools.[69] As a matter of context, it should be noted that the problem of noncompliance is not restricted to educational matters. Wasby reviewed the literature dealing with the impact of the Supreme Court and concluded that "the decisions of the Court, far from producing uniform impact or automatic compliance, have varying effects—from instances in which no action follows upon them to wide degrees of compliance (usually underreported), resistance, and evasion." [70]

Levine and Becker suggest that the impact of the Supreme Court has been limited by lower court autonomy, elite unresponsiveness, and public unawareness.[71] Each of these factors can be related to policy-oriented behavior in education. Despite the judicial principle that lower courts are to be guided by decisions in courts with superior jurisdiction, this does not always occur. Moreover, lower court decisions will not be overturned unless appealed, an action taken in only a small number of cases because it is time-consuming and expensive. The interpretation by lower courts of superior rulings can be counter to the latter's intent. An important example in desegregation law was the 1955 decision of a three-judge district court in South Carolina which held that "Nothing in the Constitution or in the decision of the Supreme Court takes away from the people freedom to choose the schools they attend. The Constitution, in other words, does not require integration. It merely

68. *Abington School District v. Schempp*, 374 U.S. 203 (1963).

69. Michael W. La Morte and Fred N. Dorminy, "Compliance with the Schempp Decision: A Decade Later," *Journal of Law and Education* 3 (July 1974): 399-407.

70. Stephen L. Wasby, *The Impact of the United States Supreme Court: Some Perspectives* (Homewood, Ill.: Dorsey Press, 1970).

71. James P. Levine and Theodore L. Becker, "Toward and beyond a Theory of Supreme Court Impact," *American Behavioral Scientist* 13 (March/April 1970): 561-73.

forbids discrimination."[72] The rationale in this case, which was not appealed, influenced district court judges until it was overturned in a 1966 decision of the Fifth Circuit Court.[73]

Levine and Becker assert that, "The real test of the Court's potency are the changes voluntarily initiated by those elites, public and private, whose activities are similar to those declared illegitimate by the Court."[74] The reluctance of leaders to act in this way has been apparent in many areas where deference to local custom and tradition overrides concern for voluntary compliance with court decisions rendered in other jurisdictions. Thus, for example, school officials in some locales have resisted desegregation, continued to encourage classroom prayers, neglected student rights to free expression and due process, and/or continue to request information on application forms that violates employee rights to privacy.

Public unawareness of court decisions is doubtless a factor in sustaining local behavior that is inconsistent with court decisions. Citizen advocacy groups have altered this condition somewhat in recent years. Indeed, some have published brochures and pamphlets informing students of their rights. Nevertheless, many students and parents remain largely unaware of the law as it applies to schools. As a consequence they may unwittingly disobey that law. They may also accept school abuses of the law without question or upon being told that the action in question represents "standard procedure."

To this point we have discussed impact from the perspective of compliance by the public at large with decisions rendered in specific cases. Another question regarding compliance is what happens to the behavior of defendants in a case after they have been found to be acting improperly. Again the record indicates that some officials may resist the implementation of court orders. Even when officials seek to comply with such orders, however, organizational realities may preclude achieving the goals mandated by the court.

72. *Briggs v. Elliott*, 132 F. Supp. 776, 777 (E.D.S.C. 1955), quoted in Read, "Judicial Evolution of the Law of School Integration," p. 13.

73. Ibid.

74. Levine and Becker, "Toward and beyond a Theory of Supreme Court Impact," p. 563.

For example, in responding to the decree in *Hobson* v. *Hansen*, the schools in Washington, D.C. found it very difficult to replace the "Track Plan" with individualized instruction and to equalize expenditures among schools.[75] Problems of measurement, processing relevant information, training personnel, and maintaining other aspects of the system can retard implementation and perhaps generate unintended consequences of court decrees.

There is little doubt that the impact of court orders can be very real in the districts that are directly affected by them. For example, Cuban refers to a report of the superintendent of the Washington, D.C. schools in 1972, in which the following results of complying with court-ordered desegregation were noted: (a) disturbance to continuity of instructional services because of possible transfer of children; (b) detrimental effects on educational planning; (c) promotion of unrest among teachers, parents, and community; (d) decrease in teacher-pupil-staff morale; (d) discontinuation of specific programs by individual teachers, by teams of teachers, and so forth.[76]

Similar observations were presented by Cunningham in a discussion of events surrounding desegregation litigation in Detroit.[77] He reports that citizen energies were mobilized on both sides of the issue, that school construction and renovations were halted for an extended time, and that the protracted period of processing appeals fatigued and demoralized citizens throughout the city as they worried about the ramifications of the litigation. Evidence from other cities indicates that compliance can bring real dollar costs. One review of several school districts that recently introduced court-ordered desegregation found that districts incurred a transportation cost of $59 to $141 per student (compared to a national average of $87 for all pupils transported).[78] Other efforts to comply with

75. See Joan C. Baratz, "Court Decisions and Educational Change: A Case History of the D.C. Public Schools, 1954-1974," *Journal of Law and Education* 4 (January 1975): 63-80; and Larry Cuban, "*Hobson v. Hansen*: A Study in Organizational Response," *Educational Administration Quarterly* 11 (Spring 1975): 15-37.

76. Cuban, "*Hobson v. Hansen*: A Study in Organizational Response," p. 35, quoting from the "Superintendent's Report on Compliance," July 18, 1972.

77. Cunningham, "Influence of the Courts."

78. *Desegregation Update*, no. 5, November, 1976, p. 4. Published by the Citizens' Council for Ohio Schools, Cleveland, Ohio.

desegregation orders, such as providing human relations training and establishing magnet schools, also have budget implications. Likewise, districts that have been ordered to establish bilingual programs and/or expand educational opportunities for handicapped children have noted the effects of such orders on their budgets.

Another way in which the courts affect educational policy is by helping to build policy agendas for other governmental bodies.[79] Several examples can be cited. Recent efforts by state legislatures to reform public school funding arrangements have been given impetus by court cases in this area. Desegregation decisions have spawned legislation to assist schools in desegregation (for example, the Emergency Schools Assistance Act) and a spate of bills and proposed constitutional amendments (at state and federal levels) designed to discourage busing to achieve desegregation. Supreme Court rulings against public assistance to nonpublic schools have been followed in some states by legislation designed to counter the objections of the Court. Decisions that expand the educational rights of handicapped children are followed by legislation providing for such opportunities. Decisions that allow boards of education to bargain with teachers are followed by school board policies establishing such relationships. Court rulings establishing due process requirements for disciplinary procedures are followed by school board actions to clarify such procedures. The list could go on; the basic point is that calling attention to inequities in existing policies often encourages (or in some cases, even compels) federal, state, and local officials to enact new legislation.

Finally, the fact that courts have heard cases dealing with education and have increasingly demonstrated willingness to rule against school officials has influenced the educational policy-making process. At one level, it has made educators more conscious of their potential liability and the legal ramifications of their actions. As a consequence, they are more likely than formerly to seek liability insurance and to seek legal counsel in advance of formal actions.[80]

79. Wasby, "The Impact of the United States Supreme Court," p. 13 ff.

80. A check with one insurance company that provides liability insurance for educators revealed a 28.3 percent increase in the number of policies issued from 1970 to 1975 and a 78 percent increase in the frequency of claims filed over the same period.

Attorney fees represent a growing portion of many school system budgets.

As educators have become more aware of legal factors, so also have students and citizens. The litigious tendencies reflected in medical malpractice suits and consumer advocacy have their parallel in educational affairs. Encouraged by the fact that courts have forced educators to modify some practices, and unable to achieve their goals by direct appeal to school boards and legislators, many would-be school reformers have focused their attention on the courts. In some instances, they act as individuals; in others, they represent an organizational base and a coordinated plan to achieve widescale reform by pursuing similar cases in various locales.

Knowledge that the courts represent an avenue of appeal for dissatisfied clients has likely influenced the policy process not only by making those who participate in it more sensitive to legal concerns but also by encouraging them to broaden participation in the process itself. Policies and practices rooted in consensus are less likely to be challenged in the courts than those created in disregard for the affected parties. Thus in addition to their direct participation from time to time, the courts have contributed indirectly to the growing complexity of educational policy making just by being available to speak to matters that cannot be resolved to the satisfaction of all interested parties.

## Conclusion

The thrust of the argument in the preceding pages has been that the role of the courts in developing educational policy has been essentially conservative, rooted in precedents, mindful of constitutional requirements, and respectful of the professional qualifications of educators. In some situations, court mandates have been dramatically and forcefully enforced. In some others they have been overlooked or evaded. More generally, the courts have been identified as a resource that may be drawn into the policy process and have established some precedents that provide bases for predicting their position with respect to particular issues.

We see little reason to believe that tendencies to involve the courts in matters of educational policy will slacken in the near future. Insofar as plaintiffs can relate their concerns to basic constitutional rights, the courts have proven to be a valuable resource to school reformers. Many of these reformers believe injustices remain in the system and seek their redress. To them, the courts are an important vehicle for achieving social change.

How the courts will respond to this continued press upon them is not entirely clear. Mr. Justice Powell argued in his dissent to *Goss* that the willingness of the Court to extend due process protections to students who are to be suspended may logically lead to similar protections for the "student who is given a failing grade, who is not promoted, who is excluded from certain extracurricular activities, who is assigned to a school reserved for children of less than average ability, or who is placed in the 'vocational' rather than the 'college preparatory' track." [81] One effect of such dicta will undoubtedly be to encourage the filing of suits that test these and other points. On the other hand, the tendency of the Court to reaffirm the policy-making prerogatives of local officials in the *Hortonville,*[82] *Pasadena,*[83] and *Austin*[84] decisions suggests that the courts will likely continue to respect the professional judgment of policy actors and perhaps even seek to disengage somewhat from educational matters.

81. *Goss v. Lopez*, 419 U.S. 565, 598 (1975).

82. *Hortonville Joint School District No. 1 v. Hortonville Education Association*, 462 U.S. 482 (1976).

83. *Pasadena City Board of Education v. Spangler*, 427 U.S. 424 (1976).

84. *Austin Independent School District v. United States*, 426 U.S. 952 (1976).

# CHAPTER III

# The Balance between Lay and Professional Control

H. C. HUDGINS, JR.

## Introduction

Basic textbooks in education traditionally have referred to education as a state function. School districts are creatures of the state constitution and, more specifically, the state legislature. In order to fulfill their responsibility of providing for education, legislatures have created these local school districts headed by a board of education. The major responsibility of boards of education is the creation of policy not inconsistent with the constitution and statutes of the nation and the given state.

The delegation of state authority to the local school district has historically generated the notion of local control of education. Knezevich has defined local control as meaning the "placement of policy-making authority, within legislatively defined limits, for the direct operation of education with the people or their designated representatives within a legally defined civil subdivision of the state known as the school district."[1]

Since the powers of school boards are derived from the legislature, board members cannot delegate those powers to others. Their decisions involve debate and discretion, which can transpire only when all members have the opportunity to participate. To allow other individuals or groups to make such decisions for the board could be construed as an abrogation of its responsibility.

Within the context of the policy-making function of the school board, Knezevich has identified five general responsibilities of all boards: (a) establishing general objectives, goals, or missions of

---

1. Stephen J. Knezevich, *Administration of Public Education*, 3d ed. (New York: Harper and Row, 1975), p. 227.

the corporation; (b) determining the district's major operating policies; (c) determining the organizational structure; (d) selecting major executives of the organization; and (e) appraising the performance of executives to whom responsibilities have been delegated and evaluating how well the goals have been achieved.[2]

Within the last few years there have been a number of developments challenging or competing with local boards of education for control of schools. These developments have arisen in part from pressure groups within and outside the school district, from increased federal involvement, and from foundation grants. Another major influence has been that of collective bargaining. Teachers have organized in order to assert more authority in the decision-making process. Their collective action has often clashed with the notion of school board authority.

As recently as 1959 Wisconsin became the first state to initiate collective bargaining for teachers. As of 1975, more than half the states allowed unionization of teachers.[3] Since 1971-72, bills have been introduced for a federal labor relations law applicable to teachers, but as of 1976 Congress had not enacted such a bill.

The content and coverage of the state negotiation laws vary considerably. The subjects usually thought of as being bargainable and often negotiated include wages, hours, and conditions of work. It is not clear, however, what is included by the term "conditions of work." It often covers, but is not necessarily limited to, length of day, length of year, class size, preparation periods, sabbatical leaves, retirement, and evaluation. The actual subject of negotiations is the focus of this chapter, that is, what subjects are bargainable and to what degree have these issues altered the concept of the control of local school districts by boards of education?

2. Ibid., p. 319.

3. According to the Education Commission of the States, thirty-one states had some form of mandatory meet-and-confer or collective bargaining law in 1975. The nineteen states that did *not* have such a law were Alabama, Arizona, Arkansas, Colorado, Georgia, Illinois, Kentucky, Louisiana, Mississippi, New Mexico, North Carolina, Ohio, South Carolina, Tennessee, Texas, Utah, Virginia, West Virginia, and Wyoming. Of these states, four had permissive coverage but no legislation (Illinois, Kentucky, New Mexico, and Virginia). Education Commission of the States, *A Legislator's Guide to Collective Bargaining in Education*, Research Brief, vol. 3, no. 4 (Denver, Colo.: Education Commission of the States, 1975), pp. v-x.

## Court Decisions on General Problems of Negotiation

In those states that require or permit negotiations between a school board and a teachers' association, the question arises as to what is negotiable. Statutes may often cite specific areas as being within the ambit of bargainable issues, but they are often silent on specific, narrow topics. When a question arises as to whether a specific issue is negotiable, the courts have decided whether negotiation is mandatory, permitted, or forbidden with respect to that issue.

Several nonschool cases are reviewed here first because they are applicable to the question. For example, a Delaware Court of Chancery held in 1973 that, although items asked for (including premium time for holidays, time off for union leaders, and other issues) fall broadly under the statute requiring negotiations, they clearly violate statutes applicable to other state personnel and are thus not negotiable.[4]

The Pennsylvania Commonwealth Court held in 1976 that the Public Employee Relations Act does not allow bargaining away of rights defined by existing legislation.[5] The act also limits the right to negotiate so that the employer retains the right to hire and fire employees for just cause.

California's Winter Act was held to be valid to the extent that it was severable from its illegal veto power provision over future board decisions.[6] The "meet-and-confer" requirement of the act gave workers a voice in wage and hour conditions, and the controller was required to grant the monies agreed to.

Once a subject is considered as being mandatory for bargaining, it remains as such. This was the essence of a decision by the Michigan Supreme Court in 1974.[7] It ruled that unclassified subjects are either "permissive" or "illegal." Illegal subjects were held to be those that are statutorily forbidden, although they can be

4. *Laborers International Union of North America, Local 1029 v. State through Department of Health and Social Services,* 310 A. 2d 664 (Del. 1973).

5. *Pittsburgh Joint Collective Bargaining Committee v. City of Pittsburgh,* 315 A. 2d 304 (Pa. Cmwlth. 1976).

6. *City and County of San Francisco v. Cooper,* 534 P. 2d 403 (Cal. 1975).

7. *Detroit Police Officers' Association v. City of Detroit,* 214 N.W. 2d 803 (Mich. 1974).

discussed. A party may act unilaterally on a permissive subject but not on a mandatory one. With respect to the specific issue in this case, that of a residency requirement for policemen, the court held that the issue is a term of employment and is negotiable. The requirement can be unilaterally imposed, however, if an impasse occurs. The court also held that if that subject was raised at the negotiation, it must be bargained.

In the last nonschool case to be considered here the Supreme Court of the United States held in 1964 that "contracting out" of work after an agreement to negotiate violates the concept of bargaining.[8] It recognized that the method of contracting out affects the terms of employment in that possible termination is involved and thus it constitutes a condition of work. If the subject is one that will abridge one's freedom to manage, there is no need to bargain. The case involved the obligation of an employer and his employee's representatives to "confer in good faith with respect to wages, hours, and other terms and conditions of employment" under the National Labor Relations Act. The petitioner had sought to contract out some of its work as a cost-saving mechanism. Since this work was taken over by persons outside the bargaining unit, the company was directed to resume its maintenance operations, reinstate the employees with back pay, and bargain with the union. In so doing, the Court held that contracting out is a statutory subject of collective bargaining when it involves the replacement of employees in the existing bargaining unit with those of an independent contractor.

Most of the court decisions on collective bargaining in the educational sector are rendered by state courts. In an exception, the federal district court in Delaware ruled that a collective bargaining statute does not impose a legal duty on boards of education to bargain on matters other than salaries and related matters, but it does permit negotiation on them, as in this case, if such negotiation is not inconsistent with other statutes.[9]

In Ohio the question was raised as to whether a school board

8. *Fireboard Paper Products Corporation v. National Labor Relations Board,* 379 U.S. 203 (1964).

9. *Morris v. Board of Education of Laurel School District,* 401 F. Supp. 188 (D. Del. 1975).

58     LAY AND PROFESSIONAL CONTROL

has the authority to enter into a collective bargaining agreement.[10] If it does, does that authority include the power to agree to the final and binding arbitration of grievances? The dispute arose over an interpretation of a contract and a formula for application of state funds. The union argued that the matter was subject to grievance procedures and an arbitration clause. The board claimed the entire contract to be unenforceable. The appellate court held that a school board can enter into individual contracts, can make a collective bargaining agreement in the absence of statutory prohibition, and can agree to binding arbitration if it applies only to an interpretation and application of the terms of the contract.

Similarly, an issue arose in Louisiana as to whether a school board has the power to engage in collective bargaining in the absence of specific legislation authorizing it. The court held that the board

has the power and authority to collectively bargain with an agent selected by the employees, if the Board determines, in its discretion, that implementation of collective bargaining will more effectively and efficiently accomplish its objectives and purposes. In our opinion the Board can select reasonable means to carry out its duties and responsibilities incidental to the sound development of employer-employee relations, as long as the means selected are not prohibited by law or against public policy.[11]

It was recognized that the board decided only with respect to terms and conditions of work; it retained the right of final decision as to the terms and conditions to which it would agree.

In *Sutherlin* it was held that a statute precluding the board of education from adopting rules inconsistent with state rules does not prevent bargaining if the rules are consistent.[12] The court ruled that the test for determining if the subject is within the scope of terms of employment, or if it falls within the ambit of managerial prerogatives, is to balance educational policy involved against the effect that the subject has on a teacher's employment.

10. *North Royalton Education Association v. North Royalton Board of Education*, 325 N. E. 2d 901 (Ohio App. 1974).

11. *Louisiana Teachers' Association v. Orleans Parish School Board*, 303 S. 2d 564, 567 (La. App. 1974).

12. *Sutherlin Education Association v. Sutherlin School District No. 130, Employment Relations Board*, 548 P. 2d 204 (Oreg. 1976).

Based on this test, the court held that teachers could bargain about disciplinary rules, about referral of students to specialists, and about exclusion of disruptive students if it is not inconsistent with statewide rules to do so.

As in the two previous cases, an Ohio court held that a school board has discretion in making negotiated agreements, if they are not in violation of duties imposed by law.[13] The court was also faced with the question of whether binding arbitration in such an agreement was valid. It answered by stating that binding arbitration is honored if it treats the interpretation and application of a contract.

An interpretation of the term "other conditions of employment" was before the Supreme Court of South Dakota in 1974.[14] Teachers sought to negotiate on the following items: elementary conferences, planning time, class size, audio-visual expansion, budget allowances, school-wide guidance and counseling program, and mandatory retirement of administrators. The court held that the Public Employee's Union Law does not mandate the negotiation of issues that are within the province of the board of education. It ruled that

"other conditions of employment" . . . means conditions of employment which materially affect rates of pay, wages, hours of employment and working conditions. . . . In our opinion the items appealed by the Association are not material items to working conditions or wages and hours, but rather are items belonging wholly to the discretion of the Board.[15]

The duty of the school board to bargain collectively and to contract with a teacher does not mean that the board must use specific kinds of contracts.[16] The form of the contract may be determined by the parties in negotiation.

13. *Dayton Classroom Teachers' Association v. Dayton Board of Education,* 323 N. E. 2d 714 (Ohio 1975).

14. *Aberdeen Education Association v. Aberdeen Board of Education, Independent School District,* 215 N.W. 2d 837 (S.D. 1974).

15. Ibid., p. 841.

16. *Detroit Federation of Teachers, Local 231 AFT, AFL-CIO v. Board of Education of School District of City of Detroit,* 396 Mich. 220, 240 N.W. 2d 225 (1976).

Notices about renewing contracts were sent out by a school board to teachers while negotiations were in progress. The association took the position that this action had a chilling effect on negotiations and asked for a restraining order. The trial judge issued such an order and later dissolved it, claiming that the union could not show just cause. On appeal, the action was upheld.[17] No bad faith had been shown by the board; had the request been granted, the union could have used the same statute just as tactically in another point in negotiations.

In 1972 a Texas court held that a state law saying that teachers could not contract for more than three years could not be superseded by a contract calling for an indefinite contract unless poor performance was seen.[18] Here, a teacher had been hired prior to the time that the law had been changed.

In Oregon the Public Employe Relations Board directed a local school district to reopen negotiations with the bargaining unit prior to the termination of an existing contract for the purpose of negotiating on matters not currently covered in the contract.[19] The school district appealed the order. The Court of Appeals held that, in the absence of an express contractual provision, issues that were not the subject of negotiation and that, by law, could not have been the subject of negotiation, except at the sufferance of the school district, were negotiable immediately upon a change in the law increasing the education association's right to bargain on such issues.

Collective bargaining is allowed but the board's topics are limited by applicable statutes.[20] A teachers' association in Ohio took the position that school board action was in violation of the master agreement. Because of unrest at a school, the board instituted new and unspecified policies. In upholding the board, the court

17. *Edgeley Education Association v. Edgeley Public School District*, 231 N.W. 2d 826 (No. 1975).

18. *Hix v. Tulso-Midway Independent School District*, 489 S.W. 2d 706 (Tex. App. 1972).

19. *Redmond School District No. 2J v. Public Employe Relations Board*, 527 P. 2d 143 (Oreg. App. 1974).

20. *Youngstown Education Association v. Youngstown City Board of Education*, 301 N.E. 2d 891 (Ohio App. 1973).

ruled that school board action can be interfered with in the exercise of managerial authority only where there is an abuse or an indiscretion in the use of such authority.

Finally, a New Jersey court was asked to decide if a requirement that teachers sign in and sign out each day constituted a term or condition of employment.[21] The school district in question had such a practice; the teachers objected to it. The court held that it was a reasonable method of checking on teachers and a prerogative of management.

## Court Decisions on Particular Issues in Negotiation

### REQUIREMENTS FOR WORKING

Several court decisions of the 1970s have dealt with various issues concerning the right of a school district unilaterally to impose conditions attendant to one's securing a job. In particular, the residency requirement and the requirement for a physical examination have been challenged.

In 1974 the Supreme Court of Michigan held that the subject of residency was an appropriate topic for negotiations.[22] It ruled that the primary obligation of both parties initially was to meet and confer in good faith. In recognizing that the exact meaning of the term "bargain in good faith" has not been rigidly defined in case law, the court observed that the judges must "look to the overall conduct of a party to determine if it has actively engaged in the bargaining process with an open mind and a sincere desire to reach an agreement."[23] Once a subject has been classified as mandatory for bargaining, the parties are required to bargain concerning the subject if it has been proposed by either party and "neither party may take unilateral action on the subject absent an impasse in the negotiations."[24] After the parties have met in

21. *Galloway Township Board of Education v. Galloway Township Education Association,* 343 A. 2d 133 (N.J. Super. 1975).

22. *Detroit Police Officers Association v. City of Detroit,* 391 Mich. 44, 214 N.W. 2d 803 (1974).

23. Ibid., p. 808.

24. Ibid.

good faith and bargained over the mandatory subjects placed upon the bargaining table, they have satisfied their statutory duty.

On another issue, two courts held that the requirement that one have a physical examination was legal as well as nonnegotiable. The Pennsylvania Commonwealth Court held in 1974 that an ordinance requiring the examination was a hiring requirement and not a condition of work.[25] The requirement violated no regulation with respect to negotiability. In the second case, the giving of an examination was held to be legal in Minnesota.[26] The giving of the examination itself was not negotiable, although the fairness of it was negotiable.

The legality of a right-to-work law for teachers in Rhode Island was questioned.[27] The court held that the law did not preclude the school board from agreeing to an agency shop in which nonmembers pay a reasonable proportion of dues.[28] More than a certain amount, however, was not arbitrable. According to the agreement in question, teachers would have to pay an amount equal to the dues in a united profession. The court's holding limited the agency shop provision to a situation that "neither requires a nonjoiner to share in the expenditures for benefits he is entitled to receive, nor exacts from him more than a proportionate share of the costs of securing the benefits confirmed upon all members of the bargaining unit."[29]

In a case cited elsewhere in this chapter, it was held that a statute requiring bargaining on conditions of employment allows the university to negotiate a union shop.[30]

25. *City of Sharon v. Rose of Sharon Lodge No. 3,* 315 A. 2d 355 (Pa. Cmwlth. 1974).

26. *International Union of Operating Engineers, Local No. 49 v. City of Minneapolis,* 233 N.W. 2d 748 (Minn. 1975).

27. *Town of North Kingston v. North Kingston Teachers' Association,* 297 A. 2d 342 (R.I. 1972).

28. In an agency shop it is required that a fee be paid to a certified labor organization by the employees who are not members of that organization but who are part of the collective bargaining unit. The following states forbid the agency shop: Alabama, Arkansas, Georgia, Iowa, Louisiana, Mississippi, Nebraska, North Carolina, South Carolina, Tennessee, Utah, Virginia, and Wyoming.

29. *Town of North Kingston v. North Kingston Teachers' Association,* 297 A. 2d 346 (R.I. 1972).

30. *State Employees Association of New Hampshire v. Mills,* 344 A. 2d 6 (N.H. 1975).

JOB SECURITY

Of all the questions surrounding the scope of negotiations, none is more important to the teacher than that of the security of his position. To the administrator, the issue is one of the degree of control he feels he needs in order to administer the school properly. To what extent, then, does a board of education have autonomy in determining, in concert with its administrators, the employment status of a teacher? What issues surrounding tenure and dismissal are negotiable? Most of the cases to be mentioned here involve recent court decisions and they are representative of an increasing number of cases on this topic.

An appellate court in Missouri held that a contract outside specified subjects is permissible. Although such subjects as teacher qualifications, tenure, compensation, and working conditions of employment cannot be negotiated, some teacher participation in discussions on those subjects is desirable.[31] One year earlier, the supreme court of New Jersey ruled that the guidelines of the Board of Higher Education on tenure, which held that negotiations on the subject were not mandatory, did not violate the state's Employer-Employee Relations Act.[32]

A board of education is not prohibited from bargaining with a teachers' association with respect to notice and termination, according to a holding of the New York Supreme Court, Appellate Division, in 1975.[33] In so holding, the court overruled an arbitrator's decision that concluded that a teacher's service had been improperly terminated and that she should be reappointed and paid for lost salary.

Five years earlier, a court in New York had held that a contract can provide for additional days of notification prior to termination of a teacher, over and above the statutory requirement, provided that the school board had negotiated such terms in the contract.[34] A New York court also held that state law supersedes a provision

31. *Finley v. Lindbergh School District*, 522 S.W. 2d 299 (Mo. App. 1975).

32. *Association of State College Faculties Inc. v. Dungan*, 316 A. 2d 425 (N.J. 1974).

33. *Board of Education, Central School District v. Harrison*, 46 A.D. 2d 674, 360 N.Y.S. 2d 49 (1974).

34. *Associated Teachers of Huntington v. Board of Education, District No. 3*, 64 Misc. 2d 443, 303 N.Y. 2d 469 (1969).

of a negotiated contract specifying that the school board or the teachers could terminate with written notice of thirty days and without cause.[35] The court held that dismissal was allowed only after a probationary period unless the superintendent gives a negative evaluation. The time period as well as the nature of the reason for the dismissal distinguished this decision from the one above. In Minnesota, it was ruled that the suspension of employees with thirty days notice without pay is a negotiable item and not a managerial prerogative.[36]

In *Elder*, an Illinois court held that a school board could adopt a regulation defining temporary incapacity on the part of a teacher.[37] It also held that the contract of a nontenured teacher could be terminated for absences beyond the specified three-month period of temporary incapacity. It was ruled that the powers of the school board in employment, salaries, discharges, grade assignments, and length of school terms cannot be delegated or limited by contracts.

A number of court decisions have treated the issue of the rights of nontenured teachers through collective bargaining. For the most part, the courts have limited the degree of freedom of teachers who have not yet attained tenure, particularly with respect to rights sought in dismissal proceedings. For example, in Delaware, a court ruled that a nontenured teacher may not receive through collective bargaining what is not secured under the statutes dealing with tenured teachers.[38] The teacher had been given notice by the board of education that she would not be tenured and that her teaching contract would not be renewed. She conceded that the defendant had no duty to rehire her, but she also invoked a grievance procedure in the hope of counteracting an unfavorable rating of her teaching. The court stated:

Beyond doubt . . . there is no statutory duty upon the Board to justify

35. *Johnson v. Nyquist*, 6 A.D. 2d 930, 361 N.Y.S. 2d 431 (1974).

36. *International Brotherhood of Teamsters, Chauffeur Warehousemen, and Helpers of America, Local 320 v. City of Minneapolis*, 257 N.W. 2d 254 (Minn. 1975).

37. *Elder v. Board of Education of School District No. 127½, Cook County*, 208 N.E. 2d 423 (Ill. App. 1965).

38. *Newman v. Board of Education of Mt. Pleasant School District*, 350 A. 2d 339 (Del. 1975).

or even discuss a decision against renewal. The legal duty on the Board is limited to bargaining about "salaries, employee benefits, and working conditions. . . . It does not necessarily follow from these provisions alone that there is a legal prohibition upon the Board to refrain from granting such rights by contract to a nontenured teacher.[39]

A question was raised in a New York court as to whether a collective bargaining agreement superseded a statute.[40] Nash, the teacher, was fired after a three-year probationary period. At the time the teacher began work, the statute provided that sixty days notice be given; it was later amended, however, to allow for the denial of tenure. The court held that a statute supersedes a collective bargaining agreement and can be amended after the original employment of teachers.

A similar question was raised in Illinois, where a school board sought to determine if it could impose upon itself conditions precedent to the dismissal of a nontenured teacher that are in excess of the school code.[41] Two teachers, subject to dismissal, alleged that a professional negotiation agreement between the board of education and the teachers gave nontenured teachers many of the rights enjoyed by tenured ones. One of the teachers was dismissed for the "best interests of the district" and the other for "unsatisfactory performance," both statutory reasons for dismissal. The court recognized that the school board is a body politic of the state for educating children; its powers are grants and, at the same time, limitations. It cannot take away procedural rights of tenured teachers and it cannot deny itself flexibility in dealing with nontenured teachers. The primary job of the school is not "on the job" training of nontenured teachers who presumably come qualified to teach, the court concluded.

In Pennsylvania, the Philadelphia teachers' union asserted a teacher's dismissal was improper.[42] It demanded that the school district

39. Ibid., p. 340.

40. Nash v. Board of Education, Union Free School District No. 13, 362 N.Y.S. 2d 26 (N.Y. 1974).

41. Wesclin Education Association v. Board of Education, 331 N.E. 2d 335 (Ill. App. 1975).

42. Board of Education of School District of Philadelphia v. Philadelphia Federation of Teachers Local No. 3, 346 A. 2d 35 (Pa. 1975).

agree to arbitrate the propriety of discharging a nontenured teacher. The board objected to arbitration on the ground that it would be an unlawful delegation of the exclusive power of the board. The court held that the school board may agree to arbitrate the matter. It recognized that the issue dealt with wages, hours, or conditions of work and thus was not out of the purview of collective bargaining. The action was also viewed as not inconsistent with any state directive. It was the prerogative of the school board to agree to this issue and the subject of bargaining was not voided by its inclusion in a bargaining agreement.

In 1976, an Illinois court held that the dismissal of a probationary teacher was in accordance with state law. It held that a school board may not delegate the discretionary powers conferred upon it by the legislature.[43]

It has been primarily in the 1970s that the issue of reduction in force because of economic reasons or a drop in enrollment has been a real problem. State laws, once somewhat vague on the subject, have been reexamined in terms of both substance and procedure. Teachers whose job security has been threatened or who have been notified of their dismissal for such reasons have sought clarification as well as protection in the courts. A New York court held in 1973 that a school district cannot negotiate the abolition of a position for economic reasons; it can only negotiate terms of employment.[44] That same year a court in the state of Washington held that the school board could not be required to "bump" another teacher, even if the one not renewed was qualified and had more seniority.[45] In that case, a teacher's contract had not been renewed for economic reasons. In its holding, the court ruled:

Under the law, length of service of a certified teacher gives certain rights such as salary increments, pension rights, and leave benefits, and when the teacher transfers from one district to another, those rights

43. *Illinois Education Association, Local Community High School District 218 v. Board of Education of School District 218, Cook County*, 62 Ill. 2d 127, 340 N.E. 2d 7 (1976).

44. *Carmel Central School District v. Carmel Teachers' Association*, 348 N.Y.S. 2d 665 (N.Y. 1973).

45. *Peters v. South Kitsap School District No. 402*, 8 Wash. App. 809, 509 P. 2d 67 (1973).

follow him. . . . However, even in the case of transfer, the district to which a particular teacher applies for employment is not compelled to give his application preferred treatment over an applicant of less seniority. The legislature has seen fit to leave the question of employment solely to the discretion of a majority of the school board and once a teacher is employed, the tenure of his contract is one year.[46]

In another decision in the state of Washington, the court held that the school district is not obligated to negotiate such issues as budget cuts and nonrenewals of teacher contracts.[47] The action arose after two hundred teacher contracts were not renewed in Spokane. The teachers' association sought an action in mandamus to get the district to cease its action. In ruling against the association, the court observed that the teachers did not offer to negotiate until two days before the deadline for nonrenewals. The state act requiring negotiations mandated the budget as being a negotiable issue; it is an entrepreneurial right reserved by management, not a duty imposed by statute. The court held that the issue may be negotiated, but that a school board is not required to do so.

A school district in Pennsylvania had a contractual agreement to the effect that reduction in force would be governed by statute unless something was added to the contract. No other governing authority was mentioned in the specific section of the contract. Three teachers were suspended as provided by the school code.[48] The court held that there was no ground for grievance or arbitration where the school code clearly provides for the governance of suspension.

In *Schwab* the legality of abolishing positions for economic reasons was tested as being in conflict with the collective bargaining agreement.[49] There were no charges preferred against the teachers in question nor was there any disciplinary reason for the discharge. The court indicated its reluctance to strike down a portion of the collective bargaining agreement; it negated the action of a public employer in negotiating on matters not classified as terms and con-

46. Ibid., p. 72.

47. *Spokane Education Association v. Barnes*, 517 P. 2d 1362 (Wash. 1974).

48. *Pylke v. Portage Area School District*, 341 A. 2d 233 (Pa. Cmwlth. 1975).

49. *Schwab v. Bowen*, 363 N.Y.S. 2d 434 (1975).

ditions of employment. It held that a public employer cannot sur-render the power to abolish positions in good faith through the vehicle of a collective bargaining agreement unless the subject of the abolition of positions constitutes a term or condition of employment.

An almost identical ruling was made in New York in the same year in a case involving the same issue but not a school teacher.[50] Because of economic reasons, a sheriff's position was eliminated. The court ruled that the state's Civil Service law does not give one permanency of tenure; accordingly, an employer does not have to continue a position and budget funds for it. "A public employer does not surrender the power to abolish positions in good faith, through the vehicle of a collective bargaining agreement, unless the subject of the abolition of position constitutes a term or condition of employment." [51]

CLASS SIZE

The litigation over whether class size is a bargainable issue has been based primarily on what a statute allows or intended rather than on what it clearly provides. Litigation has revolved around whether this issue is considered a term and condition of employment.

In a far-reaching decision in Pennsylvania, class size was one of twenty-one issues over which the teachers' association sought to bargain.[52] The Commonwealth Court held in 1973 that even if a subject is a term of employment, it is not negotiable if it affects managerial prerogatives.[53] The court recognized that duties and

50. *Lippmann v. Delaney*, 48 A.D. 2d 913, 370 N.Y.S. 2d 128 (1975).

51. Ibid., p. 130.

52. The twenty-one issues in dispute were: availability of instructional materials, planning time, notice of assignments, desk space, faculty cafeteria, nonteaching duties, teaching in separate buildings, substitute teaching, chaperoning athletic activities, processing supplies, time for association meetings, access to one's personnel files, leaving during the school day, preparation time for special teachers, class size, calendar, closing time for holidays, time of day for staff meetings, time for parent conferences, number of teaching periods per week, and planning for elementary teachers.

53. *State College Education Association v. Pennsylvania Labor Relations Board*, 9 Pa. Cmwlth. 229, 306 A. 2d 404 (1973).

prerogatives of school boards under the school code cannot be subjects of collective bargaining. Although the employer is not required to negotiate on policy, he must meet and discuss. The term "inherent managerial policy" refers to matters belonging to the public employer as a natural prerogative or essential element of the right to manage the affairs of business. Such subjects as wages and hours limit but do not require bargaining in other areas such as class size. Duties and responsibilities of public employers as imposed by statute are not subject to collective bargaining.

With respect to the twenty-one items at issue, the board offered to meet and discuss with teachers but it refused to bargain on any of them. It alleged that the items fell within the purview of the state's Public Employee Relations Act and were matters of inherent managerial policy.

The court held that "other terms and conditions of employment" refers to such matters as:

the various physical conditions of one's working surroundings; what quantity and quality of work is required during one's work period; what safety practices prevail at and near the job site; what sick and hospital benefits are available and what vacation benefits are available; what retirement benefits will be provided and how eligibility will be determined.[54]

The case was appealed to the state Supreme Court, which rendered a decision in 1975.[55] In reviewing the case, the court first established criteria in determining if items were mandatory, permissive, or prohibitive subjects of bargaining. It ruled that items are mandatory if they are of fundamental concern to the employee's interest in wages, hours, and other conditions of employment, even to the extent that the items touch on basic policy. They are mandatory where the impact of the issue on the employee in wages, hours, and other conditions of employment outweighs its probable effect on the basic policy of the system as a whole. Items are permissive where the impact on the basic policy of the system as a whole outweighs the impact of the employee's interest. If the issue is one

54. Ibid., p. 412.

55. *Pennsylvania Labor Relations Board v. State College Area School District*, 337 A. 2d 262 (Pa. 1975).

of inherent managerial policy, the board is required to meet and discuss it, if requested; however, the board is not required to bargain on such issues. The matter was remanded to the state Labor Relations Board for resolution of the items in dispute.

A board of education in New York refused to negotiate with its teachers on the issue of class size.[56] The school board sought to retain administrative control and flexibility of class size in order to provide for program diversity and innovation. The teachers' proposal suggested varying limitations on different classes and provided for exceptions upon mutual agreement by teachers and principal. The board's position was that class size was not a term and condition of employment. The court essentially agreed with the board and held that it was not required to negotiate on class size as a number:

Mandatory negotiation of numerical class size would necessarily involve mandatory determinations of the number of classes, and ultimately it would constitute negotiation of capital construction. This is not to preclude the negotiation of the impact of the board's determination on class size in relation to terms and conditions of employment but the ultimate determination of numerical class size must be a permissive item on the part of the board of education.[57]

In a second case in New York, the court held that a school board is not compelled to negotiate on class size but it can voluntarily do so.[58] In this case a school board agreement with the teachers had a provision about class size. A teacher filed a grievance, claiming that the science and physical education classes were too large. An arbitrator ruled in the teacher's favor, whereupon the board alleged that the arbitrator's decision was in violation of public policy. The court held that since the board had voluntarily agreed to a provision for class size in the contract, it was also free to agree to submit disputes about class size to arbitration. Here, the arbitrator's award was held not to be in violation of public policy.

Due to a budget reduction, the school board in Susquehanna,

56. *West Irondequoit Teachers' Association v. Helsby*, 42 A.D. 2d 808, 346 N.Y.S. 2d 418 (1973).

57. Ibid., p. 419.

58. *Board of Education v. Greenburgh Teachers' Federation*, 381 N.Y.S. 2d 517 (N.Y. 1976).

New York, decided to increase class size. The teachers' association tried to arbitrate this; the board sought a stay in court.[59] Its position was that budget reduction and class size are managerial prerogatives and thus not subject to arbitration. The court held that the issue was arbitrable, for the board had agreed to arbitrate a matter outside the scope of mandatory bargaining in the original contract and the subject was one not clearly prohibited by statute.

Can an arbitrator force negotiations on class size? That issue was before the Maine Supreme Judicial Court in 1975.[60] It originated when the school district increased the number of classes for junior high school teachers from four to five and increased the size of typing classes. All grievance steps were followed up to binding arbitration, and at each step it was ruled that the parties should negotiate. The supreme court ruled that the requirement in the contract to negotiate the work day and class size does not require binding arbitration.

WORK LOAD

The question of who has the responsibility for determining the work load of teachers has been before the courts. Like other subjects in this chapter, the issue has involved a resolution of the question of whether management or the teachers' association can determine work load. Seven cases are presented here, three of them not involving education.

In the first case, a school district in New Jersey attempted to consolidate two department chairmanships.[61] The question was whether consolidation was an educational policy decision or one subject to arbitration and/or negotiation. The state supreme court heard the case. It held that the issue was neither arbitrable nor negotiable; the problem was not directly related with terms of employment and therefore one for management to resolve.

A year later, also in New Jersey, another decision was handed

59. *Susquehanna Valley Central School District v. Susquehanna Valley Teachers Association*, 376 N.Y.S. 2d 427 (N.Y. 1975).

60. *Superintending School Committee v. Portland Teachers' Association*, 338 A. 2d 155 (Me. 1975).

61. *Dunellen Board of Education v. Dunellen Education Association*, 64 N.J. 17, 311 A. 2d 737 (1973).

down on this subject.[62] It involved the question of whether a board of education could assign homerooms to department chairpersons. Those positions had previously not carried with them homeroom responsibilities; the association took the position that a homeroom was an extension of one's work load. The court held that the subject was severable from direct educational policy and so closely related to "wages, hours, and other terms and conditions of employment" as to be negotiable.

A case involving higher education grew out of action by the Board of Higher Education in New Jersey to regulate outside employment.[63] The board promulgated a Code of Ethics, the provisions of which were designed to avoid a conflict of interest over a faculty member's responsibility to his institution. The following guidelines were set forth: (a) a teacher's employment shall not be in substantial conflict with his duties; (b) the assignment shall not be secured through one's official position in obtaining unwarranted privileges; (c) the teacher shall not act on matters in which he has an interest and where his objectivity might be impaired; and (d) the teacher shall not accept gifts or other things of value which might be inferred as influencing his behavior.[64]

Two years later, other guidelines were added. They provided that a full-time employee of a public institution of higher education or of the Department of Higher Education may engage in outside employment only under three conditions: (a) the assignment shall not constitute a conflict of interest; (b) the assignment does not occur at a time the employee is expected to discharge his assigned duties; and (c) the assignment shall not diminish the employee's effectiveness in performing his primary work.[65] The state supreme court ruled that these later restrictions on outside employment related to terms of employment rather than to educational policy and thus were negotiable. The earlier guidelines were found to be acceptable.

62. *Board of Education of West Orange v. West Orange Education Association,* 319 A. 2d 776 (N.J. Super. 1974).

63. *Association of New Jersey State College Faculties v. New Jersey Board of Higher Education,* 66 N.J. 72, 328 A. 2d 235 (1974).

64. Ibid., p. 235.

65. Ibid., p. 236.

Three noneducation cases relate to the issue and are treated briefly. In one, it was held that case load is negotiable despite the Local Public Employee's Law prohibiting discussion of "merits, necessity or organization of any service or activity" done for the good of people.[66] Terms and conditions relating to case load can be discussed without involving those prohibited areas.

The second noneducation case involved the negotiability of the number of firemen needed to fight a fire.[67] The issue was raised after thirteen firemen had been dismissed. It was held that the number of firemen could not be negotiated, but the number of men per piece of equipment was negotiable, as was the impact of job termination.

An opposite decision was reached by a New Jersey court over the issue of combining two jobs.[68] A sheriff was enjoined from consolidating the jobs of a court and a process-serving employee into one title. The court ruled that the state Employer-Employee Relations Act requires consultation and negotiation before any change in working conditions, even if they are miniscule or beneficial to the employees.

The final case in this section involved a teacher who was assigned to nonteaching duties, among them the supervision of athletic events and dances.[69] The teacher alleged that the activities did not fall within the scope of his duties as a teacher under the conditions of his employment and that the activities were unprofessional. In ruling against the teacher, the court recognized that schools are primarily for the benefit of students, not teachers. Since boards of education are entrusted with the responsibility of seeing that children are educated, they can thus regulate assignments for teachers.

### FINANCIAL BENEFITS

A number of court decisions have been rendered with respect to negotiating on matters of salary. The law is well settled in that,

66. *Los Angeles County Employees Association, Local 660 v. County of Los Angeles*, 108 Cal. Rptr. 625 (Cal. App. 1973).

67. *Burke v. Bowen*, 373 N.Y.S. 2d 387 (N.Y. App. 1975).

68. *Patrolmen's Benevolent Association Local #208 v. Camden County Board of Chosen Freeholders*, 304 A. 2d 784, (N.J. Super. 1973).

69. *McGrath v. Burkhard*, 280 P. 2d 864 (Cal. App. 1955).

where school boards have the authority or discretion to enter into a negotiated agreement, they can negotiate salaries of teachers. Other issues related indirectly to salary have been litigated.

The Kansas Supreme Court held in 1973 that a school board was compelled to negotiate, but only in a limited manner.[70] Its decision was based on a reading of the state Professional Negotiations Act of 1970. The court ruled that the terms and conditions of that act include issues with direct impact on the well-being of individual teachers as opposed to matters affecting the operation of the school as a whole. The crucial determination was judged to be the direct impact of the bargaining. The court stated:

It does little good to speak of negotiability in terms of "policy" versus something which is not "policy." Salaries are a matter of policy, and so are vacation and sick leaves. Yet we cannot doubt the authority of the Board to negotiate and bind itself on these questions. The key, as we see it, is how direct the impact of an issue is on the well-being of the individual teacher as opposed to its effect on the operation of the school system as a whole.[71]

It was held not to be a policy matter when an Arizona school district sought to reduce teacher compensation.[72] The court held that the matter involved a breach of contract, even if the school board sought the action to keep within a 6 percent budget limitation. The court reasoned that because a school district can statutorily enter into employment contracts, ordinary law applies. The school district cannot unilaterally change the terms of the contract, for it implicitly includes all obligations of teachers, according to the statutes.

In Massachusetts, a school district and a teachers' association agreed to a salary adjustment for persons approaching retirement. Specifically, a teacher nearing retirement would have his salary adjusted up for days worked in excess of 170. When an order was presented for payment of sums due eligible teachers, the auditor refused to approve on the ground that the action had been improper.

70. *National Education Association of Shawnee Mission v. Board of Education*, 212 Kan. 741, 512 P. 2d 426 (1973).

71. Ibid., p. 435.

72. *Carlson v. School District No. 6 of Maricopa County*, 12 Ariz. App. 179, 469 P. 2d 944 (1970).

The court held that the agreement was a valid exercise of the bargaining committee. The provision was viewed as resembling a bonus, an issue that had been approved earlier by this same court. "Days in excess of 170 worked in a given year represent unused sick leave or personal leave. The provision thus has the effect of rewarding lengthy and continuing service by teachers and discourages frivolous use of sick leave."[73] The court held further that a lack of appropriation to cover the sums due was an irrelevant issue. It pointed out that the school committee might use funds allocated for other purposes so long as the committee did not exceed its total appropriation.

A school committee can negotiate a sick leave provision as part of a package.[74] This has been judged to be a traditional part of collective bargaining agreements. The court recognized that a state possesses not only the powers expressly given it but also those not excepted by the state constitution or the courts.

Like a sick leave provision, a dental plan can be negotiated under state laws giving municipalities the power to negotiate conditions of employment.[75] A Delaware Chancery Court held that health insurance is considered a term of employment and is thus negotiable.[76] Even though money for the insurance had not been appropriated, it was deemed to be a priority when the money became available.

The question of a disparity in bonuses awarded to teachers of special education was decided by a New Jersey court in 1975.[77] Certified teachers were given bonuses of $400 and those provisionally certified were given $100. Later, the school board unilaterally eliminated the bonuses for the provisionally certified teachers. After losing in various grievance procedures, the teachers' association sought relief in the courts. It argued that the subject involved a working condition; the school board alleged that the issue was one

73. *Fitchburg Teachers' Association v. School Committee*, 271 N.E. 2d 646, 648 (Mass. 1971).

74. *Allen v. Town of Sterling*, 329 N.E. 2d 756 (Mass. 1975).

75. *New Jersey Civil Service Association Camden County No. 10 v. Mayor and City Council of City of Camden*, 343 A. 2d 154 (N.J. Super 1975).

76. *State of Delaware v. AFSCME, AFL-CIO Local 1726, Division of Adult Correction*, 292 A. 2d 362 (Del. 1972).

77. *Bridgeton Education Association v. Board of Education of City of Bridgeton*, 334 A. 2d 376 (N.J. Super 1975).

of policy. The court held that the compensation was a term of employment and thus must be negotiated.

Unlike the above decision, one handed down by a New Hampshire court was more strict.[78] It recognized a limitation on bargaining by holding that a statute requiring bargaining on conditions of employment did not require it on money matters. A right-to-work law allowed the university not to negotiate union shop, and compulsory arbitration was not mandatorily negotiable in a no-strike situation.

A board of education in New Jersey was not required to negotiate away its right to withhold salary increments for inefficiency or other good cause.[79] The court ruled that a negotiated agreement need not specify this right since the right is a statutory one. The judgment of the quality of a teacher's performance is a managerial prerogative beyond the scope of negotiations. To hold otherwise would be to destroy an inherent right of the board of education.

### THE CALENDAR AND SCHOOL DAYS

The question of whether the school calendar is negotiable has been raised a number of times in the courts. Litigation has focused on the formulation of the calendar itself as well as adjustments to it during the year. The decisions do not reflect a unanimity of agreement among the courts. The issue has often revolved around the question of whether the calendar is a part of the contract and thus negotiable or whether it is a managerial prerogative.

A 1971 decision by the Supreme Court of Wisconsin held that a school calendar is a condition of employment and is thus negotiable.[80] Under the state Public Employees law, teachers' unions were empowered to negotiate about terms of employment, a matter that affects hours and other related subjects.

In New Jersey, two decisions in 1973 treated the subject of the negotiability of the school calendar. Both involved higher education.

---

78. *State Employees Association of New Hampshire Inc. v. Mills*, 344 A. 2d 6 (N.H. 1975).

79. *Clifton Teachers Association Inc. v. Board of Education*, 136 N.J. Super. 336, 346 A. 2d 107 (1975).

80. *Board of Education of Unified School District No. 1 v. Wisconsin Employment Relations Commission*, 191 N.W. 2d 242 (1971).

The faculty at Burlington County College alleged that the issue was negotiable as a term of employment; the administration took the position that it was a managerial prerogative.[81] The court held it to be an exclusive right of management in keeping with its responsibility for the management and control of the college. It ruled that the board may not abdicate this right but it can negotiate on terms of employment. It was noted that the faculty had been somewhat involved in the formulation of the calendar through a committee that had helped create it. In the second New Jersey case, an appellate court held that the school calendar itself is not negotiable, although the impact of it is.[82]

A school district in Missouri adjusted the calendar and scheduled days not originally indicated in the calendar that had been sent to teachers with their contract. The court held that the school calendar is not part of the contract.[83] Teachers could not enjoin the district from holding school on the three designated days even if the days had not been listed in the original calendar. Moreover, the school board had initially contracted the right to fix the number of days and therefore possessed unilateral power on this subject.

The issue of the school calendar was one of several placed before the Supreme Court of Connecticut in 1972.[84] The question was whether the subjects were to be considered as terms and conditions of work. The court held that "The significance of calling something a 'condition of employment' is that it then becomes a mandatory subject of collective bargaining. . . . The duty to negotiate is limited to mandatory subjects of bargaining. As to other matters, however, each party is free to bargain or not to bargain." [85]

A similar issue arose in Portsmouth, New Hampshire, when

81. *Burlington County College Faculty Association v. Board of Trustees,* 311 A. 2d 733 (N.J. 1973).

82. *Rutgers Council of American Association of University Professors v. New Jersey Board of Higher Education,* 312 A. 2d 677 (N.J. Super. 1973).

83. *Adamich v. Ferguson-Florissant School District,* 483 S.W. 2d 629 (Mo. App. 1972).

84. *West Hartford Education Association v. DeCourcy,* 162 Conn. 566, 295 A. 2d 526 (1972). The other issues involved length of school days, assignment of extracurricular activities, class size, and work load.

85. Ibid., p. 533.

teachers were required to work on two Saturdays for time missed because of bomb threats.[86] In addition to unilaterally selecting the make-up days, the school board also ruled that the teachers would not be paid for them for two reasons: (a) the teachers did not appeal the plan to the State Commissioner when it had been proposed, and (b) they were required by contract to work on Saturdays. The teachers claimed that they had contracted for only 183 teaching days. The court held that the days in question were to be interpreted as being teaching days and the teachers were to receive *quantum meruit* pay.

In New Jersey, a teachers' association went to arbitration over three grievances, one of them being an extended school day.[87] The issues were deemed by the court to be subjects for negotiation in that they are directly financial and personal. The grievances also involved an interpretation of the "savings clause" that protects existing benefits prior to the effective date of agreement unless otherwise stated in the contract.

A four-day week and a ten-hour day for policemen was held to be negotiable under state statutes.[88] The court held that the city of Huntington Beach could not unilaterally change schedules without meet-and-confer action.

In New York, after a school district had unilaterally reduced some twelve-month administrative posts to eleven and ten months, the teachers' association filed an unfair labor practice.[89] The school district maintained that its action was a managerial prerogative relating to the operating costs within the budget. The court ruled otherwise, holding that the length of the work year is a function of hours of work and is thus a term of employment. The subject

86. *Association of Portsmouth Teachers v. Portsmouth School District,* 312 A. 2d 573 (N.H. 1973).

87. *Board of Education of Englewood v. Englewood Teachers' Association,* 311 A. 2d 729 (N.J. 1973). The other two issues involved reimbursement to teachers for courses taken and a teacher's salary being increased for earning a Master's degree plus thirty credits.

88. *Huntington Beach Police Officers Association v. City of Huntington Beach,* 129 Cal. Rptr. 893 (Cal. App. 1976).

89. *City School District of City of Oswego v. Helsby,* 346 N.Y.S. 2d 27 (N.Y. App. 1973).

must therefore be negotiated, particularly since it was not forbidden by statute.

## TEACHER AIDES AND SUBSTITUTES

Like the reduction in the teaching staff, some school districts have reduced the number of paraprofessionals as a cost-saving device. This action has not passed unchallenged. In Massachusetts a school committee reduced the number of aides in order to dilute their majority status.[90] An appellate court held that this action was not a matter of educational policy and was thus negotiable.

In another case involving teacher aides, the legality of reducing their number was questioned.[91] The pivotal issue was whether the action was deemed to be a management decision or a matter subject to collective bargaining. After having bargained with the teachers' association on salaries for teacher aides, the school board then reduced their number. The state Labor Relations Board ruled that the action was unfair and claimed that the board had hired volunteer, nonpaid aides to replace those not reappointed. This ruling was overturned by the Commonwealth Court of Pennsylvania, which held that the school board had acted to save money as a policy matter and had thus acted within its jurisdiction.

In a related matter, the issue of hiring qualified teachers as substitutes was raised.[92] The teachers' association viewed the matter as a subterfuge to avoid tenuring the individuals in question. An appellate court held that the number of teachers and the terms applying to their employment as well as the scope of the use of substitutes are bargainable issues. The court reiterated the long-established principle that hiring qualified teachers is statutorily required of a board of education; in this case, hiring them for the purpose indicated was in violation of the statutes.

To what extent can students who are interns, residents, and post-

90. *School Committee of Stoughton v. Labor Relations Commission*, 346 N.E. 2d 129 (Mass. App. 1976).

91. *Pennsylvania Labor Relations Board v. Mars Hill Area School District*, 344 A. 2d 284 (Pa. Cmwlth. 1975).

92. *Detroit Federation of Teachers, Local 231 AFT, AFL-CIO v. Board of Education of School District of Detroit*, 213 N.W. 2d 839 (Mich. App. 1973).

doctoral fellows negotiate?[93] That question was placed before the Michigan Supreme Court when students at the University of Michigan attempted to gain recognition. The court held that these classified individuals have the right to organize and negotiate but the right is limited. It is limited by the constitutionally set function of the University, and although students cannot negotiate on educational matters, they can negotiate with respect to hours and wages.

ACADEMIC FREEDOM

The subject of the academic freedom of a teacher has been litigated very little insofar as the issue involves negotiations. The issue has more often been in the courts on an alleged restraint of an individual's constitutional rights. With respect to academic freedom and negotiations, two cases are treated here, each of them involving both of these notions.

In an almost unique situation, an association attempted to arbitrate the issue of academic freedom.[94] The contract provided that a subject was proper for teaching if it was appropriate to the maturation level of students. A seventh grade teacher attempted to have a class debate on the subject of abortion. On learning of the teacher's plan, the superintendent directed that the debate not take place. The case got into the courts, where it was held that "the selection of courses to be presented to students and the subjects to be presented or discussed cannot be a 'term or condition of employment.' "[95] The teacher was not entitled to have the issue of an alleged violation of the contract and the issue of academic freedom filed as a grievance.

A California court ruled that a school board could restrict a union member's freedom of speech.[96] The teachers' association sought to circulate in elementary and secondary schools a petition on school finance that would go to the Governor, the State Super-

93. *Regents of University of Michigan v. Michigan Employment Relations Commission*, 204 N.W. 2d 218 (Mich. 1973).

94. *Board of Education v. Rockaway Township Education Association*, 120 N.J. Super. 564, 295 A. 2d 380 (1972).

95. Ibid., p. 383.

96. *Los Angeles Teachers Union, Local 1021, AFT v. Los Angeles City Board of Education*, 74 Cal. Rptr. 461 (Cal. 1969).

intendent of Public Instruction, and the Los Angeles City Board of Education. The court stated:

> We see no justifiable reason to question the credibility of testimony to the effect that political activities on the part of teachers in circulating petitions dealing with controversial political issues on school campuses and during school hours would tend to generate dispute and discord among the teachers and lead to the development of political factions, all to the detriment of the cooperative efforts of the members of the faculty essential to the proper functioning of an educational institution.[97]

### PROFESSIONAL GROWTH ACTIVITIES

To what extent can teachers negotiate on rewards for professional growth? The subject is often considered in concert with a salary package. Three cases are treated here in that they deal specifically with the matter of a salary change as a result of one's improving his professional skills.

In a 1971 Wisconsin case, a minority union association was represented at a convention and the teachers in attendance lost their pay for the time missed in work.[98] The members claimed discrimination and were upheld by the Employment Relations Commission. The state supreme court overruled the Commission and held there was no discrimination in the board's action. It was within the board's discretion to act as it had since state law did not specifically provide for days off for the convention of the minority union and the board had not agreed to pay for them under terms of the contract.

More recently an Illinois court held that a school board could freeze the salary of a teacher but not fire her for lack of professional growth.[99] It held that if there are no specific rules in a situation such as existed here, then the relevant general rules of the state and the policy of the school district should apply. In this case, however, the general rules about hiring and firing teachers were superseded

97. Ibid., p. 567.

98. *Board of Education of Unified School District No. 1 v. Wisconsin Employment Relations Commission,* 191 N.W. 2d 242 (Wis. 1971).

99. *Hefner v. Board of Education of Morris Community High School District, No. 101, Grundy County,* 335 N.E. 600 (Ill. App. 1975).

by specific stipulations about a salary freeze for lack of professional growth.

The refusal to pay a teacher a salary increment for courses taken was litigated in Massachusetts in 1976.[100] The teacher had added a vocational certificate to his regular certificate but was given no salary increase. The court held that this action amounted to, or was equivalent to, paying him as little as possible and thus was not educational policy.

## Concluding Statement

The subject of lay versus professional control of educational policy is timely and has become more acute in the last fifteen years. It is difficult to generalize on the topic, however, for several reasons. State laws vary greatly with respect to rights of teachers to negotiate and the degree to which they can do so. In those states where negotiation is legal, the subject matter of what is negotiable likewise varies considerably. Court decisions are often framed in very narrow and limited terms, and their general application is often restricted to the district in question or certainly to the confines of the state. The reader is cautioned, therefore, that a decision in one jurisdiction may well not be applicable in another.

Teacher negotiations exist under several conditions. There is mandatory bargaining, in which a board of education is required to negotiate with the teachers' organization and to negotiate in good faith. There is permissive bargaining, in which the school board exercises the option of meeting and conferring or of bargaining. If a board agrees to meet and confer, it is not usually bound to go beyond that and reach an agreement. If the board elects, however, to bargain under permissive legislation, it then is bound by the agreement it effects with the association. Finally, there are situations where the statutes are silent on bargaining, and in such circumstances no obligation is conferred upon the school board.

Where school boards have negotiated, courts have ruled that a resolution of the items cannot be in conflict with existing laws or with managerial prerogatives, that is, with the policy-making func-

100. *School Committee of Leominster v. Gallagher*, 344 N.E. 2d 203 (Mass. App. 1976).

tion of the board. The legal definition of policy is not patently clear; courts have made no definitive statement but have considered it in terms of the limited question in dispute. In spite of this, teacher organizations have clearly become greater partners or adversaries in decision making. Fewer unilateral decisions are being made by school boards. It seems likely that there may be even fewer such decisions in the years ahead.

CHAPTER IV

# Issues in School Desegregation Litigation

CLIFFORD P. HOOKER

The contemporary judicial landscape is cluttered with school desegregation decrees, many of which are enmeshed in controversy. Both liability and remedy questions persist and new issues emerge as more desegregation orders are implemented. Is the practice to be corrected or eliminated sufficiently harmful to justify the consequent costs entailed in complying with the order? Is the state or the school district responsible for segregation in schools? Do school boards have an obligation to eliminate segregation regardless of its source? When has a school board fully complied with a court order? These troublesome questions and related issues are discussed in this chapter. The focus is on the litigation involving black plaintiffs. While many of the legal arguments treated here apply with equal validity to all minorities, there are unique equity and remedy issues for each group.

## The Background: From Brown to Swann

In 1954, four separate cases—from Kansas, South Carolina, Virginia, and Delaware[1]—were consolidated for argument in the Supreme Court. The Court framed the issue before it as being whether "segregation of children in public schools solely on the basis of race, even though the physical facilities and other tangible factors may be equal, deprives the children of the minority group of equal educational opportunity."[2] The Court answered in the affirmative, holding that the Fourteenth Amendment forbids state-imposed seg-

---

1. *Brown v. Board of Education of Topeka,* 98 F. Supp. 797 (1951); *Briggs v. Elliot,* 103 F. Supp. 920 (1952); *Gebhart v. Belton,* 33 Del. Ch. 144 (1952); *Davis v. County School Board,* 103 F. Supp. 337 (1952).

2. *Brown v. Board of Education of Topeka,* 347 U.S. 483, 493 (1954).

regation of races in public schools: "In the field of public education the doctrine of 'separate but equal' has no place. Separate
educational facilities are inherently unequal."[3]

The Court accepted the language of the Kansas district court,
which stated:

Segregation of white and colored children in public schools has a
detrimental effect upon the colored children. The impact is greater
when it has the sanction of law; for the policy of separating the races
is usually interpreted as denoting the inferiority of the Negro group.
A sense of inferiority affects the motivation of a child to learn. Segregation with the sanction of law, therefore, has a tendency to retard the
educational and mental development of Negro children and to deprive
them of some of the benefits they would receive in a racially integrated
school system.[4]

*Brown II*[5] was decided the following year, with the Court giving these directions as it remanded the cases:

In fashioning and effectuating the remedies, the courts will be guided
by equitable principles. Traditionally, equity has been characterized by
a practical flexibility in shaping its remedies and by a facility for adjusting and reconciling public and private needs. These cases call for the
exercise of these traditional attributes of equity power. At stake is the
personal interest of the plaintiffs in admission to public schools as soon
as practicable on a nondiscriminatory basis. . . . Courts of equity may
properly take into account the public interest in the elimination of such
obstacles in a systematic and effective manner. But it should go without
saying that the vitality of these constitutional principles cannot be
allowed to yield simply because of disagreement with them.[6]

For almost twenty years following *Brown*, the Court was constantly defining and redefining the nature of the constitutional
right of black children to public education in the South. This exercise was undertaken to decide concrete cases, and to resolve
under *Brown* the conflicting claims of parties—black children and
their parents on the one hand and school authorities on the other—
but it also was undertaken against the backdrop of increasing na-

3. Ibid., p. 495.

4. Ibid., p. 494.

5. *Brown v. Board of Education of Topeka*, 349 U.S. 294 (1955).

6. Ibid., p. 300.

tional concern over what limits, if any, the Court would eventually impose on the *Brown* doctrine.

*Brown*, of course, was a precise application of the Fourteenth Amendment, clearly mandated in the context of the cases under consideration. The facts were limited to school systems that historically had maintained schools that unmistakenly violated the Fourteenth Amendment, and in those cases the condition that offends the Constitution was clear.

It was then a relatively simple step beginning with *Brown II* to launch the case-by-case development from *Brown* to *Swann*.[7] The problem of establishing a constitutional violation rarely presented itself since the cases arose almost exclusively in states in which segregation had been constitutionally or statutorily mandated. The questions before the courts related to remedying admitted state-imposed segregation. In the few cases that arose outside the South, some courts found only de facto segregation and hence no state action requiring desegregation. No nonsouthern case reached the Supreme Court until *Keyes*[8] in 1973.

*Swann* is representative of the cases coming before the courts prior to *Keyes*. It ended the era of unanimous Supreme Court opinions in school desegregation cases and set the stage for attacks upon what was presumed to be de facto segregation in the North. In the Charlotte-Mecklenburg school system there was an admitted past history of district-wide de jure segregation, which had not been completely disestablished. The school board argued, however, that the segregated pattern of school attendance was not due to deliberate assignment by race on the part of school officials but rather to the nature of residential patterns, a form of de facto segregation. In other words, the board argued, since there was no longer a statute requiring segregated schools and since there were no deliberate acts on the part of school officials to segregate the schools, there was no constitutional violation to be remedied.

The Court agreed with the school authorities that there was no discrimination practiced by the school district in its present method

7. *Swann v. Charlotte-Mecklenburg Board of Education*, 402 U.S. 1, 46 (1970).

8. *Keyes v. School District No. 1*, 413 U.S. 189 (1973).

of assigning pupils. The Court, however, saw a causal link between past discrimination and the continued pattern of segregated schools. The plaintiff, according to the Court, could invoke a presumption that the present segregated patterns were "vestiges" of past state-imposed segregation. The Court even pointed out that plaintiffs could establish a prima facie case of a violation of the equal protection clause when "it is possible to identify a 'white school' or a 'Negro school' simply by reference to the racial composition of teachers and staff, the quality of the school building and equipment, and the organization of sports activities."[9]

Accordingly, the Court was saying that in a school district where there is a past history of de jure segregation it is the *effect* of decisions made by school officials that is important, and not whether those decisions were made with *intent* to maintain segregation.[10]

## Harmful Effects of Segregation

A strict reading of the Constitution leads one to conclude that a finding of "harm" is a requisite condition for invoking the equal protection clause of the Fourteenth Amendment. Indeed, the practice complained of must not just be harmful and sanctioned by law, but it must be especially harmful to an identifiable class. This class-centered quality enables the harm to be seen as a form of unequal treatment and, therefore, a matter of concern under the equal protection clause. As noted above, the Court accepted the language of the Kansas district court in *Brown* in the matters of harm, the identifiable class, and state sanctions. It went on to support this finding by citing the research reports of numerous social scientists in what has become the controversial "footnote eleven."[11]

In the past two decades, however, courts generally have not inquired whether segregation is psychologically or educationally

9. *Swann v. Charlotte-Mecklenburg Board of Education*, 402 U.S. 1, 18.

10. The Court seems to have reversed positions of the intent-effect dichotomy in *Milliken v. Bradley*, 418 U.S. 717, 802 (1973). The point is discussed in more detail later in this chapter.

11. *Brown v. Board of Education of Topeka*, 347 U.S. 483, 494, note 11.

harmful to black and/or white children, nor have they inquired whether desegregation would "benefit" children in terms of improved pupil performance or ability to compete in the marketplace. The courts are inclined to rely on the principle stated in *Brown* that "separate educational facilities are *inherently* unequal." [12]

The harmful effects, and thus the constitutional issues, become much more complex, however, when a purely de facto segregated school system is challenged. Presumably, to find that the constitutional rights of black and/or white students are being impinged, the de facto racial imbalance would have to be shown to be educationally or psychologically harmful. Therefore, while proof of harm is relevant in a de jure situation, unless *Brown* is overturned, the recent articulation by the U.S. Supreme Court of the distinction between de jure and de facto segregation in the Denver and Pasadena cases suggests that an affirmative duty to correct pure de facto segregation might have to be based on a showing that such segregation inflicted the same educational harm as the statutorily imposed segregation outlawed in *Brown*. The courts were confronted with elements of this question in *Bradley v. School Board, City of Richmond.*[13] Since the three school districts involved (Chesterfield County, Henrico County, and the City of Richmond) in the proposed interdistrict remedy had previously dismantled their former dual systems and were operating unitary systems, the courts could have addressed the question of the harmful effects, and thus the constitutional issue, of de facto segregation. Abundant testimony regarding the harm of school segregation was introduced into the record by Professor Thomas Pettigrew and others. The trial court, however, chose to rule for the plaintiffs on the de jure question rather than address the harmful effects of segregation per se. The Fourth Circuit reversed the metropolitan area remedy ordered by the trial court, finding no proof that the actions of authorities in the outlying counties, which are mostly white, were taken with segregative intent and effect.[14]

12. *Swann v. Charlotte-Mecklenburg Board of Education*, 402 U.S. 1, 11.

13. *Bradley v. School Board, City of Richmond, Virginia*, 462 F. 2d 1058 (4th Cir. 1972); affirmed by an equally divided Court, 412 U.S. 92 (1973).

14. *Bradley v. School Board, City of Richmond, Virginia*, 338 F. Supp. 67, 184-86 (1972).

Possibly weary from a consideration of the multivaried issues in this case, the Fourth Circuit finally concluded:

Whatever the basic cause [of the concentration of blacks in the inner city] it has not been school assignments, and school assignments cannot reverse the trend. That there has been housing discrimination in all three units is deplorable, but a school case, like a vehicle, can carry only a limited amount of baggage.[15]

An evenly divided Supreme Court (Mr. Justice Powell took no part in the proceedings) allowed the Fourth Circuit opinion to stand.

The plethora of statements about the alleged harm which school segregation inflicts on blacks can be reduced to three theories:

1. *Segregation deprives blacks of the opportunity to learn from the dominant group and therefore perpetuates their subordinate position.* Advocates of this "peer-group learning theory" walk precariously between firm pedagogical ground and the quicksand of racial tension. Educators know that students learn many important facts and concepts from one another. Clearly, the desegregated school provides the setting for black children to learn more about white children. Many blacks however, see this theory as an insult because there is the not so subtle suggestion that a black child must sit in a classroom with a majority of whites in order to receive a good education. Nowhere in the theory is there even a suggestion that white children also benefit by integrated schools. In the opinion of some blacks this theory is nothing more than a plan to obliterate the black culture, leaving blacks powerless in the control of the schools.

2. *Segregation inevitably results in the reduction of the financial and physical resources available to all-black schools because these schools are attended only by members of the least powerful group.* Even the most casual reading of history shows the merits of this argument. The oldest central city schools are often populated by large numbers of black children, while the newer schools around the fringe of the city and in the suburbs are white schools. While some changes in resource allocations have occurred in recent years,

15. *Bradley v. School Board, City of Richmond, Virginia,* 462 F. 2d 1058, 1066.

the cumulative effect of decades of neglect can be found in every major city of the nation. This harmful neglect has been the target of much of the school desegregation litigation in the past twenty-two years.

3. *Segregation is a symbol of inferiority.* Again, the historical basis for this assertion is well established. Separate and unequal schools are a wretched part of the history of public education in the United States. It follows, according to this argument, that the stigmatization of blacks occurs in racially identifiable schools.

While there are substantial counter movements among blacks, as represented by the Congress on Racial Equality (CORE), for example, an overwhelming majority of blacks feel that integrated schools are in their best interest. Mr. Justice Marshall articulates this view with great fidelity, having never cast a vote that would limit or restrict school integration. His votes, often recorded as dissents, seem to suggest that the Constitution requires integrated schools. Accordingly, black and white children have both the right *and duty* to attend integrated schools. Illustrative is the comment Marshall included in his dissent in the Detroit case, in which he recalled the language in *Swann* that school authorities must make "every effort to achieve the greatest degree of actual desegregation." He insisted:

If these words have any meaning at all, surely it is that school authorities must, to the extent possible, take all practicable steps to ensure that Negro and white children in fact go to school together. This is, in the final analysis, what desegregation of the public schools is all about.[16]

The theories outlined above provided much of the social science argument before the *Brown* court. While there were few empirical data to support these theories, the arguments were nonetheless persuasive. Paradoxically, better data are now available, but we seem to have increased our doubts. As Robert Crain has related:

Twenty years ago there was no respectable social science evidence tending to show that segregation was harmful, and yet social scientists were nearly unanimous in believing that it was. Today there is respect-

16. *Milliken v. Bradley*, 418 U.S. 717, 802 (1974).

able evidence tending to show that it is harmful, but no one in the profession believes it.[17]

This paradox, Crain speculated, is due to the growing disbelief in the possibility of social betterment through government intervention—a disbelief not limited to social scientists nor to the problem of school desegregation.

A second source of doubt springs from the escalation of the remedial costs. While some assert that the violation of a constitutional right must be corrected regardless of cost, there is a compelling precedent for a court to consider the remedial costs when determining whether there is a violation. The due process and equal protection clauses are especially suitable to this form of judicial discretion. Consider the following language in *Milliken* v. *Bradley*:

Entirely apart from the logistical and other serious problems attending large-scale transportation of students, the consolidation would give rise to an array of other problems in financing and operating this new school system. Some of the more obvious questions would be: . . .[18]

The Court continued with a long list of policy and administrative questions having nothing to say about equity. The Court finally answered its list of questions by pointing out that:

The District Court will become first, a de facto "legislative authority" to resolve these complex questions and then the "school superintendent" for the entire area. This is a task which few, if any, judges are qualified to perform and one which would deprive the people of control of schools through their elected representatives.[19]

When the harmful practice could be clearly identified as a state-imposed racial assignment no remedial cost seemed too great. But once the perceived harmful practice became segregation that was attributed to agencies and individuals outside the reach of the school boards, the perceived cost of the remedy, when weighed

17. Statement made at the conference on Courts, Social Science, and School Desegregation, Hilton Head Island, S.C., August 20, 1974, on file at the office of the journal *Law and Contemporary Problems*, Duke University, Durham, N.C.

18. *Milliken v. Bradley*, 418 U.S. 717, 743 (1974).

19. Ibid., pp. 743-44.

against the alleged harm, seemed too great. An awareness of these costs has given rise to some second thoughts about the harmfulness of segregation. The question then turns on whether segregation is that harmful. Some even wonder if it is harmful at all.

## The De Jure-De Facto Dilemma

Circuit courts deciding the question have consistently refused to characterize de facto segregation as unconstitutional state action. Some federal district courts before *Keyes*, however, have indicated that they would find de facto segregation constitutionally impermissible. Other courts, in ruling on situations analogous to de facto segregation, have established substantial support for its elimination. Some district courts and at least one circuit court have even held that, because segregation was a foreseeable result of the use of school zone boundaries that conformed to residential dividing lines, such segregation was de jure. In these instances the Fourteenth Amendment was seen as a mandate for the state to take affirmative steps to avoid harm or injury to its citizens. Finding no evidence of state action that created racial segregation in the schools, these courts have simply equated "state inaction" with state action to bring the issue within the scope of the Fourteenth Amendment. In so doing, they have inferred segregative intent from school board actions having the foreseeable effect of fostering segregation. Thus the courts have engrafted the tort principle, that a person is responsible for the natural consequences of his actions, onto school desegregation cases in order to establish "intent." A holding of the Second Circuit illustrates the point:

[A] finding of de jure segregation may be based on actions taken, coupled with omissions made, by governmental authorities which have the natural and foreseeable consequences of causing educational segregation.[20]

In *Hobson* v. *Hansen* the district court for the District of Columbia set itself the task of differentiating between de jure and de facto segregation.[21] According to the court in *Hobson*, de jure segregation "adverts to segregation specifically mandated by law or

20. *Hart* v. *Community School Board*, 512 F. 2d. 37, 50 (1975).

21. *Hobson* v. *Hansen*, 269 F. Supp. 401 (D.D.C., 1967).

by public policy pursued under color of law." [22] The Court also noted that de jure segregation has been clearly denounced as unconstitutional by the Supreme Court in *Bolling* v. *Sharpe*[23] and in *Brown*. According to Judge J. Skelly Wright in the *Hobson* case, however, segregation is de facto in an instance resulting from "social or other conditions for which government cannot be held responsible." [24]

In contrast to the above clear declarations by the *Hobson* court, there are many who feel that to differentiate the two types of segregation absolutely would result in an artificial distinction. The starting point of the disagreement is in the approaches taken to the meaning of the terms *de facto* and *de jure*. Advocates of the exclusion of a de facto form of segregation from equal protection would accept Judge Wright's view of the existence of two identifiable types of segregation. On the other hand, Mr. Justice Powell concluded in his dissent in *Keyes* that it should be irrelevant whether the existing segregation is "state-assisted" or "state-perpetuated," since public schools are created under the auspices of the state. In his dissent in *Keyes*, Mr. Justice Douglas seems to be saying that the Constitution condemns discrimination whether accomplished ingeniously or ingenuously. Accordingly, it seems that Justices Powell and Douglas are saying that the Constitution should be used to protect citizens from the evils of prejudice, public or private, a morally plausible proposition of questionable constitutional relevance. Or, put another way, there is the assumption that all observable segregation is the product of some form of state action. Opponents of this view would respond by saying that the role of the Supreme Court is to interpret the law and not necessarily to encourage the moral and condemn the amoral acts of private citizens. It follows, therefore, that some quantum of state action, and not simply state inaction, would be required for a holding that the isolation of a minority group is condemned by the Constitution. Continuing the argument, the legislative branch of

22. Ibid., p. 493.

23. *Bolling v. Sharpe,* 374 U.S. 497 (1954).

24. *Hobson v. Hansen,* 269 F. Supp. 401, 493.

government is the appropriate body to act when there is an educational need and no constitutional violation is involved.

The response to the argument that all segregation is the product of some form of state action is a bit more complicated. Currently, school segregation exists, especially in the northern industrial cities, because of several factors: (a) the absence of overt state action to avoid it; (b) residential patterns; (c) the neighborhood school policy; (d) the selection of construction sites for new schools; and (e) white flight to the suburbs. These, and many more factors, have created racial segregation in the schools. The causes of such segregation and the interrelatedness of the factors motivated the Fourth Circuit Court of Appeals to conclude:

[T]he root causes of the concentration of blacks in the inner cities of America are simply not known. . . . [Any] action the counties may seem to have taken to keep blacks out is slight indeed compared to the myriad reasons, economic, political, and social, for the concentration of blacks in Richmond and does not support the conclusion that it has been invidious state action which has resulted in the racial composition of the three school districts.[25]

Similarly, in a concurring comment in the Detroit case, Mr. Justice Stewart was unwilling to agree with Mr. Justice Marshall in his dissent. When Marshall said that black children in Detroit had been confined by (external) intentional acts of segregation, Mr. Justice Stewart responded:

Segregative acts within the city alone cannot be presumed to have produced—and no factual showing was made that they did produce—an increase in the number of Negro students in the city as a whole. It is this essential fact of predominantly Negro school population in Detroit—caused by unknown and perhaps unknowable factors such as in-migration, birth rates, economic changes, or cumulative acts of private racial fears—that accounts for the "growing core of Negro schools," a "core" that has grown to include virtually the entire city. The Constitution simply does not allow federal courts to attempt to change that situation unless and until it is shown that the State, or its political subdivisions, have contributed to cause the situation to exist.[26]

As the first nonsouthern school desegregation case to be heard

25. *Bradley v. School Board, City of Richmond, Virginia,* 462 F. 2d 1058, 1066.

26. *Milliken v. Bradley,* 418 U.S. 717, 756, note 2.

by the Supreme Court, *Keyes* (the Denver case) led to an articulation of the issues involved in a school system that had never been
segregated pursuant to state statutory or constitutional provisions.
The Court stated:

[W]e hold that a finding of intentionally segregative school board
actions in a meaningful portion of a school system . . . creates a presumption that other segregated schooling within the system is adventi-
tious. It establishes . . . a prima facie case of unlawful segregative design
on the part of school authorities, and shifts to those authorities the
burden of proving that other segregated schools within the system are
not also the result of intentionally segregative actions.[27]

The *Keyes* decision is significant in two respects. First, it allows
a plaintiff to effectuate city-wide desegregation with a showing of
intentional segregation in only a substantial portion of the school
district. Second, the holding indicates the approach that will be
taken by the Court in dealing with problems of desegregation in a
northern context. In grappling with the problem of the dual school
system, however, the Court seems to indicate that it may exact a
high price, in terms of national desegregation policy, for substantially easing the plaintiff's burden of proof.

Four levels of inquiry are revealed by the Court in *Keyes*. First,
was there segregation in the first instance? Secondly, assuming that
there was segregation, was that segregation intentional, that is, was
there "segregative intent" on the part of the school board? And,
if there were intentional segregation in one area, could this finding
be of value in assessing board policies throughout the rest of the
district? Finally, in the event that a plaintiff did establish a prima
facie case of unlawful segregation, what could the board do to
rebut that presumption?

Having discovered segregation in a portion of the Denver
schools, the Court then focused on whether the school board,
through its policies, displayed the "segregative intent" necessary to
invoke the jurisdiction of the Court under the equal protection
clause. The Court's use of "segregative intent" in determining cul-
pability settled a controversy that had arisen in lower courts. More
significantly, by using this standard the Court perpetuated the de
facto/de jure distinction that it had enunciated in dealing with

27. *Keyes v. School District No. 1*, 413 U.S. 189, 208.

intentional segregation in the southern context. Mr. Justice Brennan, writing for the majority, emphasized that the distinguishing factor between de facto and the unlawful de jure segregation was the "purpose or intent to segregate." The Court, however, had not been guided by this strict reading of the Constitution in all cases prior to *Keyes*.

In *Brown*, the Warren Court held that state-imposed segregation constituted a denial of "equal educational opportunity" and a violation of the equal protection clause. The thrust of the case was essentially negative. It imposed no affirmative duty on the state to desegregate, but simply prohibited the state from intentionally mandating a dual school system.

Had the Court adhered to this rationale, the de facto/de jure distinction would be based on solid legal principles. In *Green v. County School Board*, however, a dramatic shift in the Court's attitude can be seen.[28] In this instance the Court was no longer satisfied with state neutrality but charged the school officials "with the affirmative duty to take whatever steps might be necessary to convert to a unitary system in which racial discrimination would be eliminated root and branch."[29]

This was the Court's expression of dissatisfaction with a "freedom of choice" plan which had not eliminated racially identifiable schools. It was now incumbent upon the school officials to institute a plan that promised to work immediately. The school was thus held accountable not only for its positive acts but also for its acts of omission, that is, its failure to institute a plan that would promote desegregation. This was so even after all statutory provisions mandating segregation were removed.

In *Swann*, some two years later, the Court had already begun its retreat from *Green*. The Court stated:

We are concerned in these cases with the elimination of discrimination inherent in the dual school systems, not with myriad factors of human existence which can cause discrimination in a multitude of ways on racial, religious, or ethnic grounds.[30]

The Court in *Swann* clung tenaciously to its theoretical de facto/

28. *Green v. County School Board*, 391 U.S. 430 (1966).

29. Ibid., pp. 437-38.

30. *Swann v. Charlotte-Mecklenburg Board of Education*, 402 U.S. 1, 22.

de jure distinction and did not expand or even accept the "affirmative duty" doctrine of *Green*.

Similarly, the Court in *Keyes* maintained the distinction with an
emphasis upon purpose or intent to segregate. Thus the plaintiffs
now "must prove not only that segregated schooling exists but also
that it was brought about or maintained by intentional state
action." [31] Among the factors relied upon as indicators of "purpose"
or "intent" to segregate were: (a) deliberate segregative acts of
pupil assignment to schools located in a nonwhite residential area of
the city of Denver; (b) racial assignment of faculty and staff; (c)
locating a school "with conscious knowledge that it would be a
segregated school"; and (d) adopting policies that "have the clear
effect of earmarking schools according to their racial composition." [32]

With the articulation of the *purpose* or *intent* test in *Keyes*, the
Supreme Court has increased the burden of plaintiffs in de facto
cases and has all but eliminated the argument equating state inaction
with state action.

The Court applied this "purpose or intent" test in the Pasadena
case in June, 1976 when it reversed the refusal of a trial court to
lift a "no majority of any minority" order, which had been issued
in 1970. The Supreme Court held that the Pasadena School Board
could not be required to make annual adjustments in attendance
zones, once the original order to desegregate had been fully implemented, simply because of "people randomly moving into, out
of, and around the Pasadena area." [33] This most recent pronouncement by the Court leaves no doubt about its bifurcated view of
school segregation. According to the Court, school segregation
exists in two forms—de jure and de facto. The former offends the
Constitution, the latter is beyond its ambit.

## Metropolitan Area Remedies

The federal courts have been confronted with a host of plaintiffs
who maintain that school district lines should be disregarded in de-

31. *Keyes v. School District No. 1*, 413 U.S. 189, 198.

32. Ibid., pp. 201-2.

33. *Pasadena City Board of Education v. Nancy Anne Spangler*, 44 U.S.L.W.
5114 (June 28, 1976).

vising remedies for disestablishing an unconstitutional dual school system. The facts vary, but the typical scene is a central city that is losing total population to the suburban ring while the minority population within the central city increases. The proportion of minority students in the central city is increasing even more rapidly than the total minority population. As this scenario develops, and is repeated in almost every major city of the nation, it becomes more futile to order a desegregation plan confined to the city limits inasmuch as there is, or will be, no one left with whom to integrate. Thus the plaintiffs have sought a metropolitan area remedy.

The litigation regarding cross-district, or interdistrict organizational arrangements, can be classified according to the two types of remedies that have been sought by the plaintiffs. One involves the formation of a single "superdistrict" by consolidating contiguous districts in a metropolitan area—the remedy proposed by the district courts in Richmond and Detroit. The second involves the consolidation of two or more school districts that are but a part of a metropolitan area where it is alleged that school district boundaries have been modified with segregative intent. Examples of this group are found in Pittsburgh and Indianapolis.

### SUPERDISTRICTS

On May 21, 1973, an equally divided Supreme Court (Mr. Justice Powell took no part in the case) affirmed the decision of the Fourth Circuit Court of Appeals in *Bradley* v. *School Board, City of Richmond, Virginia*[34] in which the trial court order for the creation of a superdistrict for the metropolitan area was reversed. Fourteen months later, July 25, 1974, the Supreme Court ruled against mandatory busing of school children between city and suburban school districts in the Detroit metropolitan area. In the 5-4 (or as some see it, the 4-1-4) decision in *Milliken* v. *Bradley*,[35] the Court held that the plaintiffs had not established sufficient grounds of discrimination or segregation based on state action to warrant the imposition of a proposed metropolitan de-

34. *Bradley* v. *School Board, City of Richmond, Virginia,* 416 U.S. 696 (1974).

35. *Milliken* v. *Bradley,* 418 U.S. 717 (1974).

segregation plan. In doing so it overturned the opinion of the federal district court and the Sixth Circuit Court of Appeals.

Aside from the coincidence that the plaintiffs in both cases have the same surname, the cases are strikingly similar. Both were cases in which the respective district courts had ordered school desegregation accomplished by means of a metropolitan plan. In both instances, school district boundaries have remained unchanged for more than a hundred years and both had almost exactly the same percentage of black children when the respective cases were tried. Both district courts found city-only plans were inadequate because they would increase white flight and cause the system to become overwhelmingly black. Both district courts found the suburban districts were needed to accomplish desegregation in the city school districts. The Supreme Court in the Detroit case and the Fourth Circuit Court in the Richmond Case (the Supreme Court wrote no opinion in the evenly divided Richmond Case) held that there is no constitutional right of the plaintiffs to any particular degree of racial balance and that desegregation does not require any particular racial balance. Both of these courts held that unless some constitutional violation was found causing interdistrict segregation, no interdistrict remedy would be appropriate.[36]

The legal argument made by the plaintiffs in both cases, and accepted by the dissenters in *Milliken*, is straightforward enough. Since the Fourteenth Amendment speaks to the states, not its subdivisions; since the Constitution recognizes the equal protection right of blacks but does not similarly recognize a state's right to maintain political-geographic subdivisions; since these subdivisions are at most no more than a convenient administrative apparatus; and since in other contexts, specifically the reapportionment cases, the Court has required restructuring of the political subdivisions of a state for equal protection purposes; it follows that school district boundaries may give way also if that is required to prevent state denial of equal educational opportunity to black children.

The authors of the majority opinions in the Fourth Circuit and the Supreme Court were not persuaded by these arguments. Both

---

36. *Milliken v. Bradley*, 418 U.S. 717; *Bradley v. School Board, City of Richmond, Virginia*, 462 F. 2d 1058.

were inclined to pose the question much more narrowly. Judge Craven of the Fourth Circuit asked:

May a United States District Judge compel one of the states of the union to restructure its internal government for the purpose of achieving racial balance in the assignment of pupils to public schools? We think not, absent invidious discrimination in the establishment or maintenance of local governmental units.[37]

Judge Craven explained:

In his (District Court Judge Robert R. Merhige, Jr.) concern for effective implementation of the Fourteenth Amendment he failed to sufficiently consider, we think, a fundamental principle of federalism incorporated in the Tenth Amendment.[38]

Chief Justice Burger worded the question without reference to the State of Michigan in the *Milliken* case—a crucial omission as far as the plaintiffs were concerned. As he framed the question before the Court, Justice Burger explained:

We granted certiorari in these consolidated cases to determine whether a federal court may impose a multi-district, area-wide remedy to a single district de jure segregation problem absent any finding that the other included school districts have failed to operate unitary school systems within their districts, absent any claim or finding that the boundary lines of any affected school district were established with the purpose of fostering racial segregation in public schools, absent any finding that the included districts committed acts which effected segregation within the other districts, and absent a meaningful opportunity for the included neighboring school districts to present evidence or be heard on the propriety of a multidistrict remedy or on the question of constitutional violations by those neighboring districts.[39]

In contrast, counsel for black plaintiffs framed the question:

May the state of Michigan continue the intentional confinement of black children to an expanding core of state-imposed black schools within a line in a way no less effective than intentionally drawing a line around them, merely because petitioners seek to interpose an existing school district boundary as the latest line of containment? [40]

37. *Milliken v. Bradley*, 462 F. 2d 1058, 1060.
38. Ibid., p. 1061.
39. *Milliken v. Bradley*, 418 U.S. 717, 721-22.
40. Brief for Respondents, Ronald G. Bradley et al., Nos. 73-434 to 73-436, October Term, 1973, pp. 1-2.

The full significance of these decisions cannot now be accurately assessed. Mr. Justice Marshall characterized the Detroit decision as a "giant step backwards."[41] Mr. Justice White considered the majority opinion an "arbitrary limitation on the equitable power of the federal district courts, based on the invisible borders of local school districts."[42] Mr. Justice White seemed to be advocating a legal theory of "no-fault segregation" when he wrote in a dissent:

The task is not to devise a system of pains and penalties to punish constitutional violations brought to light. Rather, it is to desegregate an educational system in which the races have been kept apart.[43]

Nevertheless, Chief Justice Burger articulated the principle that an interdistrict violation is necessary before an interdistrict remedy can be ordered. Building upon the Court's holding in *Swann* he wrote: "The scope of the remedy is determined by the nature and extent of the constitutional violation."[44]

He related the basic standards that are to govern the use of cross-district remedies as follows:

Before the boundaries of separate and autonomous school districts may be set aside by consolidating the separate units for remedial purposes or by imposing a cross-district remedy, it must first be shown that there has been a constitutional violation within one district that produces a significant segregative effect in another district. Specifically it must be shown that racially discriminatory acts of the state or local school districts, or of a single school district have been a substantial cause of interdistrict segregation. . . . Where the schools of only one district have been affected, there is not constitutional power in the courts to decree relief balancing the racial composition of that district's schools with those of the surrounding districts.[45]

The Court left the door only slightly ajar on interdistrict remedies:

An interdistrict remedy might be in order where the racially discriminatory acts of one or more school districts *caused* racial segregation in

41. *Milliken v. Bradley*, 418 U.S. 717, 782.

42. Ibid., p. 781.

43. Ibid., p. 764.

44. Ibid., p. 744.

45. Ibid., pp. 744-45.

an adjacent district, or where district lines have been deliberately drawn on the basis of race.[46] (emphasis added)

Mr. Justice Stewart opened the door a bit further when, in concurring with the majority, he showed a willingness to consider segregative acts of all state agencies which may have contained blacks to Detroit. Proof of such actions by other governmental agencies would in certain circumstances permit an interdistrict remedy.

Were it to be shown, for example, that state officials had contributed to the separation of the races . . . by purposeful, racially discriminatory use of state housing or zoning laws, then a decree calling for transfer of pupils across district lines or for restructuring of district lines might well be appropriate.[47]

### CONSOLIDATION OF A PORTION OF A METROPOLITAN AREA

The Pittsburgh and Indianapolis cases[48] illustrate that the consolidation of a portion of a metropolitan area may be relatively easy to accomplish when there is a showing that the municipal and/or school district boundaries have been adjusted or maintained with segregative intent. Since both cases have been before the courts since *Milliken* they give some clues regarding lower court applications of the *Milliken* decree.

Again, the two cases chosen for discussion have many facts in common. In both instances the plaintiffs alleged that the state created or maintained school district boundaries to protect white enclosures from high concentrations of black students. Also, both cases were concerned with school districts outside the central city. Finally, relatively recent acts by the state created the conditions that were challenged by the plaintiffs. The principal difference in the facts is that the central city of Indianapolis is involved in one case while the Pittsburgh case is limited to some of the suburban districts in Allegheny County.

The Commonwealth of Pennsylvania, the State Board of Educa-

46. Ibid., p. 745.

47. Ibid., p. 755.

48. *Hoots v. Commonwealth of Pennsylvania*, 359 F. Supp. 807, 821 (1973); *U.S. v. Board of School Commissioners, City of Indianapolis*, 503 F. 2d 68, 86 (7th Cir., 1974).

tion, the intermediate unit (school district), and several individuals
as officials of those agencies were defendants in a suit brought by
black plaintiffs alleging that school authorities in preparing, approv-
ing, and adopting plans of reorganization for the central eastern
area of Allegheny County deprived them of rights, privileges, and
immunities guaranteed them by the Constitution. The issue was
brought to trial following the adoption of a plan for school district
consolidation that was developed pursuant to an act of the Pennsylvania legislature. At issue was an interpretation of State Board
Standards for Approval of Administrative Units. One of the standards directed that "neither race nor religion shall be a factor in
determining administrative unit boundaries." The district court
found that:

the natural, foreseeable and actual effect of combining Braddock, North
Braddock, and Rankin into one school district was to perpetuate, exacerbate and maximize racial segregation within the public schools of
this central eastern portion of Allegheny County.[49]

This finding was based on a showing that the three districts, which
were merged into the newly created General Braddock School District, all had heavy concentrations of black students—more than 50
percent in two of the former districts—while all the excluded districts had student enrollments which were less than 10 percent
black.

The court then ordered the Pennsylvania State Board of Education to submit a comprehensive plan for school district reorganization which would be "educationally sound and a practical plan of
desegregation that promises now and hereafter to achieve the greatest possible degree of desegregation within the public schools.[50]

The State Board of Education encountered resistance from all
quarters as it attempted to comply with this order. The affected
local school districts moved to protect their interests. A multitude
of plans were considered, hearings were conducted, and expert witnesses were invited to testify as to the viability of the many proposals. Finally, the court rejected the state's plan, issuing new directions that restricted the options by ordering that the constituent

49. *Hoots v. Commonwealth of Pennsylvania,* 359 F. Supp. 807, 821.

50. Ibid., pp. 824-25.

school districts of General Braddock (Braddock, North Braddock, and Rankin) be distributed three ways and that the plan involve as few school districts as possible; all of which was another way of saying that the court wanted exactly three reorganized units.

This series of court orders, with detailed instructions to the state board, finally produced a plan which the affected school districts maintain is the court's plan and not the plan of the state board. This is a crucial point because several of the school districts are anxious to launch an appeal, while the Commonwealth of Pennsylvania seems willing to accept any solution that satisfies the plaintiffs and the court. Several of the affected local school districts have argued that since there is no showing of a constitutional violation on their part or any collusion between and among them which contributed to the containment of blacks in the General Braddock School District, and since the statutes in Pennsylvania do not permit the state board to modify their boundaries, the law as established by *Milliken* and the Pennsylvania statutes exempt them from the remedy. An appeal at this time would be premature, however, because the court has not ordered the implementation of the plan.

The district court in the Indianapolis case sought to impose a metropolitan area remedy to include all of Marion County, the county in which Indianapolis is located, as well as several school districts beyond the county line. Relying upon the Supreme Court opinion in the Detroit case, the Seventh Circuit Court reversed the district court's opinion with regard to the area beyond Marion County. The court did not reverse, but vacated and remanded for further finding that part of the district court's remedy which included school districts within the county boundaries. The Seventh Circuit made this application of *Milliken* because in 1969 the Indiana legislature created "Uni-Gov" which, by the statute, consolidated the municipal governmental functions of the City of Indianapolis and the County of Marion. In Indiana, school boards or "school cities" have historically been separate and distinct from municipal governments. Accordingly, "Uni-Gov" excepted from that consolidation "any school corporation, all or a part of which is in the consolidated city or county." Therefore the eleven school systems in Marion County remained independent from the unified municipal government for Indianapolis. On remand, the federal appellate court asked the district court to determine whether the establishment of Uni-Gov boundaries "warrants an interdistrict remedy within Uni-Gov in accordance with *Milliken*." [51] The district court then held another evidentiary hearing on Uni-Gov and housing practices within Marion County. In regard to Uni-Gov, Judge S. Hugh Dillin found:

The evidence clearly shows that at the time of the passage of the Uni-Gov Act of 1969, various annexation plans and school consolidation plans had bogged down on the local level because of the aforementioned opposition of the suburban school corporations and their patrons. . . . Under existing law . . . [the General Assembly] had a duty to alleviate the segregated condition then existing in IPS [Indiana Public Schools]. When the General Assembly expressly eliminated the schools from consideration under Uni-Gov, it signaled its lack of concern with the whole problem and thus inhibited desegregation with[in] IPS.[52]

Judge Dillin then ordered the transfer of 6533 students from the Indianapolis public schools to other school districts in Marion County. An additional 3000 students were to be transferred the second year of the plan, raising the proportion of black students in the suburban schools to 15 percent.

All the defendants appealed. In a 2 to 1 opinion the United States Court of Appeals for the Seventh Circuit, on July 16, 1976, affirmed the district court's order. Circuit Court Judge Swygert, writing for the majority, specifically noted that there was no evidence that the opposition to the school district merger was racially motivated. Nonetheless, he wrote: "The record fails to show any compelling state interest that would have justified the failure to include IPS in the Uni-Gov legislation. . . . These considerations, although apparently not racially motivated, cannot justify legislation that has an obvious racial segregative impact." [53]

In August of 1976, Associate Justice Stevens of the Supreme Court entered a stay order against the order of the Seventh Circuit

51. *U.S. v. Board of School Commissioners, City of Indianapolis,* 503 F. 2d, 68.

52. *U.S. v. Board of School Commissioners, City of Indianapolis,* 419 F. Supp. 180, 183 (1975).

53. *U.S. v. Board of School Commissioners, City of Indianapolis,* Nos. 75-1730 through 75-1737, 75-1765, 75-1936, 75-1964, 75-1965 and 75-2007 (7th Cir., July 16, 1976).

Court of Appeals and of the district court for interdistrict transfer of students, pending action by the entire Court on a writ of *certiorari*. In January, 1977 the U.S. Supreme Court, in a 6 to 3 ruling, ordered the Seventh Circuit Court to reconsider the busing plan involving the city of Indianapolis and the other school districts in Marion County. In doing so, the Court strongly indicated that it will not approve judicially-ordered busing for school desegregation unless it has been proven that the intent, as well as the effect, of the policies of local officials was to discriminate against black students.[54]

## Segregative Acts of Nonschool Agencies

The obligation of school authorities to correct racial imbalances that have been exacerbated by nonschool government agencies and private persons has been debated vigorously in the federal courtrooms. The issue is especially complex, going to the essence of the distinction between de facto and de jure segregation. In theory, a purely de facto segregated school district is one where there is neither a history of statutorily imposed segregation nor intentional segregative acts on the part of school officials. The racial imbalance in the schools is fortuitous, attributed solely to a neighborhood policy superimposed on a pattern of residential segregation. Some commentators, however, and even some courts have suggested that neighborhood schools coupled with private racism should be sufficient alone to establish de jure segregation and therefore a violation of the equal protection clause. A Texas court said,

Whether or not the residential isolation of whites, blacks, and Mexican-Americans in Austin is . . . the result of state action, the acts of the school authorities in taking official action, including assigning students . . . and drawing zone lines, on the basis of these segregated housing patterns were violative of the Fourteenth Amendment.[55]

Similarly, Judge Robert R. Merhige, Jr. in *Bradley v. School Board, City of Richmond* was convinced that neighborhood schools tend to lend state sanction to the cumulative private acts of racism:

By maintaining black schools and white schools, perceived as such, to

54. *Board of School Commissioners, City of Indianapolis v. Buckley,* 45 U.S.L.W. 3500 (1977).

55. *U.S. v. Texas Education Agency,* 467 F. 2d 848, 863-64 n. 22 (5th Cir., 1972).

serve particular areas, they (school authorities) turned such force as might have been exerted by school policies to assist in eliminating housing segregation in the opposite direction. In creating new segregated facilities to accommodate the area's expanding population, school officials not only built upon the pattern of housing segregation extant in the city and counties, but also encouraged and fostered its extension in a substantial manner. The existence of a number of nearly all-white schools, together with a firm policy of refusing to relieve segregation by crossing school division lines, constituted an invitation to white persons seeking new residences in the area to discriminate in their selection according to the racial composition of the school their children would attend. As a result, the intensity and magnitude of racial separation increased.[56]

Finally, Goodman likewise recognizes the combined evils of discriminatory housing and neighborhood schools:

Residence in the ghetto, and thus membership in the class disadvantaged by the neighborhood school assignment policy, is often the immediate consequence of racially discriminatory practices in the housing market, where race directly determines place-of-residence. Grouping students in school by place-of-residence becomes, in effect, racial classification once removed. It amplifies the consequences of private discrimination; it lengthens the discriminator's arm, giving him a veto over admission to the neighborhood public schools.[57]

School authorities and a few courts have also suggested that in school desegregation cases the courts should look to actions of other governmental agencies which may have contributed to the pattern of residential segregation in order to establish that the pattern of segregated schooling constitutes de jure segregation. Mr. Justice Stewart lends credence to this position in *Milliken*:

Were it to be shown, for example, that state officials had contributed to the separation of the races, by drawing or redrawing school district lines, . . . by transfer of school units between districts, . . . *or by purposeful, racially discriminatory use of state housing or zoning laws*, then a decree calling for transfer of pupils across district lines or for restructuring of district lines might well be appropriate.[58] (emphasis added)

56. *Bradley v. School Board*, Civil Action No. 3353 (E.D. Va., Richmond div., filed Jan. 5, 1972), pp. 39-40.

57. Frank I. Goodman, "De Facto School Segregation: A Constitutional and Empirical Analysis," *California Law Review* 60 (May 1972): 320.

58. *Milliken v. Bradley*, 418 U.S. 717, 755.

The emphasis is added because this specific qualification of the Court's holding by Mr. Justice Stewart is significantly absent from the majority opinion. Further, of the three hypothetical fact patterns described, it is the only one mentioned with no prior case citations. Nevertheless, since Mr. Justice Stewart was the "one" in this 4-1-4 opinion, his vote was crucial. Presumably he would have voted with the four dissenters in *Milliken* if there had been sufficient evidence of "racially discriminatory use of state housing."

Mr. Justice Stewart's opportunity to act on these words was soon to come. In delivering the opinion for the Court in *Hills* v. *Gautreaux* in 1976 he wrote: "Nothing in the *Milliken* decision suggests a per se rule that federal courts lack authority to order parties found to have violated the Constitution to undertake remedial efforts beyond the municipal boundaries of the city where the violation occurred." [59]

In this, and in more than twenty additional references in *Hills*, Mr. Justice Stewart explained the Court's holdings, which supported a metropolitan remedy for housing (Chicago) while denying a metropolitan remedy for schools (Detroit)—all of which is reminiscent of the statement in *Hamlet*, "The lady protests too much, methinks."

*Hills* was brought to trial in 1966 by six black tenants in, or applicants for, public housing in Chicago. The action was brought against the Chicago Housing Authority (CHA) and the Federal Department of Housing and Urban Development (HUD). CHA was accused of deliberately selecting family public housing sites in Chicago to avoid the placement of black families in white neighborhoods in violation of federal statutes and the Fourteenth Amendment. The charge against HUD was for assisting in that policy by providing financial assistance and other support for the discriminatory housing project of CHA. In 1969 the district court entered judgment against CHA, which was ordered to take remedial action, but dismissed the action against HUD. The case was appealed to the Seventh Circuit Court of Appeals which reversed (1970) the lower court on HUD. Thereupon, the district court (1970) consolidated the CHA and HUD cases and proposed corrective action

59. *Hills v. Gautreaux*, 44 U.S.L.W. 4484 (1976).

in Chicago, rejecting a motion to consider *metropolitan* relief. That rejection was appealed to the Seventh Circuit Court, which reversed the district court and ordered further consideration of metropolitan relief. HUD then appealed to the U. S. Supreme Court. The question presented concerned only the authority of the district court to order HUD to take remedial action outside the city limits of Chicago. HUD contended that the *Milliken* decision bars a remedy affecting its conduct beyond the boundaries of Chicago for two reasons:

First, it assert[s] that such a remedial order would constitute the grant of relief incommensurate with the constitutional violation to be repaired. And second, it claim[s] that a decree regulating HUD's conduct beyond Chicago's boundaries would inevitably have the effect of "consolidating for remedial purposes" governmental units not implicated in HUD's and CHA's violations.[60] [Both of these arguments had been used by the majority in the Detroit court.]

The Court made short shrift of both arguments on April 20, 1976 in affirming the Seventh Circuit Court of Appeals, holding that a "metropolitan area remedy in this case is not impermissible as a matter of law." [61]

Predictably, Mr. Justice Marshall, along with Associate Justices White and Brennan, all of whom dissented in *Milliken* (Mr. Justice Douglas also dissented in *Milliken*), concurred in *Hills*, and used the occasion to complain once more about the majority opinion in *Milliken*:

I dissented in *Milliken* vs. *Bradley*, 418 U.S. 717 (1974) and I continue to believe that the Court's decision in that case unduly limited the federal court's broad equitable power to provide effective remedies for official segregation. In this case the Court distinguishes *Milliken* and paves the way for a remedial decree directing the Department of Housing and Urban Development to utilize its full statutory power to foster housing projects in white areas of the greater Chicago metropolitan area. I join the Court's opinion except insofar as it appears to reaffirm the decision of *Milliken*.[62]

History has taught us that litigation on issues far removed from

60. Ibid.

61. Ibid., p. 4487.

62. Ibid.

education may have a heavy and unforeseeable impact on public schools. A classic example was *Plessy* v. *Ferguson*,[63] a case involving a Louisiana statute that prohibited the transportation of black and white persons in the same railway cars. The upholding of that statute by the U.S. Supreme Court established the legal basis for "separate but equal" educational facilities from 1896 to 1954. *Hills*, too, may be a landmark case in school desegregation, albeit of a different order. A vigorous implementation of *Hills* by HUD will disperse the poor and minority persons from the central cities, and accomplish the goals of the plaintiffs in *Milliken* and similar cases in other cities. So, if support for metropolitan relief for school segregation can come from such an unexpected quarter, who can say what the judicial portals of the future will admit?

### School Board Duty to Retard Resegregation

At what point does the relationship between a school board's past segregative acts and the present racial segregation become so attenuated as to be incapable of supporting a finding of de jure segregation warranting judicial intervention?[64] Or, in other words, how long a period of supervision by the courts will be required before it is determined that a dual system has been dismantled? Some of the forces that created segregation in the first instance, extending well beyond the reach of school authorities, may cause the schools to slip out of compliance with the literal terms of a court order. This resegregation can be caused by changes in residential patterns as a function of "white flight"; practices and policies of government agencies in locating housing and highways; and private racism through the sale, rental, and financing of housing. Does the Constitution require school boards to retard resegregation, or more precisely, to maintain integrated schools in communities which have resegregated? The Court first addressed this issue in *Swann*, stating:

It does not follow that communities served by (unitary) systems will remain demographically stable, for in a growing, mobile society few will do so. Neither school officials nor district courts are constitutionally

63. *Plessy v. Ferguson,* 163 U.S. 537 (1896).

64. See *Keyes v. School District No. 1,* 413 U.S. 189, 211.

required to make year-by-year adjustments of the racial composition
of student bodies once the affirmative duty to desegregate has been accomplished and racial discrimination through official action is eliminated
from the system.[65]

The June 1976, holding of the U.S. Supreme Court in the
*Pasadena* case adds considerable illumination to the earlier statement from *Swann*. The Court took particular exception to the
remark of the district court in 1974 that its 1970 order "meant to
me that at least during my lifetime there would be no majority
or any minority in any school in Pasadena." [66]

The Supreme Court found this interpretation to be inconsistent
with its intervening decision in *Swann* (1971) regarding the scope
of the judicially created relief which might be available to remedy
violations of the Fourteenth Amendment, noting that *Swann* expressly disapproved the contentions that plaintiffs have the "substantial constitutional right to a particular degree of racial balance
or mixing." [67]

Speaking more precisely to the issue in Pasadena, the Court said:

While the District Court found such a (constitutional) violation in 1970,
and while this unappealed finding afforded a basis for its initial requirement that the defendants prepare a plan to remedy such racial segregation, its adoption of the Pasadena Plan in 1970 established a racially
neutral system of student assignment in PUSD. Having done that, we
think that in enforcing its order so as to require the annual readjust-
ment of attendance zones so that there would not be a majority of any
minority in any Pasadena public school, the District Court exceeded its
authority.[68]

Noting that the post-1971 changes in the racial mix of some
Pasadena schools "resulted from people randomly moving into, out
of, and around the PUSD area," the Court said:

This quite normal pattern of human migration resulted in some changes
in the demographies of Pasadena's residential patterns, with resulting

65. *Swann v. Charlotte-Mecklenburg Board of Education*, 402 U.S. 1, 31-32.

66. *Pasadena City Board of Education v. Nancy Anne Spangler et al.*, 44
U.S.L.W. 5114.

67. *Swann v. Charlotte-Mecklenburg Board of Education*, 402 U.S. 1, 24.

68. *Pasadena City Board of Education v. Nancy Anne Spangler et al.*, 44
U.S.L.W. 5117.

shifts in the racial makeup of some of the schools. But as these shifts are not attributed to any segregative actions on the part of the defendants (school board), we think this case comes squarely within the sort of situation foreseen in *Swann* (quoted above).[69]

Observing that there was no substantial disagreement to the statement that following the 1970 order, the Pasadena Board of Education had created and maintained racial neutrality in the attendance of students, the Supreme Court held that the district court was not entitled to require the school district to rearrange its attendance zones each year so as to ensure that the racial mix desired by the court was maintained in perpetuity.

The full impact of the *Pasadena* holding cannot be determined at this time. It seems predictable, however, that many school boards will be requesting district courts to dissolve orders which are contrary to this opinion. The practice of retaining jurisdiction indefinitely, now followed by most district courts, seems to be banned by the *Pasadena* decision. If school boards are to become instruments to retard resegregation, the impetus will have to be self-generated, or, if they fail to do so, hopefully, state education agencies and state legislatures will resume their appropriate roles in education.

The prospect of school boards being relieved of court supervision, once an order has been fully implemented for some period of time, possibly as little as two years, may be the most positive force in the *Pasadena* opinion. With this carrot in front, the district courts may have less need for the stick at the other end.

## Conclusion

The future course of school desegregation litigation seems more uncertain now than it did in the years immediately after *Brown*. The task then was to desegregate the schools in seventeen southern states and the District of Columbia where racially identifiable schools were maintained by law. The litigation now covers a myriad of issues, some of which seem almost unrelated to *Brown*. There is some recent evidence, however, that the courts, plaintiffs, and defendants are tiring. If this observation is accurate we may be approaching the end of a stormy epoch in public education.

69. Ibid.

The decisions of the U.S. Supreme Court in the 1970s reveal a waning enthusiasm for court intervention in school governance, absent a clear showing of state-sanctioned invidious discrimination. Clearly, the "affirmative duty to integrate" doctrine of *Green* in 1969 was not expanded in *Swann* in 1971. Also, the "intent to discriminate" test of *Keyes* in 1974 and the sharp distinction between de facto and de jure segregation in the same case were serious setbacks for desegregation proponents. *Milliken* in 1975 showed an additional reluctance of the Court to expand on earlier holdings. The *Pasadena* case in 1976, limiting the period of jurisdiction of federal courts in school desegregation cases, and the *Austin* case in the same year, restricting the use of busing as a remedy, are additional signals from the Supreme Court.[70] Similarly, the Court's agreement in January, 1977 to review the *Dayton* case,[71] at the request of the school board, was the latest in this series of steps in the direction which the Court began charting in the early 1970s. While the outcome of this case is uncertain at this time, the granting of *certiorari*, in response to the board's argument that the desegregation order was too broad, may indicate that the Court is ready to approve only such remedies as are essential to correct known violations of equal protection. Possibly the Court, in accepting the *Dayton* case, is doing some fine tuning of *Keyes* and *Milliken*. However, a holding that will limit the scope of the remedies which district courts may impose on school boards seems likely. More precisely, remedies which require a student racial balance within a fixed range in all schools, such as fifteen percentage points of the percentage of black students in the system as a whole, seem to be headed for judicially troubled waters. Comments in the March, 1977 opinion and order by Judge Duncan in the *Columbus* case clearly suggest that at least one Federal District Court expects the Supreme Court to reject this feature in school desegregation orders.[72]

70. *Austin Independent School District v. United States*, 44 U.S.L.W. 3413 (1976).

71. *Dayton Board of Education v. Brinkman*, No. 76-539 (U.S. Supreme Court, January, 1977) (cert. granted).

72. *Penick v. Columbus Board of Education*, No. C-2-73-248, U.S. District Court, S.D. Ohio E.D. (March, 1977).

Given this posture of the highest Court, and the evidence of considerable public opposition to more school desegregation litigation, the conditions suggest the need for a more amicable solution to the school desegregation problem. The 1974 consent decree in Springfield, Illinois, the first in the nation respecting the liability of a school district for a Fourteenth Amendment violation, is an example of a thoughtful solution to segregated schools and it did conserve the time of the court and the resources of the parties.[73] Similarly, the 1973 compromise plan for Atlanta provided an acceptable remedy for a judicially identified violation. This out-of-court settlement, which was approved by the district court, ended almost a decade of litigation in that city.[74]

In addition to the obvious economies in consent decrees, they offer the most flexibility in the shaping of the remedy. For instance, the court order in Springfield, Illinois, pursuant to the consent of the parties, required the defendant school district to submit a plan for racial integration "which is educationally sound, administratively efficient, and financially feasible."[75] This board mandate makes it possible for the parties to balance the advantages of proposed pupil assignment plans against the obvious strength of neighborhood schools. The press for "full integration," a racial quota system by a different name, can be evaluated more carefully by plaintiffs as well as by defendants. There is no requirement in this consent decree that the court accept the plan which is "most constitutional" or the one which completely disperses the black students to all of the schools in the district. One-race schools and neighborhood schools are not precluded and of course they are not unconstitutional nor educationally unsound per se. Moreover, plaintiffs and defendants shaping remedies according to consent decrees may wish to give preference to plans recognizing that cultural pluralism is replacing "the melting pot" as a major goal of public education. It seems clear that school desegregation plans failing to recognize this fact will not remain stable. Black students

73. *McPherson v. School District 186, Springfield, Ill.*, Civil Action No. S-Civ 74-44 (S.D. Ill., 1974).

74. *Calhoun v. Cook*, Civil Action No. 6298 (N.D. Ga.).

75. *McPherson v. School District 186, Springfield, Ill.*, S-Civ 74-44, p. 7.

and their parents will find ways to have concentrations of black students in at least some schools. Similarly, white flight from racially identifiable black schools cannot be totally disregarded by the courts.

The use of consent decrees is the latest manifestation of a changing role of the courts in school desegregation cases. While the courts in Boston and Detroit become increasingly involved in the details of a solution, the courts in the future will be likely to function as mediators rather than as monarchs. Trial judges will exercise decisive responsibility for resolving desegregation controversies, while recognizing their limited ability to implement a remedy that is of necessity largely outside their direct control. The dynamics of contemporary desegregation disputes are becoming increasingly complicated. The precise legal basis for a court ruling is often not clear, and facts may be so complex that no single resolution can command consensus. The dispute is not solely between two parties but spills over to involve a multiplicity of groups, each pressing an objective to which it attempts to give a constitutional anchor.

Courts in the future will be pressed to recognize the forces of political democracy in a pluralistic society. But pluralistic politics need not be equated with judicial abdication. Courts in desegregation cases can manage negotiations among many and diversely affected parties.

The safest prediction about the future is that school desegregation will continue. Many issues remain unresolved. Second generation problems, such as within-school segregation, will emerge. Central to future litigation is the clarification of the meaning of the purpose or intent to segregate; the equal protection clause of the Fourteenth Amendment; and the troublesome concepts of de facto and de jure segregation. With the tendency of the Court to fashion definitions out of whole cloth, we have a situation analogous to Humpty Dumpty's statement to Alice: "When I use a word, it means just what I choose it to mean—neither more nor less."

CHAPTER V

# Legal Impediments to Private Educational Options

DONALD A. ERICKSON

The focus in this chapter on private educational *options* rather than private *schools* reflects the fact, exemplified in shared time, dual enrollment practices, and in other approaches occasionally advocated,[1] that full-time private school attendance is not the only conceivable alternative to full-time public school attendance. Educational facilities, schedules, and finances could be arranged to permit the student to construct an educational mosaic from components proffered by numerous public and private agencies.[2] Furthermore, these variegated learning opportunities could be distributed across a much longer time span than the segment of life customarily devoted to formal schooling.[3] Perhaps educational reform would in fact come more quickly if public and private agencies were encouraged to specialize in particular aspects of education, unburdened by the total welter of often contradictory custodial, instructional, and "character-building" goals that most schools are asked to achieve simultaneously. But all these approaches

1. Donald A. Erickson, "The Public-Private Consortium: An Open-Market Model for Educational Reform," in *Metropolitan School Organization*, vol. 2, *Proposals for Reform*, ed. Troy M. McKelvey (Berkeley, Calif.: McCutchan Publishing Corp., 1972), chap. 2. Also see Theodore R. Sizer, *Places for Learning: Places for Joy* (Cambridge, Mass.: Harvard University Press, 1973), especially chap. 4.

2. Erickson, "The Public-Private Consortium."

3. This freedom to distribute one's tax-funded educational opportunities across a larger gamut of years is advocated in several recent reports on secondary school reform, including: Ruth Weinstock, ed., *The Greening of the High School* (New York: I/D/E/A and Educational Facilities Laboratory, 1973); *American Youth in the Mid-Seventies* (Washington, D.C.: National Association of Secondary-School Principals, 1972); James S. Coleman, ed., *Youth: Transition to Adulthood*, Report of the President's Science Advisory Committee (Chicago: University of Chicago Press, 1974).

are currently obstructed by legal frameworks discussed in the passages that follow.

Within the space limitations of the present chapter, one cannot address *all* legal handicaps on private educational options in our society. Some necessary omissions will be noted explicitly, and other areas of concern will be given only cursory treatment. The analysis will center mainly upon (a) government-imposed fiscal handicaps, with attention to reasons why these handicaps are difficult to mitigate, (b) state and federal regulations that limit the educational variety legally permitted, and (c) certain other generally overlooked rigidities that have the force of law.

## Government-imposed Fiscal Handicaps

Perhaps the most stringent limitation upon the availability of private educational options, especially among low-income families, inheres in the fact that the funds these families might otherwise use to purchase private educational options are collected by government through taxation and authoritatively allocated to the procurement of public educational options, regardless of whether parents and children prefer the former to the latter.[4] When substituting private for public educational services then parents, having already involuntarily purchased (through taxation) the public services, must find new funds to procure the private services, thus "paying twice" for their children's schooling. In an era when public school taxes burgeon more rapidly than family incomes, larger and larger proportions of the population are deprived, through these fiscal constraints, of the constitutional right to determine whether their children will be schooled, in whole or in part, under private auspices.[5] Many scholars and thoughtful citizens think these infringements upon parental choice are justified as a means of achieving more important values. It would certainly be unreasonable to demand the right to be relieved of taxation supporting any public service for which one could envision a more attractive private alternative. If we ignore the fact that an element of coercion

4. Milton Friedman, *Capitalism and Freedom* (Chicago: University of Chicago Press, 1962), chap. 6.

5. The classic Supreme Court statement concerning this right is found in *Pierce v. Society of Sisters*, 268 U.S. 510, 45 S. Ct. 571, 69 L. Ed. 1070 (1925).

exists, however, we will fail to confront the question of whether some publicly provided services impinge so fundamentally upon constitutionally guaranteed liberties that steps should be taken to restore true freedom of choice.[6] Questions in this area are particularly complex when church-related institutions are involved. Since the U.S. Supreme Court has largely preempted authoritative decision making in this respect, bringing to bear its interpretations of the two religious prohibitions of the First Amendment, attention will be directed here primarily to key U.S. Supreme Court cases, with only minor discussion of state constitutional provisions and court rulings and to the details of the pertinent legislation.

To facilitate discussion, it seems useful to distinguish four major periods in the recent history of government efforts to alleviate the financial inhibitions now legally imposed upon the sponsors and patrons of private educational options. The periods are (a) from *Everson* (1947) to *Allen* (1968), (b) from *Allen* (1968) to *Lemon I* (1971), (c) from *Lemon I* to *Pittenger* (1975), and (d) from *Pittenger* (1975) to the present.

## FROM *Everson* (1947) TO *Allen* (1968)

In the *Cochran* case of 1930, the Supreme Court unanimously affirmed the constitutionality of state provision of free textbooks to students in private schools.[7] The constitutionality of this type of peripheral, indirect, "child-benefit" aid, however, was not considered and approved in the light of the religious clauses of the First Amendment until the *Everson* case of 1947, in which the U.S. Supreme Court concluded that New Jersey public school districts could pay for the transportation of students attending church-related schools without being guilty of an establishment of religion.[8] Consequently, the modern era of conflict over "public aid" or "fiscal relief" for nonpublic educational ventures (the vast majority of which are offered under religious sponsorship) may be viewed as beginning with the *Everson* decision.

6. Marc Galanter, "Religious Freedom in the United States: A Turning Point?" *Wisconsin Law Review* 1966 (Spring 1966): 217-96.

7. *Cochran v. Louisiana State Board of Education*, 281 U.S. 370, 50 S. Ct. 335, 74 L. Ed. 913 (1930).

8. *Everson v. Board of Education*, 330 U.S. 1, 67 S. Ct. 504, 91 L. Ed. 711 (1947).

By a narrow margin of five to four, the Court in *Everson* held
New Jersey's bus rides constitutional and cited *Cochran* as a precedent, thus implying that free textbooks, too, were permissible
under the First Amendment. Moreover, the *Everson* opinion contained exceedingly strong language forbidding aid to religious institutions, and it described the bus rides for parochial school students as approaching the verge of unconstitutionality. In defense
of the bus rides, much was made of their "child-benefit" character. The resultant assistance to religiously affiliated schools was
pointedly described as indirect and incidental. It is understand-
able, then, that in the twenty-one years between *Everson* and the
next Supreme Court decision in this area (*Allen*, 1968),[9] *Everson's*
indication that only peripheral "child-benefit" aid was permissible
was reflected in most relevant legislative activity. Numerous state
legislatures enacted statutes providing tax-financed bus rides and/
or textbooks to children attending private (including religiously
affiliated) schools, although not all state courts regarded these
benefits as permissible under the state constitutions.[10] It was
widely assumed, as an examination of the bills during this *Ever-
son-to-Allen* period clearly indicates,[11] that the Supreme Court
would not tolerate *direct* grants to religiously affiliated schools,
grants that gave these schools *sizeable* (rather than minor or incidental) benefits, or grants that provided funds for the *central*
(as opposed to *peripheral* or "noncurricular") functions of these
institutions.[12] Nevertheless, some relevant legislation in this period

9. *Board of Education v. Allen*, 392 U.S. 236, 88 S. Ct. 1923, 20 L. Ed. 2d
1060 (1968).

10. August W. Steinhilber and Carl J. Sokowski, *State Law Relating to
Transportation and Textbooks for Parochial School Students and Constitutional Protection of Religious Freedom*, OE-20087, Cir. No. 795 (Washington,
D.C.: Office of Education, U.S. Department of Health, Education, and Welfare, 1966).

11. A national search of these bills was conducted in connection with my
study of Illinois nonpublic schools. See Donald A. Erickson, *Crisis in Illinois
Nonpublic Schools: Research Report to the Elementary and Secondary Nonpublic Schools Study Commission, State of Illinois* (Springfield, Ill.: the
Commission, 1970).

12. For one of the most systematic, and in retrospect, most accurate analyses
of the Supreme Court's implicit guidelines during this period, see George R.
LaNoue, *Decision for the Sixties: Public Funds for Parochial Schools?* (New
York: National Council of the Churches of Christ in the U.S.A., 1963).

may be characterized as progressively stretching the presumed boundaries of *Everson's* "child-benefit" or "peripheral, indirect, incidental assistance" posture. The extent to which the parameters in *Everson* were pushed is perhaps best illustrated by the following enactment in Michigan:

Whenever the board of education of a school district provides any of the auxiliary services specified in this section to any of its resident children in attendance in the elementary and high school grades, it shall provide the same auxiliary services on an equal basis to school children in attendance in the elementary and high school grades at non-public schools. The board of education may use state school aid funds of the district to pay for such auxiliary services. Such auxiliary services shall include health and nursing services and examinations; street crossing guards services; National Defense Education Act testing services; speech correction services; visiting teacher services for delinquent and disturbed children; school diagnostician services for all mentally handicapped children; teacher counsellor services for physically handicapped children; teacher consultant services for mentally handicapped or emotionally disturbed children; remedial reading; and such other services as may be determined by the legislature.[13]

At the federal level, Title I of the *Elementary and Secondary Education Act of 1965* (now under challenge in the U.S. district court for the Southern District of New York)[14] was another example of legislation reflecting a rather expansive view of the *Everson* doctrine. Under this title, federal funds to provide special programs and projects for "educationally deprived" children were required to be used for the equal benefit of students in nonpublic schools who fell into this category.

The quickening pace and broadening scope of pertinent lawmaking between 1947 and 1968 seem logically attributable to three major factors, among others: (a) for complex reasons that cannot be explicated here, many nonpublic schools were encountering severe financial difficulties, and thus had more reason than previously to press for public assistance; (b) Catholics, who had long sought fiscal relief for their schools, were joined in the effort by

13. Mich. C. L. Ann. 340, 622. Note, in this connection, *In Re Proposal C*, 185 N.W. 2d 9, 384 Mich. 390 (1971).

14. "Federal Parochiaid Goes to Court," *Church and State* 29 (April 1976): 3, 6.

many hitherto reluctant Lutheran, Christian Reformed, and Jewish
groups; and (c) people seeking monetary aid to private schools
began to exhibit greater political activism and expertise than previously, forming numerous state and federal lobbying organizations
and exerting systematic pressure on elected officials who needed
their votes. Almost simultaneously, a number of "anti-parochiaid"
organizations sprang up to oppose these efforts, both in the legislative halls and in the courts. (As later discussion will make clear,
there has been an unprecedented amount of litigation on questions
of government aid to church-related schools since the late 1960s.)
Since Mr. Justice Douglas, whose vote had been crucial to the
*Everson* decision, announced that he had changed his mind in the
intervening years,[15] and since the composition of the Court had
changed, there was some reason to hope (or fear) that the Court
would reverse or strictly limit its position on "child benefit" assistance. A test case was inevitable. It came when *Board of Education* v. *Allen* reached the U.S. Supreme Court.[16] *Allen* contested
the constitutionality of state-purchased textbooks for parochial
school students in the state of New York. In a manner that few
people seemed to anticipate, the *Allen* decision in 1968 heralded a
new era of legislation and litigation.

FROM *Allen* (1968) TO *Lemon I* (1971)

In *Allen*, the Supreme Court placed a stamp of constitutional
good housekeeping on New York's scheme for providing state-
purchased textbooks to children in nonpublic schools. The Court
emphasized, as in *Cochran* thirty-eight years earlier and *Everson*
twenty-one years earlier, that the child was the intended bene-
ficiary, the nonpublic school deriving only indirect, incidental
assistance. The legislation under attack was seen as having a secular
purpose and a primary effect that neither advanced nor inhibited
religion. None of this logic was surprising to students of earlier
Supreme Court cases concerning church-state issues.

But in statements that almost seem, retrospectively, to have in-

15. See his concurring opinion in *Engel v. Vitale*, 370 U.S. 421, 82 S. Ct. 1261,
8 L. Ed. 2d 601 (1962), p. 443.

16. *Board of Education v. Allen*, 392 U.S. 236 (1968).

volved a slip of the pen,[17] the Court went much further than it had done in *Everson* to provide a rationale to justify the "child-benefit" assistance. It was easy to infer that the Court's basic stance on aid to religious institutions had shifted significantly since *Everson* in 1947. The *Allen* opinion in 1968 came very close to stating that church-related schools, rather than being untouchables insofar as the flow of public money was concerned, performed some distinctly *secular* functions which, because they were not inextricably intertwined with religious activities, might justifiably be supported by the state. The Court asserted, for example:

[T]his Court has long recognized that religious schools pursue two goals, religious instruction and secular education. . . . Private education has played and is playing a significant and valuable role in raising national levels of knowledge, competence, and experience.
. . . The continued willingness to rely on private school systems, including parochial school systems, strongly suggests that a wide segment of informed opinion, legislative and otherwise, has found that those schools do an acceptable job of providing secular education to their students. This judgment is further evidence that parochial schools are performing, in addition to their sectarian function, the task of secular education.
Against this background of judgment and experience, unchallenged in the meager record before us in this case, we cannot agree with appellants either that all teaching in a sectarian school is religious or that the processes are so intertwined that secular textbooks furnished to students by the public are in fact instrumental in the teaching of religion.[18]

In a stinging dissent Mr. Justice Black, who had written the *Everson* decision with its strong statements about a "high and impregnable wall between church and state," argued that the Court's rationale in *Allen* could easily be used, not merely to justify free textbooks, but to uphold laws "providing for state or federal funds to buy property on which to erect religious school buildings or to erect the buildings themselves, to pay the salaries of

17. Giannella characterizes the Court as unintentionally going "over the verge" of constitutionality in *Allen*, and needing later "to scramble back, reaching out for any support it could find on the constitutional landscape." Donald A. Giannella, "*Lemon* and *Tilton*: The Bitter and the Sweet of Church-State Entanglement," in *Supreme Court Review, 1971*, ed. Philip B. Kurland (Chicago: University of Chicago Press, 1972), p. 148.

18. *Board of Education v. Allen*, 392 U.S. 245.

the religious school teachers, and finally to have the sectarian religious groups cease to rely on voluntary contributions of members of their sects while waiting for the Government to pick up all the bills for the religious schools."[19]

Much in keeping with Mr. Justice Black's assertion, legislators in many parts of the nation began drafting bills on the premise that government could constitutionally support the secular elements of church-related schooling. One of the best-known examples of this new lawmaking trend was Pennsylvania's Nonpublic Elementary and Secondary Education Act of 1968, which authorized the State Superintendent of Public Instruction to purchase "secular educational services" from nonpublic schools, specifically in the areas of mathematics, modern foreign languages, physical science, and physical education. The nonpublic schools providing these services were to be directly reimbursed for some of the costs of teachers' salaries, textbooks, and instructional materials. It was argued that the four subjects mentioned could readily be taught without reference to religion. Church-affiliated schools wishing to emphasize the religious implications of these areas of study could do so in religion classes, which would receive no support from the state.

In one of the most intriguing legal analyses of this period, Choper, a professor at the University of California Law School, went still further, arguing that the state should be permitted, under the First Amendment, to procure secular products from any source, so long as an adequate return for the money was received.[20] If some private agencies made a profit in the process, and if others managed to produce religious by-products while delivering what the state had purchased, no matter. The state was merely buying what it needed without regard to the source. Choper suggested, in fact, that if only nonreligious agencies were permitted to sell their goods and services at a fair price to the state, the state might well be accused of penalizing religion.

Despite Choper's logic, most relevant bills passed in this *Allen-*

19. Ibid., p. 252.

20. Jesse H. Choper, "The Establishment Clause and Aid to Parochial Schools," *California Law Review* 56 (April 1968): 260-341.

to-*Lemon I* period (1968 to 1971) contained provisions to ensure, not merely that the state would get its money's worth (though presumably it would, given the level of funding provided and the services expected in return), but also that the public funds in question would not be "diverted" or "diffused" so as to abet the religious functions of sectarian schools, except in the incidental sense that church funds hitherto allocated to secular instruction might now be "released," as a result of government support, for avowedly religious purposes. Some prophylatic measures in these bills were amusing, as for example the provision in Rhode Island that teachers used for religious instruction (and apparently contaminated thereby) could not also teach sectarian subjects and receive state salary supplements for doing the latter.

The legislation of this period (*Allen-to-Lemon I*, 1968 to 1971) generally represented such a radical departure from pre-*Allen* judicial guidelines that an early court challenge was predictable. The Supreme Court's assessment of two representative laws (one from Pennsylvania and one from Rhode Island) was announced on June 25, 1971, in the companion case of *Lemon* v. *Kurtzman*,[21] which came later to be known as "*Lemon I*," and *Earley* v. *DiCenso*.[22]

## FROM *Lemon I* (1971) TO *Pittenger* (1975)

While *Lemon* v. *Kurtzman* and *Earley* v. *DiCenso* were moving their way through the judicial system to the Supreme Court, students of this area of law began to see inklings of a shift away from the judicial attitude suggested in *Allen*.[23] On May 4, 1970, in *Walz* v. *Tax Commission of New York City*, the Supreme Court approved property tax exemptions for religious and other non-profit groups, but in the process enunciated a new test of constitutionality under the establishment prohibition of the First Amendment.[24] The new test concerned the degree of "entanglement"

21. *Lemon v. Kurtzman*, 403 U.S. 602, 91 S. Ct. 1923, 20 L. Ed. 2d 1060 (1971).

22. *Earley v. DiCenso*, 316 F. Supp. 112 (1970).

23. *Board of Education v. Allen*, 392 U.S. 236.

24. *Walz v. Tax Commission of New York City*, 397 U.S. 664, 90 S. Ct. 1409, 25 L. Ed. 2d 697 (1970).

between church and state that a given law might create. Utilizing this "excessive entanglement" criterion, a U.S. district court struck down the Rhode Island law under scrutiny in the *DiCenso* case, explaining that "government aid to purely secular activity may nevertheless involve the state so deeply in the workings of religious institutions 'as to give rise to divisive influences and inhibitions of 'freedom.' "[25]

The Supreme Court consolidated the *Lemon* and *DiCenso* cases, another unfavorable augury for those who desired financial relief for private educational ventures, for whereas the *DiCenso* record contained extensive evidence purporting to show that Rhode Island Catholic schools were permeated with religion, there was no evidence of this kind in the *Lemon* case from Pennsylvania.[26] The final *Lemon I* decision was a harsh blow to the proponents of aid to private schools. Several students of the law suggest that the Court had not intended in *Allen* to encourage a new era of legislation extending fiscal relief to private schools, and now, realizing the implications of its statements concerning the separability of secular and religious functions in church-affiliated schools, was endeavoring to bring the new movement to a sudden stop.[27] In fact, the Court's own language tends to support this view.[28] One key ruling of the Court in *Lemon I* was that the Rhode Island and Pennsylvania laws under attack had created, by means of regulations designed to ensure that state funds would be used only for secular purposes, an excessive (and thus unconstitutional) involvement of the state in the affairs of religious institutions. At the same time the Court concluded from the Rhode Island evidence mentioned earlier that, because of the purported tendency for religion to permeate Catholic schools, a "comprehensive, discriminating, and continuing state surveillance will inevita-

25. *Earley v. DiCenso*, 316 F. Supp. 112 (1970).

26. The Court has been severely criticized for simply assuming that Catholic schools in Rhode Island were typical of Catholic schools elsewhere. See Giannella, "*Lemon* and *Tilton*."

27. See footnote 16.

28. For example, "A certain momentum develops in constitutional theory and it can be a 'downhill thrust' easily set in motion but difficult to stop." *Lemon v. Kurtzman*, 403 U.S. 611.

bly be required to ensure that these restrictions are obeyed and the First Amendment otherwise respected."[29] It appeared to some observers that the Court had erected an insuperable barrier to tax assistance for nonpublic schools, since they are predominantly religiously affiliated: *without* extensive regulations to ensure that the funds would be used for secular purposes only, the laws would be demolished as providing aid to religion; *with* these extensive regulations, the laws would be condemned as requiring excessive entanglement between church and state.[30]

While discussing excessive entanglement in *Lemon I*, the Court not only stressed the danger of state involvement in religious affairs, but also the danger that the laws in question, particularly since they would require periodic legislative appropriations, would lead to bitter political strife along religious lines, "one of the principal evils against which the First Amendment was intended to protect."[31]

As a federal district court has recognized, the era from *Lemon I* (1971) to *Pittenger* (1975) was in some respects analogous to the period of extensive litigation that followed the *Brown* decision in 1954[32] concerning racial segregation in public schools.[33] Both *Brown* and *Lemon I* left many questions unanswered. In both instances, persistent efforts were made to determine how severely the Court intended to apply its new doctrines, and in both instances policies were designed and redesigned in an attempt to avoid capitulating entirely to the particular aversion the Court was apparently manifesting—aversion to racial segregation in the *Brown* case and aversion to "parochiaid" in *Lemon I*. In both instances, the Supreme Court revealed in a series of decisions that its prohibitions were far more extensive and severe than many people had imagined.

For the purposes of the present analysis only the most important cases need be mentioned. In *Americans United* v. *Oakey*

29. Ibid., p. 609.

30. Giannella, "*Lemon* and *Tilton.*"

31. *Lemon v. Kurtzman*, 403 U.S. 612.

32. *Brown v. Board of Education of Topeka*, 347 U.S. 483 (1954).

33. *Wolman v. Essex*, 342 F. Supp. 399 (1972), at 415.

(1972) a U.S. district court struck down a program under which public school teachers made their services available in religiously affiliated schools.[34] In *Public Funds for Public Schools of New Jersey* v. *Marburger* (1973) a U.S. district court dismantled a statute that reimbursed parents for the costs of a wide range of instructional materials and gave nonpublic schools some funds to purchase materials of the same type.[35] In *Americans United* v. *Paire* the practice of holding "public" classes in private schools was abruptly terminated by a U.S. district court.[36] On June 25, 1973, the Supreme Court laid down several important decisions concerning private schools and postsecondary institutions, including *Levitt* v. *Committee for Public Education and Religious Liberty*, which outlawed reimbursements to New York private schools for expenses of examinations, record-keeping, and other legally required services;[37] *Committee for Public Education and Religious Liberty* v. *Nyquist*, which condemned (among other things) tuition grants and tax credits for patrons of private schools,[38] and *Sloan* v. *Lemon*,[39] which overturned a tuition-reimbursement plan. In *Kosydar* v. *Wolman*, a U.S. district court decided, with subsequent affirmation by the Supreme Court, that a program of tax credits, which benefited not only parents whose children were in private schools but also some other parents who incurred unusual educational expenses, was unconstitutional.[40] Since the Supreme Court, with an assist from the federal district courts, was condemning a wide range of approaches to relieving the fiscal handicaps imposed on private educational ventures and their patrons, it was reasonable to ask at this point whether even the pre-

34. *Americans United v. Oakey*, 339 F. Supp. 545 (D. Vt. 1972).

35. *Public Funds for Public Schools of New Jersey v. Marburger*, 358 F. Supp. 29 (1973).

36. *Americans United v. Paire*, 359 F. Supp. 505 (1973).

37. *Levitt v. Committee for Public Education and Religious Liberty*, 413 U.S. 472 (1973).

38. *Committee for Public Education and Religious Liberty v. Nyquist*, 413 U.S. 756 (1973).

39. *Sloan v. Lemon*, 413 U.S. 825 (1973).

40. *Kosydar v. Wolman*, 353 F. Supp. 744 (S.D. Ohio 1972), aff'd 413 U.S. 901, 37 L. Ed. 2d 1021, 93 S. Ct. 3062 (1973).

*Allen* forms of peripheral, incidental, "child-benefit" assistance were constitutional within the Court's definition. In *Meek* v. *Pittenger* the Court gave a resounding answer.[41]

FROM Pittenger (1975) TO THE PRESENT

The Supreme Court administered a severe blow to the campaign to relieve the financial handicaps imposed on private educational options in *Meek* v. *Pittenger* (1975).[42] In its decision the Court imposed stringent limitations even upon the peripheral, incidental, "child-benefit" services which many states had been extending to private schools and their parents during the period between *Everson*[43] and *Allen.*[44] In numerous respects, the Pennsylvania acts under judicial scrutiny in *Pittenger* were similar to the above-mentioned "auxiliary services" statutes, which Michigan legislators had passed during the *Everson*-to-*Allen* period. Consequently, the Court was not merely blasting the type of legislation that *Allen* had the effect of encouraging, but was dooming many hopes based on the old "child benefit," "peripheral assistance" rationale. The Court had argued in *Lemon I* that teachers functioning in the employ of a religious institution could not be expected to teach even the most "value-neutral" subjects (such as mathematics and modern foreign languages) without bringing religious influences to bear, unless they were extensively monitored by the state.[45] In *Pittenger* this general line of argument was considerably extended. The Supreme Court indicated that teachers employed by *public* school systems could not provide such services as remedial reading, counseling, testing, and speech therapy in religious schools without running considerable risk of being influenced to promote the religious objectives of the school. But if Pennsylvania took regulatory steps to see that the public school personnel did not thus succumb to the religious thrust of the church-affiliated school, then, the Court asserted, the state would

41. *Meek v. Pittenger,* 421 U.S. 348, 95 S. Ct. 1753 (1975).

42. Ibid.

43. *Everson v. Board of Education,* 330 U.S. 1, 67 S. Ct. 504, 91 L. Ed. 711 (1947).

44. *Board of Education v. Allen,* 392 U.S. 236 (1968).

45. *Lemon v. Kurtzman,* 403 U.S. 602 (1971).

have become excessively entangled in church affairs. In keeping with the *Allen* decision,[46] the *Pittenger* opinion permitted Pennsylvania to provide free textbooks to students in nonpublic schools, but the anathema of unconstitutionality was cast upon the auxiliary services (remedial reading instruction, counseling, testing, speech therapy, and so forth), which the state wanted to make available, and loans of instructional materials and equipment to nonpublic schools were abolished as well.

In at least one statement, the Supreme Court came close in *Pittenger* to an explicit rejection of its position in *Allen*.[47] Whereas the *Allen* opinion had emphasized the separability of religious and secular functions in church-related schools, *Pittenger* declared that "it would simply ignore reality to attempt to separate secular educational functions from the predominantly religious role performed by many of Pennsylvania's church-related elementary and secondary schools. . . . Within the institution, the two are inextricably intertwined."[48]

In the wake of *Pittenger*, there is not much to encourage those who wish to alleviate government-imposed fiscal handicaps on private educational options. There is room to argue that the Supreme Court might find a broad-based voucher plan (one including all public and nonpublic schools in a given area, for example) constitutionally permissible,[49] but such argument is little more than academic in the light of the fact that such plans now seem politically impossible in the face of organized opposition by public educators.[50] Over a considerable period of years, it is possible that

46. *Board of Education v. Allen*, 392 U.S. 245 (1968).

47. *Meek v. Pittenger*, 421 U.S. 348 (1975).

48. Ibid., p. 365.

49. Cf. "Voucher Systems of Public Education after *Nyquist* and *Sloan:* Can a Constitutional System Be Devised?" *Michigan Law Review* 2 (March 1974); 895-915.

50. The only public school voucher scheme (apart from the old racism-tainted vouchers in the South) that was launched—at Alum Rock—was so drastically watered down in the face of the opposition of public educators that it became a travesty of the voucher concept. Daniel Weiler, *A Public School Voucher Demonstration: The First Year at Alum Rock* (Santa Monica, Calif.: Rand Corp., 1974). After extensive plans were made to experiment with vouchers in several New Hampshire communities, the idea was killed. "End of the Line for Vouchers," *Church and State* 29 (June 1976): 3.9.

public opinion could be marshalled in support of the view that, since the state is now heavily influencing parental options in favor of public schools, the Supreme Court's prohibition upon efforts to restore equilibrium in the scales of individual choice is grossly inequitable.[51] If that happened, the Court might be persuaded to alter its interpretation of the religion clauses of the First Amendment. Another possible approach would be to mitigate, and perhaps eventually remove, the fiscal impediments now imposed by law on private schools by partially or totally instituting the policy of financing *all* schools, public and private, by means of fees collected from clients at the schoolhouse door.[52] The "double-payment" penalty would thus be removed from the decision to patronize private educational ventures, yet the state could not be accused of granting public money to private schools, directly or indirectly, or of exempting the patrons of these schools from taxes that other citizens were required to pay. One may be sure, however, that intense opposition would be encountered in legislative halls by the proponents of such a strategy.

## State and Federal Regulations

Recent Supreme Court decisions concerning government assistance to religiously affiliated colleges and universities suggest strongly that the price of the assistance may be abandonment of all significant religious distinctions,[53] in which case the campaign for the assistance could hardly be characterized as a triumph. Fairly extensive exposure to the politics of aid to private elementary and secondary schools has convinced this writer that many key figures in these schools were surprisingly willing to accept virtually any type of state regulation as a trade-off for public money.[54] In the

51. Galanter, "Religious Freedom in the United States."

52. For a provocative recent exchange of views on this point see E. G. West, *Nonpublic School Aid* (Lexington, Mass.: Lexington Books, 1976).

53. *Hunt v. McNair*, 413 U.S. 734 (1973); *Roemer v. Board of Public Works*, 426 U.S. 736 (1976).

54. This exposure was acquired in connection with consultation with relevant legislative commissions in Massachusetts and Maryland, in the preparation of my report, *Crisis in Illinois Nonpublic Schools*, and in the preparation of Donald A. Erickson and George F. Madaus, *Issues of Aid to Nonpublic Schools*, Final Report to the President's Commission on School Finance, 4 vols. (Chestnut Hill, Mass.: Center for Field Research and School Services, Boston College, 1971).

eyes of these people, apparently the prospect of government control is not problematic.

Many examples could be cited, however, of individuals and groups for whom this control *is* a serious issue.[55] When these people have attempted to opt for private alternatives in education, they have encountered not merely the fiscal impediments mentioned earlier but also the direct prohibitions of the law, often enforced under threat of serious penalties.

In three cases between 1923 and 1927, the Supreme Court established the right of private schools to exist and to be free from excessive state regulation. *Meyer v. State of Nebraska* (1923) struck down a law outlawing foreign language instruction in Nebraska elementary schools.[56] "No emergency has arisen," the Court asserted, "which renders knowledge by a child of some language other than English so clearly harmful as to justify its inhibition with the consequent infringement of rights long freely enjoyed."[57] Among the rights long freely enjoyed, according to the Court, was the parent's right to control the upbringing of the child. In *Meyer*, the Court suggested that the state's power to regulate "institutions which it supports" was more extensive than its power to regulate "all schools." The former power extended to curricular prescriptions. The latter power was described by the rather ambiguous term, "reasonable regulations." In *Pierce v. Society of Sisters* the Supreme Court condemned an effort, by means of initiative referendum in the State of Oregon, to compel all children of compulsory attendance age to enroll in public schools.[58] As if to reiterate its "reasonable regulation" stance in *Meyer*, the Court observed in *Pierce* that its decision did not cast any doubt on "the power of the state reasonably to regulate all

55. For the example of the Old Order Amish, see Donald A. Erickson, *Public Controls for Nonpublic Schools* (Chicago: University of Chicago Press, 1969). Concerning a Seventh-Day Adventist mother, see also Raymond S. Moore, "Motherhood on Trial," *Liberty* (Washington, D.C.: Review and Herald Publishing Co., Jan.-Feb., 1976): 3-5. Other examples will become evident in the discussion of court cases that follows.

56. *Meyer v. State of Nebraska*, 262 U.S. 390, 43 S. Ct. 625, 67 L. Ed. 1042, 29 A.L.R. 1446 (1923).

57. Ibid., 262 U.S. 394.

58. *Pierce v. Society of Sisters*, 268 U.S. 510, 45 S. Ct. 571, 69 L. Ed. 1070 (1925).

schools."[59] Here again, little was said about the definition of "reasonable," beyond the assertion that the state could require "certain studies plainly essential to good citizenship" and could prohibit any teachings "manifestly inimical to the public welfare."[60] As I have noted elsewhere, beyond literacy, "numeracy," and perhaps a basic understanding of our political and economic systems, it is exceedingly difficult to identify any skills and understandings that are "plainly essential to good citizenship."[61] If the suggested guidelines in *Pierce* were followed in this regard, state regulation of private educational enterprises would certainly not be extensive. In *Farrington* v. *Tokushige* (1927) the Supreme Court ended an apparent attempt in Hawaii to regulate private educational ventures out of existence.[62] The Court condemned the provisions in question in the following terms:

[T]he measures adopted thereunder go far beyond the mere regulation of privately supported schools, where children obtain instruction deemed valuable by their parents and which is not obviously in conflict with any public interest. They give affirmative direction concerning the intimate and essential details of such schools, entrust their control to public officers, and deny both owners and patrons reasonable choice and discretion in respect of teachers, curriculum and textbooks. Enforcement . . . would deprive parents of fair opportunity to procure for their children instruction which they think is important and we cannot say is harmful.[63]

Here, somewhat as in *Meyer* and *Pierce*, the Court suggested that the state could not prevent the parent from obtaining a type of instruction for the child "deemed valuable" by the parent and not clearly "harmful." There is at least a strong suggestion in *Meyer*, *Pierce*, and *Farrington* that the right of the parent to direct the child's upbringing is so fundamental that the state must have a

59. Ibid., 268 U.S. 573.

60. Ibid.

61. Erickson, *Public Controls for Nonpublic Schools*. See also Donald A. Erickson, *Super-Parent: An Analysis of State Educational Controls* (Chicago: Illinois Advisory Committee on Nonpublic Schools, 1973).

62. *Farrington* v. *Tokushige*, 273 U.S. 284, 47 S. Ct. 406, 71 L. Ed. 646, 53 A.L.R. 833 (1927).

63. Ibid., 273 U.S. 298.

compelling reason for restricting it. Also several phrases tend to support the position that state regulations must be considerably more limited for private educational ventures than for the public schools.

For present purposes, a large body of litigation regarding state requirements applying to private educational ventures (including home instruction) must be summarized in terms of the following generalizations.[64] Since the 1930s the Supreme Court has shown a strong inclination (at least until a few very recent cases were decided) to *presume*, in the absence of compelling evidence to the contrary, that state regulatory legislation is justifiable.[65] There has been a notable tendency in recent decades for state regulations to demand not merely that private educational enterprises exclude elements "manifestly inimical to the public welfare" and include "certain studies plainly essential to good citizenship," but be "equivalent," sometimes in onerously specified detail, to public schools in the same areas.[66] Until very recently, parents challenging this type of regulation have been singularly unsuccessful.[67] In some cases the courts have permitted the states to outlaw instruction that was demonstrably producing the knowledge and skills defined as essential in the relevant statutes.[68] It was noted earlier in this discussion that the parental rights guaranteed in *Pierce* may have been effectively placed beyond the reach of many people as a result of government-imposed fiscal constraints. In the present context, it seems important to observe that the same rights can be effectively destroyed by regulations ensuring that private educational options are not fundamentally different from the options provided within public school systems.

The most signal departure from the established proregulatory

64. For a much more extensive treatment see Erickson, *Public Controls for Nonpublic Schools*, especially chap. 5.

65. For example, *United States v. Carolene Products Co.*, 304 U.S. 144 (1938); *Day Brite Lighting Inc. v. Missouri*, 342 U.S. 421 (1952).

66. Erickson, *Public Controls for Nonpublic Schools*.

67. Ibid., chap. 5.

68. Ibid. See also, Donald A. Erickson, "The Persecution of LeRoy Garber," *School Review* 78 (November 1969): 81-90.

stance, insofar as private educational ventures are concerned, is found in *Wisconsin* v. *Yoder* (1972), a case in which several Old Order Amish were prosecuted for refusing to send their offspring to institutions that the state was willing to define as high schools.[69] In place of conventional schooling within classroom walls, the Amish were preparing their young for adulthood by following elementary instruction with an apprenticeship-like system of informal learning-by-doing under parental tutelage on the farm. Faced with a record showing that regular high school attendance clearly violated Amish religious teachings, that the Amish educational approach effectively prepared Amish youngsters for adulthood in their rural environs, and that the Amish communities, while relying on this educational approach for generations, had been singularly free of many ills affecting the larger society, the Supreme Court found that the Wisconsin compulsory attendance statute, as applied to the Amish in the context of this case, was an unjustifiable infringement upon their religious liberty and thus unconstitutional in the light of the First Amendment.

As if extremely reluctant to allow this dramatic departure from the state's conception of essential schooling, the Court hedged its decision with far-reaching qualifiers. It came close to asserting that one would have to look much like an Amishman to be granted the liberty it awarded in this case. Purely "secular" considerations —in contrast to "deep religious conviction, shared by an organized group, and intimately related to daily living"—would not warrant the same First Amendment protection.[70] The Court stated:

Thus, if the Amish asserted their claims because of subjective evaluation and rejection of contemporary secular values accepted by the majority, much as Thoreau rejected the social values of his time and isolated himself at Walden Pond, their claim would not rest on a religious basis. Thoreau's choice was philosophical and personal rather than religious, and such belief does not rise to the demands of the Religion Clause.[71]

This tendency of the Supreme Court to show more concern for

69. *Wisconsin v. Yoder*, 406 U.S. 205 (1972).

70. Ibid., p. 211.

71. Ibid.

the protection of fundamental life preferences traditionally characterized as "religious" than for those traditionally regarded as "not
religious" has been criticized as unduly time-bound, as too extensively rooted in the circumstances that happened to be salient when
the First Amendment was written.[72] In terms of this argument, the
First Amendment is conceived as preventing government from
putting its weight behind any basic philosophy of life, whether or
not that philosophy is characterized as emanating from any organized "religious" group. The First Amendment's references to
religion are explained by the fact that organized religious groups
*were*, at the time, perhaps the fundamental originators of attempts
to curtail the freedoms in question. In an extensively secularized
society many decades later, however, to protect freedom of conscience from traditional *religious* threats exclusively may be tantamount to leaving them largely unprotected. For example, parents
whose child is alienated from them by a state-required educational
program are not likely to have their agony ameliorated by the
assertion that their way of life is "not religion," or that the way of
life promoted by the program is "not religion." And if the secular-
ization of our society continues, it is precisely these parents in
"nonreligious" life-style conflicts who will require the most protection, yet who, in the light of current Supreme Court doctrines,
will be least likely to obtain it.

It is possible, however, to view *Yoder* (the Amish school case)
as establishing judicial principles that will prove more compelling,
in the long run, than the Court's attempts to hedge them in. In
fact, two state supreme courts, both quoting *Yoder* as part of their
justification, have now rather dramatically departed, much like
the Supreme Court did in *Yoder*, from the long-established tendency to uphold state educational regulations. More important,
they have done so when faced with aggrieved parents who look
quite different from the Amish.

In *State v. Whisner* (1976),[73] twelve parents of school-age children were prosecuted for failing to send their children to a school

72. Erickson, *Super-Parent*. Essentially the same argument appears in Stephen
Arons, "The Separation of School and State: *Pierce* Reconsidered," *Harvard
Educational Review* 46 (February 1976): 76-104.

73. *State v. Whisner*, 351 N.E. 2d 750, 47 Ohio St. 2d 181 (1976).

approved under the terms of a 149-page document titled, *Minimum Standards for Ohio Elementary Schools.*[74] As the title implies, the same standards, spelled out in great detail (for example, "The learning area contains: Drinking water with slanted stream"),[75] are applied to public and private schools. As the U.S. Supreme Court had done in *Yoder*, the Ohio Supreme Court found in *Whisner* that the religious liberty of the parents had been unjustifiably infringed upon by the state regulations. In addition, the court, in language reminiscent of the *Meyer*, *Pierce*, and *Farrington* decisions roughly half a century earlier, spoke of fundamental parental child-rearing rights and the need to maintain the liberty to be different in the private school. The following passages seem particularly notable:

> This cause presents sensitive issues of paramount importance involving the power of the state to impose extensive regulations upon the structure and government of non-public education, and conversely, upon the right of these appellants to freely exercise their professed religious beliefs in the context of providing an education to their children.[76]

> [A]lthough admittedly an admirable effort to extol the secular aims of the state in assuring that each child in this state obtains a quality education, we believe that these "minimum standards" overstep the boundary of *reasonable* regulation as applied to a nonpublic religious school.[77]

> There is an additional, independent reason, ignored by the lower courts in this case, that compels upholding appellants' attack upon the state's "minimum standards." In our view, these standards are so pervasive and all-encompassing that total compliance with each and every standard by a non-public school would effectively eradicate the distinction between public and non-public education, and thereby deprive these appellants of their traditional interest as parents to direct the upbringing and education of their children.[78]

> . . . [I]t has long been recognized that the right of a parent to guide

74. Virginia M. Lloyd, *Minimum Standards for Ohio Elementary Schools* (Columbus, Ohio: Ohio State Board of Education, 1970).

75. Ibid., p. 84.

76. *State v. Whisner*, 351 N.E. 2d 751, 760.

77. Ibid., p. 764.

78. Ibid., p. 768.

the education, including the religious education, of his or her children is indeed a "fundamental right" guaranteed by the due process clause of the Fourteenth Amendment.[79]

The "minimum standards" under attack herein effectively repose power in the state Department of Education to control the essential elements of non-public education in this state. The expert testimony received in this regard unequivocally demonstrates the absolute suffocation of independent thought and educational policy, and the effective retardation of religious philosophy engendered by application of these "minimum standards" to non-public educational institutions.[80]

Under the facts of this case, the right of appellants to direct the upbringing and education of their children in a manner in which they deem advisable, indeed essential, and which we cannot say is harmful, has been denied by application of the state's "minimum standards" as to them.[81]

Somewhat similarly, according to available reports, in *Vermont v. LaBarge* (1976), a case for which the written opinion is not yet available to this writer, the Supreme Court of Vermont has held that the religious liberties of several parents have been violated by the statutory demand that their school is unacceptable under the compulsory attendance requirement unless it has received the state Department of Education's official approval.[82] It was enough, the court reportedly ruled, that the school provided the essential education the state was entitled to demand.

These three recent, dramatic decisions (*Yoder, Whisner*, and *LaBarge*) obviously do not justify any generalization concerning the demise of the deeply rooted judicial tendency to uphold state educational regulations in the face of parental challenges. Courts in other states may refuse to follow the example of the Ohio and Vermont supreme courts. The U.S. Supreme Court may refuse to broaden its repeatedly delimited stance in *Yoder*. And in none of

79. Ibid., p. 769.

80. Ibid., p. 770.

81. Ibid.

82. The information available to me concerning *State v. LaBarge* has been obtained by means of a conversation with the attorney for the parents (William B. Ball) and by means of newspaper accounts, such as: "Court Ruling Jars Board of Education," Rutland (Vermont) *Herald*, 7 April 1976.

these three cases were the "nonreligious" philosophical preferences of parents weighed against the asserted right of a state to control the educational process. It seems predictable, however, that there will be much litigation on this topic in the near future, and thus much opportunity for clarification of judicial guidelines. It is clearly possible that the courts will return to the more expansive view of parental rights and to the more constraining approach to state control that the *Meyer*, *Pierce*, and *Farrington* cases appear to embody.

Private educational ventures are not entirely unaffected by federal statutory regulations and related court rulings, although this area of concern cannot be explored in any depth in the present chapter. It is now clear, for example, that Congress may constitutionally forbid private schools, as it has done, to exclude would-be students on racial grounds:

'[T]he Constitution . . . places no value on discrimination,' . . . and while '[i]nvidious private discrimination may be characterized as a form of exercising freedom of association protected by the First Amendment,' . . . it has never been accorded constitutional protections. And even some private discrimination is subject to special remedial legislation in certain circumstances.[83]

## Other Legally Sanctioned Constraints

The opportunity to opt for private rather than public educational offerings may be curtailed, not merely by government-imposed fiscal handicaps and unduly prescriptive regulations applicable to these offerings, but also by physical and temporal arrangements in public education, enforced under the legal powers of public educational agencies at state, local, and sometimes other levels. It is arguable that many parents who cannot afford to patronize a private school *in toto* in the light of current financial arrangements nevertheless can afford to purchase private educational options made available on a piecemeal (for example, subject-by-subject) basis, and that many parents would opt to do the latter if given the opportunity. As a specific instance, a parent who is particularly unhappy about the approach of a public school to social studies, but relatively content with the rest of the program,

83. *Runyon v. McCrary*, 427 U.S. 160, 176 (1976).

should perhaps be provided with conditions permitting a student to be released from the public school during social studies periods and quickly and easily transferred to premises on which social studies would be offered by some private agency. The same circumstances would make it feasible for groups that cannot manage to sponsor a total school program to develop the discrete component(s) in which they are most interested. Elsewhere, I have described in considerable detail some of the physical and temporal arrangements that public school authorities could adopt to maximize the availability of private educational options.[84] In the light of the widespread absence of these arrangements, it seems that current legally sanctioned temporal and physical settings for public education may be characterized as a serious impediment in this regard.

Some small steps toward facilitating the availability of private educational options through conducive temporal and physical arrangements have been taken, obviously, by the relatively few public school districts that have cooperated with private schools in "shared time" or "dual enrollment" practices.[85] There is some assurance, moreover, that the courts will tend to view these small steps as constitutional.[86] But the basic principle of making private and public educational alternatives available on a component-by-component rather than a take-it-or-leave-it basis has been scarcely discussed in its logical extensions, let alone applied at all comprehensively.[87] If thus applied in the context of current Supreme Court doctrines, it might be struck down as an unconstitutional mode of assistance to, or entanglement with, church-related educational agencies. The possibilities seem strangely neglected and unexplored. There is little in the educational literature, to this writer's knowledge, to illuminate the pertinent legal questions.

84. Erickson, "The Public-Private Consortium."

85. Many specific examples of these programs are provided in Erickson and Madaus, *Issues of Aid to Nonpublic Schools.*

86. For one of the most recent cases, see *Citizens v. Porter,* 237 N.W. 232 (1975).

87. Some of the more comprehensive approaches that might be envisioned are discussed in Erickson, "The Public-Private Consortium" and in Sizer, *Places for Learning.*

# CHAPTER VI

# Control of the Curriculum

M. A. MCGHEHEY

## Introduction

The curriculum of the public schools has, from the beginning of the Republic, been a matter of continuing controversy. Public schools existed for over a hundred years prior to the development of the United States Constitution, although on a very limited basis, both as to accessibility by substantial numbers of students and as to the extent of the curriculum available. Since the curriculum of the schools depends upon current ideas of the purposes of education, the curriculum changes from time to time. In the very first public schools, established in Massachusetts under the "Old Deluder Satan Act," a chief purpose of the schools was to prepare students to read the Holy Bible, and religious influences have pervaded the curriculum during much of our history as a nation. From the outset, however, there was controversy about the place of religion in the curriculum, and the formation of Roman Catholic parochial schools may be traced directly to the strong Calvinistic influences in the curriculum of the public school system in the first half of the nineteenth century. In 1875, President Ulysses S. Grant, on the occasion of our first centennial celebration, proposed that a constitutional amendment be submitted to the legislature of each state making it the duty of the states to provide free public schools, but "forbidding the teaching in said schools of religious, atheistic, or pagan tenets."[1]

With each new generation there have been new curriculum controversies. Old issues, thought dead, have been revived as times

1. James D. Richardson, *A Compilation of the Messages and Papers of the Presidents*, 1789-1897, vol. 7 (Washington, D.C.: Government Printing Office, 1898). The entire message of President Grant appears in the *Congressional Record*, 1876, 4, pp. 175-81.

and conditions have changed. So long as the schools are "public" schools, the content of the curriculum will be subject to public pressure, which varies not only as to time, but also as to place. What may be essential to the purposes of one segment of the population may be anathema to another. Thus the avenues available for the exertion of political pressure—constitutions, statutes, litigation, and administrative regulations—will continue to be explored by those who are dissatisfied with current notions of what the public school curriculum is, or ought to be.

The term "curriculum" has been subjected to varying definitions. One school of thought holds that the curriculum is properly limited to the courses, officially prescribed for a given grade, for which credit is available, leading eventually to some form of a diploma. Another school of thought applies a broader definition of curriculum, encompassing all activities of the school, both formal and informal, that impinge upon the lives of the pupils. Morris suggests that there is an even broader view:

Courts generally use the term "curriculum" in both senses, and indeed, occasionally in a third, and broader sense. They have infrequently used the term to apply to whatever happens in school, whether the authorities want to accept responsibility for it or not.[2]

In this chapter, the narrower definition will be utilized, and the discussion will be limited to those cases dealing with the formal curriculum structure of the schools.[3]

A formal structure for the control of the curriculum of the public schools exists by virtue of provisions found in (a) state constitutions; (b) statutes; (c) rules and regulations of the state education agency, principally those providing for accreditation of schools; (d) administrative rulings, such as opinions of the attorney general, and in New York and New Jersey, decisions of the Commissioner of Education; (e) written policies, rules, and regulations of local boards of education; and (f) court decisions. The extent to which the foregoing agencies of control actually

2. Arval A. Morris, *The Constitution and American Education* (St. Paul, Minn.: West Publishing Co., 1974), p. 263.

3. For an analysis of early cases in the area of legal aspects of extracurricular activities, see J. David Mohler and Edward C. Bolmeier, *Law of Extracurricular Activities in Secondary Schools* (Cincinnati, Ohio: W. H. Anderson Co., 1968).

influence the content of the public school curriculum varies widely among the fifty states.

The curriculum is also influenced by an informal control structure that includes (a) textbook writers and publishers, (b) school administrators, (c) classroom teachers, (d) regional accrediting agencies, (e) community mores, and (f) federal programs such as those provided for under the Elementary and Secondary Education Act. In many ways, the informal structure has a greater impact than the formal structure on the day-to-day activities that establish and maintain the school curriculum. The influences of textbook writers, for example, is far more subtle and less direct than that of the statutes. But since many teachers are bound to the textbook, what goes into the textbook determines, to a very large extent, what becomes the effective curriculum of the school.

In this chapter, I shall deal only with the agencies that are part of the formal structure and particularly with court decisions that have had an impact on the curriculum of elementary and secondary schools.

## State and Local Agencies of Control

### CONSTITUTIONS

For the most part, state constitutions are silent on the broad content of the curriculum. The typical state constitution imposes a duty upon the legislature to establish and maintain a general, thorough, uniform, and efficient system of free common or public schools.[4] Some of the state constitutions, however, are quite specific in terms of curriculum requirements. Several state constitutions require instruction in the English language,[5] while the constitution of one state attempts to insure that teachers will be able to instruct

4. Language incorporating one or more of these ideas appears in the constitutions of Arizona, Arkansas, Delaware, Florida, Idaho, Illinois, Indiana, Kansas, Kentucky, Maryland, Michigan, Minnesota, Mississippi, Montana, Nebraska, Nevada, New Mexico, New Jersey, New York, North Dakota, Oklahoma, Oregon, Pennsylvania, South Dakota, Texas, Utah, Virginia, Washington, West Virginia and Wyoming. *Index Digest of State Constitutions,* 2d ed. (New York: Oceana Press, 1959), p. 373.

5. Arizona Constitution, Article XX, Section 7; Louisiana Constitution, Article XII, Section 12; Michigan Constitution, Article XI, Section 9; Nebraska Constitution, Article I, Section 27; and Oklahoma Constitution, Article I, Section 5.

Spanish-speaking pupils.[6] The North Carolina constitution requires the legislature to provide a means for education of inebriates and idiots,[7] and the Utah constitution specifically mandates the teaching of the metric system.[8] The Oklahoma constitution mandates that the legislature provide for teaching of the elements of agriculture, horticulture, stock raising, and domestic science,[9] and North Dakota requires, by constitutional provision, that instruction be given to inculcate the vital importance of truthfulness, temperance, purity, public spirit, and respect for honest labor of every kind.[10] Although most of state constitutions vest the duty to establish a school system in the legislature, the Colorado constitution provides for control of the curriculum at the school district level, a provision that has been held "to vest in the directors of every school district, the control of the instruction of the youth of that district."[11] Despite the consensus of legal scholars that constitutions should be cast in broad, general language, it appears that many states prefer to write very narrow, extensive, and specific constitutional provisions.

## STATUTES

At least twenty-two states have statutory provisions that either require or prohibit specific curriculum areas. Mandated courses in order of frequency include: reading, writing, and arithmetic; pen-

6. New Mexico Constitution, Article XII, Section 8; Article XIX, Section 1.

7. North Carolina Constitution, Article XI, Section 9.

8. Utah Constitution, Article X, Section 11.

9. Oklahoma Constitution, Article XIII, Section 7.

10. North Dakota Constitution, Article VIII, Section 149.

11. *School District No. 16 v. Union High School No. 1*, 60 Colo. 292, 152 P. 1149 (Colorado, 1915). The language of the Colorado constitution, Article IX, reads as follows:

Section 15. *School districts—board of education.* The general assembly shall, by law, provide for organization of school districts of convenient size, in each of which shall be established a board of education, to consist of three or more directors to be elected by the qualified electors of the district. Said directors shall have control of instruction in the public schools of their respective districts.

Section 16. *Textbooks in public schools.* Neither the general assembly nor the state board of education shall have power to prescribe textbooks to be used in the public schools.

manship, grammar, and spelling; social studies, including the specific subjects of anthropology, political science, psychology, sociology, civics, and the role of ethnic groups in society; geography; health and hygiene; the effects of alcohol, drugs, and tobacco on the human body; natural or physical sciences; physical education; United States history and government; the fine arts, including music, art and drawing; nature study; agricultural education; and foreign languages.

Several state legislatures have attempted to deal with the subject of sex education. The state legislature of Louisiana prohibited sex education throughout the state on a temporary basis, pending the report and recommendation of a legislative committee on the subject. The legislative committee was appointed in 1969 but the statute generally prohibiting the teaching of sex education has not yet been repealed or amended. Other states provide for excusing students from classes in sex education upon parental request, require prior notice to parents relative to the school's intention to provide such instruction and give parents the right to inspect the materials to be used, and exempt instruction in physiology, biology, and health from the bans of the sex education statutes. Michigan has abolished the discussion of birth control in the public schools.

Several states have enacted statutes prohibiting sectarian instruction in the schools, and a number of states ban teaching about communism.

Educators generally prefer that the content of the curriculum be left to educational agencies, but this position has not met with universal acceptance among state legislators. Indeed, the proliferation of statutory enactments, either specifically mandating or prohibiting curricular offerings, suggests that legislatures will continue to enact statutes in areas that become involved in political controversy.[12]

## Rules of State and Local Agencies

The rules for accrediting schools, enacted either by the state board of education or by the chief state school officer, usually are

12. For a more comprehensive treatment of statutory enactments in the area of curriculum, see Leon F. Edelman, "Basic American," *NOLPE School Law Journal 6*, no. 2 (1976): 83-122.

both quite extensive and specific in nature. Accreditation rules seldom prohibit curriculum offerings, and are ordinarily concerned exclusively with mandated courses and subjects.

In New York and New Jersey, the state commissioner of education is authorized to decide controversies arising out of the state school laws. It is not uncommon for the commissioner of education to be called upon to decide questions involving curriculum offerings. Similarly, the attorneys general are asked to interpret statutes that involve the curriculum of the schools. Rulings or opinions of these administrative agencies have legal force, if at all, only in the particular state and are not considered to have legal effect outside of the state.

The general rule is that local boards may not reduce the curriculum below state-mandated standards.[13] Local boards, however, may supplement the curriculum mandated by statute, unless there is a clear statutory prohibition,[14] or the board may delete courses not required by the state law.[15] The courts will ordinarily not interfere with board decisions as to course offerings, methods of teaching, or the adaptation of courses to changing conditions in the absence of an abuse of discretion on the part of the board of education.[16]

## Courts as Agencies of Control

In the remainder of this chapter I shall report on court decisions that have influenced the school curriculum in the following

13. *Jones v. Board of Trustees of Culver City School District,* 47 P. 2d 804, 8 Cal. App. 2d 146 (California App., 1935); *Ehret v. School District of Borough of Kulpmont,* 5 A.2d 188, 333 Pa. 518 (Pennsylvania, 1939); *Ehret v. Kulpmont School District,* 14 Northumb, L. J. 254 (Pennsylvania Com. Pl., 1940).

14. *Woodson v. School District No. 28, Kingman County,* 274 P. 728, 127 Kans. 651 (Kansas, 1929); *State Tax Commission v. Board of Education of Holton,* 73 P. 2d 49, 146 Kans. 722 (Kansas, 1937).

15. *Board of Education of Okay Independent School District, No. 1 of Wagoner County v. Carroll,* 513 P. 2d 872 (Oklahoma, 1973).

16. *State ex rel. Brewton v. Board of Education of the City of St. Louis,* 233 S.W. 2d 697 (Missouri, 1950); *in re Winters,* 146 N.Y.S. 2d 107, 208 Misc. 953 (New York, 1955); *State ex rel. Williams v. Avoyelles Parish School Board,* 147 So. 2d 729 (Louisiana App., 1962); *Thompson v. Engelking,* 537 P. 2d 635, 96 Idaho 793 (Idaho, 1975); *Schwan v. Board of Education of Lansing School District,* 183 N.W. 2d 594, 27 Mich. App. 391 (Michigan App., 1970).

selected areas: the definition of "common" schools, the rights of parents as opposed to those of the school district, the teaching of foreign language, religious instruction, the teaching of evolution, sex education, and bilingual/bicultural education.

<h2 style="text-align:center">THE "COMMON" SCHOOL</h2>

The constitutions and statutes of the states have usually described the school system in the terms of "common schools" or "public schools." In the early part of the nineteenth century, the drive for the establishment of free public schools, led by Horace Mann and others, inevitably resulted in litigation to define these terms. Many of these early cases involved the question of the upward extension of the curriculum to include high school offerings. An early Massachusetts case dealt with the legality of a girls' high school that was teaching bookkeeping, algebra, geometry, history, rhetoric, mental, moral, and natural philosophy, botany, Latin, French, and other higher branches of learning that were not offered in the grammar schools of the town. It was contended that such a school was not a "public" school. The Supreme Judicial Court of Massachusetts held that the term "public school" was sufficiently broad to authorize the raising of taxes to support the aforementioned curriculum offerings.[17]

In 1881, the Illinois Supreme Court upheld the teaching of modern languages in the common schools of that state,[18] and the Missouri Supreme Court held in 1883 that the terms "public" and "common" schools were interchangeable and that the term "school" by itself does not imply any restriction to the mere rudiments of an education.[19]

The Kalamazoo decision of 1874 is generally cited by school authorities as the landmark decision relative to the upward extension of the common schools to include high school grades, although the 1845 case in Massachusetts, cited above, really dealt with the same subject matter. Despite the absence of any express statutory authority, the Michigan Supreme Court upheld the right of a common school district to maintain a high school.[20] The decisions in

17. *Cushing v. Inhabitants of Newburyport,* 51 Mass. 508 (1845).
18. *Powell v. Board of Education,* 97 Ill. 375 (Illinois, 1881).
19. *Roach v. St. Louis,* 7 Mo. App. 567, 77 Mo. 484 (Missouri, 1883).
20. *Stuart v. School District No. 1,* 30 Mich. 69 (Michigan, 1874).

Illinois and Missouri, referred to above, were to the same effect as the Kalamazoo decision. Other states quickly followed: Kentucky in 1877[21] and Kansas in 1893.[22]

Every addition to the curriculum of the schools has apparently been challenged in one jurisdiction or another. But the courts have almost universally supported the addition of secular subjects to the curriculum unless specifically prohibited by law. Courts have approved the teaching of music,[23] domestic science,[24] speech improvement,[25] bookkeeping,[26] manual training,[27] field day exercises,[28] and dancing.[29]

The downward extension of the curriculum to include kindergarten did not receive favorable consideration by the courts in early cases, due to the fact that many state constitutions expressly provided for education of children between the ages of six and twenty (or in some instances twenty-one). Because of such limiting language in state constitutions the provision of kindergarten instruction was held to be unconstitutional.[30]

When the question was raised in California, however, as to whether or not kindergarten was a part of the "primary school system," the court, in the absence of any constitutional restriction,

21. *Newman v. Thompson,* 4 S.W. 341 (Kentucky, 1887).

22. *Board of Education of the City of Topeka v. Welch,* 51 Kans. 792 (Kansas, 1893); *Epley v. Hall,* 97 Kans. 549 (Kansas, 1916); *Koester v. Board of Commissioners of Atchison County* 44 Kans. 141 (Kansas, 1890).

23. *Epley v. Hall,* 97 Kans. 549 (Kansas, 1916); Finegan, *Decisions of New York Superintendent,* 329; *Bellmeyer v. Independent District of Marshalltown,* 44 Iowa 564 (Iowa, 1876); *State v. Webber,* 108 Ind. 31 (Indiana, 1886); *Meyers Publishing Co. v. White River District,* 28 Ind. App. 91 (Indiana App., 1901).

24. 21 *New York State Dept. Rep.* 23 (1919).

25. 22 *New York State Dept. Rep.* 565 (1920).

26. *Rulison v. Post,* 79 Ill. 567 (1875).

27. *Maxcy v. City,* 144 Wis. 238 (1910).

28. *Adams v. Schneider,* 124 N.E. 718 (Indiana, 1919).

29. *Hardwick v. Board of School Trustees of Fruitridge School District,* 205 Pac. 49 (California, 1922).

30. *Roach v. St. Louis,* 77 Mo. 484 (Missouri, 1883); *in re Kindergarten Schools,* 18 Colo. 234 (Colorado, 1893), an advisory opinion given to the legislature; *Dickerson v. Edmonson,* 120 Ark. 80 (Arkansas, 1915).

upheld the legality of kindergarten.[31] In later years, kindergarten instruction was expressly authorized by statute.

Later cases upheld the legality, under the common school rubric, of teacher-training departments in high schools,[32] and practice teaching,[33] but denied the legality of laboratory schools conducted under the auspices of normal schools.[34]

The California Supreme Court decided in 1915 that evening schools are a part of the common school system,[35] and vocational schools offering agriculture and home economics were upheld in Minnesota and California.[36] The Kansas Supreme Court, however, took the position in the same year that the authority of school boards to acquire land for sites did not authorize the purchase of land for use in teaching vocational agriculture.[37] The effect of this case was subsequently overcome by statutory enactment.

From the above, it may be seen that, with few exceptions, the courts have generally applied a liberal construction to the term "common schools" and the curriculum has gradually expanded over the years.[38]

### PARENTAL RIGHTS AGAINST THE SCHOOL DISTRICT

There is a division in the cases relative to the authority of a parent as opposed to the right of the schools with respect to the selection of courses. The relationship of the parent to the state

31. *Sinnott v. Colombet,* 107 Cal. 187.

32. *Dickerson v. Edmondson,* 120 Ark. 80 (Arkansas, 1915); *Spedden v. Board,* 74 W. Va. 181 (W. Va., 1914).

33. *Clay v. Independent School District of Cedar Falls,* 174 N.W. 47 (Iowa, 1919).

34. *School District No. 20, Spokane City v. Bryan,* 51 Wash. 498; *State v. Preston,* 79 Wash. 286.

35. *Board of Education of the City and County of San Francisco v. Hyatt,* 152 Cal. 515 (California, 1915).

36. *Associated Schools v. School District No. 83,* 122 Minn. 254 (Minnesota, 1913); *Bates v. Escondido Union High School District,* 24 P. 2d 884 (California App., 1933).

37. *Board of Education of the City of Nickerson v. Davis,* 90 Kans. 621 (Kansas, 1913).

38. For a thorough treatment of the early cases, see Otto T. Hamilton, *The Courts and the Curriculum,* Contributions to Education, no. 250 (New York: Teachers College, Columbia University, 1927).

with respect to the education of the child was defined by the
Georgia Supreme Court in 1897 in the following language: "At
common law it was the duty of parents to give to their children
'an education suitable to their station in life'—a duty pointed out
by reason, and of far the greatest consequence of any. (1 Blackstone's *Commentaries*, p. 450)"[39] The court, however, went on
to say the following:

> The common law rule being clear and unequivocal, that, while the duty
> rested upon the parent to educate his child, the law would not attempt
> to force him to discharge this duty; the child, so far as education is
> concerned, is completely at the mercy of the parent. Therefore, at
> common law the child had no right to demand an education at the
> hands of the parent.[40]

The Supreme Court of Oklahoma stated the same principle in
this fashion: "At common law the parent, and especially the father,
was vested with supreme control over the child, including its
education, and, except when modified by statute, that authority
still exists in the parent."[41]

Not all courts agree with this strict view. The Indiana Supreme
Court, in 1870 and again in 1901, held that the natural rights of
the parent are subordinate to the power of the state, and may be
restricted and regulated by municipal laws. The court said: "How
far this interference should extend is a question, not of constitutional power for the courts, but of expediency and propriety,
which is the sole province of the legislature to determine."[42]

A number of cases have been decided involving parental attempts to control the curriculum of their children. In 1859 a
parent had asked that his child be excused from writing a composition. The child had been expelled for refusal to write the composition. The Vermont Supreme Court upheld the reasonableness
of the rule and the expulsion of the pupil.[43] A local school board
rule in Ohio, which required that at certain times students should

39. *Board of Education of Cartersville v. Purse*, 101 Ga. 422 (Georgia,
1897).

40. Ibid.

41. *State v. Thompson*, 103 Pac. 578 (Oklahoma, 1909).

42. *State v. Clottu*, 33 Ind. 409 (Indiana, 1870); *State v. Bailey*, 157 Ind.
324 (Indiana, 1901).

43. *Lander v. Seaver*, 32 Vt. 224 (Vermont, 1859).

be prepared to give some rhetorical exercise before the school, was upheld as reasonable.[44] An Indiana case is frequently cited as the most extreme position upholding the power of the state. In *State* v. *Webber*, a boy had been expelled from school for refusing, upon his father's orders, to study music. The father's only reason was his right to exercise the choice of curriculum for his child. The court held that the determination of the branches of learning to be taught was vested, by statute, in the board.[45] The school board was upheld in Georgia as to an assignment that required a student to write a composition to be used as a part of a debate on the topic "Should Trial by Jury by Abolished?"[46]

Other courts, however, have found for the parents in cases of this sort. In Wisconsin, the supreme court defended the right of a parent to have his child not take geography in order that he might spend more time on arithmetic.[47] In two separate decisions the Illinois Supreme Court upheld parental rights to exclude their children from classes in bookkeeping and in grammar.[48] The Nebraska Supreme Court has ruled in favor of parental selection of curriculum in one case involving the teaching of grammar[49] and in another where a student would have been required to go to a different building, more than a mile away from the regular school, for instruction in domestic science.[50] Other cases involving rulings in favor of parents have been decided in Oklahoma[51] and in California.[52]

---

44. *Sewell v. Board of Education*, 29 Ohio St. 89 (Ohio, 1876).

45. *State v. Webber*, 108 Ind. 31 (Indiana, 1886). For a modern case on the same subject, see *Davis v. Page*, 385 F. Supp. 395 (D.C.N.H., 1974). See also *Commonwealth City of Pittsburgh v. Ross*, 330 A. 2d 290 (Pennsylvania Commonwealth, 1975).

46. *Bradford v. Samuel Benedict School*, 111 Ga. 801.

47. *Morrow v. Wood*, 35 Wis. 59 (Wisconsin, 1874).

48. *Rulison v. Post*, 79 Ill. 567 (Illinois, 1875); *Trustees v. People*, 87 Ill. 303 (Illinois, 1877).

49. *State, ex rel. Sheibley v. School District*, 31 Nebr. 552 (Nebraska, 1891).

50. *State v. Ferguson*, 95 Nebr. 63 (Nebraska, 1914).

51. *School District No. 18, Garvin County v. Thompson*, 24 Okla. 1 (Oklahoma, 1909).

52. *Hardwick v. Board of School Trustees of Fruitridge School District*, 205 Pac. 49 (California, 1921).

## PROHIBITION OF TEACHING OF FOREIGN LANGUAGE

The first case to reach the U.S. Supreme Court concerning a curriculum issue involved a 1919 Nebraska statute prohibiting the teaching of the German language in any private, denominational, parochial or public school, and imposing a criminal sanction (fine and/or imprisonment) for violation of the statute. Robert T. Meyer, a teacher, was convicted under the statute, and fined $25. His conviction was upheld by the Nebraska Supreme Court, which found that the statute in question came reasonably within the police power of the state.[53] Upon appeal to the U.S. Supreme Court, the decision was reversed on grounds that the statute was in violation of the due process clause of the Fourteenth Amendment. There were three bases for the Court's decision: (a) that the statute interfered with the professional calling of modern language teachers, (b) that it deprived students of an opportunity to obtain desired knowledge, and (c) that it interfered with the right of parents to control the education of the children.[54] *Meyer* is frequently cited in balancing the power of the state versus the rights of parents.

### RELIGIOUS INSTRUCTION

Religious instruction was regarded to be an integral part of the curriculum of colonial schools, and the King James Version of the Bible was used daily, either in the form of formal exercises at the beginning or ending of the school day, or as a basic textbook. Because of the absence of a substantial number of adherents to religious denominations other than Protestant (except in Maryland) religious teaching involving the use of the King James Version was not a source of serious controversy at the time.

It appears that the earliest challenge to the use of the Bible in the classroom occurred in Maine in 1854. A Roman Catholic pupil was expelled from the school for refusing to obey the school

53. *Meyer v. Nebraska*, 187 N.W. 100 (Nebraska, 1922).

54. *Meyer v. Nebraska*, 262 U.S. 390, 43 S. Ct. 625 (1923). See also, *Farrington v. Tokishige*, 273 U.S. 284, 47 S. Ct. 406 (1927), where a similar provision in the School Act of Hawaii was held to be unconstitutional by the U.S. Supreme Court, and *Hock Ke Lok Po v. Stainback*, 74 F. Supp. 852 (D.C. Hawaii 1947), which held unconstitutional legislation prohibiting teaching of a foreign language to children below a specified age or grade.

officials and read from the King James Bible, the regularly adopted reading textbook. A unanimous court held that the regulation adopting the King James Version did not infringe upon the constitutional rights of students, or the rights of conscience, or the right to freedom of worship.[55] The highest courts of at least thirteen states have expressly approved the reading of the Bible in their public schools.[56] The high courts of seven states have found that Bible reading violates either the state constitution or statutes.[57] Boles, writing in 1961, found that thirty-seven states permitted Bible reading in their schools at that time by statute. Only Mississippi had a constitutional provision permitting Bible reading. Twelve states required Bible reading by law. At the same time, twenty-four states had statutes prohibiting sectarian instruction in the public schools. It is obvious that the Bible was not regarded as a sectarian document in a majority of the states in 1961.[58]

In 1950, the Supreme Court of New Jersey had decided a case

55. *Donahoe v. Richards,* 38 Maine 279 (Maine, 1854).

56. *Moore v. Monroe,* 64 Iowa 367, 20 N.W. 475, 52 Am. St. Rep. 444 (1884); *Hackett v. Brooksville Graded District,* 120 Ky. 608, 87 S.W. 792, 69 L.R.A. 592, 117 Am. St. Rep. 599 (1905); *Billard v. Board of Education of the City of Topeka,* 69 Kans. 53, 76 Pac. 422, 66 L.R.A. 166, 105 Am. St. Rep. 148 (1904); *Pfeiffer v. Board of Education of Detroit,* 118 Mich. 560, 77 N.W. 250, 42 L.R.A. 536 (1898); *Kaplan v. Independent School District of Virginia,* 171 Minn. 142, 214 N.W. 18, 57 A.L.R. 185 (1927); *Spiller v. Inhabitants of Woburn,* 12 Allen 127 (Massachusetts, 1866); *Donahoe v. Richards,* 38 Maine 379, 61 Am. Dec. 256 (1854); *Lewis v. Board of Education of City of New York,* 157 Misc. 520, 285 N.Y. Supp. 164 (1935), appeal dismissed, 276 N.Y. 490, 12 N.E. 2d 172 (1937); *Doremus v. Board of Education of Hawthorne,* 5 N.J. 435, 75 A. 2d 880, 342 U.S. 429 (1952); *Church v. Bullock,* 104 Tex. 1, 109 S.W. 115, 16 L.R.A. (n.s.) 860 (1908); *People ex rel. Vollmar v. Stanley,* 81 Colo. 276, 255 Pac. 610 (1927); *Wilkerson v. City of Rome,* 152 Ga. 763, 110 S.E. 895, 20 A.L.R. 1535 (1921); *Carden v. Bland,* 288 S.W. 2d 718 (1956).

57. *People ex rel. Ring v. Board of Education of District 24,* 245 Ill. 334, 92 N.E. 251, 29 L.R.A. (n.s.) 442 (1910); *Herold v. Parish Board of School Directors,* 136 La. 1034, 68 So. 116 (1915); *State ex rel. Freeman v. Scheve,* 65 Nebr. 853, 91 N.W. 846 (1902); *Board of Education of Cincinnati v. Minor,* 23 Ohio St. 211 (1872); *State ex rel. Finger v. Weedman,* 55 S.D. 343, 226 N.W. 348 (1929); *State ex rel. Clithero v. Showalter,* 159 Wash. 519, 293 Pac. 1000 (1930); *State ex rel. Dearle v. Frazier,* 102 Wash. 369, 172 Pac. 35 (1918); *State ex rel. Weiss v. District Board of School District No. 8,* 76 Wis. 177, 44 N.W. 967 (1890).

58. Donald E. Boles, *The Bible, Religion, and the Public Schools* (Ames, Iowa: Iowa State University Press, 1961).

involving a statute requiring the daily reading of five verses from the Old Testament without comment, and permitting the recitation of the Lord's Prayer. In ruling that the statute was constitutional, a unanimous court found that neither the Old Testament nor the Lord's Prayer were sectarian. When the case reached the U.S. Supreme Court, it was dismissed as moot because the plaintiff had already graduated from school and because the economic interest of the taxpayer involved was insufficient to provide the basis for a taxpayer's lawsuit.[59]

The same issue came before the U.S. Supreme Court in 1963. Both Pennsylvania and Maryland had statutes similar to the New Jersey statute found constitutional in *Doremus*. Plaintiffs challenged the statutes under the establishment clause of the First Amendment to the U.S. Constitution. The two cases were merged for consideration, and in an 8-1 decision the Court held the statutes to be violative of the establishment clause.[60]

On two occasions, the U.S. Supreme Court has considered the question of the constitutionality of school programs in which students were released for a portion of the day in order to participate in religious instruction. The first of these cases arose in Champaign, Illinois, and was decided by the U.S. Supreme Court in 1948. Under the terms of the released time program in effect in Champaign, students were released from regular classes, upon the request of their parents, and required to attend religious courses. The religious courses were taught in the regular classrooms of the school buildings by three separate groups representing Protestant denominations, by Catholic priests, and by a Jewish rabbi. Reports of the attendance of students were made to their regular teachers. Students who did not wish to take the religious instruction were required to leave their regular classrooms and to pursue their regular secular studies in another part of the building. The Supreme Court held this practice to be in violation of the establishment clause of the First Amendment.[61]

59. *Doremus v. Board of Education of Hawthorne*, 5 N.J. 435, 75 A.2d 880 (New Jersey, 1950); 342 U.S. 429, 72 S. Ct. 394 (1952).

60. *School District of Abington Township v. Schempp*, 374 U.S. 203 (1963); *Murray v. Curlett*, 374 U.S. 429, 72 S. Ct. 394 (1952).

61. *State ex rel. McCollum v. Board of Education of School District No. 71*, 333 U.S. 203, 68 S. Ct. 461 (1948).

Four years later the question was again before the U.S. Supreme Court, but on a different set of facts. The case involved a New York plan in which the students left the school building to attend religion classes sponsored by specific churches, a practice that was held to be constitutional.[62]

The first case reviewed by the U.S. Supreme Court involving the use of prayers in the public schools originated in New York. The State Board of Regents had adopted a prayer, recommended by a committee representing Protestant, Catholic, and Jewish groups, for use in the public schools. The prayer was: "Almighty God, we acknowledge our dependence upon Thee, and we beg Thy blessings upon us, our parents, our teachers, and our country." This prayer was required by regulations of the local school board, but any student who wished could be excused from taking part. The Court found this practice to be violative of the establishment clause of the First Amendment, observing that the question of whether the practice is compulsory or voluntary is immaterial when the establishment clause is involved. When the state prescribes a prayer, it is establishing a religion, and the fact that the prayer may be denominationally neutral does not free it from the strictures of the First Amendment.[63]

School authorities tended to overreact to this decision and failed to read a footnote in the case specifically limiting the decision to exercises of a devotional type, and acknowledging that other practices, such as the use of religious songs, recitation of historical documents that include religious references, and the use of the Bible in an objective course of study, were not to be regarded as falling within the scope of the decision.

Many states have enacted statutes providing for a daily recitation of the Pledge of Allegiance. In other states the practice had been established by board regulations. Such was the case in 1935 when two children in Minersville, Pennsylvania refused to participate in the recitation of the Pledge of Allegiance, on grounds of religious conviction. The two Gobitis children, who were members of Jehovah's Witnesses, objected to the recitation of the pledge, regarding it as a form of worship of a graven image. Both the

62. *Zorach v. Clauson,* 343 U.S. 306, 72 S. Ct. 679 (1952).
63. *Engel v. Vitale,* 370 U.S. 421, 82 S. Ct. 1261 (1962).

federal district court and the circuit court of appeals had ruled for the children, but upon appeal to the U.S. Supreme Court, the case was reversed, and the validity of the board regulation was upheld.[64]

The same issue was before the United States Supreme Court again within three years. In the intervening period, three of the justices who had joined with the majority in the *Gobitis* case dissented in the case of *Jones* v. *City of Opelika*, saying: "Since we joined in the *Gobitis* case we think this is an appropriate occasion to state that we now believe that it also was wrongly decided."[65] The second case arose in West Virgina, where the state board of education, acting under authority vested in it by the state legislature, enacted a rule requiring the recitation of the Pledge of Allegiance, without exception. The three-judge federal court, relying largely upon the dissenting opinion in *Jones* v. *Opelika*, decided in favor of the students. Upon appeal, the U.S. Supreme Court, in an opinion written by Mr. Justice Jackson, reversed its opinion in *Minersville* v. *Gobitis* and found the regulation of the state board to be in violation of the free exercise clause of the First Amendment. Thus, the matter was laid to rest until 1954, when the Congress of the United States amended the Pledge of Allegiance to add the words "under God." An action was brought in New York to compel the Commissioner of Education to revoke a regulation recommending that the new form of the pledge be used in the schools. In refusing plaintiff's petition, the court upheld the commissioner's right to use the form of the pledge that included the words "under God" but at the same time held that the plaintiff had a right to disbelieve and that neither the plaintiff nor his children could be compelled to recite the words "under God" in the pledge.[66]

### THE TEACHING OF EVOLUTION

The teaching of the theory of evolution has been a matter of controversy for the past fifty years. The first case, *Scopes* v. *State*

---

64. *Minersville School District v. Gobitis*, 310 U.S. 586 (1940).

65. *Jones v. City of Opelika*, 316 U.S. 584 (1942).

66. *Lewis v. Allen*, 159 N.Y.S. 2d 807 (New York, 1957).

*of Tennessee,* received national attention because of the involvement of William Jennings Bryan as a special prosecutor for the
state and Clarence Darrow as the attorney for the defendant. The
case has also become a part of American drama. Although Scopes
was convicted in 1927, the Tennessee Supreme Court reversed his
conviction on the ground that the jury, and not the judge, should
have assessed the fine.[67]

The issue remained dormant for many years, only to be revived in Arkansas in a test case in 1964. An Arkansas statute had
been enacted in 1928, the year after the *Scopes* decision, making it
unlawful for a teacher in any state-supported school or university
"to teach the theory or doctrine that mankind ascended or de-
scended from a lower order of animals." Susan Epperson, a biology
teacher in Little Rock, received a textbook which included material
about evolution. Such a textbook was also a violation of the statute
and a case was filed to test the validity of the statute. The Arkansas
Supreme Court upheld the statute, but that decision was reversed
by the U.S. Supreme Court, which held that the Arkansas statute
constituted an establishment of religion under the First Amendment.[68]

The Tennessee legislature repealed the antievolution statute
which had provided the basis for the Scopes trial, and replaced it
with a new statute prohibiting the use of any textbook discussing
evolution if the text did not include a statement that evolution was
but a theory and not scientific fact as to the nature of the origin
of man. The statute further required inclusion of the version of
creation found in Genesis, if any version of creation at all were
mentioned. This new statute was held to be an establishment violation because it gave preferential treatment to the biblical version
of creation.[69] Earlier a Mississippi statute was struck down by
the supreme court of that state.[70]

67. *Scopes v. State of Tennessee,* 154 Tenn. 105, 289 S.W. 363 (Tennessee, 1927).

68. *Epperson v. Arkansas,* 393 U.S. 97 (1968).

69. *Daniel v. Waters,* 515 F. 2d 485 (6 California 1975).

70. *Smith v. State,* 242 So. 2d 692 (Mississippi, 1970).

## SEX EDUCATION

The inclusion of instruction relative to sexual development and maturation has produced a number of cases in recent years. The first such case was tried in Topeka, Kansas in 1970, and involved a program that had been in existence in the schools of Topeka for a number of years. The plaintiffs, an organization of parents, attacked the legality of the program under Section 1 of the Fourteenth Amendment generally, under the Ninth and Tenth Amendments, and under Section 20 of the Bill of Rights of the Kansas Constitution.[71] The findings of fact generally describe the program in existence in Topeka. In its conclusions of law the court held that the program constituted a reasonable exercise of the constitutional and statutory authority of the board of education and that it did not violate the Ninth, Tenth, or Fourteenth Amendment to the U.S. Constitution or Section 20 of the Kansas Bill of Rights.[72] The case was not appealed beyond the district court.

A case was filed in the U.S. district court in Maryland at about the same time as the Topeka case. In *Cornwell v. State Board of Education*, the plaintiff parents challenged a program approved by the state board of education on grounds that it violated the equal protection clause of the Fourteenth Amendment. The district court summarily rejected the plaintiff's contentions, and upon appeal to the Fourth Circuit the decision of the district court was affirmed.[73] The Fourth Circuit court of appeals compared the sex education program to public health measures that have been accorded wide latitude when attacked on religious grounds.

In *Hopkins v. Hamden Board of Education*, a sex education program was attacked by Catholic parents on grounds that "their religious beliefs imposed upon parents the primary obligations for education of their children and that, in the area of sexual

---

71. Section 20 of the Bill of Rights of the Kansas Constitution reads as follows: "This enumeration of rights shall not be construed to impair or deny others retained by the people; and all powers not herein delegated remain with the people."

72. *Clemmer v. Unified School District No. 501*, Case No. 112,064, District Court of Shawnee County (Kansas, 1970).

73. *Cornwell v. State Board of Education*, 314 F. Supp. 340 (Maryland, 1969); 428 F.2d 471 (4 Ca. 1970); cert. den. 400 U.S. 942, 91 S. Ct. 240 (1970).

education particularly, papal encyclicals and Vatican II directed parents to instruct their children in the home in sexual matters."[74] The court rejected this theory of exclusive parental authority and found no violation of either the due process or equal protection clauses of the Fourteenth Amendment.

Courts have upheld sex education programs in New Jersey,[75] Hawaii,[76] Michigan,[77] and California,[78] and sex education programs appear to be safe from constitutional attack where provisions are made for excusing individual students upon request of parents, and where the programs are not specifically prohibited by law.

### BILINGUAL/BICULTURAL EDUCATION

There have been a few cases in recent years in which plaintiffs whose primary language is other than English have attempted to establish a constitutional right to instruction in their native tongue. These cases have been characterized as bilingual or bicultural cases.

The first of these cases to reach the U.S. Supreme Court was *Lau* v. *Nichols,* in which plaintiffs representing a class of non-English-speaking Chinese students brought suit against the San Francisco Unified School District, alleging in substance that the failure of the school district to provide instruction in Chinese deprived them of the equal protection of the laws as guaranteed by the Fourteenth Amendment. The district court denied relief, and the court of appeals affirmed.

The U.S. Supreme Court reversed the court of appeals, but specifically declined to consider the equal protection argument advanced by plaintiffs. Instead, the Court decided the case on the narrower grounds of the Civil Rights Act of 1964, 42 U.S.D.,

74. *Hopkins v. Hamden Board of Education*, 289 A.2d 914, 970 (Connecticut, 1971).

75. *Valent v. New Jersey State Board of Education*, 114 N.J. Super. 63, 274 A.2d 832 (1971); 118 N.J. Super. 416, 288 A.2d 52 (1972).

76. *Medeiros V. Kioysaki*, 478 P.2d 314 (Hawaii, 1970).

77. *Hobolth v. Greenway*, 52 Mich. App. 682, 218 N.W. 2d 98 (Michigan, 1974).

78. *Citizens for Parental Rights v. San Mateo County Board of Education*, 124 Cal. Rptr. 68 (California App., 1975).

Section 2000 (d). No specific relief was prescribed by the Court, that matter being left to the court of appeals.[79]

In *Serna* v. *Portales*, the U.S. District Court for New Mexico held that, in view of evidence concerning the lack of achievement of Spanish-surnamed children, it was incumbent upon the school district to reassess its program for meeting the specialized needs of Spanish-surnamed students at all schools.[80] This case also was not decided on constitutional grounds.

A U.S. district court reached a different conclusion in *Morales* v. *Shannon*, holding that national origin groups are not entitled, as a matter of constitutional right, to instruction in the language of the country of their origin.[81] Although the case was not decided specifically under the U.S. Constitution, a U.S. district court in Massachusetts determined, in connection with a court-ordered school desegregation plan, that bilingual instruction must be provided where twenty or more kindergarten students attending a school were found to be in need of such instruction.[82]

Immediately following the decision of the Tenth Circuit Court of Appeals in *Keyes*, the U.S. District Court for Colorado decided *Otero* v. *Mesa County Valley School District*.[83] The district court, relying to some degree on the Tenth Circuit decision, found no constitutional right to a bilingual/bicultural program.

## Concluding Statement

A number of curriculum issues are not treated in this chapter. For example, many of the school desegregation cases involve curriculum, such as *Hobson* v. *Hansen*,[84] the Washington, D.C. case in which "tracking" was held to be unconstitutional. Similarly,

79. *Lau v. Nichols*, 414 U.S. 563 (1974).

80. *Serna v. Portales*, 351 F. Supp. 1279 (D.C.N.M., 1972); aff'd 499 F.2d 1147 (10 Ca. 1974); but see *Keyes v. School District No. 1*, 521 F.2d 465 (10 Ca. 1975), where it was decided on equal protection grounds that there is no constitutional right to bilingual/bicultural education.

81. *Morales v. Shannon*, 266 F. Supp. (D.C. Texas, 1973).

82. *Morgan v. Kerrigan*, 401 F. Supp. 216 (D.C. Mass. 1975).

83. *Otero v. Mesa County Valley School District*, 408 F. Supp. 162 (D.C. Colo. 1967).

84. *Hobson v. Hansen*, 269 F. Supp. 401 (1967).

there are a very large number of textbook cases that are, of course, directly related to the curriculum. And finally, the cases involving extracurricular activities continue to be handed down in substantial numbers.

There are a few cases upholding dismissal of teachers for departing from the established curriculum.[85] This area should be a matter for further investigation.

Over the past one hundred years or so, the courts have been called upon to decide questions involving the public school curriculum on many occasions. Many of the cases have turned upon the constitutional rights of parents to choose among course offerings, while other cases have been primarily concerned with resistance on the part of taxpayers to the expansion of the curriculum. The scope and content of the curriculum continues to be a matter of controversy and it is to be expected that students of the law will be occupied in analyzing curriculum cases for years to come.

85. *Goldwasser v. Brown*, 417 F.2d 1169 (1969); *Ahern v. Board of Education of School District of Grand Island*, 456 F.2d 399 (8 Ca., 1972); and dicta in *Mercer v. Michigan State Board of Education*, 379 F. Supp. 580 (E.D. Michigan, 1974).

# CHAPTER VII

# Constitutional Rights of Students

RALPH D. MAWDSLEY

The direction of student rights has changed gradually but perceptibly during the past decade. One change has been from a definition of student rights to compensation for the deprivation of student rights. This is not to say that the development of constitutional rights for students is no longer continuing but rather that the status of the rights has become sufficiently recognized to form the basis for both equitable and legal remedies, especially under Section 1983 of the Civil Rights Act.[1] Also, this is not to say that the formulation and clarification of student rights has been met without judicial reservation. Mr. Justice Stewart, concurring in *Tinker*, observed: "I cannot share the Court's uncritical assumption that school discipline aside, the First Amendment rights of children are co-extensive with those of adults."[2] It was Mr. Justice Black dissenting in *Tinker* who prophesied that "one does not need to be a prophet or the son of a prophet to know that after the Court's holding today some students . . . in all schools will be ready, able, and willing to defy their teachers on practically all orders."[3] Whether Black's prophecy has come to fruition is impossible to assess but there is no doubt that his judicial restraint and criticism raise the crucial question whether students can be treated differently than adults, and if so upon what basis this differentiation can be made. At stake in the entire consideration is a definition of education.

Courts may not be the proper forums to define the purpose of

1. United States Code Annotated, ch. 42, Section 1983 (1974).

2. *Tinker v. Des Moines Independent Community School District*, 393 U.S. 503, 515 (1968).

3. Ibid., p. 525.

education and to direct the administration of education, but it is inevitable that some courts will feel compelled to perform these functions. A school has been defined as "a market place of ideas," a place "to learn intelligent involvement."[4] School rules must exist but the admonition has been set forth that their enactment and enforcement "must be related to the state interest . . . lest students' imaginations, intellects, and wills be unduly stifled or chilled."[5] The caustic capstone to this judicial intervention into the definition of education has come from the pen of Mr. Justice Goldberg who observed that "perhaps it would be well if those entrusted to administer the teaching of American history and government to our students began their efforts by practicing the document on which that history and government are based."[6]

The result of such judicial supervision of the function of education has been a loosening of the school's influence over the decisions and conduct of its students, a diminishing influence that has had its impact even in the home. As if the fabric of the public educational system has not been subjected to sufficient stress by student challenges to school rules and the traditional authority structure, the fabric elasticity is being further tested today. Damage suits are being filed by students under the Civil Rights Act against administrators and school board members claiming monetary compensation for violations of their constitutional rights.

In this chapter we shall consider the current status of student rights in public schools and will project the emerging areas of conflict in the home. Only a summary cross-section will be taken of student rights in public schools because a major focus of the chapter will be upon the post-*Tinker* development of childrens' rights and its effect upon the home. Student rights, the immediate progeny of *Tinker*, have metamorphosed into childrens' rights with a definition of the home at stake. Just as the student-school relationship has been redefined by a decade of litigation, it is likely that the parent-

4. *Eisner v. Stanford Board of Education*, 440 F. 2d 803 (2d Cir., 1971).

5. *Scoville v. Board of Education of Joliet*, 425 F. 2d 10, 14 (17th Cir., 1970).

6. *Shanley v. Northeast Independent School District*, 462 F. 2d 960 (5th Cir., 1972).

child relationship will also be redefined. If constitutional rights have become part of the property of every child in school, it is conceivable that students will retain some of these rights upon leaving the school and entering the home. The rights of students in the school will be considered here under four headings: personal appearance, student publications, pregnancy and marriage, and locker searches.

## Rights of Students in the School

### PERSONAL APPEARANCE

In the matter of personal appearance, student rights are poorly defined. The status of student substantive rights has been obfuscated by the swirl of the mists of conflicting decisions in different jurisdictions. Despite the noble words of the *Tinker* court in 1968 that "students [do not] shed their constitutional rights to freedom of speech or expression at the schoolhouse gate" [7] there yet is lacking any definition of student substantive rights that approaches the firm skeletal guarantees in the procedural area. Even with respect to matters such as hairstyles, which have generally been thought to be protected under the First Amendment, there is by no means unanimity among the federal courts of appeal. The First,[8] Second,[9] Third,[10] Fourth,[11] Seventh,[12] and Eighth[13] circuits have provided relief on constitutional grounds for regulations concerning the length of students' hair. On the other hand the District of Colum-

7. *Tinker v. Des Moines Independent Community School District*, 393 U.S. 503, 506.

8. *Richards v. Thurston*, 424 F. 2d 1281 (1st Cir., 1970).

9. *Owens v. Barry*, 483 F.2d 1126 (2d Cir., 1973).

10. *Zeller v. Donegal School District Board of Education*, 517 F. 2d 600 (1975).

11. *Massie v. Henry*, 455 F. 2d 779 (4th Cir., 1972).

12. *Holsapple v. Woods*, 500 F. 2d 49 (7th Cir., 1974): *Arnold v. Carpenter*, 459 F. 2d 939 (7th Cir., 1972); *Crews v. Cloncs*, 432 F. 2d 1259 (7th Cir., 1970); *Breen v. Kahl*, 419 F. 2d 1034 (7th Cir., 1969).

13. *Bishops v. Colaw*, 450 F. 2d 1069 (8th Cir., 1971).

bia,[14] Fifth,[15] Sixth,[16] Ninth,[17] and Tenth[18] circuits have not been receptive to claims that tonsorial tastes are subsumed in substantial rights protected by the federal Constitution. As if the waters had not been muddied enough by this judicial conflict, there is even no agreement as to what the specific constitutional basis is for one's personal appearance. The constitutional guarantee has been variously described as a "sphere of liberty inherent in the due process clause," [19] "the right to be secure in one's person guaranteed by the due process clause," [20] "but having overlapping equal protection by the United States Constitution" [21] and "rights other than those specifically enumerated." [22] For the attorney desirous of fashioning a civil rights action alleging a violation of a student's constitutional right there has not been much judicial assistance to stabilize the area. It is probably not without some justification that a judge in one circuit was prompted to write:

One of the realities of this innovativeness is that the federal decisions are being made, not on the basis of visible, time-tested rules or principles of substantive law, but on the basis of jural impressionism—subjective judgments of individual judges as to what constitutes protectable "liberty" or denial of due process or equal protection.[23]

### STUDENT PUBLICATIONS

The sluggishness of courts in developing a consistent body of law regarding personal appearance must be contrasted with the demon-

14. *Fagan v. National Cash Register Co.*, 481 F. 2d 1115 (1972).

15. *Karr v. Schmidt*, 460 F. 2d 609 (5th Cir., 1972).

16. *Gfell v. Rickelman*, 441 F. 2d 444 (6th Cir., 1971); *Jackson v. Dorrier*, 424 F. 2d 213 (6th Cir., 1970).

17. *King v. Saddleback Jr. College District*, 445 F. 2d 932 (9th Cir., 1971); *Olff v. East Side Union High School District*, 404 U.S. 1042 (1972).

18. *Hatch v. Goerke*, 502 F. 2d 1189 (10th Cir., 1974); *Freeman v. Flake*, 448 F. 2d 258 (10th Cir., 1971).

19. *Richards v. Thurston*, 424 F. 2d 1281, 1284.

20. *Massie v. Henry*, 455 F. 2d 779, 783.

21. *Holsapple v. Woods*, 500 F. 2d 49, 51-52.

22. *Bishop v. Colaw*, 450 F. 2d 1069, 1075.

23. *Zeller v. Donegal School District*, 517 F. 2d 600, 604 (3d Cir., 1975).

stration by the courts of a more predictable course in the area of student publications, where student rights are well-defined. School regulations prohibiting distribution of certain kinds of material on school property have been given vigorous scrutiny. Contrary to cases involving personal appearance where the constitutional nexus is vague, the right to distribute literature on school property is clearly grounded in the First Amendment.

There appear to be two levels of consideration in dealing with student publications. First, there must be the promulgation of rules for submission of material to be distributed. As one court has noted:

There is nothing unconstitutional per se in a requirement that students submit materials to the school administration prior to distribution. Given the necessity for discipline and orderly processes in the high schools, it is not at all unreasonable to require that materials destined for distribution to students be submitted to the school administration prior to distribution.[24]

The fact that such prior submission of material is considered permissible suggests that the courts may be balancing different kinds of interests other than those concerned with the general adult nonschool public. The confined nature of school buildings, along with the captive nature of the student audience resulting from compulsory attendance statutes, makes the submission of material more reasonable than it would be if material were to be distributed on a public street. The age and maturity of the students are also factors when they are linked with the captive audience aspect of elementary and secondary students. It may also be that the educative process, which must allow for an interchange of information, nonetheless can allow for an orderly procedure for disseminating such information and thus be reconciled with a regulation requiring the prior submission of material to be distributed.

A second consideration after the promulgation of rules for submission would be the examination of the content of submitted material in light of guidelines concerning what is acceptable and what is unacceptable material for student publications. The substantive legal problem here has been the framing of a constitutionally permissible standard. Such terms as "obscene" and "libelous" have been

24. *Shanley v. Northeast Independent School District*, 462 F. 2d 960, 969 (5th Cir., 1972).

used[25] and have met with critical judicial scrutiny. Even such common language as "substantial disruption of or material interference with school activity"[26] has been objected to because of inadequate definition. When a school board regulation required submission of material to be distributed to the principal upon penalty of suspension and the principal had "reasonable cause to believe that the expression [distribution] would engender such material and substantial interference"[27] the court reinstated the student and effectively skirted the problem by declaring that "the school board's burden of demonstrating reasonableness becomes geometrically heavier as its decision begins to focus upon the content of materials that are not obscene, libelous, or inflammatory."[28] A school regulation prohibiting distribution of materials "under school jurisdiction without permission of the principal"[29] was declared inadequate under the First Amendment and the suspended student reinstated even though the material distributed exhorted fellow students "to be prepared to fight in the halls and in the classrooms . . . [and to] burn the building of our school down."[30]

Absent some evidence of disruption actually caused by the distributed material, courts appear very reluctant to place a prior censorship upon the student's First Amendment right of free expression. The student's measure of First Amendment protection in this area seems to be very similar to the general censorship standard of clear and present danger.[31] There may be some question whether courts would be willing formally to adopt the standard of a clear and present danger for schools, but the courts' tendency to evaluate the constitutional language of the regulation rather than the content of the material to be distributed certainly suggests an equivalence in the minds of many judges. The conclusion would appear to be that

25. *Nitzberg v. Parks*, 525 F. 2d 378 (4th Cir., 1975).

26. Ibid., p. 383.

27. *Shanley v. Northeast Independent School District*, 462 F. 2d 960, 970 (5th Cir., 1972).

28. Ibid., p. 971.

29. *Quarterman v. Byrd*, 453 F. 2d 54 (4th Cir., 1971).

30. Ibid., pp. 55-56.

31. See *Near v. Minnesota*, 283 U.S. 697 (1931).

such descriptive terms as "obscene," "libelous," "inflammatory," "disruptive," and so forth must accord with definitions established in nonschool First Amendment cases. In *Eisner* v. *Stanford Board of Education*[32] the Second circuit approved the application of the standard of a clear and present danger to a student challenge to a school regulation that prohibited distribution of material that "will interfere with the proper and orderly operation and discipline of the school, will cause violence or disorder, or will constitute an invasion of the rights of others."[33] A more recent court has laid down specific constitutional protections in cases of prior restraint that approach, if they do not equal, the standard of clear and present danger: (a) definition of material that can be prohibited; (b) prompt approval or disapproval of what is submitted; (c) procedural rights if a prompt decision is not made; and (d) adequate and prompt appeals procedure.[34] The drafting responsibility of school boards and administration is considerable and somehow the prodigious task is not lightened by the eloquent judicial rhetoric of one of the cases involving student publications:

*Tinker's* dam to school board absolutism does not leave dry the fields of school discipline. *Tinker* simply irrigates, rather than floods, the fields of school discipline. It sets canals and channels through which school discipline might flow with the least possible damage to the nation's priceless topsoil of the First Amendment.[35]

PREGNANCY AND MARRIAGE

The rights of pregnant and married students in school situations are as poorly defined as personal appearance. Nowhere in the compendium of school regulations are the diversities of school policy more evident than in the area concerning student pregnancies and marriages. These diversities reflect differing moral attitudes by school boards and administrators and these attitudes have been translated into a very mottled body of law. Although the situation of the unmarried pregnant students may vary somewhat from that

32. *Eisner v. Stanford Board of Education*, 440 F. 2d 803 (2d Cir., 1971).

33. Ibid., p. 805.

34. *Nitzberg v. Parks*, 525 F. 2d 378 (4th Cir., 1975).

35. *Shanley v. Northeast Independent School District*, 462 F. 2d 960, 978 (5th Cir., 1972).

of the married students, their interest in remaining in school is essentially the same. Unmarried pregnant girls have been excluded because of a desire to deter teenage pregnancies and preserve morality, to prevent disruption, and to maintain the student's health and well-being.[36] This attempt by the school to impose a moral standard upon all students has been increasingly resisted by the courts. The judicial pendulum has swung from a moral condemnation of pregnancies to a social awareness of the mother's interest in completing her education. It has been suggested that the effects of school policies penalizing unwed mothers undermine the interest of the state in strengthening the ability of its citizens to support themselves and their dependent children in order to minimize welfare demands.[37] Since the impact of a policy of exclusion from school would be to postpone completion of secondary work by a year or more, the interests of the mother *and* the child are both affected.[38] The exclusion of unmarried students because of a desire to deter teenage pregnancies and preserve morality is offset by an individual's interest in sexual privacy. The U.S. Supreme Court has stated:

> If the right to privacy means anything, it is the right of the individual, married or single to be free from unwarranted governmental intrusion into matters so fundamentally affecting a person as the decision whether to bear or beget a child.[39]

In *Eisenstadt* the court declared a Massachusetts statute prohibiting the distribution of contraceptives to unmarried persons a violation of equal protection. Whether minor girls, or boys, would come within the scope of *Eisenstadt* is not certain. The avowed interest of the school in protecting the student's health is countered by the girl's interest in her own emotional and physical well-being. If a

36. "Marriage, Pregnancy, and the Right to Go to School," *Texas Law Review* 50 (August 1972): 1220-23.

37. Ibid., p. 1219.

38. In view of the emerging equal protection rights of illegitimate children, it may be indirect discrimination against a child to impair his mother's ability to support him. See *Levy v. Louisiana,* 391 U.S. 68 (1968); *Labine v. Vincent,* 401 U.S. 532 (1971); *Weber v. Aetna Casualty and Insurance Co.,* 406 U.S. 164 (1972).

39. *Eisenstadt v. Baird,* 405 U.S. 438, 453 (1972).

girl is not attending school her feelings of ostracism and severe depression, as well as withdrawal from the services of public health nurses in schools, may jeopardize her health more than if she were in school.[40]

The interest of the married students in remaining in school has been more often protected than that of the unwed mothers. Courts have generally struck down school rules that suspend or expel married students,[41] but some courts have upheld rules that exclude married students from extracurricular activities on the basis that school attendance is a right whereas extracurricular participation is a privilege.[42] The courts supporting this distinction have dismissed the constitutional objections by relying upon curricular and social reasons. The Utah Supreme Court considered the curriculum and declared that extracurricular activities "are supplementary to the regular classes of the academic curriculum and are carried on under the discretionary powers granted to the Board of Education."[43] The Ohio Supreme Court considered the social ramifications of teenage marriages and declared:

The life expectancy of teen-age marriages is short indeed—the mortality rate thereof alarmingly high. Any policy which is directed toward making juvenile marriages unpopular and to be avoided should have the general public's wholehearted approval and support.[44]

40. See testimony of Dr. Mary Jane England in *Ordway v. Margraves* 323 F. Supp. 1155, 1157 (D. Mass., 1971).

41. *Board of Education v. Bentley*, 383 S.W. 2d (Ky., 1964); *McLeon v. State ex rel. Colmer*, 154 Miss. 468, 122 So. 737 (1939); *Carrollton-Farmers Branch Independent School District v. Knight*, 418 S.W. 2d 535 (Tex. Civ. App. 1967); *Alvin Independent School District v. Cooper*, 404 S.W. 2d 76 (Tex. Civ. App., 1966). But see also *State ex rel. Thompson v. Marion County Board of Education*, 202 Tenn. 29, 302 S.W. 2d 57 (1957), in which expulsion for the remainder of a school term following marriage was held reasonable, and *State ex rel. Idle v. Chamberlain* 39 Ohio op. 262, 175 N.E. 2d 539 (1961), in which mandatory withdrawal during pregnancy was held reasonable.

42. *Board of Directors v. Green*, 259 Iowa 1260, 147 N.W. 2d 854 (1967); *State ex rel. Baker v. Stevenson*, 27 Ohio op. 2d 223, 189 N.E. 2d 181 (1962); *Kissick v. Garland Independent School District*, 330 S.W. 2d 708 (Tex. Civ. App., 1959); *Starkey v. Board of Education*, 14 Utah 2d 227, 381 P. 2d 718 (1963).

43. *Starkey v. Board of Education*, 14 Utah 2d at 229, 381 P. 2d at 720.

44. *State ex rel. Baker v. Stevenson*, 27 Ohio op. 2d 223, 229, 189 N.E. 2d 181, 187 (1962).

These courts, which have invalidated rules prohibiting married students from participating in extracurricular activities, have advanced four reasons: (a) such a regulation is arbitrary and unreasonable when applied to students who are not a bad influence;[45] (b) "extracurricular activities are, in the best modern thinking, an integral and complementary part of the total school program" and thus to deprive a student of participation in such a program violates the state statutory provisions that require the establishment of a system of education;[46] (c) such regulations interfere with the constitutional right of marital privacy by depriving the student of an opportunity to participate in an activity that may become his future livelihood; to prohibit married students from participating in extracurricular activities would place an "unendurable strain" upon the marriage and possibly "destroy the marriage itself;"[47] (d) the establishment of two classes of students in the field of extracurricular activities—married and unmarried—amounts to an unreasonable classification and thus violates equal protection.[48] The U.S. Supreme Court will ultimately have to resolve the question of whether extracurricular activities are a right or a privilege, but given the prominence of the constitutional arguments and the importance of extracurricular programs in schools, especially sports, it is probable that the Court will declare such activities to be a right rather than a privilege.

The reasons for married students remaining in school are essentially the same as those of the pregnant girls who are unmarried, except the moral onus is absent. The arguments of the school to discourage early marriage and prevent fraternization have been rejected and one court even went so far as to suggest that a student who entered into the marriage relationship with the proper motive would be an asset to the school.[49] Overriding the entire subject area of married students are the expressions of public policy statements by the legislatures in the matter of marriages.[50] To the

45. *Cochrane v. Board of Education*, 360 Mich. 390, 103 N.W. 2d 569 (1960).

46. *Davis v. Meek*, 344 F. Supp. 298, 301 (N.D. Ohio, 1972).

47. Ibid., p. 302.

48. *Hollon v. Mathis Independent School District*, 358 F. Supp. 1269, 1270 (S.D. Texas, 1973).

49. *McLeod v. State ex rel. Colmer*, 154 Miss. 468, 122 So. 737 (1929).

50. For example, see Texas Family Code Ann., Section 1.51, 1.52 (1971).

extent that a state legislature has expressed a policy on marriageable
ages, with or without parental consent, it has been argued that
"other political subdivisions should not be allowed to substitute
their own notions of marriageable age." [51] To the extent that a
public policy has been statutorily declared, this ought to be ex-
haustive as far as student rights in school are concerned. The extracurricular restriction for married students has remained in force
in some jurisdictions despite the facts that nonacademic activities
are part of the curriculum[52] and that some legislatures have a
variety of statutes pertaining to sports and recreation facilities.

LOCKER SEARCHES

In the problem area of student locker searchers the definition
and determination of student rights has been immediate and complete in some areas but spasmodic and halting in others. The Fourth
Amendment guarantees that "the right of the people to be secure
in their persons, houses, papers, and effects, against unreasonable
searches and seizures, shall not be violated." [53] Until very recently
courts had employed a number of legal rationales to permit searches
of students and their lockers that would not be permissible outside
the school doors. In a typical set of facts the principal would receive
a tip from a student informer that a student may have contraband
such as drugs or a weapon in his locker or on his person. The principal without any further information would open the student's
locker with a pass key or would require the student to submit to a
search. Contraband would be found and the student's motion to
suppress the evidence in a juvenile or criminal proceeding would be
denied.

Relying upon language such as *"in loco parentis,"* [54] "emergency,"[55] "agency,"[56] or the nongovernmental character of the

51. "Marriage, Pregnancy, and the Right to Go to School," p. 1206.

52. James S. Coleman, *Adolescents and the Schools* (New York: Basic
Books, 1965), p. 45.

53. U. S. Constitution, Amendment IV.

54. *In re Donaldson*, 75 Cal. Rptr 220 (1969); *Mercer v. Texas*, 450 S.W.
2d 715 (1970).

55. *In re Boykin*, 39 Ill. 2d 617, 237 N.E. 2d 460 (1968).

56. *In re Fred C.*, 26 Cal. Supp. 3d 320, 102 Cal. Rptr 682 (1972).

principal,[57] courts have justified a search of the student's person or locker. Most courts have not paused to reflect upon the *Tinker* language that constitutional rights are not shed at the schoolhouse gate.

Despite the apparent deathblow of *Tinker* to the *in loco parentis* doctrine, the doctrine still appears to be alive and well in the area of search and seizure. *In loco parentis* has been viewed "as a social concept antedating the Fourth Amendment, [so] that any action, including a search, taken thereunder under reasonable suspicion should be accepted as necessary and reasonable." [58] The emergency doctrine has been fashioned to justify an otherwise illegal school search where a dangerous object such as a gun is in fact found.[59] The agency doctrine has been used to sustain an in-school search where nonschool law enforcement officers assist in the search.[60] These searches have been sustained on the grounds that the law enforcement officer's otherwise illegal search was legitimized because he was an agent of the school administrator who is not a government official.

The common denominator in these contrived judicial doctrines appears to be a judicial standard for search and seizure that is less than probable cause. School searches have been sustained where the quantum of evidence for the search of a student or his locker is "reasonable suspicion," [61] less than the "probable cause" required by the Fourth Amendment. The rationale for such a casual application of the Fourth Amendment is difficult to determine. Certainly the *in loco parentis* explanation seems to have little support in fact, because one course of action parents probably would not follow would be to enlist police assistance immediately to discipline their child.[62] Parents normally would owe some moral duty to the chil-

---

57. *In re Donaldson*, 75 Cal. Rptr. 220 (1969).

58. *In re State in Interest of G.C.*, 121 N.J. Super. 108, 112, 296 A. 2d 102, 106 (1972); *Mercer v. Texas*, 450 S.W. 2d 715 (1970).

59. *In re Boykin*, 39 Ill. 2d 617, 237 N.E. 2d 460 (1968); *People v. Lanthier*, 5 Cal. 3d 751, 488 p. 2d 625 (1971).

60. *People v. Overton*, 20 N.Y.S. 2d 360, 220 N.E. 2d 596 (1967); *In re Fred C.*, 26 Cal. App. 3d 320, 102 Cal. Rptr 682 (1972).

61. *In re Donaldson*, 75 Cal. Rptr. 220 (1969); *State v. Stein*, 203 Kan. 638, 456 P. 2d 1 (1969); *State v. Baccino*, 283 A. 2d 869 (Del. 1971).

62. See dissenting opinion in *Mercer v. Texas*, 450 S.W. 2d 715 (1970).

dren to discuss the problem, to express this concern, and to seek professional help. The agency doctrine allows police and juvenile officers to conduct searches as agents of the school administrator and escape the consequences of an otherwise illegal search. Whatever standard the administrator may be held to in his search on school premises, it would appear to be incongruous to suggest that this standard ought still to be employed if a law enforcement officer is called in. Where an administrator relinquishes his authority and effectively delegates the duties of the search to the police officer the standards for judging the reasonableness of the search should be evaluated by criminal standards rather than educational standards. The very reason for the policeman's presence on the school premises ought automatically to suggest the inadequacy of the school officials to handle a problem. The introduction of the police would seem to make the search a joint venture rather than an agency relationship.[63]

Recent cases have appeared to strike at the very heart of these legal subterfuges by ruling that school administrators and teachers are government officials and thus subject to the restrictions in the Fourth Amendment. In State v. Mora a search by an administrator of a student's wallet left in a teacher's possession was held unreasonable.[64] There was no evidence available to the teacher or administrator that the wallet contained marijuana. The court applied the full Fourth Amendment criminal standard to the school by declaring that the general rule is that a search conducted without a warrant is per se unconstitutional. "We hold that a search on school grounds of a student's personal effects by a school official who suspects the presence or possession of an unlawful substance is not an exception." [65]

The most immediate effect of the decision in Mora would appear to be the destruction of the "reasonable suspicion" basis for searches in Louisiana public schools. The Mora court has also eliminated the legal subterfuge that a teacher or administrator acting as, or in

63. See Margaret A. Mulholland, "Searches by School Officials: The Diminishing Fourth Amendment," Santa Clara Lawyer 14 (Fall 1973): 134.

64. State v. Mora, 307 S.W. 2d 317 (1975).

65. Ibid., p. 320.

concert with, a law enforcement officer is a private person and not a government official. Under the *Mora* rationale school officials will no longer be permitted to search students or their lockers to find evidence of a crime; evidence to substantiate probable cause must exist prior to the search.

However offensive the *Mora* rationale and result may appear to administrators, the decision may represent a source of light at the end of a tunnel of inconsistency, illogic, and intemperance in the conduct of student searches. If the job of the school administrator is viewed as that of a policeman responsible for law enforcement, the administrator's relationships with students are likely to be damaged. Furthermore, it is doubtful that education will thrive in an atmosphere of suspicion and distrust, or where schools have become a dragnet for crime detection.

## Rights of Children in the Home

### STATE INTERVENTION IN PARENT-CHILD RELATIONSHIP

The unstable caldron of student rights in the public schools must inevitably spill over into the homes of these students. The refinement of student rights in school settings will continue to be a developing area of law but the emergence of children's rights in the home represents the new horizon of legal action. Substantive and procedural safeguards for students having been established in the authority setting of the school, it is inevitable that there will be a press to extend some minimal level of due process even into the home. It is just such a thrust that will form the battle lines over the definition of the parent-child relationship in the courts and legislatures in the decade to come.

The parents' control over their child's decisions and destiny until recently has historically been an absolute and inviolate right. In early American life the education of children was solely the responsibility of the parents, since the home was largely a self-sufficient unit in economics, health, moral training, and in other areas.[66] Court and state legislatures have been very reluctant in the past to restrict unduly or unnecessarily the parents' sovereignty over their

66. Harold H. Punke, "Parental Choices in Education," *Alabama Lawyer* 31 (April 1970): 216.

children. Statutes prohibiting parents' abuse or desertion of children can properly be viewed as establishing some minimal parameters of the functions of parenthood.[67] The concern for the child, although not expressed in terms of childrens' rights, has been manifested in the use of life-saving techniques even over a parent's religious objections,[68] but nonlife-saving surgery, although necessary for a child's well-being, cannot be carried out over the parent's religious objections.[69] The U.S. Supreme Court has declared that parental control in the area of child labor is subordinate to child labor regulations that are to protect children.[70] A number of states have enacted legislation to eliminate the necessity of parental consent and information for treatment of minors twelve years of age and over in the areas of venereal disease and drug abuse.[71] The areas of conflict between parental prerogatives and juvenile need and care probably do not reflect juvenile rights as much as they reflect the right of the state to intervene on behalf of the child. The social threat of these abuses can be viewed as so enormous that the parental prerogatives must be sacrificed in favor of a more compelling societal interest.[72]

### CHILDREN'S RIGHTS IN THE LITERATURE

The assertion of juvenile rights over against the parents is an emerging area of law that is distinctly post-*Tinker* in development.[73] But the concept of a juvenile possessing rights in his own name, even against the parents clearly has antedated *Tinker*.[74] At

67. For example, see Minnesota Statutes Ann., sec. 260.221 (1971).

68. *People ex rel. Wallace v. Labrenzo*, 411 Ill. 618, 104 N.E. 2d 769 (1952); *Levitsky v. Levitsky*, 231 Md. 388, 190 A. 2d (1930) 621.

69. See *in re Green*, 41 L.W. 2013 (Pa. Sup. ct., 1972).

70. *Prince v. Massachusetts*, 321 U.S. 158 (1944).

71. For example, see Illinois Statutes Ann., ch. 91, sec. 18.4 (1974).

72. A comprehensive explanation of this rationale can be found in *The Age of Majority: Legal Rights and Responsibilities for Youth*, Report of the Illinois Council of Youth, Illinois Commission on Children, State of Illinois, November 1971.

73. *Tinker v. Des Moines Independent Community School District*, 393 U.S. 503 (1968).

74. See Henry H. Foster, Jr., *A Bill of Rights for Children* (Springfield, Ill.: Charles C. Thomas, 1974), pp. 3-7.

this point in legal history the concept of juvenile rights in the home has developed to a greater extent in the literature than it has in the courtroom. The common-law rule that the earnings of a son or a daughter are the legal property of the parent[75] has been attacked as an insulting anachronism that "relegates (minors) to an inferior status and at the same time is unfair." [76] The proposed rights to self-determination and alternative home environments formulated by another author would restrict or eliminate the parental right and responsibility to control the life of the child as well as allow the child options in the kind of residential living he would prefer.[77] Various bills of rights have been proposed for children, each unveiling a blueprint for the child's fullest development. These manifestos have proclaimed the rights of children to "adequate nutrition, a healthy environment, continuous loving care, a sympathetic community, intellectual and emotional stimulation, and other prerequisites for healthy adulthood." [78]

One notable legislative advance in this area has recently occurred in Minnesota. In the Minnesota Official Records Act governing the collective security and dissemination of data, a minor child under eighteen is represented by his parent or guardian "except where such minor individual indicates otherwise." [79] The language of this statute would allow any minor to preclude his parent from having access to his school records.

## POST-*Tinker* STATUS OF THE PARENT

The school discipline cases, beginning essentially with *Tinker*, are classic examples where courts appear to have sustained rights against the school without disturbing the control of parents over their children. There appears to be little doubt in *Tinker* that the majority saw the facts as a home-school conflict rather than just a

75. J. Warren Madden, *Persons and Domestic Relations* (St. Paul, Minn.: West Publishing Co., 1931), p. 439.

76. Foster, *A Bill of Rights for Children*, p. 48.

77. Richard Farson, *Birthrights* (New York: Macmillan Publishing Co., 1974).

78. Hillary Rodham, "Children under the Law," *Harvard Educational Review* 43 (November 1973): 496.

79. Minnesota Statutes Ann., sec. 15.162(4) (Supp. 1976).

student-school conflict. The *Tinker* court was careful to point out that the actions of the students in wearing black arm bands represented a political viewpoint shared by the parents.[80] Although the majority in *Tinker* considered the substantive constitutional rights of students themselves and thus not rights they might have as representing their parents, the reference to the relatively young age of the students as well as the political activity of the parents suggests that the court saw this innocuous form of protest as representing the political climate of the home.[81] Using a similar rationale and by expressly mentioning or clearly implying that the students had the support of their parents, other federal courts have asserted rights of students to express political views in the school newspaper,[82] to wear buttons expressing a political viewpoint,[83] to wear long hair,[84] and to be free from discipline by corporal punishment.[85] Even where the support of the parent is not mentioned or implied, the fact that invariably the complaint against the school authorities has been initiated by the parent on behalf of the minor lends credence to the theory that student rights over against the school have not been prosecuted in derogation of the parent's rights and interest in his child. This delicate balance between parental control and student rights appears to have been maintained until 1974 when the U.S. Supreme Court took a definite step in separating student rights in the school from parental interests in the child.

EMERGENCE OF JUDICIAL RECOGNITION OF CHILDREN'S RIGHTS

On December 6, 1973, Russell Carl, then a sixth grade student in North Carolina, was given two swats "in the presence of a second teacher and in view of other students."[86] Prior to the spanking Mrs.

80. *Tinker v. Des Moines Independent Community School District*, 393 U.S. at 504 (1968).

81. Ibid., p. 516.

82. *Zucker v. Panitz*, 299 F. Supp. 102 (S.D.N.Y. 1969).

83. *Burnside v. Byars*, 363 F. 2d 744 (5th Cir., 1966).

84. *Axtell v. LaPenna*, 323 F. Supp. 1077 (W.D. Pa. 1971); *Bishop v. Colaw*, 450 P. 2d 1069, 1075 (8th Cir., 1971).

85. *Glaser v. Marietta*, 315 F. Supp. 555 (W.D. Pa., 1972).

86. *Baker v. Owen*, 395 F. Supp. 294, 296 (M.D. N.C., 1975).

Baker, the mother of Russell Carl, had requested of the principal that her son not be spanked because "she opposed it on principle." [87] What was apparently a routine discipline became a problem of constitutional proportion because Mrs. Baker alleged "that the administration of corporal punishment over her objections violated her parental right to determine disciplinary methods for her child." [88]

A three-judge federal panel was convened to consider the constitutionality of a North Carolina statute allowing school officials to "use reasonable force in the exercise of lawful authority to restrain or correct pupils and to maintain order," [89] on the grounds that it allows corporal punishment over parental objection and without adequate procedural safeguards. The decision of the three-judge panel upholding the authority of the school to discipline without parental consent was sustained without comment by the U.S. Supreme Court.[90] In resolving the constitutional objections of the parent it was necessary for the federal district court to consider three questions, only the first of which is relevant here: (a) whether the parent's control of the discipline of this child is a fundamental constitutional right; (b) whether a student is entitled to procedural rights to avoid corporal punishment; and (c) whether a system of administering corporal punishment can be so unfair that it violates the "cruel and unusual punishment" provision of the Eighth Amendment.

The threshold question of *Baker* v. *Owen* was whether the parent could impose her views upon the school through her child, and if the response to this question is affirmative, whether the parent's rights to direct the discipline of his child is a fundamental constitutional right. In cases antedating *Tinker* the right of parents to impose their views upon schools was recognized by a number of courts. Parents have been successful in prohibiting their child's participating in the flag salute,[91] eliminating all Bible reading and

87. Ibid.

88. Ibid.

89. North Carolina General Statutes, sec. 115-146 (1975).

90. *Baker v. Owen*, 423 U.S. 907 (1975).

91. *West Virginia State Board of Education v. Barnette*, 319 U.S. 624 (1943).

prayer from the school routine,[92] removing their child from an objectionable class,[93] prohibiting restrictions on the offering of foreign language classes,[94] and in sending their children to non-public rather than public schools.[95] However, despite this impressive display of parent power and notwithstanding the precedent of *Tinker* and subsequent cases, the U.S. Supreme Court has given assent to the principle that parental control over the child in the area of discipline is not a fundamental constitutional right. The district court agreed with Mrs. Baker that *Meyer v. Nebraska*[96] and *Pierce v. Society of Sisters*[97] create a Fourteenth Amendment "right of a parent to determine and choose between means of discipline of children." [98] But this right is not a fundamental one. The district court could find no precedents that "parental control over child-rearing" has ever been ranked that high "in the hierarchy of constitutional values." [99] The difference between a protected constitutional right and a fundamental constitutional right is significant. The school could adequately satisfy Mrs. Baker's objections by proving the reasonableness of the punishment, whereas, if Mrs. Baker's claim of a fundamental right had been sustained, the school would have had to demonstrate a compelling interest. Under a compelling interest test, a school would have had to prove that corporal punishment was necessary to prevent a strong likelihood of disruption. Since such proof would be virtually impossible to establish, a compelling interest test would be tantamount to eliminating corporal punishment from the school.[100] In balancing the parental

92. *School District of Abington Township v. Schempp,* 374 U.S. 203 (1963); *Engel v. Vitale,* 370 U.S. 421 (1962).

93. *State ex rel. Kelley v. Ferguson,* 95 Neb. 63, 144 N.W., 1039 (1914).

94. *Meyer v. Nebraska,* 262 U.S. 390 (1923).

95. *Pierce v. Society of Sisters,* 268 U.S. 510 (1925).

96. *Meyer v. Nebraska,* 262 U.S. 390 (1923).

97. *Pierce v. Society of Sisters,* 268 U.S. 510 (1925).

98. *Baker v. Owen,* 395 F. Supp. 294, 299 (M.D. N.C. 1975).

99. *Ibid.*

100. See Ralph D. Mawdsley, "*Baker v. Owen:* Its Implications for the School and the Home," *Minnesota Elementary School Principal* (Winter 1976): 7.

interest in the child against the continued reasonable use of corporal punishment, the district court was not prepared to take the choice of methods of school discipline from the school and give it to the parent.

Although the parent's interests were denied the child's interests were clearly recognized. "We believe that Russell Carl does have an interest protected by the concept of liberty in the Fourteenth Amendment, in avoiding corporal punishment." [101] The parent's and child's interest in this case were similar but not identical.

In a recent case, *Ingraham* v. *Wright*, the U. S. Supreme Court had occasion to address itself to the rights of children concerning corporal punishment under the Eighth Amendment and the due process clause.[102] Whatever new directions of analysis of student rights are presented it is clear that it is only the students' "personal liberty" [103] that is at stake. The parental interests analyzed by the district court in *Baker* are relegated to only family support.[104] The *Baker* case is one of first impression because the parent's interests in the child are separated from those of the child and parent's interest is disallowed, whereas the child's interests are recognized in his own right. The *Ingraham* case supported the conclusion of *Baker*. By recognizing that parental interest in establishing a philosophy and pattern of childrearing differs from the child's interest in avoiding punishment the court appears to be moving perceptibly toward the right of a child to sue in his own behalf without parental consent. Whether courts or legislatures will be able or willing to take the next step to complete the separation by granting legal standing to a person, other than the parent or guardian, to represent the child in his claim against the school remains to be seen. Clearly the avoidance of punishment does not represent the life-and-death matter of a blood transfusion or emergency surgery and thus to elevate such avoidance to a constitutional status may well have implications for the parent-child relationship.

It is fair to say that the U.S. Supreme Court has not faced

101. *Baker* v. *Owen*, 395 F. Supp. 294, 301 (M.D. N.C., 1975).

102. *Ingraham* v. *Wright*, 45 L.W. 4364 (1977).

103. Ibid., p. 4370, 4371.

104. Ibid., p. 4369.

squarely a case in education where the child's claim was in direct opposition to that of the parent. In *Wisconsin* v. *Yoder*[105] the Court sidestepped this kind of problem despite a vigorous dissent from Mr. Justice Douglas:

> While the parents, absent dissent, normally speak for the entire family, the education of the child is a matter on which the child will often have decided views. . . . It is the student's judgment, not his parent's, that is essential if we are to give full meaning to what we have said about the Bill of Rights and of the right of students to be masters of their own destiny. If he is harnessed to the Amish way of life by those in authority over him and if his education in truncated, his entire life may be stunted and deformed. The child, therefore, should be given an opportunity to be heard before the State given the exemption which we honor today.[106]

The *Yoder* majority however left open for future consideration the question of whether "a child who expresses a desire to attend public high school in conflict with the wishes of his parents should not be prevented from doing so." [107] But because in *Yoder* the criminal complaint of violating the compulsory attendance statute of Wisconsin was brought against the parents the students were not parties to the litigation. The Court did raise cautionary signals that may presage a final decision. Calling "into question traditional concepts of parental control over the religious upbringing and education of their minor children [represents] an intrusion by a state into family decisions in the area of religious training [that] would give rise to grave questions of religious freedom." [108]

However, in interpreting *Yoder* in the light of *Baker* v. *Owen* it does not appear that the U.S. Supreme Court is adverse to recognizing a child's interests apart from his parents. It may be that a court will be more willing to recognize parental authority if that control has a definite religious mandate.[109] Even though methods of

105. *Wisconsin v. Yoder*, 406 U.S. 205 (1972).

106. Ibid., pp. 245, 246.

107. Ibid., p. 231.

108. Ibid., pp. 231-32.

109. Ibid., at 215-16. See also *West Virginia State Board of Education v. Barnette* 310 U.S. 624 (1943); Ralph D. Mawdsley, "A Legal Analysis of the School-Home Relationship" (Ph.D. diss., University of Minnesota, 1974), pp. 14-26; *State of Ohio v. Whisner* 47 Ohio St. 2d 181, 351 N.E. 2d 750 (1976).

childrearing have now been held not to be fundamental constitutional rights in *Baker*, freedom to practice one's religion is a fundamental constitutional right.[110] The Minnesota legislature has appeared to take cognizance of the distinction by providing in its statute on child abuse that "nothing in this section shall be construed to mean that a child is neglected solely because the child's parent, guardian or other person responsible for his care in good faith selects and depends upon spiritual means or prayer for treatment or care of disease or remedial care of the child." [111] Where the religious element is absent, as in *Baker*, the court appears more disposed to separate the parental and child interests.

Lending some credence to the above theory is the recent case of *Runyon* v. *McCrary*[112] prohibiting discrimination in admission by private schools. The majority in *Runyon* v. *McCrary* noted that "it may be assumed that parents have a First Amendment right to send their children to educational institutions that promote the belief that racial segregation is desirable, and that the children have an *equal right* to attend such institutions." [113] If children have an equal right to attend a school consistent with their parent's beliefs, does it also follow that a child has the same equal right not to attend the school of their parent's choice? The *Runyon* court stressed a limited application of *Yoder* "that while a State may posit (educational) standards, it may not preempt the educational process by requiring children to attend public schools." [114]

The *Runyon* court still left open the question that the *Yoder* court would not decide, that is, the extent to which children may resist parental attempts to inculcate their (the parents') attitudes and goals in their children. The U.S. Supreme Court recently struck down a provision of a Missouri statute requiring parental consent before a minor daughter could secure an abortion.[115] The court

110. See *Wisconsin v. Yoder*, 406 U.S. 205, 215-16 (1972).

111. Minnesota Statutes Annotated, sec. 221(2)(b) (1974).

112. *Runyon v. McCrary*, 44 L.W. 5034 (1976).

113. Ibid., p. 5039 (emphasis added).

114. Ibid., quoting *Wisconsin v. Yoder* 406 U.S. 205, 239 (1972).

115. *Planned Parenthood of Central Missouri v. Missouri* 44 U.S. L.W. 5197 (1976).

countered the potential threat to the authority of the parents over their daughters by observing that "it is difficult . . . to conclude that providing a parent with absolute power to overrule a determination made by the physician and his minor patient to terminate the patient's pregnancy will serve to strengthen the family unit." [116] The full implications of this decision remain to be seen because the plaintiffs challenging the statute were physicians and not minor, unwed daughters. However sweeping the language, the case does not yet represent a significant departure from the sovereignty of the parents over their children. But no court will be able to resolve this question without realizing that not just a legal matter of student rights is at stake but a sociological definition of the family as well.

THE RIGHT OF CHILD SOCIALIZATION

Child socialization, the choice of educational methods and content to prepare a child for society, has not often found expression among courts, perhaps because socialization is often seen as reflecting social class[117] and no court wants to have to choose the socialization patterns of one class over another. But the *Baker* court was willing to take what amounted to judicial notice of the fact that "a parent's absolute disapproval of reasonable corporal punishment . . . [would not achieve] the kind of societal respect that is clearly accorded the desire to expose one's child to certain fields of knowledge, to send him to private or parochial school, or to pass on one's religious heritage to him." [118] By rejecting the parental choice over discipline in the school, the *Baker* court has limited parental control over child socialization in the area of discipline but at the same time the court may have given a child a recognizable right in his own socialization.

The question of child socialization was raised by the Supreme

116. Ibid., p. 5204.

117. See Melvin L. Kohn, "Social Class and the Exercise of Parental Authority," *American Sociological Review* 24 (June 1959): 354; Frank Musgrove, *The Family, Education and Society* (London: Routledge and Kegan Paul, 1966), p. 85; Urie Bronfenbrenner, "Socialization and Social Class through Time and Space," in *Readings in Social Psychology*, ed. Eleanor E. Maccoby, Theodore M. Newcomb, and Eugene L. Hartley (New York: Holt, Rinehart and Winston, 1958), p. 419.

118. *Baker v. Owen*, 395 F. Supp. 294, 300 (M.D. N.C. 1975).

Court in *Yoder* and by a number of state courts. In *Yoder* the majority found inescapable the conclusion that

secondary schooling, by exposing Amish children to worldly influences in terms of attitudes, goals, and values contrary to beliefs, and by substantially interfering with the religious development of the Amish child and his integration into the way of life of the Amish faith community at the crucial adolescent state of development, contravenes the basic religious tenets and practice of the Amish faith, both as to the parent and the child.[119]

The *Yoder* court, however, cautions that it is not predisposed to protect the child socialization philosophy of parents for a "recently discovered . . . 'progressive' or more enlightened process for rearing children for modern life." [120] The more able a parent is to place his philosophy in a religious framework the better appear to be his chances of success in imposing his socialization ideas upon his child.[121]

State courts have been called upon to resolve this question of child socialization in the area of home instruction and instruction in nonpublic schools. The right of a parent to remove a child from public schools and educate the child at home "has been resolved by careful, sometimes tortured, readings of state statutes rather than by constitutional adjudication." [122] Although the legal question has always been one of "equivalent" education the underlying issue has been the right of parents to select the forum for their child that satisfies their desires for the child.[123] Where the parent has been unsuccessful in his or her claim, emphasis has not been placed upon the rights of the child but upon the ability of the school to meet the needs of children for "discipline and health habits," "character

119. *Wisconsin v. Yoder* 406 U.S. 205, 218 (1972).

120. Ibid., p. 235.

121. For example, ibid., pp. 215-19; *State of Ohio v. Whisner*, 47 Ohio St. 2d 181, 351 N.E. 2d 750 (1956).

122. Joel S. Moskowitz, "Parental Rights and State Education," *Washington Law Review* 50 (1975): 623, 625.

123. *People v. Levisen*, 404 Ill. 574, 90 N.E. 2d 213 (1950); *Stephens v. Bongart*, 189 A. 131 (1947); *State v. Massa*, 231 A. 252 (1967); *Shoreline School District No. 412 v. Superior Court*, 55 Wash. 2d 177, 346 P. 2d 999, cert. denied, 363 U.S. 814 (1960).

education" and "a social setting." [124] Where the parent has been successful in removing a child from the public school to be taught at home or in a parochial school the court has bowed even to such an ephemeral parental argument as "she desired the pleasure of seeing her daughter's mind develop. She felt she wanted to be with her child when the child would be more alive and fresh." [125] At no time do courts consider attendance at public schools a matter of right for children. The socialization process as far as the forum of education is concerned is presumed by courts to be a parental choice with the countervailing choice not being the rights of the children but the ability of the parental choice to meet the state-determined educational needs of the child. The ultimate question invariably is "the right of parents to have their children taught where, when, how, what, and by whom they may judge best." [126]

### FUTURE PROBLEMS AND DEVELOPMENTS

The future legal developments in the child-parent relationship await an opportunity for a child to express his desires in opposition to his parents. Not many remedies are available to allow a child a forum where his interests can be placed in juxtaposition to those of his parents. In a misdemeanor charge against the parents for their child's truancy[127] the question of any legal rights of the child does not arise because he is not a party to the action.[128] A proceeding against the minor child under a Juvenile Court Act[129] does not properly raise any substantial questions of childrens' rights over against the parents because a quasi-judicial juvenile proceeding serves only to compare a child's behavior to state-established norms. Where children are defendants in a juvenile proceeding because of their alleged criminal acts, it is not very conceivable that any substantive rights of minors could be raised as far as the home is

124. *Stephens v. Bongard*, 189 A. 131 (1947).

125. *State v. Massa*, 231 A. 2d 252 (1967).

126. *People v. Stanley*, 81 Colo. 276, 255 p. 610, 613 (1927).

127. For example, Minnesota Statutes Ann., sec. 120.12; 127.20 (1975).

128. See, for example, *Wisconsin v. Yoder*, 406 U.S. 205, 230-31 (1972); *State v. LaBarge*, 357 A. 2d 121 (Vt. 1976).

129. For example, Minnesota Statutes Ann., sec. 260.185, 191 (1975).

concerned, since there is no constitutional right to commit a crime. Even where a child is removed from a home for parental neglect the issues raised are not those of the substantive rights of minors in the home but of the overriding interest of the state to intervene to correct a neglectful or abusive situation.

If any development in the area of childrens' rights is to occur it will have to begin in a forum other than the courtroom. Whether legislatures are willing to intrude into the sanctity of the home and define childrens' rights is doubtful. "The family is the primary and the most fundamental influence on children." [130] It may well be that courts and legislatures will be satisfied to establish legal parameters for permissible parental conduct and intervene or permit interventions only where there is reported abuse or neglect.[131] To go farther would result in a complete restructuring of the basic child-parent relationship. It is one thing for the courts to alter the traditional authority relationship in the school but it is quite another to disrupt parent-child relationships in the home. It may be that courts have gone too far to reverse themselves, but in the absence of some judicial restraint the adversary system, now part of the routine of the public schools, may become an integral part of normal child-rearing patterns in the home.

## Conclusion

One hesitates to wax prophetic and project the demise of school and home authority because of these latest trends in the student-school-home relationship. However, one does not need be "a prophet or son of a prophet," as Mr. Justice Black so plainly expressed himself in *Tinker*, to see the debilitating effect that such trends may have upon school administrators, school board members, and parents. Caution simply cannot become the byword in school or home discipline and education when the concern ought instead to be for control; fear of legal reprisals by students ought not to replace firmness in dealing with problem students in the school or

130. See 1975 Family Services Act, sec. 2(9)(1).

131. The 1974 Minnesota Child Abuse Statute contains the following phrase as part of its public policy ". . . to strengthen the family and make the home safe for children through improvement of parental and guardian capacity for responsible child care." Minnesota Statutes Ann., sec. 221(1) (1974).

home. No one desires to foster a system of education where administrative rules and parental demands are irrational and school and parental discipline is unreasonable; but, on the other hand, courts or legislatures ought not to force educators and parents into a constitutional and statutory straitjacket so that the processes of education and discipline become anesthetized by a judicial or legislative fatalism akin to the mournful lament of Lady Macbeth: "What is done cannot be undone."

# CHAPTER VIII

# The Right to a Free Appropriate Public Education

JEFFREY J. ZETTEL
and
ALAN ABESON

Establishing the constitutional right of an individual to obtain a free and appropriate public education has been a major concern of educational jurisprudence since the early 1950s. To understand many of the complexities that bear upon this area of public policy requires an awareness of many of the changes that have occurred during the past twenty-five years with regard to: (a) the basic definition of equality of educational opportunity; (b) the emergence of the federal judiciary as a strong and viable force in support of this concept as a result of decisions regarding student classification, the right to education, due process of the law, educational placement in the least restrictive environment, and the right to an education that is "free"; and finally (c) the passage of a series of state and federal statutes that followed in the wake of these decisions and have had considerable impact upon past and present educational policy relating to the responsibility of a state to provide a free, appropriate public education to all of its children of school age.

## Equal Educational Opportunity: A Changing Concept

The concept of equal educational opportunity has changed in meaning at least four times over the past century. Prior to 1850, it was often thought to be a responsibility of the state to provide all of its school-age children with a free, tax-supported, common educational experience. Implicit in this early definition was the existence of a reciprocal relationship between the state and the individual—it was the responsibility of the state to provide a common school and a uniform curriculum, but, at the same time, it was the responsibility of the individual to take advantage of it.[1] Therefore, as long as a school district provided "each child with an opportunity to acquire the basic minimum skills necessary for the enjoyment of the rights of speech and full participation in the political process,"[2] the state was deemed to have met its obligation and the public interest was satisfied.

During the late nineteenth century this definition of equal educational opportunity changed. Although most judicial analysis focused upon what went into a school (that is, its facilities and resources), a new dimension was added to the "equal" definition in 1896 when the U. S. Supreme Court ruled that equality did not necessarily have to mean one and the same. According to this newer interpretation, separate educational facilities could exist or be established for a particular class of children (such as a social, economic, or racial class) as long as they remained "separate but equal."[3]

This second phase or interpretation of equal educational opportunity, however, came to an abrupt end in 1954 when the Supreme Court ruled that legal separation by race inherently constituted inequality of opportunity. In *Brown* v. *Board of Education* the Court rejected the "separate but equal" doctrine on the basis that it was violative of the equal protection clause of the Fourteenth Amendment to the U. S. Constitution.[4]

Thus, it became apparent that educational equity could not be determined solely by examining the facilities or resources of a school. The courts, for example, began to consider other factors such as the prestige of the school, the composition of its student body, and the impact of the institution upon those it served.[5] Moreover, a number of comprehensive studies such as the Coleman

1. James S. Coleman et al., *Equality of Educational Opportunity* (Washington, D. C.: U. S. Government Printing Office, 1966).

2. *San Antonio Independent School District v. Rodriguez*, 36 L. Ed. 2d 45 (1973).

3. *Plessy v. Ferguson*, 163 U. S. 537 (1896).

4. *Brown v. Board of Education of Topeka*, 347 U. S. 483 (1954).

5. *Sweatt v. Painter*, 339 U. S. 620 (1950); *McLaurin v. Oklahoma State Regents*, 339 U. S. 637 (1950).

Report[6] substantiated the need for a newer definition of equal educational opportunity and the importance of considering the population of a school in terms of racial, social, and economic factors in determining this new definition.

A third definition of equal educational opportunity began to appear in state and federal litigation and legislation during the 1960s. This definition was concerned with "equality of results given different individual inputs."[7] The definition suggested that educational equality would exist within a public school when all of its students, regardless of their entry behaviors or conditions, would be able to achieve the same or similar educational objectives.

To help achieve the implementation of this interpretation, the United States during the 1960s set out upon what has been referred to as its "compensatory period,"[8] "educational decade,"[9] or "one" of the largest most sustained educational reform movements in [its] history."[10] In 1965, Congress approved the Elementary and Secondary Education Act (ESEA), which provided for "the greatest financial commitment to education in the history of the world."[11] Likewise, a multitude of instructional interventions and strategies flooded the schools—team teaching, modular scheduling, nongraded schools, programmed learning, and computer-assisted instruction, to name a few.

The results of this monumental effort to reform schools and produce equality of educational opportunity were at best disap-

6. Coleman et al., *Equality of Educational Opportunity*.

7. Frederick J. Weintraub and Alan Abeson, "New Educational Policies for the Handicapped: The Quiet Revolution," *Phi Delta Kappan* 55 (April 1974): 526-27.

8. Ibid.

9. Charles E. Silberman, *Crisis in the Classroom: The Remaking of American Education* (New York: Random House, 1970), p. 159.

10. Ibid.

11. Mary M. Bentzen and Kenneth A. Tye, "Effecting Change in Elementary Schools," in *The Elementary School in the United States*, Seventy-second Yearbook of the National Society for the Study of Education, Part II, ed. John I. Goodlad and Harold G. Shane (Chicago: University of Chicago Press, 1973), p. 351.

pointing. Studies conducted by the Kettering Foundation, the Rand Corporation, and the Ford Foundation concluded that curriculum reform and money alone were not the answers to bring about decisive and innovative improvements within the public schools.[12] Furthermore, according to yet another critic:

Many of these attempts started with, and were dependent upon external funding. When the funds ran out, few innovations survived. Some of the attempts employed a change-agent strategy. Someone from the outside was going to come in and change the schools for the local community. The change agent's perception of local needs may have been quite different from the perceptions of teachers, students, and parents. But perhaps the most significant aspect of most of these reform attempts was that they were designed for everyone. The New Math was for all students (and teachers). Flexible scheduling was for all. The school would move from one program for every student to another program for every student.[13]

The basic flaw with this third interpretation was that it assumed that all children have innate capabilities for common educational attainments. Instead of looking at individual students and attempting to meet individual needs, the reform movement of the late 1960s attempted to design a new overall instructional approach to fit education in general. With the failure of this movement and the expenditure of millions of state and federal tax dollars, there were many who came to regard the concept of educational equality as being practically unobtainable.

### EQUAL ACCESS TO DIFFERING RESOURCES FOR DIFFERING OBJECTIVES

Beginning in the early 1970s, another interpretation of equal educational opportunity evolved. Unlike previous attempts to discover a single method or way to meet the educational needs of all students, this newer definition called for educational programmers

12. For details as to the failure to reform public schools through monetary and curriculum reform, see John I. Goodlad, M. Frances Klein, et al., *Looking behind the Classroom Door* (Belmont, Calif.: Wadsworth Publishing Co., 1974) and Harvey A. Avrich et al., *How Effective is Schooling? A Critical Review and Synthesis of Research Findings* (Santa Monica, Calif.: Rand Corp., 1972).

13. Vernon H. Smith, *Alternative Schools: The Development of Options in Public Education* (Lincoln, Neb.: Professional Educators Publications, 1974), p. 9.

and practitioners to look at individual students and their individual needs. This newest interpretation rests, therefore, on a premise of "providing individuals with equal access to differing resources for differing objectives." [14]

This fourth and most recent definition provides the basis for much of the ensuing discussion. In essence, a substantial portion of the remainder of this chapter will deal with the attempts of a particular segment or minority of the school-age population to gain access to equal educational opportunity.

The children who form the newest group to seek the right to a free and appropriate public education have often been described as children with special learning needs. They include the mentally retarded, the learning disabled, the serious emotionally disturbed, the speech and language impaired, as well as the visually, hearing, physically, and multiple handicapped. They are estimated to be approximately eight million in number and comprise between 10 and 15 percent of the school-age population. As a group, they have endured a long history of discrimination and segregation and to-day they actively seek delivery of their right to an equal educational opportunity. Collectively these children constitute a group called "the handicapped."

To establish this newest definition of equality of educational opportunity, the handicapped initially went to court. Beginning in 1971 with a series of landmark decisions establishing the right to education for all children, including the most severely handicapped, they have successfully litigated in five closely related areas that collectively constitute the right to a free and appropriate public education. Specifically, the following legal rights have been established: (a) the right to an appropriate education; (b) the right to a "free" public education; (c) the right to due process of law; (d) the right to placement in the least restrictive environment; and (e) the right to nondiscriminatory testing and evaluation procedures. Furthermore, following in the wake of this wave of litigation came the passage of state and federal mandates to set educational policies that reinforce the previously established judicial directives.

14. Frederick J. Weintraub and Alan Abeson, "Appropriate Education for All Handicapped Children: A Growing Issue," *Syracuse Law Review* 23, no. 4 (1972): 1056.

## The Right to an Education

In 1954, the Supreme Court affirmed the rights of all children to an equal education when it proclaimed:

In these days, it is doubtful that any child may reasonably be expected to succeed in life if he is denied the opportunity of an education. Such an opportunity, where the state has undertaken to provide it, is a right which must be made available to all on equal terms.[15]

Despite such an explicit decree from the nation's highest court, the Children's Defense Fund (CDF) in 1974 estimated that there were nearly two million children between the ages of seven and seventeen who were still being excluded from public schools. In describing the type of child most often excluded, CDF found:

If a child is not white, or white but not middle class, does not speak English, is poor, needs special help with seeing, hearing, walking, reading, learning, adjusting, growing up, is pregnant or married at age 15, is not smart enough or is too smart, then in too many places, school officials decide that school is not the place for that child. In sum, out-of-school children share a common characteristic of differentness by virtue of race, income, physical, mental or emotional "handicap," and age. They are, for the most part, out of school not by choice but because they have been excluded. It is as if many school officials have decided that certain groups of children are beyond their responsibility and are expendable. Not only do they exclude these children, they frequently do so arbitrarily, discriminatorily, and with impunity.[16]

The legality of denying a public education to any child by exclusion, postponement, or by any other means is increasingly being challenged. The basis for this challenge rests in the equal protection clause of the Fourteenth Amendment to the Constitution, which guarantees equal protection of the laws to all the people. In other words, where a state has undertaken to provide a benefit to the people, such as a public education, the benefits must be provided on equal terms to all the people unless the state can demonstrate a compelling reason for doing otherwise.

Frequently, the compelling reasons used for the exclusion of certain types of students centered on the presumed inability of

15. *Brown v. Board of Education of Topeka*, 347 U. S. 483 (1954).

16. Children's Defense Fund, *Children out of School in America* (Cambridge, Mass.: Children's Defense Fund, 1974), pp. 3-4.

some children to learn or benefit from an education. Today, as the result of judicial intervention and increasing legislative mandate, it is illegal for any public school to deny an education to a child because of behavioral difficulties, an inability to learn, or any handicapping condition. The language of the courts makes this clear:

A sentence of banishment from the local educational system is, insofar as the institution has power to act, the extreme penalty, the ultimate punishment; . . . stripping a child of access to educational opportunity is a life sentence to second-rate citizenship.[17]

We hold that G.H. is entitled to an equal educational opportunity under the Constitution of North Dakota, and that depriving her of that opportunity would be an unconstitutional denial of equal protection under the Federal and State Constitutions and of the due process and privileges and immunities clauses of the North Dakota Constitution.[18]

Congress has decreed a system of publicly supported education for the children of the District of Columbia. The Board of Education has the responsibility of administering that system in accordance with law and of providing such publicly supported education to all of the children of the District, including these exceptional children.[19]

### ESTABLISHING THE PRECEDENT: THE RIGHT TO AN EDUCATION

Two of the most heralded and precedent-setting "right to education" cases occurred in the early 1970s in Pennsylvania and the District of Columbia. In January 1971, the Pennsylvania Association for Retarded Children (PARC, now known as Pennsylvania Association for Retarded Citizens) brought suit against the Commonwealth of Pennsylvania for the alleged failure of the state to provide all school-age retarded children with access to a free public education.[20] In addition to PARC, the plaintiffs included fourteen mentally retarded school-age children who represented

17. *Lee v. Macon County Board of Education*, 490 F. 2d 460 (5th Cir., 1974).

18. *In the interest of G. H., a Child v. G. H., B. H., F. H.*, Williston School District No. 1, Civil No. 8930 (Supreme Court, State of North Dakota, April 30, 1974).

19. *Mills v. Board of Education of the District of Columbia*, 384 F. Supp. 866 (D.D.C., 1972).

20. *Pennsylvania Association for Retarded Children v. Commonwealth of Pennsylvania*, 343 F. Supp. 279 (E. D. Pa., 1972), Consent Agreement.

themselves and "all others similarly situated." The defendants included the state board of education, the state secretaries of education and public welfare, and thirteen named school districts, representing the class of all school districts of Pennsylvania.

The suit, heard by a three-judge panel in the U.S. District Court of the Eastern District of Pennsylvania, specifically questioned state policy as expressed in law, policies, and practices that excluded, postponed, or denied free access to public education opportunities to school-age, mentally retarded children who could benefit from such education.

Expert witnesses for the plaintiffs presented testimony that focused on the following educational principles which were dealt with by the suit:

1. The provision of systematic educational programs for mentally retarded children will produce learning.

2. Education cannot be defined solely as the provision of academic experiences for children. Rather, education must be seen as a continuous process by which individuals learn to cope with and function within their environment. Thus, for children to learn to clothe and feed themselves is a legitimate outcome achievable from a public school program.

3. The earlier mentally retarded children are provided with educational experiences, the greater the amount of learning that can be predicted. This principle relates directly to the provision in some school districts of preschool programs for nonhandicapped children—programs to which preschool mentally retarded children were denied entry.

A June 1971 stipulation and order and an October 1971 injunction, consent agreement, and order resolved the suit. The order decreed that the state could not apply any policy that would postpone, terminate, or deny mentally retarded children access to a publicly supported education, including a public school program, tuition or tuition maintenance, and homebound instruction. Further, by October 1971, the plaintiff children were to have been reevaluated and placed in programs, and by September 1972, all retarded children between the ages of six and twenty-one were to be provided a publicly supported education.

Following in the footsteps of the *PARC* case, a second and more impressive federal ruling occurred in 1972 in the District of Columbia. In *Mills* v. *Board of Education*[21] the parents and guardians of seven District of Columbia children brought a class action suit on behalf of all out-of-school handicapped children against the Board of Education of the District, the Department of Human Resources, and the Mayor for failure to provide all children with a publicly supported education.

The plaintiff children ranged in age from seven to sixteen and were alleged by the public schools to present the following types of problems that led to denial of their opportunity for an education: slightly brain damaged, hyperactive behavior, epilepsy and mentally retarded, and mentally retarded coupled with an orthopedic handicap. Three of the plaintiff children resided in public, residential institutions with no educational program. The others lived with their families and when denied entrance to public school programs were placed on a waiting list for tuition grants to enable purchase of a private educational program. In none of these cases, however, had the tuition grants been provided.

Also at issue was the manner in which the children were denied entrance to or were excluded from public education programs. Specifically, the complaint said that

plaintiffs were so excluded without a formal determination of the basis for their exclusion and without provision for periodic review of their status. Plaintiff children merely have been labeled as behavior problems, emotionally disturbed, or hyperactive.[22]

Further, it was pointed out that

the procedures by which plaintiffs were excluded or suspended from public school are arbitrary and do not conform to the due process requirements of the Fifth Amendment. Plaintiffs are excluded and suspended without: (a) notification as to a hearing, the nature of offense or status, any alternative or interim publicly supported education; (b) opportunity for representation, a hearing by an impartial arbiter, the presentation of witnesses, and (c) opportunity for periodic review of the necessity for continued exclusion or suspension.[23]

21. *Mills* v. *Board of Education of the District of Columbia*, 348 F. Supp. 866 (D. D. C., 1972).

22. Ibid.

23. Ibid.

In December 1971, the court issued a stipulated agreement and order providing for the following: (a) the named plaintiffs were to be provided with a publicly supported education by January 3, 1972; (b) by the same date, the defendants were to provide to the court a list of every child of school age not receiving a publicly supported education; (c) also by January 3, the defendants were to initiate efforts to identify all other members of the class not previously known; and (d) the plaintiffs and defendants were to consider the selection of a master to deal with special questions arising out of this order. The defendants failed to comply with the order, resulting in the filing by the plaintiffs, on January 21, 1972, of a motion for summary judgment and a proposed order and decree for implementation of the proposed judgment.

On August 1, 1972, U. S. District Judge Joseph Waddy issued such an order and decree providing (a) a declaration of the constitutional right of all children, regardless of any exceptional condition or handicap, to a publicly supported education and (b) a declaration that the defendant's rules, policies, and practices which excluded children without a provision for adequate and immediate alternative procedures denied the plaintiffs and the class rights of due process and equal protection of the law.

In testimony prior to issuance of the August 1 order the defendants claimed that it would be impossible for them to afford the relief specified in the original order unless the Congress appropriated more funds or unless funds were diverted from other educational services for which they had been appropriated. The court responded:

The defendants are required by the Constitution of the United States, the District of Columbia Code, and their own regulations to provide a publicly supported education for these "exceptional" children. Their failure to fulfill this clear duty to include and retain these children in the public school system or otherwise provide them with publicly supported education, and their failure to afford them due process hearing and periodical review, cannot be excused by the claim that there are insufficient funds. In *Goldberg* v. *Kelly*, 397 U.S. 254 (1969), the Supreme Court, in a case that involved the right of a welfare recipient to a hearing before termination of his benefits, held that constitutional rights must be afforded citizens despite the greater expense involved. . . . Similarly the District of Columbia's interest in educating the excluded children clearly must outweigh its interest in preserving its financial resources. *If sufficient funds are not available to finance all of the services and programs that are needed and desirable in the system then the available funds must be expended equitably in such a manner that no child is entirely excluded from a publicly supported education consistent with his needs and ability to benefit therefrom. The inadequacies of the District of Columbia Public School System, whether occasioned by insufficient funding or administrative inefficiency, certainly cannot be permitted to bear more heavily on the "exceptional" or handicapped child than on the normal child.*[24] (italics added)

The basic precedent emerging from these two cases was that all school-age children, regardless of the severity of their handicap, were entitled to a free public education. These rulings demonstrated the intention of courts that handicapped children were to have equal access to all public school programs—academic, vocational, and extracurricular—that are afforded to their nonhandicapped peers.

### LEGISLATION AND THE RIGHT TO EDUCATION

Following the judicial precedents established by the *PARC* and *Mills* decisions, the "right to education" principle became further solidified through the promulgation of a number of state and federal regulations as well as through the passage of state and federal legislation.

In 1972, for example, it was reported that almost 70 percent of the states had adopted mandatory legislation requiring the education of all eligible handicapped children as defined in the policies of each state.[25] The remaining states continued to operate with permissive statutes, which in effect allowed local school agencies to decide whether or not they would provide educational programs to handicapped children. By 1975, a survey of state law indicated that all but two states had adopted some form of mandatory legislation. The survey further revealed that thirty-seven of the forty-eight states with mandatory legislation had adopted their current

24. Ibid.

25. Alan Abeson, "Movement and Momentum: Government and the Education of Handicapped Children," *Exceptional Children* 39 (September 1972): 63-66.

special education legislation since 1970.[26] The tone of the mandates in state legislation, exemplied by the following statute, demonstrates that the provision of appropriate educational opportunities for handicapped children is no longer considered an option by state legislatures:

It is the policy of this State to provide, and to require school districts to provide, as part of free public education, special education services sufficient to meet the needs and maximize the capabilities of handicapped children. The timely implementation of this policy to the end that all handicapped children actually receive the special education services necessary to their proper development is declared to be an integral part of the policy of this State. This section applies to all handicapped children regardless of the schools, institutions or programs by which such children are served.[27]

With the passage of the Education Amendment of 1974 (signed August 24, 1974) the U.S. Congress affirmed the right to education thrust previously established by state and federal courts and cast into law by state legislatures.[28] In Title VI-B, the Congress ordered state educational agencies to develop and submit to the U.S. Commissioner of Education long-range, detailed state plans to achieve full educational opportunity for all handicapped children within each state. This mandate was again affirmed by the same Congress when P.L. 94-142 (the Education of All Handicapped Children Act of 1975) became law. Among the purposes of the act cited by the Congress was "to assure that all handicapped children have available to them . . . a free appropriate public education." [29] Further, the act specified that "a free appropriate public education will be available for all handicapped children between the ages of three and eighteen within the state not later than September 1, 1978."[30]

26. U. S. Congress, Senate, *Education for All Handicapped Children Act,* S.6 (94th Congress, 1st Session, June 2, 1975), Report No. 94-168.

27. Tennessee Code Annotated, chap. 839, sec. 1, 1972.

28. U. S. Congress, Public Law 93-380, Education Amendments of 1974 (August 21, 1974).

29. U. S. Congress, Public Law 94-142, Education for All Handicapped Children Act (November 29, 1975).

30. Ibid.

## The Right to Nondiscriminatory Testing and Evaluation

### THE CLASSIFICATION AND LABELING OF STUDENTS

Prior to and during the time that federal courts were considering the right to education cases, another line of litigation focused on the identification, evaluation, and placement of children in special education classes and programs. Evidence was developed supporting the claim that schools too often assigned labels, subjected children to individual psychological assessments, and altered their educational status without the appropriate supporting data and often without parental knowledge, permission, or participation.

Among the well-known adverse effects of inappropriate labeling are the following:

1. Labeled children are often victimized by stigma associated with the label. This may be manifested by isolation from usual school opportunities and taunting and rejection by both children and school personnel. In the latter instance, it may be overt or unconscious.

2. Assigning a label to a child often suggests to those working with him that the child's behavior should conform to stereotyped behavioral expectations associated with that label. This often contributes to a self-fulfilling prophecy in that the child, once labeled, is expected to conform with the stereotyped behavior associated with the label and ultimately does so. When a child is labeled and placement is made on the basis of that label, there is often no opportunity to escape from either the label or the placement.

3. Children who are labeled and placed in educational programs on the basis of that label may often not need special education programs. This is obviously true for children who are incorrectly labeled, but it also applies to children with certain handicaps, often of a physical nature. The fact that a child is physically handicapped does not necessarily mean that a special education is required.[31]

There are those who argue that labels are needed, despite the potential negative effects. This position is based on the premise that the primary intent and benefit of a label is that it enables a

31. Alan Abeson, Nancy Bolick, and Jayne Hass, *A Primer on Due Process: Education Decisions for Handicapped Children*, (Reston, Va.: Council for Exceptional Children, 1975), p. 5.

particular child in need of special services and benefits to receive them. This dilemma is perhaps best summarized by Hobbs:

Children who are categorized and labeled as different may be permanently stigmatized, rejected by adults and other children, and excluded from opportunities essential for their full and healthy development. Yet categorization is necessary to open doors to opportunity: to get help for a child, to write legislation, to appropriate funds, to design service programs, to evaluate outcomes, to conduct research, even to communicate about the problems of the exceptional child.[32]

Classification of exceptional children is essential to get services for them, to plan and organize helping programs, and to determine the outcomes of the intervention efforts. We do not concur with sentiments widely expressed that classification of exceptional children should be done away with. Although we understand that some people advocate the elimination of classification in order to get rid of its harmful effects, their proposed solution oversimplifies the problem. Classification and labeling are essential to human communication and problem solving; without categories and concept designators, all complex communicating and thinking stop.[33]

Adding to this debate were a number of studies that began to question the alleged preponderance of minority group children placed in special education classes. Studies conducted by the California State Department of Education in 1966-67, for example, discovered that while children with Spanish surnames comprised only 13 percent of the total school population, they accounted for more than 26 percent of the 85,000 children in classes for the educable mentally retarded.[34] Similarly, a study conducted in eleven Missouri school districts in 1971 concluded that the students in learning disability classes tended to be middle- and upper-class white children, while those in educable mentally retarded programs were disproportionately black.[35] Because of the dual concerns

32. Nicholas Hobbs, *The Futures of Children* (San Francisco, Calif.: Jossey-Bass, 1975), p. 3.

33. Ibid., p. 5.

34. Frederick J. Weintraub, "Recent Influences of Law regarding the Identification and Educational Placement of Children," *Focus on Exceptional Children* 4 (April 1972): 1-11.

35. David J. Franks, "Ethnic and Social Status Characteristics of Children in EMH and LD Classes," *Exceptional Children* 37 (March 1971): 537.

of disproportionate minority group representation for special education programs and the evils of labeling, attempts to seek resolution were taken to the nation's judiciary.

### TESTING AND LITIGATION

In January 1970, a significant case, *Diana v. State Board of Education*,[36] was filed in the District Court of Northern California. This suit was brought on behalf of nine Mexican-American students, ages eight to thirteen, who came from homes in which Spanish was the principal spoken language. All had been placed in classes for the mentally retarded on the basis of intelligence quotients ranging from 30 to 72. When the plaintiffs were retested in Spanish, however, seven of the nine scored higher than the IQ cutoff point for placement in classes for the mentally retarded and the lowest score was only three points below the designated cutoff score. The average gain for the group was fifteen points.

On the basis of these data, plaintiffs charged that the testing procedures used to determine placement in classes for the mentally retarded were in fact prejudical. They further argued that such tests placed heavy emphasis on the use of verbal skills requiring facility with the English language, that the test questions were culturally biased, and that the tests were standardized on white, native-born Americans. To substantiate their claim, the plaintiffs demonstrated statistically that while Spanish surnamed students only comprised about 18.5 percent of the student population of Monterey County (the county where the plaintiffs resided and went to school), they accounted for nearly one-third of the children in classes for the educable mentally retarded. The suit filed was a class action suit on behalf of all the bilingual Mexican-American children placed in classes for the mentally retarded and for all such children who in the future were in danger of being inappropriately placed in these classes.

A stipulated agreement was signed by both parties to resolve the issues. The agreement required that (a) children were to be tested in their primary language and interpreters were to be used when a bilingual examiner was not available; (b) Mexican-American

36. *Diana v. State Board of Education*, Civil Action No. C-70 37 R.F.P. (N. D. Cal., Jan. 7, 1970 and June 18, 1973).

and Chinese children presently in classes for the educable mentally retarded were to be retested and reevaluated; and (c) the state was to undertake immediate efforts to develop and standardize an appropriate intelligence test.

A second landmark decision concerning the testing and classification of students was a class action suit filed in late 1971 on behalf of six black, elementary school-aged children attending school in the San Francisco Unified School District. In *Larry P. v. Riles*, the plaintiffs charged that they had been inappropriately classified and placed in classes for the educable mentally retarded on the basis of testing procedures that failed to recognize their unfamiliarity with white middle-class culture. Moreover, they alleged that their misplacement in classes for the educable mentally retarded carried with it a stigma and "a life sentence of illiteracy."[37]

Statistical evidence was compiled demonstrating that the San Francisco Unified School District, as well as the State of California, had a disproportionate number of black children enrolled in programs for the retarded. Furthermore, it was demonstrated that even though code and regulatory procedures regarding the identification, classification, and placement of the mentally retarded were changed to be more effective, inadequacies in the process still existed.

On June 20, 1972, the court enjoined the San Francisco Unified School District from placing black students in classes for the mentally retarded on the basis of a single IQ score, if the consequence of using such tests was the obvious racial imbalance it caused in the composition of classes for the educable mentally retarded.

### LEGISLATION AND THE RIGHT TO NONDISCRIMINATORY TESTING AND EVALUATION

Concern has likewise been demonstrated by state and federal governments with regard to various procedures and materials used to label and classify students in need of special education. Based largely upon the precedents which evolved from *Diana* and *Larry P.*, present California law now calls for the use of verbal or nonverbal individual intelligence tests in the child's primary home language for children being considered for placement in classes

37. *Larry P. v. Riles*, Civil Action No. 6-71-2270 343 F. Supp. 1036 (N. D. Cal., 1972).

for the mentally retarded.[38] Moreover, in addition to specifying the scores required for placement, assurances are included in California law to force consideration of the score in relation to the child's "developmental history, cultural background, and school achievement." [39] Further, the psychologist administering the instrument must be fluent in the child's home language,[40] and the assessment must include estimates of adaptive behavior.

Beyond California, the home of the litigation, additional state laws and regulations are increasingly prohibiting the placement of children in special education programs solely on the basis of an IQ score or the recommendations of a single professional. In Georgia, for example, regulations required that "each school system shall insure that whenever testing of a child is required or permitted by these regulations, the results of ability, aptitude, or achievement tests shall not be used exclusively or principally as the basis for any finding or conclusion." [41] Similiar provisions are contained in Massachusetts statutes, which also include the requirement that department-approved tests must be "as free as possible from cultural or linguistic bias or whenever necessary, separately evaluated with reference to the linguistic and cultural group to which the child belongs." [42]

As with the right to education principle, the Congress also reacted to the problems initially raised by *Diana* and *Larry P*. In the same acts mentioned earlier (P.L. 93-380 and P.L. 94-142) prohibitions were written to eliminate inappropriate identification, evaluation, and placement activities. Essentially, these provisions require that state agencies select, adapt, and use testing and evaluation materials that are not "racially or culturally discriminatory." In P.L. 94-142 a further prohibition was added that "no single procedure shall be the sole criterion for determining an appropriate educational program for a child." [43] This last requirement is a

38. California Education Code, Section 6902.07.

39. Ibid., Section 6902.08.

40. Ibid., Section 6902.085.

41. Georgia Department of Education, "Special Education Regulations and Procedures," (Atlanta, Ga.: Georgia Department of Education, 1975).

42. Massachusetts General Laws, chap. 71B, sec. 7, 1971.

43. Public Law 94-142, Education for All Handicapped Children Act.

further attempt to control the degree to which single intelligence test scores can be used in decision making.

A final requirement of P.L. 94-142 relating to nondiscriminatory evaluation focuses on using assessment instruments in ways that reflect what they are intended to measure. An example is the frequent inclusion of performance or manipulative tasks on standardized tests. Because of their physical difficulties many physically handicapped children do not succeed at these tasks and consequently score low. If the tasks are designed to measure agility, that scoring is appropriate. If, however, the intention is to determine whether the child knows where to place an object, such scoring is not appropriate. The child may in fact possess the knowledge and intelligence, but because of physical difficulties cannot demonstrate that knowledge. P.L. 94-142 requires that evaluation of children be done with respect to their "mode of communicating," a requirement that is intended to deal with this problem.

As more litigation and legislation evolved concerning the labeling, classification, and placement of handicapped children, it became apparent that students were often being misplaced and misclassified, not only as a result of inappropriate evaluation instruments and/or procedures, but also because of arbitrary and capricious decision making on the part of school personnel. To provide procedural safeguards against such practices and decisions, the courts recognized the importance and necessity for due process procedures in the identification, placement, and reassignment of children with regard to special education.

## The Right to Due Process of Law

There is no mystery as to why parents, advocates, legislators, judges, and others have demanded that public school officials provide due process safeguards to handicapped children and their families when making educational decisions. As has been indicated, the abuses are numerous and the actions that occurred have often been characterized by arbitrary and capricious behavior. In many instances, parents have literally been denied the chance of effectively participating in decisions having significant implications for the total lives of their children:

Harris, my only son is ten and is somewhat small for his age but has always been very active, playing with friends in his neighborhood. Last spring I got a note asking me to come to school. The pupil adjustment counselor told me that Harris and another boy, who had been his friend, had been fighting and that Harris was not to return to school for a week. When he returned to school he was immediately sent home again for no specific length of time, but with the message that he couldn't return again until he "learns to behave." When I again went to school to see his teacher, I learned that Harris had been placed in a class for retarded children since last year. I became very upset because I had never been told of this. I did get a note from someone last year saying that Harris was receiving some special help with his studies, but it said nothing about a class for retarded children. I visited the school several times about this and asked to see Harris's records and test scores, but was told that I couldn't because the information was "confidential." The teacher did say that Harris's work had been better than the others, and that he could be smart when he wanted to, and that she didn't really understand him. It seemed as though he had been placed in the class because of his behavior. Since I wasn't satisfied, I had him tested at a private clinic and was told by the psychologist that he had an IQ of 96, a normal score and that he definitely should not be in a class for mentally retarded children since that probably would only cause him to act up more, rather than helping him. Finally, a lawyer at the agency called the principal and the Director of the Department of Special Classes (for mentally retarded), and got Harris into a regular class. I'm happy now and Harris is doing better, but a neighbor told me that several other parents whose children go to Harris's school are upset because their children also have been put in those classes.[44]

Due process requirements for the public schools with regard to special education were first, and perhaps most clearly, established in the *Pennsylvania Association for Retarded Children (PARC)* v. *Commonwealth of Pennsylvania*. Moreover, as part of that order, a highly specific twenty-three step procedure establishing due process was placed into force.

In commenting on the opportunity for hearings and due process achieved by the *PARC* litigation, Thomas Gilhool, attorney for the Pennsylvania Association for Retarded Children, indicated that:

A mechanism (has been) created to assure that the educational program fits the child. The mere fact of a hearing opportunity on change in

44. Frederick J. Weintraub and Alan Abeson, "Appropriate Education for All Handicapped Children: A Growing Issue," p. 1044.

assignment and every two years thereafter will of course keep all the field professionals on their toes. There is a new instrument for account-ability—to the child, to the parent, to the Secretary of Education and to the teacher as a professional.[45]

While *PARC* was limited to the mentally retarded, in the subsequent *Mills* decision the court ordered the implementation of due process procedures for the identification, evaluation, and placement of all handicapped children. The legal basis came from the due process clauses of the Fifth and Fourteenth Amendments to the U.S. Constitution.

STATE AND FEDERAL LEGISLATION

A 1974 survey of state policies regarding due process conducted by the State-Federal Information Clearinghouse for Exceptional Children revealed that twelve states were required by statute to provide such procedures and thirteen were similarly required by regulation.[46]

The constitutional responsibility of each state to afford its residents due process procedures was further affirmed by the passage of the education amendments of 1974. Through P.L. 93-380 Congress ordered an immediate assurance from the states that procedures were in place to guarantee that all handicapped children within each state and their parents would be assured of procedural safeguards in all decisions regarding identification, evaluation, and educational placement of handicapped children. Thus, the main-tenance of fundamental due process procedures was not only acknowledged by the Congress in 1974, it was also made a condi-tion upon the states for continued receipt of federal monies for the education of their handicapped children. Furthermore, with the passage of P.L. 94-142, all states wishing to receive federal assistance under this act are required to establish and maintain procedures that will include, but not be limited to:

1. an opportunity for the parents or guardian of a handicapped child

45. Leopold Lippman and I. Ignacy Goldberg, *Right to Education* (New York: Teachers College Press, 1973), p. 58.

46. Nancy Bolick, ed., *Digest of State and Federal Laws: Education of Handicapped Children*, 3d ed. (Reston, Va.: Council for Exceptional Chil-dren, 1974).

to examine all relevant records with respect to the identification, evaluation, and educational placement of the child . . . and to obtain an independent educational evaluation of the child;

2. procedures to protect the rights of the child whenever the parents or guardian of the child are not known or are unavailable, or when the child is a ward of the state, including the assignment of an individual (who shall not be an employee of the state educational agency, local educational agency, or intermediate educational unit involved in the education or care of the child) to act as a surrogate for the parents or guardian;

3. written prior notice to the parents or guardian of the child whenever such agency or unit proposes to initiate or change, or refuses to initiate or change the identification, evaluation, or educational placement of the child;

4. procedures designed to assure that [this] notice . . . fully informs the parents or guardian, in the parents' or guardian's native language;

5. an opportunity to present complaints with respect to any matter relating to the identification, evaluation, or educational placement of the child, or the provision of a free appropriate public education to such child.[47]

Furthermore, once a complaint has been rendered, the parents or guardians shall have the opportunity for an impartial due process hearing at which all persons concerned shall be guaranteed (a) the right to be accompanied and advised by counsel and by individuals with special knowledge or training with respect to the problems of handicapped children; (b) the right to present evidence and confront, cross-examine, and compel the attendance of witnesses; (c) the right to a written or electronic verbatim record of the hearing; and (d) the right to written findings of fact and decisions.[48]

## The Right To Be Educated in the Least Restrictive Environment

Closely related to due process procedures and contributing to the position that all children need to have an individually designed educational program to meet their unique needs, is a child's right (and particularly a handicapped child's right) to be educated in the least restrictive environment. The basis for this concept stems

47. Public Law 94-142, Education for All Handicapped Children Act.
48. Ibid.

from recognition of the existence of a variety of learning environments in which any child may be educated. In the case of a handicapped child there is a continuum of placements ranging from the
least restrictive (that is, being placed in a regular classroom setting
with ample opportunity to interact with nonhandicapped children)
to the most restrictive setting, which might include a special
school, or even a nonpublic program such as an institution with
very little if any contact with nonhandicapped individuals. In the
past, few options existed beyond the regular program, the special
class or school, or nonpublic school programs such as institutions.
In the absence of options, mildly handicapped children were often
unnecessarily placed in special classes with little or no opportunity
to participate in the regular program of the school. Gallagher, for
example, reported that "in a number of large-city school systems
far less than 10 percent of the children placed in special education
classes are ever returned to regular education."[49]

In discussing the legal ramifications of the principle of least
restrictive environment, Johnson commented as follows:

In essence, this doctrine provides that, when government pursues a legitimate goal that may involve the restricting of fundamental liberty, it
must do so using the least restrictive alternative available. Applied to
education, courts have ruled in principle that special education systems
or practices are inappropriate if they remove children from their expanded peer group without benefit of constitutional safeguards. Placement in special environments for educational purposes can, without appropriate safeguards, become a restriction of fundamental liberties.
It is required, then, that substantive efforts be made by educators to
maintain handicapped children with their peers in a regular education
setting, and that the State (as represented by individual school districts)
bear the burden of proof when making placements or when applying
treatments which involve partial or complete removal of handicapped
children from their normal peers.[50]

Reference to this same concept was mentioned in the early right
to education cases. In *PARC*, for example, the court held that:

49. James Gallagher, "The Special Education Contract for Mildly Handicapped Children," *Exceptional Children* 38 (March 1972): 529.

50. Richard A. Johnson, "Renewal of School Placement Systems for the
Handicapped," in *Public Policy and the Education of Exceptional Children*,
ed. Frederick J. Weintraub et al. (Reston, Va.: Council for Exceptional
Children, 1976), p. 60.

It is the Commonwealth's obligation to place each mentally retarded child in a free, public program of education and training appropriate to the child's capacity, within the context of a presumption that, among the alternative programs of education and training required by statute to be available, placement in a regular public school class is preferable . . . to placement in any other type of program of education and training.[51]

LEGISLATION AND THE CONCEPT OF

LEAST RESTRICTIVE ENVIRONMENT

In addition to being the focus of litigation, the principle of least restrictive environment has also become embodied in federal and state law. As of 1974, six states were required by law and eleven by regulation to adhere to the principle of least restrictive alternative during the placement of handicapped children.[52] Moreover, in October 1975, the National Education Association reported that in a survey of forty-four of their state affiliates, "twenty-two or 50 percent reported that there was a state law or regulation in effect that handicapped children are to be placed in regular classes at least some of the time."[53]

Perhaps one of the clearest and most comprehensive statutory definitions of least restrictive environment as it applies to the handicapped can be found in the following 1972 Tennessee law:

To the maximum extent practicable, handicapped children shall be educated along with children who do not have handicaps and shall attend regular classes. Impediments to learning and to the normal functioning of handicapped children in the regular school environment shall be overcome by the provision of special aids and services rather than by separate schooling for the handicapped. Special classes, separate schooling or other removal of handicapped children from the regular educational environment, shall occur only when, and to the extent that the nature or severity of the handicap is such that education in regular classes, even with the use of supplementary aids and services, cannot be accomplished satisfactorily.[54]

51. *Pennsylvania Association for Retarded Children v. Commonwealth of Pennsylvania*, 343 F. Supp. 279.

52. Bolick, *Digest of State and Federal Laws.*

53. National Education Association, "Schools Must Face Serious Problems Posed by Integrating Handicapped, NEA President Says," NEA Press Release, Washington, D. C., 10 October 1975.

54. Tennessee Code Annotated, 49-2913 (Supp. 1973).

Federal legislation speaks similarly of this concept. Public Law 94-142 requires that all handicapped children "to the maximum extent appropriate" shall be educated "with children who are not handicapped." Furthermore, this act mandates that special classes, separate schooling, or other removal from the regular educational environment will occur only when "the nature or severity of the handicap is such that education in the regular class with the use of supplementary aids and services cannot be achieved satisfactorily."[55]

The implementation of such directives has been interpreted by some to mean that all handicapped children, regardless of the severity of their handicap, are to be placed in regular classroom programs. To others, these mandates mean that all handicapped children are to be placed in self-contained special education classes. Neither is correct, for what is required is the availability of an existing continuum of program options or the capacity to create or arrange options that will meet the specific individual needs of children.[56]

## The Right to a "Free" Public Education

Even with the variety of state and federal court rulings clearly stipulating that physical exclusion from the opportunity for a public education was unlawful, some educational agencies found yet another more subtle way to exclude the handicapped. This occurred through the use of tuition grant programs, which enabled state and local education agencies to offer public funds to parents of handicapped children when needed educational services were not available within the local public schools. Such funds were then used to purchase programs from private educational facilities. This procedure, however, created two major problems: (a) such provisions served as disincentives to develop programs for certain handicapped children, for it was believed to be easier and less costly for a local public education agency to send such

55. Public Law 94-142, Education for All Handicapped Children Act of 1975.

56. Alan Abeson, "Education for Handicapped Children in the Least Restrictive Environment," in Michael Kindred et al., *The Mentally Retarded Citizen and the Law* (New York: Free Press, 1976), pp. 515-16.

children to private agencies than to develop the special programs and services they needed; and (b) the tuition grant payments were often insufficient to cover the entire cost of a private education. Thus, if a family was unable to pay the difference, the handicapped child was once more subjected to either exclusion or inappropriate placement.

Recent judicial rulings have made it clear, however, that school-age handicapped children, regardless of the degree of mental, physical, or emotional disability, have a right to equal access to a public education. One of the early cases to deal with the right to a "free" public education was *Maryland Association for Retarded Children* v. *State of Maryland*. In this particular case, the court stipulated that when a state undertakes to provide education for any child and does so through the use of public or private programs as a matter of public policy, then the state must assume full financial responsibility for all children:

> The Court declares that it is the established policy of the State of Maryland to provide a free education to all persons between the ages of five and twenty years, and this includes children with handicaps, and particularly mentally retarded children, regardless of how severely and profoundly retarded they may be.[57]

State and federal litigation have spoken to the right to education issue in terms of equal protection. In *PARC*, *Mills*, and *LeBanks* v. *Spears*[58] the courts have specified that what must be provided is *free* public education. But, in addition to such general right to education cases, there have been at least two New York State decisions clearly dealing with this form of economic discrimination. In *In re Downey* the court said:

> To order a parent to contribute to the education of his handicapped child when free education is supplied to all other children would be a denial of the constitutional right of equal protection (United States Constitution, Amendment XIV; New York State Constitution, Article XI, Section 1). Legislation which singles out one class for special burdens and liabilities from which all others are exempt denies equal protection of the laws.

57. *Maryland Association for Retarded Children* v. *State of Maryland*, Equity No. 100-182-77676 (Circuit Court, Baltimore, Md., 1974).

58. *LeBanks* v. *Spears*, Civil Action No. 71-2897 (E.D. La., April 24, 1973).

Furthermore, it is the child who is given the right to an education, not the parent and his right should not be abridged or limited by the willingness of a parent to become financially liable for the education. To limit the right to an education in this manner would discourage many parents from seeking the appropriate facilities for their child.

In conclusion, while at first blush this may seem like a substantial outlay of funds for one child, when compared with the dollar cost of maintaining a child in an institution all his life or on public assistance the cost is minimal, not to speak of the incalculable cost to society of losing a potentially productive adult.[59]

In the second case, the court asserted that:

it would be a denial of the right of equal protection and morally inequitable not to reimburse the parents of a handicapped child for monies they have advanced in order that their child may attend a private school for the handicapped when no public facilities were available while other children who are more fortunate can attend public school without paying tuition and without regard to the assets and income of their parents.[60]

The use of such words as "free" and "public" make it clear that parents must not be required to contribute to the cost of educating a handicapped child when the state or local education agency prescribes a setting requiring tuition for the education of that child.

While a number of states specify "free," the most comprehensive legislation is found in Public Law 94-142, which requires that all handicapped children of ages three through eighteen within a state be provided with free appropriate public education by September 1, 1978, and that such education should be provided for all handicapped children of ages three through twenty-one by September 1, 1980. This statute also provides that a handicapped child who requires placement in a public or private residential program should be so placed and that the cost of the program, including room and board, must be at no cost to the parents of that child.[61]

59. *In re Downey*, 340 N.Y.S. 2d 690 (1973).

60. *In re K.*, 74 Misc. 2d 872, 347 N.Y.S. 2d 271 (1973).

61. "Proposed Rules: Education of Handicapped Children and Incentive Grants Program," *Federal Register* 41, no. 252 (30 December 1976): 56984-85.

## The Right to an Appropriate Education

While all of the previously described policy developments for handicapped children are of major consequence, perhaps the most significant is the emerging mandate that all handicapped children are entitled to an education that is appropriate to meet their unique needs. It can be said that this thrust has been a guiding direction for American education and has been in force for many years. Although this goal has been actively stated it has rarely been implemented, especially for handicapped children who present the greatest degree of individual variance. No distinction needs to be made here between legislative and litigative history, except to mention that since 1972 statutory and judicial emphasis have reinforced this goal as it applies to handicapped children.

State and federal statutes and judicial directives regarding the education that should be provided for handicapped children abound with words such as "suitable," "specialized instruction," "appropriate to the child's capacity," and "designed to develop the maximum potential of every handicapped person." In some states regulations have already been adopted enacting this intent. In Illinois regulations, for example, it is required that as part of placement activities a multidisciplinary staff conference will "develop an educational plan which indicates specific objectives to be attained by the child."[62] Wisconsin statutes provide that when a multidisciplinary team recommends a child for special education, it shall recommend an educational program fitted to the individual child's needs.[63] Similarly, Massachusetts also maintains detailed regulations requiring that each child with special needs be provided with an extensive individual education plan.[64]

Again, as has been described previously, the most specific and comprehensive statement regarding the development of individual educational programs for handicapped children is contained in the Education for All Handicapped Children Act of 1975. The desire

62. State of Illinois, *Rules and Regulations to Govern the Administration and Operation of Special Education*, 1974, p. 6.

63. Wisconsin Statutes Annotated, sec. 115.80(3).

64. Massachusetts Department of Education, *Bartley-Daly Act 766 Massachusetts Regulations*, Sec. 322, Springfield, Mass., 1974.

of Congress was to have each handicapped child provided with an "appropriate public education . . . designed to meet their unique needs." So strong was the concern of the Congress that it adopted the following definition of what must be provided in each child's written individual education program:

The term "individualized education program" means a written statement for each handicapped child developed in any meeting by a representative of the local educational agency . . . who shall be qualified to provide, or supervise the provision of, specially designed instruction to meet the unique needs of handicapped children, the teacher, the parents or guardian of such child, and, whenever appropriate, such child, which statement shall include (a) a statement of the present levels of educational performance of such child, (b) a statement of annual goals, including short-term instructional objectives, (c) a statement of the specific educational services to be provided to such child, and the extent to which such child will be able to participate in regular educational programs, (d) the projected date for initiation and anticipated duration of such services, and (e) appropriate objective criteria and evaluation procedures and schedules for determining, on at least an annual basis, whether instructional objectives are being achieved.[65]

It is important to understand two essential concepts related to this requirement. First, the development of the individualized education program itself must carefully delineate the rationale for the least restrictive alternative program. Second, program placement decisions cannot be made prior to determination of the individualized education program. The clear requirement is that handicapped children will not be placed in programs merely because the programs exist or for administrative convenience but rather they will be placed in programs that are designed or available to meet the goals and objectives specified in the individualized education program.

## Concluding Statement

It has been the intent of this chapter to report the impressive legal advances made during recent years that will enable handicapped children to receive the same educational benefits as are presently available to most nonhandicapped children. By virtue of the administrative, legislative, and judicial directives that have been

65. Public Law 94-142, Education for All Handicapped Children Act.

and will continue to be established to support the educational rights of this class of children historic discriminatory practices will be eliminated. From implementation of these mandates will come the provision that will provide appropriate educational services to all handicapped children.

As educators and makers of policy decisions move to refine and implement these policies, their definition of handicapped children must not be narrowly construed. The directives must be applied also to native American handicapped children who are located on or near reservation areas across the country as well as to those in existing educational communities; to abused and neglected children who because of their mistreatment become handicapped children and possess unique learning needs that require special education; and to a long neglected population of handicapped children who are found wallowing in the nation's correctional programs for juveniles.

Finally, as educators and in fact the entire society move to provide handicapped persons with their rights as citizens they should be aware of Section 504 of the Vocational Rehabilitation Amendments of 1973. This small section of law reads "no otherwise qualified handicapped individual in the United States . . . shall solely by reason of his handicap be excluded from the participation in, be denied the benefit of, or be subjected to discrimination under any program or activity receiving federal financial assistance." [66] In many respects this section of law supersedes all public policy at all levels of government and clearly establishes that handicapped persons are, like all other American citizens, entitled to full participation in American life.

66. Public Law 93-112, Vocational Rehabilitation Act of 1973, Section 504, July 26, 1973.

# CHAPTER IX

# Litigation Concerning Educational Finance

DAVID C. LONG

## Introduction

Litigation seeking to reform the ways in which states finance elementary and secondary education has been actively pursued since the late 1960s. The vitality of this reform movement sprang from the decision of the California Supreme Court in *Serrano* v. *Priest*,[1] but the focus quickly swung to the federal courts, culminating in the adverse decision of the U.S. Supreme Court in *San Antonio Independent School District* v. *Rodriguez*.[2] Since *Rodriguez*, virtually all the action has been in state courts. State cases have gone both ways, but significant victories by those aggrieved by school finance inequities in California, New Jersey, and other states mean that states are likely to face litigation if they continue to make educational opportunities depend on educationally irrelevant factors such as the size of the tax base of a school district and fail to address real differences among school districts in educational costs and burdens.

The educational and fiscal inequalities and inadequacies generated by most state systems of public school funding do not result from a single cause. They typically stem from the aggregation of at least several deficiencies. Overreliance on the local property tax to fund public education has resulted in educational opportunities varying with the size of a school district's tax base. Even if tax bases were equalized, however, not all school districts are equally

1. *Serrano* v. *Priest*, 5 Cal. 3d 584, 96 Cal. Rptr. 601, 487 P.2d 1241 (1971).

2. *San Antonio Independent School District* v. *Rodriguez*, 411 U.S. 1 (1973).

able or willing to tax themselves for education. The residents of some districts have greater personal incomes to pay property taxes than others. Districts with high concentrations of the elderly, of childless couples, and of parents with children in private and parochial schools often would rather not support the public education of other people's children. In addition, a greater proportion of the tax base in some districts may be necessary to provide non-educational services than in other districts; that is, although a district may look relatively well-off in terms of the amount of taxable wealth per child theoretically available, that property wealth may be illusory if most of it is needed to pay for essential noneducational municipal services. Reduced educational opportunities, whether caused by little taxable wealth or the lack of ability or inclination to support education, have the same effect on the children subject to them. Furthermore, the educational tasks that districts must perform are not equal. Some districts serve highly motivated children from middle-class homes. Other districts must respond to the educational deficiencies of large numbers of children from low-income families.

All these problems may overlay the system of school finance in a single state. Most cases, however, have addressed only one of these issues—the relationship between educational opportunities and the taxable wealth of a school district. This is more a reflection of the greater ease of managing a single issue in litigation and the utilization of a constitutional theory developed in the *Serrano* case than a judgment that the other serious problems in statewide systems of school finance are less worthy of judicial attention. Furthermore, school districts, parents, and children affected by voter unwillingness or inability to provide a level of education adequate for the educational tasks of the district are increasingly seeking judicial enforcement of the direct obligation of the state to children to insure equal and adequate educational opportunities, irrespective of the cause of the deficiencies in the educational program.

In this chapter, the major school finance cases challenging the relationship between taxable wealth and educational opportunities and other causes of inequality and inadequacy in educational opportunities resulting from state educational finance systems will be discussed.

## Litigation Concerning Fiscal Neutrality

It has long been recognized that the size of the property tax base is a major determinant of the educational expenditures of a school district. The larger its tax base and the fewer children it has, the wealthier the district will be in terms of its ability to support public education from the local tax base. For this reason a district's "wealth," which provides a measure of its ability to support public schools, is typically expressed as the amount of equalized assessed valuation of taxable property per pupil.[3] Districts with great taxable wealth are able to raise large amounts of revenue for the schools at modest tax rates. Districts "poor" in assessed valuation per pupil are able to raise only small amounts of revenue even at very high tax rates.[4]

In most states there are vast differences among districts in their taxable wealth per pupil.[5] These differences in district wealth then become a major determinant of the level of educational resources available in a school district; yet such variation is wholly unrelated to any educational factor. These wealth-caused differences bear no relation to a district's educational tasks or burdens, the needs of its children, or its costs. Rather, they have their origin in factors irrelevant to education—whether the school district has within it a utility, expensive homes and few children, or a factory, or whether it contains small homes and many children, poor farm land, or is unattractive for development. In many states differences in such factors, rather than those related to educational needs, costs, and aspirations, fuel the machinery that allocates educational resources to children.

3. Many states adjust reported assessed valuations to full market value or a common percentage thereof because local assessors typically do not assess property at the same percentage of fair market value. The failure to adjust for different local assessment practices will give a distorted picture of the relative wealth of school districts within a state.

4. For example, consider the case of two districts, one with $100,000 assessed valuation per pupil and the other with $10,000 assessed valuation per pupil. A 1 percent tax (10 mills) will raise $1,000 in the wealthier district. The same rate will only raise $100 per pupil in the poorer district. To raise $1,000 per pupil the poorer district would have to levy a virtually confiscatory tax of 10 percent (100 mills) per year.

5. For example, the range in equalized assessed valuation per pupil in New Jersey in 1971-72 was from $3,921 to $62,598,621 per pupil. *Robinson v. Cahill,* 118 N.J. Super. 223, 282-285 (1972).

Prior to the recent wave of litigation in school finance, most states recognized the effects of district wealth on educational opportunities and attempted to obviate, often ineffectually, the impact of differences in district wealth. Many states have so-called "foundation programs" to insure that every district at a minimum tax rate will have a certain "foundation" level of expenditure. Each district is credited with the amount it would raise at that tax rate, and the state makes up the difference between that amount and the foundation amount. Wealthier districts, of course, raise more funds at this tax rate than poorer districts and thus receive less from the state. The foundation amount, however, is generally set well below the level of funds sufficient to run even the most minimal educational program. This means that poorer districts have to struggle with higher taxes to provide minimum educational opportunities while wealthier districts can provide far more at lower tax rates.

Furthermore, foundation programs and other types of equalizing mechanisms used by states have frequently been undermined by other state aid provisions that minimize or cancel their equalizing effects. For example, flat grants, minimum aid provisions, or provisions that hold districts harmless against changes in state aid formulas often insure that wealthy districts receive large amounts of aid.[6] Indeed, states such as Connecticut make little pretense of equalization, distributing virtually all state aid as a flat grant.[7] In many states the school finance system is a "porkbarrel" in which a modest amount of state aid is permitted to be used to assist poor districts so long as wealthier districts are able to preserve their natural advantages.

This perception of the problem of school finance and the historic inability of most state legislatures to address the problem rationally have motivated both the scholars, who see the problem as involving a constitutional issue, and the courts which have agreed, to take the position that it is unconstitutional for educational opportunities to be made a function of the size of a school district's tax base. Rather, they suggest that the Constitution requires a

6. See, for example, *San Antonio Independent School District v. Rodriguez*, 411 U.S. 1, 79-81 (1973), Mr. Justice Marshall, dissenting.

7. *Horton v. Meskill*, 332 A.2d 113, 116 (1975).

fiscally neutral educational finance system, one in which educational opportunities in any district are determined by the wealth of the state as a whole.[8]

THE 1971 DECISION IN *Serrano* v. *Priest* (*Serrano* I)

The doctrine of fiscal neutrality was first adopted as a constitutional principle in 1971 in the landmark decision of the California Supreme Court in *Serrano* v. *Priest*.[9] Based upon the great dependence on local property taxes in the California system of financing public schools, which allegedly resulted in wide disparities in expenditures and educational opportunities among school districts, the court stated: "[w]e have determined that [the California] funding scheme invidiously discriminates against the poor because it makes the quality of a child's education a function of the wealth of his parents and neighbors."[10] The court's finding that the California system was unconstitutional was based upon the equal protection provisions of both the federal Constitution and the California constitution. However, the court's analysis relied largely on federal precedent under the Fourteenth Amendment. This legal analysis set the pattern for later school finance cases in both federal and state courts.

The central issue for the court was what standard of review to apply. The "two-level test" of the U.S. Supreme Court for measuring legislative classifications formed the basis for the court's analysis. Under this test classifications such as those affecting economic interests are presumed constitutional and in order to be upheld must merely "bear some rational relationship to a conceivable legitimate state purpose."[11] Where "suspect classifications" (for example, race) or "fundamental interests" (for example, equal voting rights) are involved, however, federal courts have more strictly scrutinized laws or practices which embody such classifications to determine

8. This doctrine was thoroughly explored in John Coons, William Clune, and Stephen Sugarman, *Private Wealth and Public Education* (Cambridge, Mass.: Harvard University Press, 1970) and in Arthur Wise, *Rich Schools, Poor Schools* (Chicago: University of Chicago Press, 1968).

9. *Serrano v. Priest*, 5 Cal. 3d 584, 96 Cal. Rptr. 601, 487 P.2d 1241 (1971).

10. *Serrano v. Priest*, 487 P.2d 1241, 1244.

11. Ibid., p. 1249.

whether they serve some compelling state interest and whether the distinctions in such laws or practices are necessary to further that interest.[12]

The court accepted the plaintiffs' contention that the California system classified school districts on the basis of wealth, measured by the assessed valuation of property per pupil. The court found that allocating more educational dollars to children in certain districts merely because of the "fortuitous presence" of a large commercial and industrial tax base "is to rely on the most irrelevant of factors as the basis for educational financing."[13] Such wealth discrimination, the court held, was constitutionally suspect.

The plaintiffs had also suggested that the court should condemn this discrimination because it affected an interest (education), which should be considered constitutionally fundamental. The court agreed,[14] finding support in the indispensable role of education in the modern industrial state in (a) determining an individual's chances for economic and social success and (b) in exercising a "unique influence on a child's development as a citizen and his participation in political and community life."[15] The court pointed to the universal relevance of education from which all can benefit and to the fact that it is considered so important to the state as to be made compulsory. Its uniqueness was found to distinguish it from other services.

The state asserted that its interest in promoting local control justified the California system despite its conceded inequities. The court found that the system was not necessary to promote local administrative control. It further found that it did not need to decide whether decentralized financial decision making is a compelling state interest since such control is a "cruel illusion" for poor districts that "cannot freely choose to tax [themselves] into an excellence which [their] tax rolls cannot provide."[16] Such control was a prerogative of the rich districts alone. The court pointed

12. Ibid.
13. Ibid., pp. 1252-53.
14. Ibid., pp. 1255-59.
15. Ibid., pp. 1255-56.
16. Ibid., p. 1260.

to the plaintiffs' allegation that property-poor Baldwin Park taxed itself at over twice the rate of wealthy Beverly Hills, but was able to spend only about half as much as Beverly Hills.[17] Because of the sweeping pronouncements of the California Supreme Court, it was widely assumed that the *Serrano* case was over. The California court, however, ruled only on the plaintiffs' allegations.[18] Consequently, the court merely held that the complaint stated a claim which plaintiffs still had to prove. Following that decision, the case was remanded to the superior court for trial.

LITIGATION FOLLOWING *Serrano I*

In the months following the 1971 *Serrano* decision, over thirty cases were filed challenging schemes of school finance in other states.[19] These cases were about evenly divided between federal and state courts. Rulings applying the doctrine of *Serrano* quickly followed in federal district courts in Minnesota and Texas.[20] State trial courts in Arizona, Kansas, and New Jersey followed suit.[21] In Michigan, the state supreme court took original jurisdiction and, in an action filed by the governor, ruled the Michigan system unconstitutional.[22] In Wyoming, the supreme court rejected a school district consolidation plan because of the inequalities in taxable

17. Ibid.

18. The state trial court in which the plaintiffs had filed had dismissed the complaint and this decision had been affirmed by the California appellate court.

19. See *A Summary of Statewide School Finance Cases* (Washington, D.C.: Lawyers' Committee for Civil Rights under Law, 1974).

20. *Van Dusartz v. Hatfield*, 334 F. Supp. 870 (D. Minn., 1971); *Rodriguez v. San Antonio Independent School District*, 337 F. Supp. 280 (W.D. Tex. 1972) *rev'd*, 411 U.S. 1 (1973).

21. *Hollins v. Shofstall*, No. C-253652 (Super. Ct. Ariz., 1972), *rev'd*, 110 Ariz. 88, 515 P.2d 590 (1973); *Caldwell v. Kansas*, No. 50616 (Dist. Ct. Kans., decided August 30, 1972); *Robinson v. Cahill*, 118 N.J. Super. 223, 287 A.2d 187 (1972), aff'd as modified 62 N.J. 473, 303 A.2d 273 (1973). A New York trial court ruled the New York system constitutional. *Spano v. Board of Education of Lakeland School District No. 1*, 68 Misc. 2d 804, 328 N.Y.S. 2d 229 (Sup. Ct., Westchester County, 1972).

22. *Milliken v. Green*, 389 Mich. 1, 203 N.W.2d 457 (1972), vac'd 390 Mich. 389, 212 N.W.2d 711 (1973).

wealth per pupil between districts that would result from its implementation.[23]

The initial ground swell of judicial activity following *Serrano* was quickly levelled by a quirk concerning the choice of courts in *Rodriguez*, the Texas suit. The case had been tried and won before a three-judge federal court. A direct appeal could be taken from a decision of a three-judge court to the U.S. Supreme Court, bypassing the circuit court of appeals. The State of Texas appealed, placing the issue squarely before the U.S. Supreme Court before the seed of reform in school finance had had an opportunity to germinate adequately in the lower courts.

*Rodriguez.* In *San Antonio Independent School District* v. *Rodriguez* the Supreme Court divided sharply on the issue of whether wealth-based inequalities in the Texas system of school finance violated the equal protection clause of the Fourteenth Amendment.[24] Mr. Justice Powell, writing for the five-member majority, completely undermined the federal constitutional basis for *Serrano* and the decisions in other pending cases challenging inequalities in school finance. This had the effect of placing the issue of inequities in school finance squarely in the lap of state courts, under state constitutional provisions. The broad sweep of the majority opinion virtually barred the doors of the federal courts to school finance cases and much other litigation challenging educational inequities and other inequalities burdening the poor. Moreover, the issues dividing the majority and the four dissenters became the framework for consideration of school finance inequalities in subsequent state court proceedings.

The first issue for Justice Powell was what standard of review to apply in measuring the constitutional impact of the Texas interdistrict inequalities. The Court held that education is not a fundamental interest because it is not a right "explicitly or implicitly

---

23. *Sweetwater County Planning Commission v. Hinkle*, 491 P.2d 1234 (Sup. Ct. Wyo., 1971), juris. relinquished, 493 P.2d 1050 (Sup. Ct. Wyo., 1972).

24. *San Antonio Independent School District v. Rodriguez*, 411 U.S. 1 (1973).

guaranteed by the Constitution"[25] and that, therefore, the constitutionality of the classification would be determined by applying the "minimum-rationality" standard. In contrast, Justices Brennan, Douglas, and Marshall, in their dissenting opinions, agreed with the *Serrano* decision that education should be considered fundamental because of its relation to participation in the electoral process and the rights of free speech and association.[26] The dissenting Justices also argued that the "minimum-rationality" test adopted by the majority was inconsistent with the Court's past recognition of the fundamentality of certain interests not implicitly or explicitly guaranteed by the Constitution, for example, the right to procreate,[27] the right to vote in state elections,[28] and the right to appeal from a criminal conviction.[29] These are rights which the Court has recognized as fundamental even though they do not spring from the text of the Constitution itself.

Justice Powell, writing for the majority, found that district wealth was not a suspect classification for purposes of the federal Constitution, in part because the "class of disadvantaged 'poor' cannot be identified in customary equal protection terms."[30] The Court also characterized the deprivation here as relative rather than absolute in an attempt to distinguish inequalities in educational opportunities from previous decisions involving wealth-related deprivations.[31] In response, Mr. Justice Marshall accused the majority of attempting to rewrite constitutional history by denying that in past cases the deprivations resulting from poverty often had been relative rather than absolute.[32]

25. Ibid., p. 33.

26. Ibid., pp. 62-3, 110-117.

27. *Skinner v. Oklahoma*, 316 U.S. 535 (1942).

28. *Reynolds v. Sims*, 377 U.S. 533 (1964).

29. *Griffin v. Illinois*, 351 U.S. 12 (1966); *San Antonio Independent School District v. Rodriguez*, 411 U.S. 1, 99-103.

30. *San Antonio Independent School District v. Rodriguez*, 411 U.S. 1, 19.

31. Ibid., pp. 18-29.

32. Ibid., pp. 117-120. For example, the lack of a transcript in *Griffin v. Illinois*, 351 U.S. 12 (1956) did not prevent appellate review of the criminal conviction, nor did the lack of counsel on appeal in *Douglas v. California*, 372 U.S. 353 (1963) impose a bar to an appeal.

The majority rejected the contention that discrimination based upon district wealth would trigger strict judicial scrutiny.[33] While conceding that district poverty may not create the same stigma as personal poverty, Justice Marshall's dissent argued that the local district wealth bore no relationship to the interests of school children in education and was a factor determining educational opportunities over which "the disadvantaged individual has no significant control."[34] Moreover, in contrast to other decisions in which individual poverty is produced by the private sector, wealth discrimination among school districts is much more the result of governmental action.[35]

Finding that the Texas system neither created a suspect classification nor infringed upon constitutional protected rights, the Court refused to subject the system's wealth-produced inequalities to searching judicial scrutiny. Having made this decision, Justice Powell did not recognize any intermediate standard of judicial review between strict scrutiny and the least searching standard of review, which merely requires that classifications "be shown to bear some rational relationship to legitimate state purposes."[36] Justice Marshall criticized the majority for ignoring the intermediate standard which the Court has applied in other contexts. Previous cases had evidenced the application of a "spectrum of standards" for review of alleged discrimination. This sliding scale of judicial scrutiny has depended "on the constitutional and societal importance of the interest adversely affected and the recognized invidiousness of the basis upon which the particular classification is drawn" balanced against the "asserted state interests in support of the classification."[37]

Ignoring any intermediate tests, the Court proceeded to apply

33. *San Antonio Independent School District v. Rodriguez,* 411 U.S. 1, 25-29.

34. Ibid., p. 122.

35. Ibid., pp. 123-24.

36. Ibid., p. 40.

37. Ibid., pp. 98-99. Indeed, Justice Powell appeared to have adopted this test in speaking for the Court in *Weber v. Aetna Casualty and Surety Co.,* 406 U.S. 164, 173 (1972).

the more lenient "rational basis" standard. Under this test, the Court found the Texas school finance system rationally related to the promotion of local control, which was not undermined by the existence of "some inequality" in the manner in which this objective was achieved.[38] Mr. Justice Stewart's indictment of the system as "chaotic and unjust," while at the same time concurring in the majority opinion, set the stage for the dissenters' attack on the Texas system as having no rational basis to sustain it.[39] Justice White could find no rational relationship between the Texas system and the state's asserted interest in the promotion of local control because the system effectively denied local control to property-poor districts.[40] The majority had "stacked the deck" by framing the local control issue in terms of the state's power to permit political subdivisions to "tax local property to supply revenue for local interests."[41] In fact, under state law education is almost universally considered a constitutional function of state government and school districts are generally considered agents of the state, not units of local government, for carrying out this constitutional duty.[42] The Court thus failed to make a distinction between frequent popular perceptions of education serving local interests and the actual legal relationship between school districts and the state.

*Rodriguez* returned the issue of school finance to the states. In an apparent attempt to minimize the impact of the majority opinion, Justice Marshall advised that "[o]f course nothing in the court's decision today should inhibit further review of state educational funding schemes under state constitutional provisions."[43]

*Serrano II. Rodriguez* was decided before the *Serrano* trial. Consequently the first issue for the state trial court was whether

38. *San Antonio Independent School District v. Rodriguez*, 411 U.S. 1, 50-51.

39. Ibid., p. 59.

40. Ibid., pp. 63-70; see Justice Marshall, dissenting, 411 U.S. 1, 126-30.

41. Ibid., p. 40.

42. See, for example, *Barth v. School District of Philadelphia*, 143 A.2d 909 (Pa. Sup. Ct. 1958) and cases collected in LeRoy J. Peterson, Richard A. Rossmiller, and Marvin M. Volz, *The Law and Public School Operation* (New York: Harper and Row, 1969), pp. 33-34, 43-44, 159.

43. *San Antonio Independent School District v. Rodriguez*, 411 U.S. 1 133 n. 100.

the 1971 decision of the California Supreme Court in *Serrano* was independently based upon the equal protection provisions of the California constitution.[44] The trial court answered in the affirmative and pointed out that the California constitution, unlike the federal Constitution, requires the financing of public schools. Having made this determination, the court saw itself as bound in large part by the determinations made earlier by the California Supreme Court that it is unconstitutional to make educational opportunity a function of district wealth. Two major questions, however, remained for resolution by the trial court: (a) Did SB 90, a school finance reform measure enacted after *Serrano I*, eliminate the unconstitutional features of the California system? and (b) What was the proper measure for determining whether wealth-caused inequalities in educational expenditures produced unequal educational opportunities?

SB 90 had substantially raised the foundation level of the state aid formula and had placed certain limitations on increases in expenditures which were designed to permit poor districts, over time, to increase expenditures more than wealthier districts. Substantial wealth-caused disparities, however, were actually perpetuated by SB 90. High-wealth districts continued to receive basic aid payments; it would have taken up to twenty years for expenditures in rich and poor districts to converge; and districts could override expenditure limitations by voter referenda.[45] The court found that because of these inherent deficiencies, the unconstitutional features of the present system had not been eliminated by SB 90.

The defendants had asserted that the plaintiffs should not prevail unless they could prove that additional expenditures would raise the standardized achievement test scores of children in low-spending poor districts. Even though the court agreed that some evidence showed a positive relationship between increased expenditures and student achievement, it rejected this relationship as a test of unequal educational opportunities. Rather, the court

44. *Serrano v. Priest*, No. 938,254 (Los Angeles Super. Ct., Memoranda re Intended Decision, April 10, 1974).

45. Voted overrides were of substantially greater benefit to wealthy districts than to poor districts.

held that educational opportunities should be measured by the educational inputs or offerings that school districts make available to their students. Educational offerings were demonstrably inferior in the low-wealth, low-spending districts.

Consequently, on April 10, 1974 the Los Angeles Superior Court held the California school finance system unconstitutional. In its subsequent judgment the court gave the state six years to reduce wealth-caused disparities between school districts in per pupil expenditures (apart from categorical special need programs) to less than $100 per pupil.[46] The state was given the same length of time to reduce wealth-related variations in tax rates to "nonsubstantial variations."[47]

Wealthy school districts, which had intervened as defendants, appealed from the decision of the trial court, giving the California Supreme Court an opportunity to reconsider *Serrano I* in light of *Rodriguez*.[48] On December 30, 1976, the California Supreme Court affirmed the finding of the trial court that the school finance system was unconstitutional.[49] In declining to reach the same result as the U.S. Supreme Court in *Rodriguez*, the California court asserted the "independent vitality" of the equal protection provisions of the California constitution. It thus became the first state supreme court to hold that unequal educational opportunities among districts are unconstitutional under the equal protection provisions of a state constitution, unaided by the Fourteenth Amendment.

While the court could have applied the same analysis as in *Rodriguez* to find that education was a constitutionally fundamental interest, because it is explicitly mandated by the state constitution, it declined to do so. The court, however, did find education to be of fundamental importance. The treatment of education in the constitution, although a significant consideration, was

46. Judgment entered August 30, 1974, paragraph 3(c).

47. Ibid., paragraph 3(d).

48. None of the state defendants championed the system's constitutionality in this second appeal. The state treasurer, Ivy Baker Priest, filed a notice of appeal but this was subsequently abandoned by her successor, Jesse Unruh, who filed a brief in support of plaintiffs.

49. *Serrano v. Priest*, 45 U.S.L.W. 2340 (*Serrano II*).

not conclusive of this result. Rather, the court held that "strict and searching judicial scrutiny" would be given to "legislative classifications which, because of their impact on those individual rights and liberties which lie at the core of our free and representative form of government, are properly considered 'fundamental.' "[50] Moreover, the court agreed with the assessment of the trial court that the asserted state interest purporting to justify the present system, that is, local control, was "chimerical from the standpoint of those districts which are less favored in terms of taxable wealth per pupil."[51] Although finding it unnecessary to consider whether, applying the rational relationship standard, the finance system violated the equal protection provisions, the court observed that it perceived "no rational relationship between the asserted governmental end of maximizing local initiative in a system which provides realistic options to exercise such initiative only in proportion to district wealth per ADA [average daily attendance]."[52]

In affirming the findings of the trial court, the California Supreme Court rejected the defendant's assertion that up to 10 percent of total state and local education revenues should be permitted to be outside of any state aid formula which equalized for differences among districts in taxable wealth. It also rejected the argument that educational quality should be defined in terms of performance on statewide achievement tests, and agreed with the trial court that "[t]here is a distinct relationship between cost and the quality of educational opportunities afforded."[53] Indeed, except for the standard for determining "fundamental interests," the California Supreme Court affirmed completely the judgment of the trial court that the school finance system was unconstitutional.

OTHER FISCAL NEUTRALITY RULINGS SINCE *Rodriguez*

Most states have equal protection provisions, and all but two have clauses in their state constitutions which require the state to

50. Ibid., Slip Op., pp. 63-64. The court also found that district wealth in this case was a suspect classification.

51. Ibid., p. 65.

52. Ibid., pp. 66-67, n. 49.

53. Ibid., pp. 36-44, 26.

provide public schools.[54] In the wake of *Rodriguez, Serrano* has been the leading state case on the issue of fiscal neutrality. This does not mean that other state courts have been silent. These other courts have ruled both ways on plaintiffs' claims that educational finance systems that saddle children in tax-poor districts with low expenditures, while advantaging those in high-wealth districts, are unconstitutional under the education clause and equal protection provisions of state constitutions.

In *Horton v. Meskill,* a Connecticut trial court held the Connecticut school finance system unconstitutional because it discriminated on the basis of district wealth, and this judgment has been affirmed by the Connecticut Supreme Court.[55] The heavy reliance of Connecticut school districts on unequal endowments of property wealth, combined with state aid that is largely distributed as a nonequalizing flat grant, resulted in substantial inequalities in expenditures among districts. The court found this system to violate the state equal protection provision because of the explicit constitutional protection given education under the state constitution. Here, the court applied the same test for fundamental interests as *Rodriguez.* The court also determined that education is a state duty, that the delegation of that duty to local school districts "does not discharge it,"[56] and that any legislation that delegates this duty to local units must be "appropriate" under the requirement that the state's education duty shall be implemented by "appropriate legislation."[57] The court found that the disparities inherent in the Connecticut scheme for school finance made it inappropriate legislation for discharging the state's duty.

By narrow margins, supreme courts in several other states have failed to declare their school finance systems unconstitutional. Challenges to discrimination arising from differences in wealth in Idaho and Washington met this fate.

54. These state constitutional provisions are collected in *State Constitutional Provisions and Selected Materials Relating to Public School Finance* (Washington, D.C.: U.S. Department of Health, Education, and Welfare, 1973).

55. *Horton v. Meskill,* 31 Conn. Sup. 377, 332 A.2d 813 (1974), aff'd 38 *Connecticut Law Journal* No. 42 (Conn. Sup. Ct., April 19, 1977).

56. Ibid., p. 116.

57. Connecticut Constitution, Article VIII, section 1.

In *Thompson* v. *Engelking* the Idaho Supreme Court, dividing three to two, upheld Idaho's educational finance system.[58] The majority reversed a decision of a state trial court, which had held the system unconstitutional for failure to insure a "general, uniform, and thorough" system as required by Article IX, Section 1 of the Idaho constitution.[59] Several factors permitted the majority to reject the findings and conclusions of the trial court. First, the trial record, which consisted of only documentary evidence, appeared "sketchy and incomplete"[60] and contained no evidence with respect to the harm to children from unequal expenditures. Second, the trial court opinion did not make clear to what extent the system denied "equal educational opportunities" because of expenditure variance related to disparities in district wealth or inequalities caused by other factors.

The two dissenting justices based their disagreement with the majority on their belief that education is a fundamental interest because of its special place in the Idaho constitution: they would have found the wealth-related inequalities among districts to violate the equal protection provision of the state constitution.[61]

In *Northshore School District No. 417* v. *Kinnear*, a sharply divided Washington Supreme Court turned aside a fiscal neutrality challenge to inequalities in expenditures resulting from differences in the wealth of districts.[62] The six members of the court that made up the majority could agree on only one thing: that plaintiffs had failed to prove their case. Only three of the nine justices unqualifiedly endorsed the present system as constitutional. In rejecting the plaintiff's claim under the equal protection provision of the constitution of the State of Washington, Chief Justice Hale, writing for these three justices, stated that this provision should be construed like the Fourteenth Amendment, while ignoring the test for fundamental interests applied in *Rodriguez*.

58. *Thompson v. Engelking*, 537 P.2d 635 (1975).

59. Civil No. 47055 (Ada County District Court, Nov. 16, 1973).

60. *Thompson v. Engelking*, 437 P.2d 635, 640-41.

61. Ibid., pp. 658-71.

62. *Northshore School District No. 417 v. Kinnear*, 84 Wash. 2d 685, 530 P.2d 178 (1974).

The plaintiffs in *Northshore* also challenged the system on the basis of the education article of the state constitution, which made it a "paramount duty of the state to make ample provision for education of all children residing within its borders, without distinction or preference on account of race, color, caste, or sex"[63] and mandated the legislature to "provide for a general and uniform system of public schools."[64] Chief Justice Hale disposed of the "ample provision" argument with the assertion that there was no proof that the state had ever failed to discharge this duty.[65] He dealt with the terms "uniform and general" by interpreting them as only mandating some "minimum" level of education.[66]

The plaintiffs in *Northshore* did not show to what extent inequalities in educational expenditures per pupil resulted in unequal educational opportunities for the school children affected. It was only on this point, that is, the absence of evidence showing harm to children's education, that two of the three concurring justices could agree with the three-member plurality.[67] Because of the plaintiffs' failure to show that harm resulted from inequalities in expenditure, these two concurring justices agreed that the plaintiffs had not proved their case. They expressed their personal opinion, however, that the state was in fact not providing an ample opportunity for all students and that the contribution of the state to the cost of educating children was inadequate.[68] In this regard the concurring justices appeared closer to the dissenters than the plurality—and thus kept the court's door open for future cases.

Under the constitutional test proposed by the three dissenting

63. Washington Constitution, Article IX, section 1.

64. Ibid., section 2.

65. *Northshore School District No. 417 v. Kinnear*, 530 P.2d 178, 184.

66. Ibid., p. 202. The court strained the plain meaning of the word "uniform," which on its face is most reasonably interpreted as a specific equal protection requirement pertaining to education. As one commentator has stated, "the generality and uniformity clause relates to interparty fairness in the allocation of whatever educational resources the state provides. A system which is minimally adequate could still be nonuniform." William R. Anderson, "School Finance Litigation in Washington: The Northshore Litigation and Beyond," *Washington Law Review* 50 (March 1975): 853, 892.

67. *Northshore School District No. 417 v. Kinnear*, 530 P.2d 178, 203-204 (opinion of Justice Rosellini concurring in the result).

68. Ibid., p. 203.

justices, the record abundantly supported the unconstitutionality of
the school finance system of Washington state. The dissenting
opinion found that the education provisions of the state constitution created an absolute right to an ample education. It found a
requirement of equality of treatment both in the provision for
ampleness and in the mandate for a "general and uniform system
of public schools."[69] It found that discrepancies in dollar input per
pupil were highly relevant to the measurement of the quality of
education children receive, and that the state's heavy reliance on
special voter-approved levies for meeting operating costs deprived
children in low-wealth school districts of equality of treatment.
The dissenters refused to believe that the constitutional level of
ampleness was merely the expenditure per pupil of the lowest-
spending district in the state.[70] One of the justices who concurred
in this dissent also put forth the view that the state was constitutionally required to finance directly the basic operating and maintenance budget of schools, and could not make this depend on the
whims of local voters.[71]

The only unqualified defeat for the plaintiffs occurred at the
hands of the Oregon Supreme Court in *Olsen* v. *Oregon*.[72] Con-

69. Ibid., p. 218.

70. Ibid., p. 220.

71. Ibid., p. 224 (Justice Utter concurring in the dissent).

72. *Olsen v. Oregon*, 276 Oreg. 9, 554 P.2d 139 (1976). Two other state
supreme courts, faced with constitutional challenges to wealth discrimination,
disposed of the claims on the basis of factual peculiarities or legal technicalities without full consideration of the merits. In *Milliken v. Green*, 389 Mich.
1, 203 N.W. 2d 457 (1972), vac'd, 390 Mich. 389, 212 N.W. 2d 711 (1973),
the Michigan Supreme Court originally held the system unconstitutional on
state equal protection grounds, but subsequently, on rehearing, vacated its
order on a technicality. The case was brought by the attorney general and
governor in the state supreme court under the court's original jurisdiction
powers. Without adverting to the merits, it vacated its earlier ruling on the
ground that the governor's request for certification of questions for consideration by the supreme court under its original jurisdiction was improvi-
dently granted. For a more extended discussion of the Michigan saga, see
Elwood Hain, "*Milliken v. Green*: Breaking the Legislative Deadlock," *Law
and Contemporary Problems* 38 (Winter-Spring, 1974): 350. In the interval
between the original decision and its being vacated the Michigan legislature
revised its school finance formula to decrease substantially inequalities related
to tax base. Ibid.

In *Shofstall v. Hollins*, 110 Ariz. 88, 515 P.2d 590 (1973), the Arizona
Supreme Court refused to find the Arizona education finance scheme un-

ceding that the heavy reliance of the Oregon school finance system on local property taxes, taken in combination with significant differences in assessed valuation per pupil among districts, produced wide disparities in expenditures and "substantial deficiencies in educational opportunities," the court viewed the state's interest in promoting local fiscal control as the sole and sufficient prop for the constitutionality of the system, even while agreeing that poor districts had significantly less local control than wealthy districts.

The court refused to follow Justice Powell's *Rodriguez* test for fundamental interests, opting instead for an equal protection test under the state constitution which balanced the "detriment to the education of the children of certain districts against the ostensible justification for the scheme of school financing." [73] The court's actual basis for refusing to find the system unconstitutional on equal protection grounds, however, appears to be its fear of undermining the legitimacy of wealth-related disparities in the distribution of other service facilities, for example, police and fire protection and paved streets. [74]

The court read the term "uniform" in the education clause of the state constitution [75] as insuring only minimum educational opportunities in a district. It concluded, without discussion, that

---

constitutional, but its ruling was limited by a quirk in the trial court's finding. In ruling on cross motions for summary judgment, the trial court had found that there was no evidence that the finance system discriminated against children. Instead, it held the system unconstitutional because it discriminated against taxpayers. Consequently, under the trial court's formulation the issue for resolution by the Arizona Supreme Court was whether the state could discriminate against taxpayers in the funding of a fundamental interest—education. The supreme court held that it could. In *dicta* the court indicated that it saw education as fundamental only up to some level that assures a basic education. The court also indicated that the suit might be moot because the legislature had prospectively repealed the statutory framework for school financing.

73. *Olsen v. Oregon*, Slip Op., p. 14.

74. Ibid., p. 21. The court noted that the constitution protected home rule for cities and counties in Oregon, but missed the point that this distinguishes services provided by those jurisdictions, such as police and fire protection, from education, which is a state-mandated service.

75. "The Legislative Assembly shall provide by law for the establishment of a uniform, and general system of Common Schools." Oregon Constitution, Article VIII, section 3.

*Robinson* v. *Cahill* (which reached a different result in New Jersey)
was distinguishable on the basis of different constitutional and
legislative histories.[76]

### THE LIMITED NATURE OF THE FISCAL NEUTRALITY DOCTRINE

To understand the doctrine of fiscal neutrality is to understand
more what a school finance system cannot be than what it must be:
educational expenditures, and ultimately educational opportunities,
may not be a function of the size of a school district's tax base.

The doctrine of fiscal neutrality does not require equal expenditures. The state can decide to provide more funds for children
whose circumstances dictate more costly programs or districts with
higher costs. The doctrine does not directly determine how state
aid is to be distributed except that if local districts are permitted
to rely on their local tax bases, the state must eliminate disparities
resulting from districts being unequally endowed with taxable
wealth, for example, by insuring that at any given tax rate all districts can raise the same amount of revenue—a method of funding
often termed "district power equalizing."[77] Of course, a state not
desiring to preserve local fiscal control could fund the educational
system totally from state revenues. The point is that the fiscal neutrality doctrine dictates neither the precise manner in which state
aid must be distributed nor what needs or costs the state must
equally or differentially fund.

Any system of local funding has two elements: (a) the size of
the tax base and (b) the tax rate levied on that base, either or both
of which can vary to produce differences in expenditure per pupil.
Fiscal neutrality deals only with the former variable—the size of
the tax base. The tax rate can still vary. Indeed, one of the virtues
of fiscal neutrality for those anxious to preserve or enhance local
fiscal control is that fiscal neutrality would require such control
to be equally distributed. Once district wealth is eliminated as a
cause of expenditure variation, however, differences in tax effort
may continue to produce significant differences among districts in
expenditures per pupil.

76. *Olsen v. Oregon*, Slip Op., pp. 24-25.

77. See Coons, Clune, and Sugarman, *Private Wealth and Public Education*.

The possibility that this result might occur is not necessarily a criticism of fiscal neutrality per se. Fiscal neutrality clearly would eliminate arbitrary expenditure variations flowing from inequalities in district wealth—a major determinant of educational expenditures in many states today. It would not, however, require the elimination of inequalities in educational opportunities resulting from differences in the abilities or willingness of districts or voters to tax themselves for education. Fiscal neutrality has been criticized because it does not *require* the elimination of expenditure inequalities resulting from fluctuations of the tax rate, and does not *require* higher expenditures in districts with higher costs or districts serving children requiring more intensive levels of service, for example, handicapped children, or educationally disadvantaged children from poor families.[78] In this regard the fiscal neutrality doctrine is no panacea. It does not deal with every inequity in school funding. This recognition does not undermine the validity of the doctrine, since few concede the rationality of making educational opportunities a function of property wealth.

Notwithstanding, the critics are certainly correct in pointing out that other factors in addition to the amount of assessed valuation per pupil are highly relevant to a rational system of educational finance. For example, educational tax rates can vary from district to district for reasons bearing no relation to education. High-income communities may be more willing than their low-income counterparts to tax themselves for education. Large cities in particular have high noneducational costs due to the need to provide additional municipal services because of high concentrations of the poor, the unemployed, and elderly residents. While total local tax rates in big cities are frequently the highest in their states, the high taxes needed to fund noneducational services commonly result in lower than average tax rates for education. This phenomenon of high noneducational costs taking a large bite of local revenues in cities is often referred to as "municipal overburden." Tax rates for education in large cities also are often de-

78. See, for example, defendant's assertions in *Serrano*, summarized in *Serrano II*, Slip Op., pp. 44-50; John E. Coons, "Introduction: Fiscal Neutrality after *Rodriguez*," *Law and Contemporary Problems* 38 (Winter-Spring, 1974): 299.

pressed by the unwillingness of voters in those cities to support public education. Elderly voters, for example, are frequently unwilling to give that support, as are voters whose children are in parochial schools. Similarly, white voters are frequently unwilling to support public education when a majority of the public school children are black or Hispanic-American. Rural areas often have comparable problems: educational tax rates are often depressed by the fact that farmers have a large proportion of their assets tied up in real property and lack the annual income to pay high property taxes.

Furthermore, the fiscal neutrality doctrine does not require the state to respond to the higher costs or greater educational tasks of certain districts.[79] The costs of providing educational services are not generally the same for all districts within a state. Costs in rural areas typically are less than in suburban areas. And extra expenses for security, vandalism, insurance, the maintenance of older buildings, and seniority payments for larger numbers of older and more senior teachers often push the costs of education in central cities above those of surrounding suburbs.[80] The problems of many central city school districts are compounded by having been delegated difficult educational tasks not present in other districts. Central city districts must provide education for large concentrations of children who come from impoverished families and who are behind grade level. These are children who, without intensive educational services, will fall further and further behind their middle-class peers as they proceed through school. Moreover, academic problems are not the only ones with which central cities must cope: many of their children come to school with a vast array of other problems (for example, emotional and nutritional problems) and a higher proportion of their children have well-

79. But see Coons, Clune, and Sugarman, *Private Wealth and Public Education*, p. 310.

80. See Betsy Levin, Thomas Muller, and Corazon Sandoval, *The High Cost of Education in Cities: An Analysis of the Purchasing Power of the Education Dollar* (Washington, D.C.: The Urban Institute 1973) and Norman Drachler, "The Large-City School System: It Costs More to Do the Same," in *Equity for Cities in School Finance Reform* (Washington, D.C.: Potomac Institute, 1973).

recognized handicaps calling for the full range of special educational services.

The fiscal neutrality doctrine does not require that a state respond to these problems in designing a finance system. Given the limited focus of the doctrine, it should not be surprising that other suits should seek direct redress for those inequities which this doctrine does not consider. In the following section cases dealing with educational inequities in school finance systems stemming from the factors described above are considered. The section is headed "Litigation Concerning Resource Inequalities and Inadequacies" because it focuses more directly on the educational resources children actually receive than on equalization of district fiscal capacities, although fiscal capacity is an issue in many of these cases as well.

## Litigation Concerning Resource Inequalities and Inadequacies

Cases in New Jersey, Washington, Ohio, and New York have begun to grapple with the problems not directly addressed in the fiscal neutrality suits. Opinions favorable to plaintiffs have been issued by the New Jersey Supreme Court and a trial court in Washington state, while decisions have not been reached in the other two states.

In *Robinson* v. *Cahill*, the New Jersey Supreme Court struck down the school finance system for violation of a provision of the state constitution that requires the legislature to "provide for the maintenance and support of a thorough and efficient system of free public schools."[81] The school districts involved in *Robinson*

81. *Robinson v. Cahill*, 62 N.J. 473, 303 A.2d 273 (1973). Subsequent proceedings are reported at 63 N.J. 196, 306 A.2d 65 (1973); 67 N.J. 35, 335 A.2d 6 (1975); 69 N.J. 133, 351 A.2d 713 (1975); 69 N.J. 449, 355 A.2d 129 (1976); 70 N.J. 155, 358 A.2d 457 (1976). The trial court had ruled the system unconstitutional on the basis of the equal protection and tax uniformity provisions of the state constitution as well as the education clause. The New Jersey Supreme Court rejected the equal protection and tax uniformity provisions as grounds for unconstitutionality. See 303 A.2d 273, 282-90. The *Robinson* decision is more fully discussed in Paul Tractenberg, "Reforming School Finance through State Constitutions: *Robinson v. Cahill* Points the Way," *Rutgers Law Review* 27 (Winter 1974): 365 and in idem, "*Robinson v. Cahill*: The Thorough and Efficient Clause," *Law and Contemporary Problems* 38 (Winter-Spring 1974): 312.

were not only poor in property wealth per pupil and below average in educational expenditures, but also served urban poor and minority children whose educational achievement was well below state norms.[82] While the effect of district wealth on expenditures was of substantial concern, this was not the only factor producing inequalities among districts that the court treated.

The central issue was whether the system had failed to insure every child a "thorough and efficient" education. The court construed this constitutional phrase as a mandate for "an equal educational opportunity for children."[83] The court found that the constitutional level of equality had not been met "on the basis of discrepancies in dollar input per pupil,"[84] and that a thorough and efficient education "must be understood to embrace that educational opportunity which is needed in the contemporary setting to equip a child for his role as a citizen and as a competitor in the labor market."[85] Thus, "thorough and efficient" is a concept applicable to output or achievement, as well as to input.

The court did not attempt to spell out the details of the educational opportunities which the state must provide. It was not willing, however, to believe that the district with the lowest per pupil expenditure in the state set the standard for the state's constitutional mandate. Rather, it concluded that the state "has never spelled out the content of the constitutionally mandated educational opportunity."[86]

Voter unwillingness or inability to support education appeared to be of as much concern to the court as deficiencies in tax capacity. Once the constitutional obligation is determined, the state, if it continues to rely on local levies, must "compel" districts to raise the funds necessary to provide that educational opportunity.[87]

---

82. The opinion of the New Jersey Supreme Court gives little description of the facts. The trial court, however, goes into some detail concerning the factual circumstances. See *Robinson v. Cahill*, 118 N.J. Super. 223, 287 A.2d 187 (1972).

83. *Robinson v. Cahill*, 303 A.2d 273, 294.

84. Ibid., p. 295.

85. Ibid., pp. 295, 297.

86. Ibid.

87. Ibid., p. 297.

Moreover, the court recognized that the tax base in major cities was overloaded with other demands for local service (municipal overburden), and expressed doubt that the obligation to provide a "thorough and efficient" system of schools "can realistically be met by reliance upon local taxation."[88]

*Robinson* appears to impose a direct obligation on the state to remedy deficiencies in the educational opportunities provided children. The state is obliged to insure that the requisite opportunity is provided, irrespective of a district's disinclination to fund education. Thus, under *Robinson*, neither inadequate tax effort nor an inadequate tax base justifies the failure to provide a "thorough and efficient" education.

The level of educational opportunity that the state must constitutionally provide, either for the state as a whole or for particular children, has not yet been determined. The court made clear that this was the job of the legislative and executive branches.[89] This obligation imposes more than a simple calculation of expenditures per pupil; it also includes determination of the components of such a system, including educational standards, goals, and methods for measuring their accomplishment.[90]

Although the New Jersey Supreme Court ruled that an act passed by the New Jersey legislature in 1975 to replace the school finance provisions struck down by the court in 1973 was constitutional on its face, the court indicated that it would not give further consideration to the state's constitutional obligation until the empirical effects of the new law were known.[91]

The New Jersey courts in *Robinson* were not at all antagonistic toward the fiscal neutrality doctrine; however, the state's constitutional obligation would not necessarily be satisfied with the elimination of wealth-related disparities in expenditures. To the New

---

88. Ibid.

89. See *Robinson v. Cahill,* 69 N.J. 133, 351 A.2d 713, 718-19 (1975).

90. See *Robinson v. Cahill,* 351 A.2d 713, 719 and 355 A.2d 129 (1976). The court did not require strict equality among all districts or children and, further, implied that once the system provides all children with a thorough and efficient education, districts would be permitted to provide additional educational opportunities for their children. See *Robinson v. Cahill,* 303 A.2d 273, 294-5, 298.

91. *Robinson v. Cahill,* 355 A.2d 129, 131-32.

Jersey courts, the state's obligation encompassed more. While the parameters of this obligation have not yet been fully explored, *Robinson* provides the doctrinal foundation for dealing with serious inequities and inadequacies in educational opportunities in addition to those flowing from the size of a district's tax base.

A recent decision from the State of Washington, *Seattle School District No. 1* v. *Washington*,[92] directly addressed the problem created by the refusal of local voters to support the public schools. The failure of state aid to education to keep pace with rising educational costs required Seattle to raise nearly 40 percent of its budget for the 1975-1976 school year from a special excess levy. The voters in Seattle, however, rejected excess levies twice in 1975. These levy failures plunged Seattle into a severe fiscal and educational crisis.[93]

Under the Washington constitution "it is the paramount duty of the state to make ample provision for the education of all children,"[94] and Seattle argued that the state could not fulfill this duty merely by delegating its responsibility to local voters who had no legal obligation to provide funds for Seattle. The state trial court agreed, ruling the Washington educational finance system unconstitutional because it failed to insure sufficient funding for all children to receive a basic program of education. It held that under the constitution the state must either directly fund the basic program of education or provide a dependable and regular tax source for utilization by school districts. Resort to the voters through special excess levies was not a permissible means of discharging the state's duty.[95]

92. *Seattle School District No. 1* v. *Washington*, No. 53950 (Thurston County Super. Ct., Jan. 14, 1977).

93. About 1600 employees received layoff notices. A special act of the legislature reduced the actual layoffs to about 400.

94. Washington Constitution, Article IX, section 1.

95. The court distinguished *Northshore School District No. 417* v. *Kinnear* (see note 62 above) on the ground that a majority of the Washington Supreme Court there could only agree on one proposition—that plaintiffs had failed to sustain the necessary burden of proof on the issue of ample support. *Seattle School District No. 1* v. *Washington*, Slip Op., pp. 3-4.

Like the New Jersey Supreme Court in *Robinson*, the Washington court found that the state had not defined its constitutional obligation concerning education. Ultimately, this determination was for the legislature. In the absence of a legislative definition, however, the court applied three different criteria for determining whether Seattle was able to provide a basic program of education without resort to special excess levy elections: (a) the collective wisdom approach, for example, the pupil-to-staff ratios generally provided in the state; (b) the state board of education's definition of a program of basic education; and (c) the state board's accreditation standards. The court found that without passage of special excess levies, Seattle could not meet any of these presumptive standards for a basic program of education.

In both *Seattle* and *Robinson* the courts have indicated that a "thorough and efficient" or "basic program of education" requires more than minimal educational opportunities.[96] Both courts indicated, however, that the legislature can permit districts to opt for expenditures above the level of the state's obligation.[97] To what extent legislatures will attempt to preserve the inadequacies and inequalities of the present system by attempting to define the state's educational obligation at some bare minimum level, remains to be seen.[98] Such a response would likely produce further litigation.

*Serrano's* fiscal neutrality doctrine does not permit the state, in determining its obligation to equalize the tax capacities of school districts, to distinguish between a basic program of education and educational expenditures which exceed that level. Yet fiscal neutrality does not address the problem faced by Seattle, which is relatively wealthy in assessed valuation per pupil, and where recalcitrant voters were unwilling to support the public schools. There is no

96. If this were not the case, it would have been rather simple for the court merely to assume that districts with the fewest educational resources meet the constitutional mandate.

97. Neither the New Jersey nor the Washington courts have decided whether any district enrichment leeway must be equalized for district wealth differences, although the plurality opinion in *Northshore* (see note 62 above) would permit unequalized excess expenditures.

98. One commentator fears that this will occur. See John E. Coons, "Recent Trends in Science Fiction: *Serrano* among the People of Number," *Journal of Law and Education* 23 (January 1977): 36.

inconsistency between the constitutional principles. A state, while insuring a "thorough and efficient" education or a "basic program of education" for all children, could still be called upon to eliminate the effects of tax-based disparities, if districts are permitted to spend above those levels. The justification for permitting districts to spend above those levels could only be the state's interest in promoting local fiscal control. As in *Serrano*, assuming this is an interest worthy of preservation, its exercise should not depend on the fortuity of the size of a district's tax base.

OTHER PENDING CASES

*Board of Education, Cincinnati v. Essex.* In *Board of Education, Cincinnati v. Essex*, the plaintiffs—the Cincinnati Board of Education, school children, parents, and taxpayers—also challenge the delegation of the state's educational obligation to the whim and caprice of local voters.[99] In order to increase property taxes for education, the Cincinnati board must seek voter approval. None of the four tax increase referenda voted on since 1969 has passed. Thus educational revenues in Cincinnati have remained relatively static during a time of sharply rising costs, forcing substantial cutbacks in educational programs and staff. The effect of these cutbacks is exacerbated by the need to provide more intensive educational services for the increasing concentrations of children of low-income and minority families. Moreover, the problems of the school finance system in Ohio are not confined to Cincinnati alone: a number of districts were forced to close their schools early during the 1976-77 school year for lack of funds. Cincinnati faces this prospect in the near future.

The plaintiffs claim that the State of Ohio has failed to provide children with an equal opportunity to obtain a "thorough and efficient" education under the education and equal protection provisions of the Ohio constitution.[100] Plaintiffs argue that a "thorough

99. *Board of Education of the City School District of the City of Cincinnati v. Essex*, No. A 7662725 (Hamilton County Court of Common Pleas, filed April 5, 1976).

100. Like New Jersey, the Ohio constitution requires a "thorough and efficient system of common schools" (Article VI, section 2) and has several equal protection provisions (Article I, section 2 and Article II, section 26).

and efficient" system of education must take into account the differences in educational tasks among school districts (for example,
some have greater concentrations than others of educationally deprived children) and, in measuring the fiscal capacities of school
districts, the system must take into consideration the unavailability
for education of much of the property tax base in large cities because of (a) competing demands (municipal overburden) and
(b) the unwillingness of local voters to support education. The
trial will be completed and a decision is likely by early 1978.

*Board of Education, Levittown v. Nyquist.* In *Board of Education, Levittown v. Nyquist,* a suit which began as a fiscal neutrality challenge, other issues have been raised as a result of the intervention of plaintiffs from three large cities in New York State.[101]
The cities claim that the school finance formula arbitrarily and
inadequately measures local incapacity to support education solely
on the basis of property wealth per pupil. Consequently, the cities
appear wealthy when in fact they are poor due to municipal overburden and to higher school costs, because (a) educational services
cost more in the large cities, and (b) there are high concentrations
of children needing more extensive educational services. As a result
of the state's failure to correct for this fiscal incapacity, the city
districts get less general education aid than districts with fewer
fiscal and educational burdens.

State aid is based on the number of children in average daily
attendance rather than the number enrolled. This basis is challenged
on the grounds that while a high rate of absenteeism deprives the
cities of state funds, they must still budget and plan for all enrolled
children (indeed, the same children are not absent each day) and
must actually spend additional funds for attendance services and
educational remediation needed because of absenteeism. A lengthy
trial has been completed, and a decision is expected toward the
end of 1977.

## Conclusion

Born in state courts, constitutional challenges to inequalities in
educational opportunities caused by statewide school finance sys-

101. *Board of Education, Levittown v. Nyquist,* Index No. 8208/74 (Nassau
County Sup. Ct.).

tems have returned to those courts after a brief foray into federal courts. It had been hoped that the U.S. Supreme Court would be receptive and announce a federal constitutional standard of fiscal neutrality which would eliminate dependency upon a school district's taxable wealth as a determinant of educational opportunities. *Rodriguez* made clear that this was not to be.

The school finance cases which have continued in state courts have emphasized that education is a state, rather than a federal, obligation and that state courts have greater reasons than their federal counterparts to be concerned about discrimination or inadequacy in the distribution of educational resources. Until recently, state courts have been relatively untested on issues pertaining to the rights of individuals, stemming from the establishment by the Warren Court of the federal courts as the chief protectors against government-caused discrimination where important interests or suspect classifications were involved. The era of an "activist" federal judiciary has passed, for the time being at least. Yet in the years immediately after *Rodriguez* was decided, several state courts, in thoroughly prepared challenges to educational finance inequalities, have ruled their finance systems unconstitutional. Even courts which have not gone this far have shown that these issues are likely to merit serious consideration.

Furthermore, legislative reform in a number of states has demonstrated that the barriers to reform are not conceptual or technical.[102] Alternatives to equitable finance systems are no longer untried, thus making untenable the argument that the status quo had to be maintained in the absence of any viable alternatives.

The substantial inequalities in educational opportunities among school districts resulting from state decisions about how to finance elementary and secondary education are a consequence of often separable but overlapping problems, for example, inequalities in district wealth, disequalizing formulas for state aid, unequal educational tasks, municipal overburden, and local voter disinterest in

---

102. For summaries of recent school finance reform in state legislatures, see *School Finance Reform: A Legislator's Handbook* (Washington, D.C. National Conference of State Legislatures, 1976) and W. Norton Grubb, "The First Round of Legislative Reforms in the Post-*Serrano* World," *Law and Contemporary Problems* 38 (Winter-Spring 1974): 459.

public education. Generally, litigation has not dealt with all of these at once. In no case, however, has judicial treatment of one issue precluded a rational response to others. In this regard school finance is not substantially different from many other areas, for example, a judicial pronouncement with respect to racial discrimination generally neither resolves nor precludes resolution of the sex or age discrimination claims of others.

The precise future of school finance litigation is difficult to chart, involving as it does the judicial systems in many different states. To a great extent this is in the hands of state legislatures. A satisfactory response by the legislative branch to irrational inequalities in educational opportunities caused, for example, by the fortuity of a district's taxable wealth or by the fiscal and educational deficiencies of districts serving concentrations of poor and minority children, would obviate the need for litigation. To the extent that legislatures do not meet the challenge, they confirm the need for litigation to insure that the educational obligation of a state under its constitution is more than a disregarded platitude and political football.

# CHAPTER X

# Educational Malpractice: One Jurisdiction's Response

DAVID A. ABEL AND LINDSAY A. CONNER

## Introduction

Can a student recover damages from his school district for his failure to learn because of teacher negligence?[1] The California courts have recently offered an answer to this question. The question of recovery in tort for educationl malpractice was first posed in 1972.[2] A recent high school graduate, alias Peter Doe, filed a complaint with a California superior court, asserting that after thirteen years of regular attendance in the San Francisco public school system he was functionally illiterate.[3] Peter Doe alleged that his inability to read and write resulted from, among other accusations, the negligence of his instructors. Plaintiff Doe asked the court to hold the school district liable to him and award him in excess of $500,000.

The trial judge dismissed the above case without opinion, sustaining the defendant school district's demurrer (a motion con-

1. See David Abel, "Can a Student Sue the Schools for Educational Malpractice?" *Harvard Educational Review* 44 (November 1974): 416-36.

2. A tort is a civil wrong for which the court will provide a remedy in the form of an action for damages. The primary function of the law of torts is to determine when loss shall be shifted from one to another and when it shall be allowed to remain where it has fallen. Malpractice is defined as "any professional misconduct or any unreasonable lack of skill or fidelity in the performance of professional or fiduciary duties; . . . objectionable or wrong practice; . . . practice contrary to rule." *Board of Examiners of Veterinary Medicine v. Mohr*, 485 P. 2d 235 (1971).

3. The Original Complaint was filed November 20, 1972. The plaintiff's First Amended Complaint, *Peter Doe v. San Francisco United School District*, No. 653-312 (Cal. Super. Ct., September 6, 1974), which is considered here, was filed October 31, 1973 and is hereinafter cited as *Complaint*.

tending that even if all of the plaintiff's factual charges are true, they are insufficient in law to support the plaintiff's action.) A court of appeal upheld the ruling of the superior court,[4] and on September 29, 1976, the California Supreme Court declined the plaintiff's request for a hearing.[5] Thus, to the question of recovering for educational malpractice, the California courts have for the present answered "no."

*Doe* v. *San Francisco Unified School District* raises legal and policy questions that are the subject of this chapter. Should a school district be held liable in damages to a functionally illiterate student, if that student's educational deficiencies are the result of the negligence of school personnel? What professional obligations do schools legally have to their students? Are the courts an appropriate forum in which to assess negligence in meeting those obligations? Could the quality of instruction be improved through such legal action?

We address these questions by first examining the legal issues raised by the plaintiff's complaint and by the defendant's demurrer. We then move to a consideration of the plaintiff's appeal and the appellate court's reasons for rejecting that appeal. After discussing the legal implications of the court's rulings and the potential for future educational malpractice actions, we conclude with an assessment of the policy implications of such litigations.

## Peter Doe's Complaint

The plaintiff, Peter Doe, graduated from high school in 1972. School records indicate that he is Caucasian, that his intelligence is average or slightly higher, and that he was never involved in any serious disciplinary action. He maintained an average attendance record throughout his school career and received average grades. While Peter was enrolled in the public schools, his parents made repeated attempts to secure accurate information about his educational progress. In response to these inquiries, school employees repeatedly offered assurances that the plaintiff was per-

---

4. *Peter Doe v. San Francisco Unified School District,* 60 C.A. 3d 814 (1976.)

5. 131 Cal. Rptr. 854 (1976).

forming at or near grade level and that no special, remedial, or compensatory instruction was necessary.

Shortly after graduation, Peter's parents had him examined by two reading specialists who separately concluded that the young man was a functional illiterate: he had a reading and writing ability of approximately fifth-grade level at the time of his graduation. The plaintiff could not, for example, read a job application or fill out the forms an auto accident might require; he felt inadequate to hold any job in which reading was demanded. This prompted his mother, a college graduate, to seek legal counsel.[6] Her son began to receive private tutoring and made significant improvement in his reading level—two grade levels in the first eight months of special work.

Citing these facts, Peter Doe's attorneys drafted a complaint against the San Francisco public schools relying upon, among other legal theories, the common law tort of negligence.[7] The plaintiff in *Doe* specifically contended that the school system negligently and carelessly "failed to use reasonable care in the discharge of its [common law] duties to provide plaintiff with adequate instruction, guidance, counseling and/or supervision . . . and to exercise the degree of professional skill required of an ordinary prudent educator."[8] The plaintiff claimed that such conduct amounted to professional malpractice, and sought to hold the defendant liable for the foreseeable consequences of such negligence. Specifically, he alleged in his complaint that the school district, through its employees:

1. negligently and carelessly failed to take notice of plaintiff's reading disabilities, despite evidence found in plaintiff's reading test scores, class performance, and parental inquiries from which defendants with exercise of reasonable care knew or should have known the existence of plain-

6. Doe's mother went to see an attorney who filed a private damage claim and referred the plaintiff to an attorney with the Youth Law Center of San Francisco, who then acted as Doe's advocate throughout the course of the case.

7. In addition to the general negligence claim, Doe also asserted misrepresentation and breach of constitutional and statutory duty. See Gary Saretsky, "The Strangely Significant Case of Peter Doe," *Phi Delta Kappan* 54 (May 1973): 589-92.

8. *Complaint*, p. 6.

tiff's severe reading disabilities, disabilities from which serious injury
to plaintiff would follow with near certainty unless adequate and competent reading instruction was promptly provided to him;

2. negligently and carelessly assigned plaintiff to classes where the
books and other materials were too difficult for a student of plaintiff's
reading ability to read, when defendants knew, or with the exercise
of reasonable care should have known, that said books and other
materials were too difficult for a student of plaintiff's reading ability to
read, comprehend, or benefit from;

3. negligently and carelessly allowed plaintiff to pass and advance from
a course or grade level although the defendants knew, or with the exercise of reasonable care and skill should have known, that plaintiff had
not achieved the knowledge, understanding or skills required for completion of said course or grade level and necessary for him to succeed
or benefit from subsequent courses;

4. negligently and carelessly assigned plaintiff to classes with instructors
not qualified or unable to teach the particular subject, and to classes not
geared toward students with his reading abilities and disabilities; and

5. negligently and carelessly permitted plaintiff to graduate from high
school although he was unable to read above the eighth-grade level, as
required by Education Code Section 8573, effective on the date of plaintiff's graduation from high school, thereby depriving him of additional
instruction in reading and other academic skills.[9]

Doe contended that except for the negligent acts and omissions
of the defendants, he would have attained an eighth-grade reading
ability prior to his graduation from high school. The suit claimed
that as a direct result of these acts and omissions, Doe (a) graduated
with only a fifth-grade reading ability; (b) suffered a loss of
earning capacity because of his limited ability to read and write;
(c) was unqualified for any employment other than the most
demeaning, unskilled, low-paid manual labor which requires little
or no ability to read or write; and (d) suffered mental distress,
pain, and suffering. Therefore, the plaintiff charged that the
defendants had injured him and were liable under tort law, and

---

9. Ibid., pp. 7-8. Section 8573 of the California Education Code, effective
on the date of the plaintiff's graduation from high school, in effect required
school districts to adopt standards for high school graduation which would
require that students graduating from high school demonstrate competence
in reading at an 8.0 grade equivalency or have taken a one-semester reading
course focusing on diagnostic and remedial instruction. Interestingly enough,
shortly after the institution of the Doe suit, the statute was amended to
specify that an eighth-grade level of proficiency in reading is not mandatory.

asked for $500,000 in general damages, plus private tutoring, court costs, and any other relief the court deemed just.

## Obstacles to Obtaining a Hearing

No reported case has allowed public school students to recover for loss of educational benefits resulting from teacher negligence. Two formidable legal obstacles explain the absence of such precedent. The first is the common law doctrine of sovereign immunity, under which policy a public entity is immune from tort liability for the negligent acts of its agents or employees, unless it consents to such a suit. The second obstacle involves the historical aversion of courts to considering novel applications of negligence concepts where judges fear that problems in establishing standards of negligence and proving injury and causation will lead to fraudulent claims and a flood of litigation.

### SOVEREIGN IMMUNITY

The principle that the state is not liable for damages if injuries result from the negligence of its officers, agents, and employees is deeply embedded in the common law.[10] In its pure form, the doctrine of nonliability renders a state immune from liability from tort unless its consent is granted by laws permitting suit. School districts, as state agents, traditionally have enjoyed this immunity and so have protected themselves from legal attack.[11]

In recent years, however, the doctrine of sovereign immunity

---

10. The origins of the principle lie in the sixteenth century belief in the divine right of kings and in the allied concepts later enunciated by Blackstone: "The King can do no wrong. The King, moreover, is not only incapable of doing wrong, but even of thinking wrong; he can never mean to do an improper thing; in him there is no folly or weakness." William Knaak, *School District Tort Liability in the 70s* (St. Paul, Minn.: Marric Publishing Co., 1969), p. 8, quoting Sir William Blackstone, *Commentaries on the Laws of England* (London: A. Strahan, T. Cadell, et al., 1787). On the relation of the principle to common law, see William Prosser, *Handbook of the Law of Torts*, 4th ed. (St. Paul, Minn.: West Publishing Co., 1971), p. 970; also, see generally Edwin Bouchard, "Governmental Responsibility in Tort," *Yale Law Journal* 40 (June 1956): 759-813.

11. Prosser, *Handbook*, p. 395; John Mancke, "Liability of School Districts for the Negligent Acts of Their Employees," *Journal of Law and Education* 1 (January 1972): 110. See also Lee Garber and Eugene Benedetti, *The Law and the Teacher in California* (Danville, Ill.: Interstate Printers and Publishers, 1967), p. 146.

has been eroded. State courts and legislatures have recognized that invocation of sovereign immunity may bar relief where justice and common sense demand it. Although the doctrine still is used in some states, the national trend is to limit its application, and almost all of the states have found some means to insure governmental responsibility.[12]

Fortunately for Peter Doe, California has gone farthest in delimiting the application of sovereign immunity.[13] In *Muskopf v. Corning Hospital District,* the California Supreme Court traced the history of the doctrine of governmental immunity, found the doctrine to be "an anachronism without rational basis," which "existed only by force of inertia," and concluded that "when there is negligence, the rule is liability, immunity is the exception."[14] Shortly after this decision, legislation was passed severely limiting the scope of governmental immunity,[15] and subjecting all public entity activities to tort liability.[16] In essence, the general provisions of the legislation[17] hold that (a) public entities are vicariously liable for the consequences flowing from the negligent conduct of employees acting within the scope of their employment if the employee is liable therefor, and (b) employees are liable only for injuries that result from the performance of a "ministerial act," not from the discharge of "discretionary" duties.

12. Mervin Nolte, *Guide to School Law* (West Nyack, N.Y.: Parker Publishing Co., 1969), p. 103. See also *Sewaya v. Tucson High School District No. 1,* 78 Ariz. 389 (1955); *Koehn v. Board of Education,* 193 Kan. 263 (1964); *Hoy v. Capelli,* 48 N.J. 81 (1966); *Holtz v. City of Milwaukee,* 17 Wis. 2d 26 (1962); *Hargrove v. Town of Cocoa Beach,* 96 So. 2d 130 (Fla. 1957). See generally, Mancke, *Liability of School Districts,* p. 111.

13. Prosser, *Handbook,* p. 987.

14. *Muskopf v. Corning Hospital District,* 55 Cal. 2d 211 (1961).

15. California Tort Claims Act of 1963, now encompassed in the California Government Code, sections 810 through 966.6.

16. The legislation provides numerous specific immunities for governmental activities that the legislature deemed deserving of exception from the general policy. See "Notes: California Tort Claims Act," *Hastings Law Journal* 19 (January 1968): 565. School districts, however, were not specifically excepted, so their liability is governed by the general provisions of the act.

17. Most importantly, Section 815.2 and Section 820.2, California Government Code.

Such legislation thus requires a court to determine whether acts cited in a complaint were discretionary and thus immune from tort liability, or were indeed ministerial. Courts making such decisions rely on relevant policy considerations rather than on narrow semantic distinctions.[18] While they are reluctant to interfere with discretionary policy or planning decisions of other branches of government, the courts are willing to characterize as ministerial the operational aspects of implementing set policies. This principle is enunciated in *Johnson v. State:* ". . . although a basic policy decision . . . may be discretionary and hence warrant governmental immunity, subsequent ministerial actions in the implementation of that basic decision still must face case-by-case adjudication on the question of negligence."[19]

The *Johnson* court determined that revoking immunity would not substantially hurt individual employees, noting California's provisions for indemnification.[20] The court added that employee concern for the liability of the agency, if it existed at all, would be wholesome.[21] Finally, the court rejected the contention of the state agency that negligence suits would impair the provision of important public services, declaring that immunity could not be granted in the absence of a legislative declaration of an agency's unique importance.[22]

In rejecting the state's discretionary immunity defense, the *Johnson* court added that since the loss fell peculiarly on a plaintiff who had no administrative recourse, the plaintiff could only achieve vindication in the courts. The court concluded: "Since the entire populace of California benefits from the activity of the [state agency], it should also share equally the burden of injuries negligently inflicted on individual citizens; suits against the state provide a fair and effective means to distribute these losses."[23]

18. For example, see *Sava v. Fuller*, 249 A.C.A. 313, 57 Cal. Rptr. 312 (1967); *Romos v. Madera*, 484 P. 2d 93, 94 Cal. Rptr. 421 (1971).

19. *Johnson v. State*, 447 P. 2d 352, 73 Cal. Rptr. 240, 250 (1968).

20. *Johnson v. State*, 73 Cal. Rptr. 240, 246.

21. Ibid., p. 248. For an analogous set of facts but involving the Federal Tort Claims Act, see *Costler v. United States*, 181 F. 2d 723 (5th Cir. 1950).

22. Ibid., p. 252.

23. Ibid., p. 251.

The decisions and legislation cited above exemplify a national trend away from sovereign immunity toward public entity responsibility. Erosion of this doctrine was forcefully asserted by Peter Doe in his arguments to the California courts. In its ruling on Peter Doe's appeal, the court of appeal affirmed that a plaintiff *may* state a cause of action in negligence against a school district; that sovereign immunity alone did not bar recovery from a school district. The court hastened to add, however, that holding that a plaintiff *may* state a cause of action for negligence did not mean that he *has* stated one, nor did it relieve him of the pleading requirements he must meet for success in such an action.[24]

### A NOVEL THEORY: LIABILITY FOR EDUCATIONAL MALPRACTICE

The San Francisco Unified School District responded to Peter Doe's complaint, in which he alleged failure to learn because of teacher negligence, not by denying the complaint's allegations, but by filing a demurrer and by moving to dismiss the complaint. As indicated above, the school district contended that even if all the plaintiff's assertions were true, they were insufficient in law to support the plaintiff's legal claim to relief.[25] In order to prove negligence, a plaintiff must show that the defendant owed the plaintiff a legal duty to perform with reasonable care.[26] In essence, the school district, relying on the absence of precedent for Doe's theory of the case, argued that no cognizable legal action had been set forth in the plaintiff's complaint because teachers do not legally owe students a duty to teach nonnegligently.

The absence of precedent for adopting Peter Doe's novel application of negligence concepts necessitates that a court look to declarations of social policy—to the Constitution, to fundamental principles, and to judicial and legislative trends—to determine whether school personnel ought to be held legally accountable to students whose failure to learn is the *but for* result of teacher

24. *Peter Doe v. San Francisco Unified School District*, 60 C.A. 3d 819.

25. Demurrer of Defendants on First Amended Complaint, *Peter Doe v. San Francisco Unified School District*. No. 653-312 (Cal. Super. Ct., September 6, 1974), hereinafter cited as *Demurrer*.

26. In addition, the plaintiff must show that there was a *breach* of that duty which was a *proximate cause* of *injury* to the plaintiff.

negligence. Should the court find public policy support for recognizing a student's right of action in such cases, it will then concern itself with whether it is judicially feasible to enforce that right. Judges will be interested in determining whether viable standards of proof exist, in order to limit the possibility of fraudulent claims and a flood of litigation. Inquiry into the merits of a particular case becomes relevant only in the event a court is persuaded of both the appropriateness and feasibility of holding school personnel legally accountable to students for negligent teaching.

Recent statements of public policy, including the enactment by legislatures of accountability legislation and the decisions of courts in school cases,[27] indicate an emerging trend that offers support for an adventurous court to hold school districts accountable for a teacher's negligence in the discharge of instructional duties. But while the cited examples give evidence of evolving public policy support for a conclusion that a right of action in a case like *Peter Doe* is appropriate, substantial problems relative to the feasibility of enforcement remain. Problems of proof and delineation of liability mitigate against entertaining such a suit. To what standard of skill and care are teachers to be held? How is a jury to determine whether a student has been injured, as well as the extent and cause of an injury?

Attorneys for the San Francisco Unified School District hammered at these problems of proof in argument before the court. The district asserted that school personnel had no legal duty in common, statutory, or constitutional law to exercise reasonable care, except in the physical protection of students. They contended, first, that legal standards of conduct could not be established: The "pedagogical process of transferring knowledge and cognitive skills is so complex, and as yet so inadequately understood, as not properly to be the subject of the imposition of a duty in tort."[28]

27. For example, see California Education Code annotated, 12101-12501 (amended 1967). See also, Maureen Webster, "Statewide Testing Legislation and Educational Policy," in Miriam Clasby, Maureen Webster, and Naomi White, *Laws, Tests, and Schooling* (Syracuse, N.Y.: Educational Policy Research Corp., 1973), pp. 1-78. One of the most striking court decisions came in *Serrano v. Priest*, 487 P. 2d 1241 (1971).

28. *Demurrer*, p. 16.

Further, the defendants contended that the plaintiff had no cognizable legal interest and had therefore not been injured. They maintained, among other things, that "when the state imposes on itself the obligation to provide an extraordinary public service such as public education . . . it should not be held accountable for negligence in its failure to fully accomplish that undertaking."[29] A third point relative to the negligence issue was that the recognition of the legal duty sought by Doe would begin a flood of litigation, often meritless, against school districts, which "would render public education economically unfeasible."[30]

## The California Courts Respond

### THE SUPERIOR COURT DISMISSES

Unfortunately for Peter Doe, the absence of precedent for suing in negligence for teacher-caused educational deprivation proved an insurmountable obstacle to his recovering damages from the San Francisco Unified School District. The case was dismissed by the trial court, which sustained the demurrer of the school district "on all grounds stated by the defendants." The merits of the specific allegations were never addressed by the court.

### THE PLAINTIFF'S APPEAL

From the decision of trial court, Peter Doe took his case to a California court of appeals, asking the higher court to require that his case be decided on the merits after a full hearing. Doe's attorneys recognized that reversing the ruling of the trial court on the defendant's demurrer required the plaintiff to persuade the appellate court that school professionals ought to be held liable for breach of what Doe asserted is a duty to teach nonnegligently; further, that students did have a legal interest in educational results; and, lastly, that public policy supported Peter Doe's right to recover damages proximately resulting from educational malpractice.

29. Quoted in Appellant's Opening Brief, *Peter Doe v. San Francisco Unified School District*, 1 Civil No. 36851 (Court of Appeal, July 25, 1975), hereinafter cited as *Appellant's Brief*.

30. *Demurrer*, p. 17.

Doe supported his contention that school professionals had a duty to teach nonnegligently by drawing upon three asserted common law principles and by proposing standards for determining whether a teacher had taught nonnegligently. Among the common law principles relied upon, the plaintiff maintained first that "where an individual or a public entity undertakes to perform an act, even one voluntarily or gratuitously assumed, it is under a duty to exercise reasonable care and not perform the act in a negligent manner."[31] Doe noted that several state courts and the U.S. Supreme Court had affirmed this principle.[32] Application of the principle to the school district meant, argued the plaintiff, that although the schools, in assuming the educational function, did not have to guarantee that every student would be taught to read, they did have a legal obligation to "exercise reasonable care" in the teaching of basic skills.[33] If the state wanted to educate, it would have to do so in a reasonably prudent way.

The plaintiff also argued that the school's duty of care was supported by a special relationship between the student and the educator. Since schooling is compulsory, "courts have observed that the imposition of the obligation to attend school presupposes the existence of some meaningful educational service at the school house."[34] The California Constitution and the California Education Code both mandate that public schools provide students with an education—an education that will prepare students for "legitimate remunerative employment."[35] The plaintiff, therefore, contended

31. *Appellant's Brief*, p. 11.

32. In a suit against the federal government for the negligent operation of a lighthouse by the Coast Guard, the Supreme Court said: "The Coast Guard need not undertake the lighthouse service. But once it exercised its discretion to operate a [lighthouse] and engendered reliance on the guidance afforded by the light, it was obligated to use due care to make certain the light was kept in good working order. . . ." *Indian Towing Co. v. U.S.*, 350 U.S. 61, 69 (1957). See also *Sava v. Fuller*, 57 Cal. Rptr. 312, 249 Cal. App. 2d 281 (1967), and *Morgan v. County of Yuba*, 41 Cal. Rptr. 508, 230 Cal. App. 2d 928 (1964).

33. *Appellant's Brief*, p. 13.

34. Ibid., p. 14, citing, among others, *Mills v. Board of Education of the District of Columbia*, 348 F. Supp. 866 (district court, District of Columbia, 1972).

35. California Constitution, Article IX, Sections 1 and 5; California Education Code, Section 7504.

that common law, common sense, and the requirements of public policy confer upon school employees the minimum duty to use reasonable care.

Lastly, the plaintiff maintained that California courts had long recognized the teacher's tort liability where physical injury had resulted from failure to exercise reasonable care in instruction.[36] Although the type of harm suffered might be different, Doe argued that the harm in his case was no less real and no less foreseeable.[37] The plaintiff analogized to the medical malpractice of a surgeon and a psychiatrist. The harm is physical in one case and mental in the other, but both have a recognized duty to exert reasonable care.[38]

Doe also responded to the problem of establishing minimum standards of professional conduct. He argued that courts have affirmed the principle that "teachers, like other governmental employees, may be held simply to a standard of care which persons of ordinary prudence charged with the duty of instruction would exercise."[39] The plaintiff declared that expert witnesses could testify relative to negligence in educational cases, just as they do in malpractice cases involving doctors, engineers, and the like.[40] In such situations, the difficulties of establishing standards cannot be a bar to litigation. The plaintiff cited as authority for this proposition a decision of the recent California Supreme Court: "But whatever difficulties the courts may encounter in evaluating the expert judgments of other professions, those difficulties cannot justify total exoneration from liability."[41]

In addition to the above arguments for recognizing that the

36. See, for example, *Bellman v. San Francisco High School District*, 81 P. 2d 894, 11 Cal. 2d 576 (1938), *Damgaard v. Oakland High School District*, 298 P. 983, 212 C. 316 (1931), *Dutcher v. City of Santa Rosa High School District*, 319 P. 2d 14, 156 Cal. App. 2d 256 (1958).

37. Foreseeability of risk is a common standard in negligence liability.

38. *Appellant's Brief*, p. 21.

39. Ibid., p. 41, citing *Bellman v. San Francisco High School District* and *Pirkle v. Oakdale Union Grammar School*, 253 P. 2d 1, 40 Cal. 2d 207 (1953).

40. See generally, Louis N. Massery, II, ed., *Handling the Professional Liability Case* (Reno, Nev.: Association of Trial Lawyers of America, 1976).

41. *Tarasoff v. Regents*, 13 Cal. 3d 177, 118 Cal. Rptr. 136 (1975).

defendants owed students a duty of care, plaintiff Doe attempted also to rebut contentions of the defendant school district that he had suffered no legally recognized harm, that is, that he had no legal interest in educational results. Doe argued that suffering the loss of an expectancy—in the plaintiff's case, receiving an education —is recompensable in analogous cases. Legal malpractice cases, for example, have allowed plaintiffs to recover for benefits that they probably would have received under will or from lawsuits but for the negligence of a lawyer.[42] The *Restatement of the Law of Torts* explains that "where a person can prove that but for the tortious interference of another, he would have received a gift or a specific profit from a transaction, he is entitled to full damages for the loss which has thus been caused to him."[43] Courts have allowed recovery where the receipt of the benefits was not certain but only highly probable. The novelty of suing to recover damages to compensate for failure to learn, argued the plaintiff, should not act as a bar to the relief requested. The common law, according to the California Supreme Court, "is constantly expanding and developing,"[44] and the courts have recognized the emergence of new tort claims.[45]

The last major obstacle to adoption of Doe's negligence theory, namely the court's fear that entertaining Peter Doe's complaint would result in a flood of similar cases, required that the plaintiff argue that dismissing his case on the strength of such a defense contravened the purpose of tort law. He cited Prosser's statement that "it is the business of the law to remedy wrongs that deserve it, even at the expense of a 'flood of litigation,' . . ."[46] (The plaintiff tactfully did not include the conclusion of Prosser's sentence: "and it is a pitiful confession of impotence on the part

42. "Comment: Educational Malpractice," *University of Pennsylvania Law Review* 124 (January 1976): 775.

43. *Restatement of the Law of Torts* (St. Paul, Minn.: American Law Institute Publishers, 1939), Section 912, comment f, p. 584.

44. *Rodriguez v. Bethlehem Steel Co.*, 12 Cal. 3d 395, 115 Cal. Rptr. 772 (1974).

45. *Custodia v. Bauer*, 251 C.A. 2d 303, 59 Cal. Rptr. 463 (1963); *State Rubbish Collectors Association v. Siliznoff*, 38 Cal. 2d 330, 240 P. 2d 282 (1952).

46. Prosser, *Handbook*, p. 51.

of any court of justice to deny relief on such grounds.")[47] Significantly, Doe cited the assertion of the California Supreme Court that the fallibility of the judicial process:

offers no reason for substituting for the case-by-case resolution of causes an artificial and indefensible barrier. Courts not only compromise their basic responsibility to decide the merits of each case individually but destroy the public's confidence in them by using the broad broom of "administrative convenience" to sweep away a class of claims a number of which are meritorious.[48]

To conclude his argument on public policy factors, Doe asserted that the imposition of tort liability would have a highly beneficial effect on school districts by deterring negligent conduct in the future; in addition, he recalled the words of the *Johnson* court declaring that where citizens had been wronged, "suits against the state provide a fair and efficient means to distribute these losses."[49] The plaintiff, in sum, asked the court to find that the defendants had a legal duty to him, that he had a legal interest in any educational losses he might have suffered, and that public policy required a full-dress trial on the merits of the case.

APPELLATE COURT'S RESPONSE

The court of appeal rejected Doe's arguments, and once again shut the courtroom door on a full hearing by dismissing the case.[50] Although the court concurred that public policy considerations formed the crux of the dispute, it took a view of public needs much closer to that of the defendant school district than that of the plaintiff.

In its decision, the court confirmed the demise of sovereign immunity as a bar to litigation in California: The judges noted the *Muskopf* decision with approval. They did say, however, that "liability is the rule 'only' when there is negligence." Therefore, they concluded, while *Muskopf* allows a plaintiff to bring to the

47. Ibid.

48. *Dillon v. Legg*, 69 Cal. Rptr. 78.

49. *Johnson v. State*, 73 Cal. Rptr. 240, 251.

50. *Peter Doe v. San Francisco Unified School District*, 60 C.A. 3d 814 (1976).

court a cause of action for negligence, it does not automatically confer liability.[51]

The court then formally recognized the key issue in the negligence action: Did the defendants owe the plaintiff a duty of care?[52] The judges realized that Doe's success or failure rode on the resolution of this issue, and began by addressing the three arguments Doe propounded to support recognition of a teacher's duty to teach nonnegligently. The court rejected all three arguments without much explanation, generally declaring that the precedents cited were not directly applicable to a case alleging nonphysical injuries due to educational malpractice.[53]

After declaring that the precedents cited by the plaintiff were not germane, the court then moved to a discussion of the public policy considerations involved in educational malpractice suits. In disposing of the plaintiff's appeal, the court declared: "Judicial recognition of [duty of care] in the defendant . . . is initially to be dictated or precluded by considerations of public policy."[54]

On public policy grounds, the court then determined that Doe's complaint stated no legally cognizable cause of action. The principal thrusts of the court's reasoning were, first, that there could be no appropriate standards to determine duty of care by educators, and second, that allowing the suit would leave school districts open to costly and endless litigation.

51. Ibid., p. 819.

52. We recognize that "duty," in this case duty to teach nonnegligently, is a conclusory term. Prosser writes: "The statement that there is or is not a duty begs the essential question—whether the plaintiff's interests are entitled to legal protection against the defendant's conduct. . . . It is a shorthand statement of a conclusion, rather than an aid to analysis in itself. . . . It should be recognized that 'duty' is not sacrosanct in itself, but only an expression of the sum total of those considerations of policy which lead the law to say that the particular plaintiff is entitled to protection." Prosser, *Handbook*, pp. 325-26. Nonetheless, in this chapter we shall retain the term, since it is used by judges. See "Comment: Educational Malpractice," p. 768.

53. *Peter Doe v. San Francisco Unified School District*, 60 C.A. 3d 814, 820-21. In regard to the first theory (duty by virtue of assuming the educational function), the court seemingly misconstrued the plaintiff's argument into a discussion on discretionary immunity. In the second and third theories, Doe argued for an imposition of duty by extending the logic of statutes and precedents; the court did not address the extensions of logic, and merely rejected the precedents.

54. Ibid., p. 822.

On the question of standards, the judges noted that where the California Supreme Court had allowed new grounds for tort litigation, the issues in those cases "were both comprehensible and assessable" within the terms and models of existing laws and procedures. They declared, however, that "this is simply not true of [issues] allegedly involved in educational malfeasance. Unlike the activity of the highway or the marketplace, classroom methodology offers no readily acceptable standards of care, or cause, or injury."[55] Further, the court maintained that there were a multitude of theories on how children should be taught, implying that the court would not or could not interpose itself in a wide-open academic debate. Finally, the court cited professional authorities to the effect that academic achievement is influenced by a host of factors beyond the control of education professionals. As a result of the lack of a workable rule of care to measure the conduct of defendants, the lack of certainty that Doe suffered a legal injury, and the difficulty of connecting cause and effect in education, the court declared that these policy considerations alone precluded imposing a duty to teach nonnegligently upon education professionals.

To complete its decision, however, the court briefly examined the judicial implications of allowing the Doe case to go to trial. The judges decided that such a precedent "would expose [public schools] to the tort claims—real or imagined—of disaffected students and parents in countless numbers."[56] In terms of time and money, they said, the precedent would place an overwhelming burden on the schools, and they refused to establish such a precedent.

### ROUND THREE: THE SUPREME COURT

From the decision of the court of appeal, Peter Doe appealed to the California Supreme Court. On September 29, 1976, that court refused to hear the Doe case, without prejudice and on purely discretionary grounds. The most explicit implications of this result, which leaves the decision of the court of appeal standing,

55. Ibid., p. 824.
56. Ibid., p. 825.

are those for Peter Doe himself. He will have to cope as best he can without recovering damages from the San Francisco School District.

The immediate implications for the broader concerns of educational policy and practice are no less explicit. School districts, as a result of the disposition of the Doe case by the courts of California, remain immune from such malpractice suits, albeit no longer as a result of sovereign immunity. The status quo remains basically undisturbed, although one could argue that the filing of the *Doe* suit and its course through the courts deposited a residue of caution over the practices of school personnel.

The future implications of the refusal of California courts to entertain the *Doe* case—to recognize a cause of action for failure to learn resulting from teacher negligence—are far from clear. The unanswerable question is the extent to which the decision of the court of appeal in *Doe* is a negative precedent that subsequent and similar suits for educational malpractice must overcome. Future plaintiffs who wish to test Peter Doe's theory of recovery could at least take hope from the fact that the appellate court decided the case based on its own perceptions of public policy imperatives, and did not put forward any legal principles or precedents to block it. Further, the absence of a decision from the California Supreme Court leaves open the possibility of persuading one of the other four courts of appeal in California to take a view of public policy different from the *Doe* court, and to allow a suit to go forward.

## Potential for Future Malpractice Suits

Future plaintiffs who seek to follow Peter Doe's lead will have to overcome the judiciary's traditional reluctance to recognize a novel right of action—in this case, a right of recovery for failure to learn as a result of teacher negligence. They must persuade a court that viable standards for delineating negligent conduct and for proving compensable injury and causation exist.

### RECOGNIZING A NOVEL RIGHT OF ACTION

Courts traditionally are reluctant to consider novel applications of negligence concepts, often rationalizing that they are fearful of "legislating," or that they are uneasy about the negative consequences of tampering with the existing precedents. In recent years, however, a number of courts and legal commentators have asserted the need and propriety of judicial "responsibility for the upkeep of the common law."[57] As one legal authority notes, "the progress of the common law is marked by many cases of first impression, in which the court has struck out boldly to create a new cause of action, where none had been recognized before."[58] Indeed, it has been widely argued that there is a necessity for judicial adaptation to changing social conditions and evolving concepts of justice.[59] The argument is made: "When it becomes clear that the plaintiff's interests are entitled to legal protection against the conduct of the defendant, the mere fact that the claim is novel will not of itself operate as a bar to recovery."[60] One might logically assert that just as a wide variety of other interests have been recently recognized through acknowledgment of a right of recovery in tort,[61] the courts should not bar educational malpractice suits solely because of a lack of supporting precedents.

## VIABLE STANDARDS

The opinion of the California court of appeal in *Peter Doe* suggests that its strongest objection to the plaintiff's theory of the case concerned the difficulty of establishing standards of instructional due care and of proving injury and causation. In each of these areas, however, future plaintiffs could meet the court's

57. *Rodriguez v. Bethlehem Steel Co.*, 115 Cal. Rptr. 772.

58. Prosser, *Handbook*, p. 3.

59. See generally Henry M. Hart and Albert Sacks, "The Legal Process: Basic Problems in the Making and Application of Law," tentative edition, 1958, pp. 386-650; Prosser, *Handbook*, pp. 3-4; "Note: The Child's Right to Sue for Loss of a Parent's Love, Care, and Companionship Caused by Tortious Injury to the Parent," *Boston University Law Review* 56 (June 1976): 728-29. See also, *Miller v. Monsen*, 228 Minn. 400, 406, 37 N.W. 2d 543, 547 (1949); *Custodia v. Bauer*, 251 Cal. App. 2d 303, 59 Cal. Rptr. 463 (1967).

60. Prosser, *Handbook*, pp. 3-4.

61. Examples include the right of action for loss of spouse's consortium, prenatal injuries, unwanted childbirth, and intentional infliction of mental distress, to name but a few.

concern. They, in argument, could propose viable standards and
tests for determining negligence.

For a standard of care, the plaintiffs might well adopt standards
from analogous court decisions that currently hold professionals
in law and medicine liable in malpractice suits.[62] Negligence in such
cases is tied to "failure to exercise good judgment," "omission to
use reasonable care and diligence," and failure in "rendering reasonably prudent care."[63] Like attorneys, whose negligence involves
nonphysical injury, teachers need not guarantee "the correctness of
[their] work or . . . the results which will be attained," but they
may be held liable for "negligent failure to use . . . requisite care
or skill."[64] Negligence for psychotherapists, which typically also
involves nonphysical injury, is defined by "deviation from professional standards," "extreme professional misconduct," or "shocking"
behavior.[65] Further, under English precedent for psychotherapists,
where "the very nature of the acts complained of bespeaks improper treatment," the burden of proving nonnegligence is actually
with the defendant.[66]

The courts could reasonably adopt any of these traditional
tests of professional negligence as viable standards by which teachers' instructional conduct could be measured. Should the courts
desire a more empirical standard, however, a comparative model
using "the level of skill and learning of the minimally acceptable
teacher in the same or similar communities" has been suggested.[67]
Actual comparisons could be made within the specific community
or even a particular school to set a more definite standard for the
case.[68]

62. See Massery, ed., *Handling the Professional Liability Case.*

63. John W. Wade, "The Attorney's Liability for Negligence," in *Pro-
fessional Negligence* (Nashville, Tenn.: Williams Printing Co., 1960), p. 224;
Ted M. Warshafsky, "Approaches to Hospital Negligence," in *Case and
Comment* 5 (Sept.-Oct. 1974): 12.

64. Wade, "The Attorney's Liability for Negligence," p. 222.

65. "Tort Liability of the Psychotherapist," in Massery, ed., *Handling the
Professional Liability Case,* pp. 435, 437.

66. Ibid., p. 438.

67. "Comment: Educational Malpractice," p. 756.

68. Ibid., p. 797. Here the suggested standard is made by comparing the

Thus, far from being beyond the reach of judicial cognition, it appears that viable standards of care for classroom teachers could be established, either by relying upon standards other professionals are subject to in malpractice cases, or by a parochial professional community standard.

The means for applying such standards entail hearing from experts—persons with considerable credentials—who will testify concerning generally accepted practices in the teaching profession. The fact that experts will sometimes disagree does not require the conclusion that no professional standards exist. "Courts," as one commentator noted, "are routinely called upon to evaluate conflicting expert opinions and to resolve technical controversies in areas outside judicial expertise." [69] The California Supreme Court recently held, in a highly technical case, that "whatever the difficulties the courts may encounter in evaluating the expert judgments of other professions, those difficulties cannot justify total exoneration from liability." [70] In short, the courts should not justify denying relief to a future Peter Doe because of an asserted inability to apply a viable standard of care.

Viable standards for proof and assessment of injury can also be propounded. Such standards could be based on the educational level the student probably would have attained had the teacher performed nonnegligently. In many states, already existing guidelines for minimum progress might be used as a baseline criterion in determining injuries. [71] In such cases, circumstantial evidence (such as a student's rapid improvement under private tutoring, or comparative statistics on the progress of similar students under different teachers) [72] could aid the court or jury in determining

---

performance of virtually identical groups of students under different teachers. The article notes that an additional appeal of this community-based approach for the courts is that negligence suits could not then be used to force general upgrading of education within a commuity. See pp. 756-57; 771.

69. "Comment, *Wyatt v. Stickney* and the Right of Civilly Committed Mental Patients to Adequate Treatment," *Harvard Law Review* 86 (May 1973): 1282, 1297.

70. *Tarasoff v. Regents*, 13 Cal. 3d 177, 118 Cal. Rptr. 136 (1975).

71. See, for example, Frederick McDonald, *A Design for an Accountability System for the New York City School System* (Princeton, N.J.: Educational Testing Service, 1972).

72. See generally "Comment: Educational Malpractice," especially p. 756.

what a plaintiff would have achieved, *but for* the negligence of the defendants.[73]

Peter Doe's claims that he "suffered mental distress, pain, and suffering"[74] are very difficult to prove and, therefore, undermine a plaintiff's attempt to move a court to recognize a novel right of action. On the other hand, suits seeking relief for economic loss for the consequences of a failure to learn essential skills[75] present less difficult problems for a court. Besides being more susceptible to proof, allegations of such injury are more analogous to tort precedents that support award of damages for nonphysical injuries. Thus, it is fair to conclude that the courts could make a reasonable assessment of injuries and resulting damages.[76]

The standards for proof of causation are somewhat more difficult to establish, and might be the most difficult obstacle for a potential plaintiff to overcome. Because the student is affected by a broad mix of social and psychological factors outside the school environment, proving that the defendant's negligent acts directly caused the injury might be a tough proposition. Nonetheless, Prosser wisely declares that "if the defendant's conduct was a substantial factor in causing the plaintiff's injury . . . he will not be absolved from liability merely because other causes have contributed to the result."[77] Further, a possible standard of circumstantial evidence has been proposed that might be useful in isolating proximate cause. This has been called "the comparative method," because it compares a given student's (or a class's) progress with the progress of students of similar background whose educational environment

73. Prosser declares that negligence may be proved through circumstantial evidence. See *Handbook*, p. 212.

74. Quoted in "Comment: Educational Malpractice," p. 760.

75. Nonphysical injuries resulting from malpractice by lawyers, accountants, psychotherapists, and the like are commonly recognized. In educational malpractice, the economic impact on the student would be the difference between the plaintiff's earning at his actual educational level, and what he would have learned *but for* the teacher's negligence. The latter value could be found as the average earnings for people at that educational level, or some reasonable variant thereof.

76. "Note: The Child's Right to Sue for Loss of a Parent's Love, Care, and Companionship Caused by Tortious Injury to the Parent," p. 734.

77. Prosser, *Handbook*, p. 240.

was exactly the same except for the defendant teacher or other school employee.[78] Other circumstantial arguments might also lead to a demonstration of direct cause.

After assessing the legal arguments for and against recognizing a right of recovery for educational malpractice, it is fair to conclude that a future Peter Doe could break through the above barriers. A court might well be convinced that viable standards exist for determining if a teacher was negligent, and for proving compensable injury and causation. A novel suit like Doe's, however, cannot succeed to a hearing on the merits with formal *legal* arguments alone. A plaintiff in such a case will have to include *social policy* arguments demonstrating that public policy imperatives will not be undermined, but will be well served, by permitting recovery for failure to learn.

## Policy Implications

In order to overcome the public policy obstacles that barred relief for Peter Doe, a future plaintiff must persuade a court that precedent set by allowing recovery for educational malpractice will not place an undue burden administratively on the court system or financially on a school district. Further, a plaintiff must show that the nonfinancial impact of such a precedent will not have a negative effect on the quality of educational services delivered. The latter may prove to be the highest barrier of all.

Courts traditionally fear that allowing a novel right of action will lead to a flood of similar cases, many of them meritless. To overcome such a fear, a future plaintiff may argue that it is the responsibility of a court to deal with each suit on its merits, regardless of the administrative problems involved.[79] As one legal authority commented, "it is the business of the law to remedy wrongs that deserve it, even at the expense of a 'flood of litigation'."[80]

78. "Comment: Educational Malpractice," pp. 790-91.

79. "Note: The Child's Right to Sue for Loss of a Parent's Love, Care, and Companionship Caused by Tortious Injury to the Parent," p. 732; *Dillon v. Legg*, 69 Cal. Rptr. 78.

80. Prosser, *Handbook*, p. 51.

Additionally, the argument might be made that as a practical matter the court is able to avoid hearing most meritless cases by devising a means to separate the wheat from the chaff.[81] For example, before permitting trial on the particular facts of a case, courts might require the plaintiff to introduce evidence that permits a court to infer that, *but for* the teacher's negligence, the plaintiff would not have failed to progress at least at grade level. Such evidence would not establish teacher negligence; it would merely spur the court to begin an inquiry, through means of a trial, into the facts of the case.

Over and above any burden on the court system are the implications for public education if teachers, and vicariously, school districts, are subject to malpractice suits. Awarding substantial damages to a plaintiff/student arguably could bankrupt a public school district. Mr. Justice Cardozo rejected awarding damages for such nonphysical consequences of negligence, saying such a result would produce "liability in an indeterminate amount for an indeterminate time to an indeterminate class."[82]

A plaintiff might argue, however, that the award of damages be limited to the costs of remedial instruction in order to raise the plaintiff to minimum standards of competence. Where remedial instructions alone will not provide compensation, money damages could be limited to the direct loss of potential earnings as a result of the plaintiff's educational deficiency.[83] If the amount of recovery was thus limited, and if school districts secured adequate liability insurance (currently available at relatively low cost),[84] the district could probably bear the loss better than the individual student/plaintiff. Of course, if a damage judgment would have the effect of substantially reducing the quality of services that schools could provide, a court will most likely decide that the social need for educational services outweighs the interest of any partic-

81. See Fleming James, Jr., "Limitations on Liability for Economic Loss Caused by Negligence: A Pragmatic Appraisal," *Journal of the Society of Public Teachers of Law* 12 (July 1972): 111.

82. *Ultramares Corporation v. Touche*, 255 N.Y. 170, 179; 174 N.E. 441, 444 (1931).

83. See generally "Comment: Educational Malpractice," especially p. 758.

84. See Knaak, *School District Tort Liability in the 70s*, pp. 93-94.

ular student/plaintiff in recovering for educational benefits denied by teacher negligence.

Educational malpractice suits, it must be noted, have non-financial implications for educational quality beyond the policy arguments discussed above. These are difficult to predict, however, without experience. Nonetheless, a court will have to weigh arguments relative to these implications.

By way of example, a plaintiff might argue that imposing liability on school personnel could prove to be a deterrent to negligent teaching and the hiring of incompetent teachers. In rebuttal, however, one could contend that the threat of liability and fear of being disgraced in a courtroom might discourage people from becoming teachers, and have a chilling effect on innovation in education. A plaintiff also might argue that liability for educational malpractice would force schools to provide special services to students with deficiencies in basic skills. In response, however, one could assert that to avoid liability, teacher certification standards and minimum standards of pupil achievement could be lowered through legislation. Further, it might be argued that a concentration on achieving minimum standards would lower the overall quality of a school program.

In sum, examination of public policy places a heavy burden on a plaintiff to satisfy a court that the public will be well served, rather than harmed, by holding school districts liable when instructors fail to teach nonnegligently.

## Conclusion

California has closed its courtroom doors to Peter Doe's suit against the San Francisco Unified School District. Doe is left without relief, to cope as best he can. The way in which the case was decided, however, leaves open the possibility that a future Peter Doe might succeed in obtaining a full hearing on the question of liability for educational malpractice. The ruling of a California court of appeal in the *Doe* case is based on its own perspective of public policy needs, rather than laws or precedents. Changing social contexts, or a different panel of judges, may affect the results in a subsequent suit.

While the possibility of a judicial change of heart remains, the chances for a prospective plaintiff's success are not great in the immediate future. Citing the California court of appeals. judges again may conclude that educators have no legal duty to teach nonnegligently, resting this conclusion on a lack of statutory or common law authority, and the difficulty of establishing standards of care and proof of injury and causation. We hope that this would not be the rationale, for, after reviewing the arguments above, we believe that the absence of precedent should not preclude recovery, and that standards and proof are achievable.

On the other hand, we feel that holding school districts liable for educational malpractice raises a question of public policy that might legitimately serve as a basis for precluding recovery. The court's fear of a "flood of litigation" could probably be avoided by adequate screening. The potentially adverse financial and non-financial impact of successful suits on school districts, however, may not be so easily avoided. Because such an impact might well threaten the quality of educational services, we are led to the conclusion that the courts should impose liability, if at all, only in the most outrageous cases of educational malpractice.

# CHAPTER XI

# Privacy

KELLY FRELS AND ANN RYAN ROBERTSON

The Press is overstepping in every direction the obvious bounds of propriety and of decency. Gossip is no longer the resource of the idle and of the vicious, but has become a trade, which is pursued with industry as well as effrontery. To satisfy a prurient taste the details of sexual relations are spread broadcast in the columns of the daily papers. . . . The intensity and complexity of life, attendant upon advancing civilization, have rendered necessary some retreat from the world, and man, under the refining influence of culture, has become more sensitive to publicity, so that solitude and privacy have become more essential to the individual; but modern enterprise and invention have, through invasions upon his privacy, subjected him to mental pain and distress, far greater than could be inflicted by mere bodily injury.

> Samuel D. Warren and Louis D. Brandeis
> "The Right to Privacy"
> *Harvard Law Review*, 1890

Privacy, a basic tenet of American philosophy, is constitutionally acknowledged in the Bill of Rights. These rights, while prohibiting unreasonable searches and the compulsion of testimony against one's self, recognize religious privacy and the sanctity of the home. These fundamental freedoms, however, are only a skeletal framework of the privacy rights that have evolved to meet the demands of a computerized, multimedia society. The purpose of this chapter is to review the emerging privacy rights of teachers and students, with particular attention to defamation, invasion of privacy, liberty interests, self-incrimination, freedom of association, and the recently enacted Family Educational Rights and Privacy Act.

## Defamation

Defamation, the injury of a person's character, fame, or reputa-

tion by false and malicious statements, consists of libel and slander.[1]
Libel refers to written or printed words while slander implies oral
communication; inherent in the definitions of both is the concept
of publication. While publication does not require that the communication be written or printed, it does require that defamatory
information be communicated to someone other than the person
alleging defamation.[2] Without publication to a third person, one
cannot successfully bring a suit for defamation. As a defense to an
accusation of defamation, a defendant may plead that he was legally
entitled to make the statement. Therefore, the communication was
privileged and he is immune from liability.[3]

The defense that the communication was privileged is conditioned upon the societal interest being protected and can be sub-
divided into two types: (a) absolute privilege or immunity, and
(b) qualified or conditional privilege. The absolute privilege, which
is applicable to judicial proceedings, legislative proceedings, and executive communications, is restricted to publication within the
domain of a defendant's authorized functions.[4] Absolute privilege
is predicated on the premise that

there are a few instances in which the interest of the public is esteemed
more important than that of the individual and occasions in which public [sic] rights must yield to public good. In these cases there is no
penalty attached to malice or falsehood. The utmost liberty is deemed

1. *Black's Law Dictionary*, 4th ed. (St. Paul, Minn.: West Publishing Co.,
1951), p. 505.

2. Modern technological advances have modified this distinction. The focus
is no longer on how the defamatory information is transmitted but rather on
how it is received. Thus, that which is communicated by sight is considered
libel and that which is heard is slander. William Prosser, *Handbook of the
Law of Torts*, 4th ed. (St. Paul, Minn.: West Publishing Co., 1971), Section
111, pp. 751-52.

3. Ibid., Section 114, p. 776. The defense of privilege or immunity emanates
from the common law recognition that in some instances the interest of the
individual must be waived in order to further a competing social policy.

4. Ibid., pp. 776-84. New York has extended its absolute privilege to cover
a variety of positions—in *Sheridan v. Crisona*, 149 N.Y. 2d 108, 249 N.Y.S. 2d
161, 198 N.E. 2d 359 (1964) to executives of municipal government; in *Lom-
bardo v. Stoke*, 18 N.Y. 2d 394, 276 N.Y.S. 2d 97, 222 N.E. 2d 721 (1966) to
a member of the Board of Higher Education; and in *Thompson v. Union Free
School District*, 45 Misc. 2d 916, 258 N.Y.S. 2d 307 (1965) to members of a
school board.

allowable, and communications that under other circumstances would be actionable are treated as permissible.[5]

Providing lesser protection for a defendant is the qualified or conditional privilege. In this instance, the social policy being furthered is not of the magnitude of that being protected by an absolute privilege, and the pivotal point is the interest of the person communicating the defamatory information.[6]

Attached to the qualified privilege is the condition that the privilege be exercised in a reasonable manner and for a proper purpose.[7] Four events will result in the forfeiture of immunity:

1. the defendant does not believe the defamatory matter to be true, or believing it to be true, has no grounds on which to base this belief;

2. the defamatory matter was published for some purpose other than that for which the privilege was given;

3. the publication was made to some person not reasonably believed necessary for the accomplishment of a particular privilege;

4. the publication included defamatory matter not reasonably believed to be necessary to accomplish the purpose for which the privilege was given.[8]

Thus, a qualified privilege can be, and in many instances is, lost due to a defendant's abuse of the privilege.

5. *Tanner v. Stevenson*, 138 Ky. 578, 128 S.W. 878, 881 (1910).

6. The qualified privilege has been described as follows: "[A] communication made *bona fide* upon any subject matter in which the party communicating has an *interest*, or in reference to which he has a *duty*, is privileged, if made to a person having a corresponding *interest* or *duty*, although it contained criminating matter which, without this privilege, would be slanderous and actionable; and this though the duty be not a legal one, but only a moral or social duty of imperfect obligation. . . . Such privilege is known as a 'qualified privilege.' " *Segall v. Piazza*, 46 Misc. 2d 700, 260 N.Y.S. 2d 543, 546 (1965), citing *Byam v. Collins*, 111 N.Y. 143, 150, 19 N.E. 75 (1888). See also, *Calero v. Del Chemical Co.*, 288 N.W. 2d 737, 744 (Wis. 1975); *Coopersmith v. Williams*, 468 P. 2d 739, 741 (Colo. 1970); *Johnson v. Langley*, 247 Ky. 7, 57 S.W. 2d 21, 25 (1933); *Toogood v. Spyring*, 1 C.M.&R. 181, 193, 149 Eng. Rep. 1044, 1049-50 (1834).

7. *Ranous v. Hughes*, 30 Wis. 2d 452, 141 N.W. 2d 251, 259 (1966); Prosser, *Handbook*, Section 115, p. 792.

8. *Ranous v. Hughes*, 141 N.W. 2d 259; Prosser, *Handbook*, pp. 791-95.

## EDUCATION AND COMMON LAW DEFAMATION

Generally the courts agree that a public official who makes an employment recommendation enjoys a qualified privilege.[9] This assertion is a natural extension of the "common interest" theory that undergirds a qualified or conditional privilege, and so long as the communication is made to a person "who has a legitimate interest in the subject matter,"[10] the immunity will remain intact. This premise is true even though the defamatory information was given voluntarily rather than upon request.[11] However, since it is a conditional privilege, the immunity it affords can be lost by the school official's misuse of the situation. In Burish v. Rice,[12] the court, relying on the four instances which will result in loss of privilege, found that the superintendent did not believe the defamatory matter to be true, or believing it to be true, had no reasonable grounds on which to base his belief. Consequently, he lost the protection the privilege afforded and was found liable to the plaintiff.

Conversely, a teacher must also endure certain personal comments made by parents to the principal. In Martin v. Kearney, parents wrote letters to the principal complaining about the teacher's fitness to teach typing and her classroom conduct.[13] The court found that the parents had a conditional privilege predicated upon a group of interested persons communicating mutual concerns involving education to other interested persons. It said:

> One of the crosses a public school teacher must bear is intemperate complaints addressed to school administrators by overly-solicitous parents concerned about the teacher's conduct in the classroom. Since the law compels parents to send their children to school, appropriate channels for the airing of supposed grievances against the operation of the school system must remain open.[14]

9. McAulay v. Maloff, 369 N.Y.S. 2d 946, 948 (1975); Hett v. Ploetz, 20 Wis. 2d 55, 69, 121 N.W. 2d 270, 272 (1963).

10. Burr v. Atlantic Aviation Corp., 332 A. 2d 154 (Del. Super. Ct. 1974); 50 American Jurisprudence 2d Libel and Slander, Section 275 (1970).

11. Sindorf v. Jacron Sales Co., 341 A. 2d 856 (Md. 1975); Fresh v. Cutter, 73 Md. 87, 92-94, 20 A. 774, 775 (1890).

12. Manitowoc County, (Cir. Ct. Wis, September 16, 1974).

13. Martin v. Kearney, 51 Cal. App. 309, 124 Cal. Rptr. 281 (1975).

14. Ibid., p. 283. Cf. Monnin v. Wood, 86 N.M. 460, 525 P. 2d 387 (1974).

The conditional privilege hinges on the commonality of interest between the two parties, that is, the parents and school officials. Once this interest is established, the interest is scrutinized in light of the four instances that can cause this privilege to be lost. If no abuse can be ascertained from the communication, the speaker will not be liable.

## THE SUPREME COURT

Against this common law backdrop of libel and slander, a series of U.S. Supreme Court decisions have incorporated many aspects of the qualified privilege into a broad constitutional privilege under the free press and free speech mandates of the First Amendment. The impact of these decisions has had a far-reaching effect on the states' libel laws.

*The public official.* The landmark case of *New York Times* v. *Sullivan*[15] brought into issue the extent to which the constitutional protections for speech and press limit a state's power to award damages in a libel action brought by public officials against critics of their official conduct. Sullivan, one of three elected Commissioners of the City of Montgomery, Alabama, contended that he was libeled by statements appearing in a full-page advertisement in the *New York Times* on March 29, 1960. Relying on the rationale that there is a profound national commitment to the principle that debate on public issues should be uninhibited,[16] the Court denied Sullivan any damages because he was a "public official" and because he failed to show that the advertisement was published with "actual malice" toward him.[17]

The "actual malice" requirement of *New York Times* v. *Sullivan* differs from the common law standard of malice, which focuses on a speaker's or writer's attitude toward another person.[18] Common law malice is established by evidence that a statement is made with ill will, hatred, evil or corrupt motive, intention to

15. *New York Times v. Sullivan*, 376 U.S. 254 (1964).

16. Ibid., pp. 270-71.

17. Ibid., pp. 279-80.

18. *Carson v. Allied News Co.*, 529 F. 2d 206, 209 (7th Cir. 1976).

injury, spite, enmity, or hostility.[19] The "actual malice" standard of the *New York Times* case concentrates on the defendant's attitude toward the truth or falsity of the material published.[20] The question becomes one of whether it was published "with knowledge that it was false or with a reckless disregard of whether it was false or not."[21] Later decisions have extended the "public official" doctrine to cover public employees of inferior stations, including a lieutenant of police,[22] an ordinary patrolman,[23] a school principal,[24] and a part-time accountant for a public waterworks.[25]

*The public figure and the public interest theory.* Following *New York Times* v. *Sullivan,* the Supreme Court in the companion cases of *Curtis Publishing Co.* v. *Butts* and *Associated Press* v. *Walker*[26] extended the "actual malice" test to include public figures as well as public officials. Thus, in order for a public figure to recover for defamation, the public figure must prove "highly unreasonable conduct constituting an extreme departure from the standards of investigation and reporting ordinarily adhered to by responsible publishers."[27] In essence, the *Walker* case extended the constitutional privilege to cover those who by their actions or professions have taken a position in the public eye.

19. Ibid.

20. Ibid.

21. *New York Times* v. *Sullivan,* 376 U.S. 279-80.

22. *Pape* v. *Time, Inc.,* 354 F. 2d 558 (7th Cir.) *cert. denied,* 384 U.S. 909 (1965).

23. *Tucker* v. *Kilgore,* 388 S.W. 2d 112 (Ky. 1965).

24. *Reaves* v. *Foster,* 200 So. 2d 453 (Miss. 1967).

25. *Krutech* v. *Schimmel,* 27 App. Div. 2d 837, 278 N.Y.S. 2d 25 (1967).

26. *Curtis Publishing Co.* v. *Butts* and *Associated Press* v. *Walker,* 388 U.S. 130 (1967).

27. Ibid., p. 155. The underlying rationale behind the extension was expressed by Chief Justice Warren in his concurring opinion, as follows:
Increasingly in this country, the distinctions between governmental and private sectors are blurred. . . . In many situations, policy determinations which traditionally were channeled through formal political institutions are now originated and implemented through a complex array of boards, committees, commissions, corporations, and associations, some only loosely connected with the government. This blending of position and power has also occurred in the case of individuals so that many who do not hold public

The Supreme Court's plurality opinion in *Rosenbloom* v. *Metromedia, Inc.*,[28] further expanded the *New York Times* doctrine to encompass all matters of a public or general nature when it held that "if a matter is a subject of public or general interest, it cannot suddenly become less so merely because a private individual is involved, or because in some sense the individual did not 'voluntarily' choose to become involved."[29] Therefore, if the event is one of a public nature, the individual must prove "actual malice" —knowing and reckless disregard of the truth—in order to recover in an action for defamation.

*The private individual.* The broadsweeping mandate of *Rosenbloom* was short-lived. Through *Gertz* v. *Robert Welch, Inc.*,[30] the Supreme Court circumscribed the plurality decision in *Rosenbloom*. Gertz, an attorney labeled a "Communist-fronter" by the defendant's magazine, had been denied recovery because of his failure to prove that the story was published with "actual malice." Recognizing the state's legitimate interest in protecting its citizens from injurious falsehoods, the Supreme Court reversed. In rejecting the public interest theory it had propounded three years earlier, the Court maintained that the "public or general interest test" not only inadequately served the needs of the private individual who is being injured by the defamatory statements, but also the publisher or broadcaster who erroneously concludes that the issue was of public or general interest.[31] The Court, therefore,

---

office at the moment are nevertheless intimately involved in the resolution of important public questions. . . . Our citizenry has a legitimate and substantial interest in the conduct of such persons, and freedom of the press to engage in uninhibited debate about their involvement in public issues and events is as crucial as it is in the case of 'public officials'. Ibid., p. 163.

28. *Rosenbloom* v. *Metromedia, Inc.*, 403 U.S. 29 (1971). The plaintiff brought an action against a radio station which had repeatedly broadcast a news story concerning the plaintiff's arrest for possession of obscene literature. The Court, finding that the radio station was not liable, centered its decision on the newsworthy event rather than on the individual involved and held that the distinction between public and private makes no sense in terms of the First Amendment guarantees.

29. Ibid., p. 43.

30. *Gertz* v. *Robert Welch, Inc.*, 418 U.S. 323 (1974).

31. Ibid., p. 346.

concluded that so long as a state does not impose liability without fault, the state may define its own libel laws when the defamatory falsehoods are directed at a private individual.[32] The Court further delineated the term "public figure" and posed two criteria for ascertaining whether an individual is subject to the *New York Times* "actual malice" test. An individual is a public figure if:

1. he has achieved such persuasive fame and notoriety that he has become a public figure for all purposes and in all contexts, or

2. he has voluntarily injected himself or has been drawn into a particular controversy, and has thus become a public figure for a limited range of issues.[33]

The crux of whether one is a public figure is no longer the newsworthiness of an event, but rather the nature and extent of an individual's participation in the event. Consequently, one is not a public figure for all phases of one's life.[34]

### PUBLIC OFFICIALS, PUBLIC FIGURES, AND EDUCATION

The series of Supreme Court decisions establishes the proposition that the media are afforded the protection of the First Amendment if the person alleging defamation falls within the ambit of the "public official-public figure" doctrine. Private individuals alleging defamation by the media may still recover under the less strict standards applicable to state libel laws. Left untouched by the Supreme Court's decision is private defamation; but, however logical and clear-cut these decisions may be, the application of these standards by the lower courts remains in a state of flux. Under the original *New York Times* v. *Sullivan* case the courts had no difficulty extending "public official" to include such lower echelon officials as a recreation supervisor,[35] a police chief,[36] a county

---

32. Ibid., pp. 346-47.

33. Ibid., p. 351.

34. Ibid., p. 352.

35. *Rosenblatt v. Baer*, 383 U.S. 75 (1966).

36. *Henry v. Collins*, 380 U.S. 356 (1965).

clerk,[37] a deputy sheriff,[38] a judge,[39] members of a school board,[40] a student senator of a university,[41] and a dean of a university law school.[42] The "public figure" doctrine of *Associated Press* v. *Walker* in 1967 increased the likelihood that educators would be included within that category. Recent lower court decisions have established a decided pattern of cases where educators were denied recovery because they were public figures.

A college basketball coach and former professional player was unable to recover for libel even though he had been retired from professional basketball for nine years.[43] The court relied on the theory that the coach had failed to shed his public image since the esteem in which he was held as a coach was derived from his former career. A college track coach with no professional record was also found to be a "public figure"[44] and was denied recovery because he did not show "convincing proof that the defamatory falsehood was made with knowledge of its falsity or with reckless disregard for the truth."[45] Furthermore, the court stated that a reporter may "without a high degree of awareness of their probable falsity, rely on statements made by a single source even though they reflect only one side of the story, without fear of libel prosecution."[46]

Two cases which have turned on the "public figure-public of-

37. *Beckley Newspaper v. Hanks*, 389 U.S. 81 (1967).

38. *St. Amant v. Thompson*, 390 U.S. 727 (1968).

39. *Garrison v. Louisiana*, 379 U.S. 64 (1964).

40. *Pickering v. Board of Education*, 391 U.S. 563 (1968); *Cabin v. Community Newspaper, Inc.*, 27 App. Div. 2d 543, 275 N.Y.S. 2d 396 (1966); *Fegley v. Mortheimer*, 204 Pa. Super. Ct. 54, 202 A. 2d 125 (1964).

41. *Klahr v. Winterble*, 4 Ariz. App. 158, 418 P. 2d 404 (1966). The case involves a campus newspaper.

42. *Gallman v. Carnes*, 254 Ark. 987, 497 S.W. 2d 47 (1973).

43. *Time, Inc., v. Grayson*, 448 F. 2d 378 (4th Cir. 1971); see also, *Grayson v. Curtis Publishing Co.*, 72 Wash. 2d 999, 436 P. 2d 756 (1967), where the court held that a coach is a public figure in which the public has an interest.

44. *Vandenburg v. Newsweek, Inc.*, 507 F. 2d 1024 (5th Cir. 1975).

45. Ibid., p. 1025, quoting *Gertz v. Robert Welch, Inc.*, 418 U.S. 323, 342.

46. Ibid., p. 1028, quoting *New York Times v. Connor*, 365 F. 2d 567, 576 (5th Cir. 1966).

ficial" classification have involved school principals. In *Reaves* v. *Foster*, a school principal alleged defamation following the distribution of a pamphlet which accused him of being "an Uncle Tom, a traitor to his race, a stooge, a stool pigeon, an informer, and a traitor to his people."[47] The court concluded that, in the absence of proof of malice, it was a fair comment. In a more recent case, *Kapiloff* v. *Dunn*, a Maryland court also classified a principal as a "public official-public figure" and subjected his right of recovery to the *New York Times* "actual malice" test.[48] Stating that " 'actual malice' demands more than a showing of unreasonable conduct," the court denied recovery.[49] The court further posited a distinction between facts and opinions under the *New York Times* test. The *Kapiloff* court maintained that while true statements of facts concerning the conduct of public figures are absolutely privileged, false statements of fact are protected if not knowingly or recklessly made with a disregard of the truth. Furthermore, opinions based on false facts are also protected, provided the publisher was not guilty of actual malice with regard to the supporting facts.[50]

Two cases have even ascertained that school teachers are public figures. *Schulze* v. *Coykendall*, by way of dicta, stated that teachers are considered to be involved in the area of public employment, and flowing from this statement is the natural inference that a teacher must satisfy the demanding *New York Times* test.[51] The 1974 case of *Basarich* v. *Rodeghero* involved teachers and coaches who brought an action individually and on behalf of a labor organization against the publishers of a newsletter.[52] The court maintained that the plaintiffs were public figures, that they were hired by the school board and paid with public funds, and

47. *Reaves v. Foster*, 200 So. 2d 453 (Miss. 1967).

48. *Kapiloff v. Dunn*, 343 A. 2d 251 (Md. 1975); cf. *Cox Broadcasting Co. v. Cohn*, 420 U.S. 469 (1975).

49. *Kapiloff v. Dunn*, 343 A. 2d 270.

50. Ibid., pp. 262-63.

51. *Schulze v. Coykendall*, 545 P. 2d 392 (Kans. 1976).

52. *Basarich v. Rodeghero*, 321 N.E. 2d 739 (Ill. 1974).

that as teachers they held a highly responsible position in the community.[53] Thus, they came within the confines of the "public official-public figure" doctrine and were required to prove "actual malice" on the part of the publisher before they could recover for defamation.

None of these cases involves educators in their capacities as solely private citizens. The elemental factor in each case is the fact that the educators are suing to recover damages for some slur on their professional status. Following the *Gertz* rationale, it would appear that an educator, suing as a private individual, would be afforded the protection of state libel laws that require less stringent standards to establish compensable malice.

## Invasion of Privacy

Since the 1890 article by Warren and Brandeis,[54] the right to privacy has been a source of consternation to the courts and legal commentators. Although the courts have often obfuscated the laws of privacy and defamation, the fundamental difference between the two is that a right to privacy concerns one's own peace of mind, while defamation concerns the state of one's reputation in the community. In addition, while truth is a defense to a claim of defamation, truth never justifies an invasion of one's privacy.[55] The differentiation between defamation and invasion of privacy is further complicated by the quadripartite nature of the right to privacy. An invasion of privacy is not a single tort but a composite of four types of intrusion[56] into one's personal affairs:

1. unreasonable intrusion upon the seclusion of another;[57]

53. Ibid., p. 742.

54. Samuel D. Warren and Louis D. Brandeis, "The Right to Privacy," *Harvard Law Review* 4 (December 1890): 193-220.

55. *Themo v. New England Publishing Co.*, 306 Mass. 54, 27 N.E. 2d 753, 755 (1940).

56. *Deaton v. Delta Democrat Publishing Co.*, 326 So. 2d 471 (Miss. 1976); *Restatement (Second) of the Law of Torts* (Tentative Draft no. 13, 1967), Sections 652A-652E; Prosser, *Handbook*, Section 117.

57. Prosser, *Handbook*, Section 117, p. 814. Unreasonable intrusion upon the seclusion of another requires that the invasion be of something secret.

2. appropriation of another's name or likeness;[58]
3. unreasonable publicity given to another's private life;[59]
4. publicity which unreasonably places another in a false light before the public.[60]

### THE COURTS AND INVASION OF PRIVACY

The courts have been faced with a myriad of cases alleging invasion of privacy, yet suprisingly, few of these cases involve school personnel. One of the earliest cases, *Reed v. Orleans Parish School*, questioned the right of a school board to inquire into matters of a private nature that related to a teacher's activities after school.[61] The teacher had failed to complete a questionnaire which was designed to determine how many teachers were involved in war work after school and the number of hours they were devoting to the program. The court maintained that such an action in no way invaded the teacher's privacy. Had the school board's purpose been to harass the teacher or to otherwise pry into her private life, the plaintiff's contention of invasion of privacy might have had some basis.[62] Since the facts requested were

58. Ibid., p. 805. The appropriation of another's name or likeness involves the benefit the wrongdoer derives from his use of the plaintiff's name. In order to be held liable for appropriation, the wrongdoer must have utilized for his own advantage the plaintiff's name or likeness.

59. Ibid., p. 810; *Restatement (Second) of the Law of Torts*, Explanatory Notes, Section 652 D, comment. The third branch of invasion of privacy, unreasonable publicity given to another's private life, embraces two requirements: (a) that the disclosure of the facts must be public (although the disclosure need not be written) and (b) that the facts so disclosed must be private facts. Consequently, public disclosure of private facts entails not only the infringement of secrecy but also the publication of the purloined information. There is no liability if the wrongdoer simply gives publicity to information which is already public.

60. Prosser, *Handbook*, p. 813. The final component, false light in the public eye, is juxtaposed with the tort of defamation, and these two areas of tort law often coalesce. False light, like public disclosure of private facts, depends on publicity and requires that a falsity or fiction be present. This fictive statement or situation must be something that would be objectionable to an ordinary, reasonable man under the same circumstances. The scope of this essential requisite is much broader than the narrow limits of defamation and will in many instances provide relief when defamation will not.

61. *Reed v. Orleans Parish School*, 21 So. 2d 895 (La. 1945).

62. Ibid., p. 897.

of public nature, rather than private, the teacher was unable to complain when an occupation she engaged in publicly was called to public attention.[63]

A recent nonschool case, which also turns on the public nature of the facts disclosed, is *Cox Broadcasting Corp. v. Cohn*.[64] The Supreme Court, holding that "the interests in privacy fade when the information involved . . . appears on public record,"[65] determined the identification of a rape victim during television coverage of a trial was permissible. The victim's name had been obtained from judicial records, which were open to public inspection. The Court centered its decision not only on the public nature of judicial records but also on the First and Fourteenth Amendments coupled with the public's interest in maintaining a vigorous press. Closely aligned with *Cox* is a case involving four school children who were the "stars" of an unsolicited newspaper article.[66] The article, which featured a public school special education class, described the four children as "retarded" and supplied the names and photographs of the children. Unlike the *Cox* decision, however, the court found that the privacy of the students had been invaded and maintained that while there is the consideration of "freedom of the press," the Supreme Court has never adopted a view of absolute constitutional immunity from liability for newspapers.[67] Moreover, while *Cox* involved disclosure of information available from public records, the records of these children, from which the information was taken, were by state law unavailable to the public.

Because of the propinquity of disclosure of private facts and the false-light theory of invasion of privacy to the laws of defamation, it was inevitable that the two would overlap. *Time, Inc. v. Hill*[68] brought the two branches of invasion of privacy that turn

63. Ibid.; Prosser, *Handbook*, Section 117, p. 810, n. 89.

64. *Cox Broadcasting Co. v. Cohn*, 420 U.S. 469.

65. Ibid., pp. 494-95.

66. *Deaton v. Delta Democratic Publishing Corp.*, 326 So. 2d 471, (Miss. 1976).

67. Ibid., p. 476.

68. *Time, Inc. v. Hill*, 385 U.S. 374 (1967).

on publicity within the scope of the constitutional privilege which had been afforded defendants in libel and slander cases.[69] In *Time, Inc.* v. *Hill*, Hill alleged that *Life* magazine had falsely reported that a new play portrayed an experience suffered by his family. Relying on a public interest test, the Court stated:

> where the interest at issue is privacy rather than reputation and the right claimed is to be free from the publication of false or misleading information about one's affairs, the target of the publication must prove knowing or reckless falsehood where the materials published, although assertedly private, are "matters of public interest."[70]

Thus, the constitutional privilege and its application to public figures is the same in actions for defamation and for invasion of privacy.[71] This privilege is not without its limits. In *Deaton* v. *Delta Democratic Publishing Co.*, which involved the four special education children, the court, while cognizant of the holding in *Time, Inc.* v. *Hill*, refused to find that the simple enrolling of a child in a public school was sufficient to make that child a "public figure."[72] It appears that a public figure will continue to experience difficulties in maintaining actions for invasion of privacy without establishing the requisite "actual malice" prescribed by *New York Times*. Since the courts have repeatedly held teachers to be public figures, teachers will no doubt encounter this difficulty when alleging an invasion of privacy as it relates to their professional lives.

## Liberty Interests

The due process clause of the Fourteenth Amendment to the U.S. Constitution protects an individual from the deprivation of life, liberty, or property. This protected liberty interest encompasses the basic tenets and freedoms of the American philosophy: freedom from bodily restraint, the right to contract freely, freedom to engage in any of the common occupations of life, freedom to marry, establish a home, and raise children, freedom to worship

69. Prosser, *Handbook*, Section 118, pp. 826-27.

70. *Time, Inc. v. Hill*, 385 U.S. 387-88.

71. Prosser, *Handbook*, Section 118, pp. 826-27.

72. *Deaton v. Delta Democratic Publishing Co.*, 326 So. 2d 471, 474 (Miss. 1976).

or not to worship God, and freedom to enjoy those privileges that are essential to the orderly pursuit of happiness.[73] The abridgment or deprivation of any one of these liberty interests by the government entitles an individual to a hearing with its procedural due process elements. Liberty interests, however, are not without peripheral limitations, and certain conditions must be met before an infringement can be successfully alleged.

### LIBERTY INTEREST AND EDUCATION

The concept of liberty recognizes two particular interests in the area of public employment: (a) the protection of an individual's good name, reputation, honor, and integrity, and (b) an individual's freedom to take advantage of other employment opportunities.[74] Teachers must, therefore, be afforded a hearing when nonretention by a school board imposes upon them a stigma or disability foreclosing future employment opportunities.[75] Teachers are also entitled to a hearing if the board's actions seriously damage their standing and association within the community.[76] Not every dismissal of a public employee constitutes a deprivation of liberty, and there are few judicial guidelines available for ascertaining when a liberty interest has been infringed. Only in instances involving publicly made charges that either foreclose future employment opportunities or damage the teacher's reputation in the community will the courts find an infringement of the teacher's liberty interest.[77] The mere presence of derogatory information in confidential files does not constitute an abridgment of a liberty interest.[78]

73. *Board of Regents of State Colleges v. Roth*, 408 U.S. 564, 572 (1972).

74. Ibid., pp. 573-74. See also, *Weathers v. West Yuma County School District*, 530 F. 2d 1335, 1338 (10th Cir. 1976); *Lipp v. Board of Education of Chicago*, 470 F. 2d 802, 805 (7th Cir. 1972).

75. *Buhr v. Buffalo Public School District No. 38*, 509 F. 2d 1196, 1199 (8th Cir. 1974); *Board of Regents of State Colleges v. Roth*, 408 U.S. 564 (1974); *Perry v. Sindermann*, 408 U.S. 593 (1972).

76. Ibid.

77. *Kaprelian v. Texas Women's University*, 509 F. 2d 133, 137 (5th Cir. 1975).

78. Ibid. See also, *Sims v. Fox*, 505 F. 2d 857, 863 (5th Cir. 1974) (en banc); *Collins v. Wolfson*, 498 F. 2d 1100, 1104 (5th Cir. 1974).

*The infringement of liberty.* In a recent Delaware case involving a black teacher who had been discharged because of false accusations of insubordination, the court held that she should be afforded an opportunity to clear her name and awarded damages for the injury incurred between the time of her discharge and the time when the burden on her right to pursue her teaching career was lifted.[79] The court stated that the school board knew of the potential injury to her career and that the oral rather than written dissemination of the reasons for discharge in no way mollified the injury.[80] Tantamount to the decision was the fact that the charges were untrue and that the superintendent deliberately inflicted the injury. Liberty is not offended by the mere dismissal from employment; it is offended, however, if the dismissal is based upon an unsupported charge which could foreclose future employment or wrongfully injure the employee's reputation.[81] Therefore, uncomplimentary accusations which do not impart serious character defects such as immorality or dishonesty have been held not to infringe liberty.

In *Gray* v. *Union County Intermediate Education District*, a special education teacher advised a pregnant student that she had a right to a therapeutic abortion.[82] Difficulties with the Welfare Department ensued, and the school board partially based its nonrenewal decision on the incident involving the pregnant girl. The allegations against the teacher included a letter from the Welfare Department stating that she was deliberately undermining the united planning of the community's professional social agencies and a letter from her former director of special education maintaining incompetence, hostility to authority, insubordination, and aggressive behavior.[83] The court found that personality differences or difficulty in getting along with others are not the types of ac-

79. *Morris v. Board of Education*, 401 F. Supp. 188, 213 (D. Del. 1975).

80. Ibid., p. 211.

81. *Arnett v. Kennedy*, 416 U.S. 134 (1974); *accord, Sims v. Fox*, 505 F. 2d 857 (5th Cir. 1974).

82. *Gray v. Union County Intermediate Education District*, 520 F. 2d 803 (9th Cir. 1975).

83. Ibid., p. 806.

cusations that warrant a hearing as prescribed by *Board of Regents of State Colleges* v. *Roth* and by *Perry* v. *Sindermann*.[84] In a similar instance, a report alleging "anti-establishment" behavior was found not to be a deprivation of liberty.[85]

In *Weathers* v. *West Yuma County School District* the Tenth Circuit has instituted a "practical test" to be utilized when fore-closure of employment opportunities has been alleged.[86] The "practical test" requires that the district court look to the grounds for nonrenewal and determine if they will substantially interfere with opportunities for subsequent employment.[87] Thereby, although an employee may be "less attractive" to future employers because of the facts surrounding a previous discharge, the employee's liberty interest has not been infringed.[88] Any reason for a teacher's dismissal is to some extent a negative reflection on the individual's ability; however, not every dismissal is of constitutional magnitude. Only those stigmas which seriously foreclose employment opportunities are of constitutional concern.[89]

*Recent Supreme Court decisions.* Two recent Supreme Court decisions have refined the concept of liberty interest, and may have severely restricted its viability as applied to public employment. In *Paul* v. *Davis*, the police chief of Louisville distributed

84. Ibid.; *Board of Regents of State Colleges v. Roth*, 403 U.S. 564 (1972); *Perry v. Sindermann*, 408 U.S. 593 (1972). See, for example, *Irby v. McGowan*, 380 F. Supp. (S.D. Ala. 1974) and *Courter v. Winfield-Mt. Union School District*, 378 F. Supp. (S.D. Iowa 1974).

85. *Lipp v. Board of Education of Chicago*, 470 F. 2d 805. Cf. *Wisconsin v. Constantineau*, 400 U.S. 433, 437 (1971) and *Joint Anti-Fascist Refugee Committee v. McGrath*, 341 U.S. 123 (1951).

86. *Weathers v. West Yuma Country School District*, 530 F. 2d 1335 (10th Cir. 1976).

87. Ibid., p. 1339. See also, *La Boarde v. Franklin Parish School Board*, 510 F. 2d 590 (5th Cir. 1975); *Blair v. Board of Regents*, 496 F. 2d 322 (6th Cir. 1974); *Wellner v. Minnesota State Junior College Board*, 487 F. 2d 153 (8th Cir. 1973); *Lipp v. Board of Education of Chicago*, 470 F. 2d 802 (7th Cir. 1972).

88. *Weathers v. West Yuma County School District*, 530 F. 2d 1339.

89. Ibid.; see *Board of Regents of State Colleges v. Roth*, 408 U.S. 573; *Gray v. Union County Intermediate School District*, 520 F. 2d 806; *Jablon v. Trustees of California State Colleges*, 482 F. 2d 997, 1000 (9th Cir. 1973) *cert. denied*, 414 U.S. 1163 (1974).

photographs of known shoplifters to the businessmen of the metropolitan area.[90] Although Davis had been charged with shoplifting, his guilt or innocence had never been resolved. Nevertheless, the flyer labeled him a "known shoplifter." Subsequent to the issuance of the photographs, the charges against Davis were dropped. Davis's employer, the *Louisville Courier-Journal and Times*, learning of the accusation against him, warned Davis that he "had best not find himself in a similar situation." In denying Davis's claim, the Supreme Court recited that "imputing criminal behavior to a person is generally considered defamatory per se, and actionable without proof of special damages."[91] The Court held that defamation standing alone does not give rise to a claim in federal court. Without the additional loss of a right under state law, such as employment, damage to one's reputation alone does not invoke the protection of procedural due process.

In *Bishop* v. *Wood*, a city policeman was discharged without a hearing.[92] Among the allegations communicated to him privately were his failure to follow orders, his poor attendance at police training classes, and the unsuitability of his conduct. The policeman denied the allegations and claimed he had been deprived of a liberty interest because the reasons given for discharge were false and so serious as to constitute a stigma that might seriously damage his reputation. The Supreme Court, holding that he had not been deprived of a liberty interest, stated that even if the reasons for his discharge were false, they had no impact on his reputation because they were communicated to him privately. Furthermore, to hold otherwise would penalize forthright and truthful communication between employer and employee and allow every employee to assert a constitutional claim merely by alleging that his or her former supervisor made a mistake.[93]

90. *Paul v. Davis*, 424 U.S. 693, 96 S. Ct. 1155 (1976).

91. *Paul v. Davis*, 424 U.S. 697, 96 S. Ct. 1159.

92. *Bishop v. Wood*, 426 U.S. 341, 96 S. Ct. 2074 (1976). Another recent case involving a police officer and the abridgement of liberty is *Codd v. Velger*, — U.S. —, 45 U.S.L.W. 4175 (February 22, 1977). From the examination of a personnel file, a prospective employer gleaned that the plaintiff had been dismissed because of an apparent suicide attempt. The plaintiff failed to allege that the suicide report was substantially false. The absence of such an allegation was fatal to his claim that he should be afforded a hearing.

93. *Bishop v. Wood*, 426 U.S. 349, 96 S. Ct. 2080.

With the resignation of Mr. Justice Douglas, the Supreme Court has become increasingly restrictive in involving the federal courts in public employment matters. Perhaps no statement of this restriction is more revealing than that made in *Bishop* v. *Wood*:

> The federal court is not the appropriate forum in which to review the multitude of personnel decisions that are made daily by public agencies. We must accept the harsh fact that numerous individual mistakes are inevitable in the day-to-day administration of our affairs. The United States Constitution cannot feasibly be construed to require federal judicial review for every such error. In the absence of any claim that the public employer was motivated by a desire to curtail or to penalize the exercise of an employee's constitutionally protected rights, we must presume that official action was regular and, if erroneous, can best be corrected in other ways. The Due Process Clause of the Fourteenth Amendment is not a guarantee against incorrect or ill-advised personnel decisions.[94]

In essence, the Fourteenth Amendment will no longer be the balm of plaintiffs alleging an infringement of their liberty because recovery under the Fourteenth Amendment will no doubt become increasingly more difficult as the Supreme Court endeavors to lessen the involvement of the federal courts by returning many controversies to the state courts.

## Self-incrimination

The Fifth Amendment to the U.S. Constitution provides that no individual "shall be compelled in any criminal case to be a witness against himself." The exercise of this privilege can not be taken as equivalent to either a confession of guilt or a conclusive presumption of perjury.[95] Although the Fifth Amendment specifies "criminal case," the privilege against self-incrimination can be invoked during civil proceedings if the fruits of the answers could be used in a subsequent criminal trial. The Fifth Amendment is most frequently invoked in cases involving policemen who have refused to answer questions during the course of a disciplinary hearing. Although a public employee can not be dismissed for invoking this constitutional right, the employee can be discharged

94. Ibid.

95. *Slochower v. Board of Higher Education of the City of New York*, 350 U.S. 551, 557-58 (1956).

if the questions asked are specific, narrowly drawn, and directly related to the performance of the employee's official duty.[96] Therefore, a public employee can be terminated from employment for not replying if the employee is adequately informed that not replying can be a reason for discharge and that the replies and their fruits can not be employed against the employee in a criminal case.[97] Thus, teachers can not be placed in a situation in which they are in fear of being discharged for refusal to answer on the one hand and in fear of self-incrimination on the other.[98] Situations of this nature have been aptly described by the courts as "a choice between the rock and the whirlpool"[99] and have been declared constitutionally unacceptable. It therefore appears that, as related to public employees, the courts have carved out or are carving out an exception. Employees may be discharged as to matters concerning their employment into which the employer is entitled to inquire, but if the employees do testify, their answers may not be used against them in a subsequent criminal proceeding.[100]

A somewhat different standard has been applied when the subject of the questioning is a student. In a case involving a student who was suspended after having thrown coffee on a teacher, the student was not compelled to testify in a meeting with the principal because the teacher had filed a criminal complaint against the student.[101] In *Caldwell* v. *Cannady*, four high school students were suspended for an alleged violation of a policy prohibiting possession of drugs.[102] The issue centered around the refusal of a student to testify before the school board concerning his alleged violation of the policy. Relying on the rationale that no constitu-

96. *Uniform Sanitation Men's Association* v. *Commissioner of Sanitation of the City of New York*, 392 U.S. 280 (1968); *Garner v. Broderick*, 392 U.S. 273 (1968).

97. *Kalkines v. United States*, 473 F. 2d 1391 (Ct. Cl. 1973). See also, *Garrity v. State of New Jersey*, 385 U.S. 493 (1967).

98. *Garrity v. State of New Jersey*, 385 U.S. 493 (1967).

99. Ibid., p. 496, quoting *Stevens v. Marks*, 383 U.S. 234, 243 (1966), quoting *Frost Trucking Co. v. Railroad Commission*, 271 U.S. 583, 593 (1926).

100. *Grabinger v. Conlisk*, 320 F. Supp. 1213, 1218 (N.D. Ill. 1970).

101. *Green v. Moore*, 373 F. Supp. 1194 (N.D. Tex. 1974).

102. *Caldwell v. Cannady*, 340 F. Supp. 835 (N.D. Tex. 1972).

tional rights are lost by virtue of status as a student, the court held that a student has a right to remain silent and that such silence can not be construed as an admission of guilt.[103] The court further distinguished the student's position from that of police officers. Police officers are under a duty to explain their conduct or face removal from the force because they are representative members of law enforcement and their conduct must be above reproach.[104] Unlike students, police officers and teachers are in positions of trust, which they have voluntarily chosen to assume and which they are under no pressure to retain. Furthermore, because of considerations of age, a student should be afforded greater constitutional protection.[105] Consequently, while under certain circumstances a teacher may be compelled to answer, a student apparently enjoys greater protection from self-incrimination.

### Freedom of Association

Basic to the American philosophy of privacy is the right of free association.[106] Only in the face of a legitimate, overriding state interest may a state inquire about an individual's associations and thereby circumscribe the right to associate freely with others.[107] The courts have focused particular attention on the First Amendment right of association and its relationship to teachers as public employees. The Arkansas statute that required public school teachers to file affidavits giving names and addresses of all organizations to which they had belonged or contributed within the preceeding five years as a prerequisite to employment was invalidated in *Shelton* v. *Tucker*.[108] The government's purpose in requiring

103. Ibid., p. 839. See *Tinker v. Des Moines Independent Community School District*, 393 U.S. 503 (1969).

104. *Caldwell v. Cannady*, 340 F. Supp. 841.

105. Ibid.

106. Mr. Justice Douglas, dissenting in *Moose Lodge v. Irvis*, 407 U.S. 163 (1973), wrote: "The associational rights which our system honors permit all white, all black, all brown, and all yellow clubs to be formed. They also permit all Catholic, all Jewish, or all agnostic clubs to be established. Government may not tell a man or woman who his or her associates must be. The individual can be as selective as he desires." (pp. 179-80)

107. *Baird v. State Bar of Arizona*, 401 U.S. 1, 6 (1973). Cf. *Shelton v. Tucker*, 364 U.S. 479 (1960).

108. *Shelton v. Tucker*, 364 U.S. 479 (1960).

loyalty oaths may be legitimate and substantial, but that objective cannot be pursued by means that broadly stifle the fundamental personal liberties of association and where the end can be more narrowly achieved. The narrowness with which a loyalty oath must be drawn was unclear until 1972, when the Court approved the oath complained of in *Cole* v. *Richardson*.[109]

A result similar to *Shelton* was reached in *Keyishian* v. *Board of Regents of University of State of New York*.[110] Keyishian and other teachers were terminated because of their refusal to sign a certificate or to advise the President of the State University of New York whether they were communists. The *Keyishian* court further illuminated the principle of *Shelton* v. *Tucker* that teachers do not lose their constitutional rights of association by becoming faculty members.[111]

Without a doubt, a state has a right to investigate the competence and fitness of those whom it hires to teach in the schools. For a teacher, fitness depends upon a broad range of factors, and there is no requirement that a teacher's classroom conduct be the sole basis for determining fitness for teaching.[112] The criteria used to determine fitness, however, must have a bearing on professional competence.[113]

The concept of free association often arises when a school board dismisses a teacher because of the teacher's conduct outside the classroom. To justify such a dismissal, a board must show that the teacher's conduct " 'materially and substantially' interfered with the school's work or the rights of the students."[114] In *Fisher* v. *Snyder*, a teacher's contract was terminated because of

109. *Cole v. Richardson*, 405 U.S. 676 (1972).

110. *Keyishian v. Board of Regents of University of State of New York*, 385 U.S. 589 (1967).

111. *Shelton v. Tucker*, 364 U.S. 479 (1960).

112. Ibid., p. 485.

113. *Beilan v. Board of Education*, 357 U.S. 399 (1958).

114. *Fisher v. Snyder*, 346 F. Supp. 396, 401 (D. Neb. 1972); *accord, Pickering v. Board of Education*, 391 U.S. 563 (1968); *Battle v. Mulholland*, 439 F. 2d 321 (5th Cir. 1971); *Bruns v. Pomderleau*, 319 F. Supp. 58 (D. Md. 1970); *Storch v. Board of Directors of Eastern Montana Region Five Mental Health Center*, 545 P. 2d 644 (Mont. 1976).

alleged conduct that was deemed to be unbecoming a teacher.[115] The teacher, on occasion, had allowed a young man, her twenty-six year old son's friend, to stay overnight in her apartment. The court, while recognizing that the school board has the power to inquire into a teacher's personal association, differentiated between making inquiry and using impermissible inferences arising from the inquiry.[116] Since the teacher's activities were having no effect on her work, the most she could be guilty of was a lack of good judgment. Therefore, her dismissal violated her right of free association guaranteed by the First and Fourteenth Amendments.

A school district cannot decline to hire a teacher simply because the teacher is married to a controversial community figure.[117] In addition, state statutes authorizing inquiry into a teacher's associational ties must not be unlimited and indiscriminate.[118] When dealing with the right of free association, there must be a balancing of the state's interest in making the inquiry with the teacher's right of freedom of association.

## The Family Educational Rights and Privacy Act

Balancing the individual's rights against the needs of government to compile, store, and disseminate information and protecting the citizen against growing government intrusion within the framework of the common law have become complex. The weighing of the privacy rights of public school students and their parents and guardians as opposed to the modern record requirements of the schools, which to a large part are imposed by the federal government, has become an enormous task. The fragility and sensitivity of privacy in the school environment led Congress to enact the Family Educational Rights and Privacy Act of 1974 (FERPA).[119] Through the spending powers of the United States, Congress it-

115. *Fisher v. Snyder*, 346 F. Supp 401.

116. Ibid., p. 398.

117. *Randle v. Indianola Municipal Separate School District*, 373 F. Supp. 766 (N.D. Miss. 1974).

118. *Shelton v. Tucker*, 364 U.S. 479, 490 (1960).

119. 20 *United States Code*, Section 1232g (Supp. 1975); Public Law No. 93-380 (August 21, 1974); Public Law No. 93-568, Section 2 (December 31, 1974).

self has struck the balance between the privacy rights of students, parents, and guardians and the requirements and needs of the schools.[120] The FERPA, which is applicable to those educational institutions that receive federal funds for programs administered by the Commissioner of Education, does not leave this delicate process to chance or to the interpretation of the courts under the common law or the laws of individual states.

Like most congressional acts, the FERPA provides the basic statutory framework but leaves the interpretation and enforcement to a regulatory agency, the Department of Health, Education and Welfare (HEW). With unbelievable speed, HEW responded to the FERPA with "Proposed Regulations" on January 7, 1975. The FERPA was amended by Congress and signed by the President on December 31, 1974.[121] After extensive comment by public school, college, and university personnel, together with the advocates of greater restriction on the use of student records, HEW published the "Final Rule on Educational Records" on June 17, 1976.[122]

The FERPA has two basic thrusts: (a) to guarantee parents, guardians, and students over the age of eighteen or who attend a postsecondary school access to student records;[123] and (b) to assure these same individuals privacy of these records by restricting the people who have access to them and by limiting the use of the records. The sanctions for noncompliance are a denial or termination of federal funds administered by the Commissioner of Education. The HEW Rules and Regulations are directed toward the objectives of guaranteeing access to student records and of protecting the individual's privacy.[124] Provisions for investigation

120. 20 *United States Code*, Section 1232g (Supp. 1975).

121. *Federal Register* 40, no. 3 (January 7, 1975).

122. *Federal Register* 41, no. 118, Part II (June 17, 1976) 45 *Code of Federal Regulations* 99. All references in these footnotes will be to the *Code of Federal Regulations* (C.F.R.) where references to the *United States Code* (U.S.C.) are made. Regulations for Subsection (c) of the FERPA related to surveys and data-gathering activities are not included, but will be published later. *Federal Focus* 1, no. 9 (September 1976).

123. Students over the age of eighteen or who are enrolled in postsecondary schools will be referred to as "eligible students." Whether or not students under the age of eighteen have rights in addition to those provided by the FERPA depends upon the state's laws.

124. *Federal Register* 41, no. 118, Part II (June 17, 1976) 45 C.F.R. 99.

of complaints and the termination of funding are, of course, included. The Rules and Regulations leave most procedural considerations in the hands of the school authorities but direct the local officials to adopt regulations and prescribe the substance of what must be included.

## DEFINITIONS

An understanding of the definitions given in the HEW Rules and Regulations are essential to an understanding of the FERPA and its implementation. Parents have rights of access to student records until the student reaches the age of eighteen or enters a postsecondary school. When the student becomes eighteen or enters a postsecondary school, all rights of access become exclusively those of the student except when the student is a dependent under Section 152 of the Internal Revenue Code.[125] A parent is a natural parent or a person acting as a parent or guardian in the absence of the child's natural parent, that is, a person *in loco parentis*.[126] Unless there is a court order terminating or restricting the rights of a divorced or separated parent, both parents have equal rights of access to student records.[127]

A student is a person who has actually been enrolled in school, and student records are those that are directly related to the student *and* that are maintained by an educational agency or person acting for the school. Records are any information provided in any medium including handwriting, printing, tapes, film, microfilm, or microfiche.[128]

The individual records in the sole possession of faculty members and administrators and not available to anyone other than a substitute are not student records. Other limited exceptions have been recognized for law enforcement and employee records. Certain medical records of students in postsecondary schools are also excepted.[129]

125. 45 *Code of Federal Regulations*, Sections 99.3 and 99.31 (a) (8).

126. Ibid., Section 99.3.

127. Ibid., Section 99.11.

128. Ibid., Section 99.3.

129. Ibid.

A student record is personally identifiable if it (a) contains the name of the student, the student's parent, or other family member; (b) gives the address of the student; (c) personally identifies the student through a Social Security number or otherwise; (d) lists personal characteristics which would enable the student to be identified; or (e) contains other information which would make the student's identity easily traceable. As reviewed below, directory information may be made available to the public if specific prerequisites are met. Directory information includes such items as the student's name, address, telephone number, date and place of birth, major field of study, participation in officially recognized activities and sports, weight and height of members of athletic teams, dates of attendance, degrees and awards received, the most recent previous school attended, and other similar information.[130]

### ACCESS TO AND AMENDMENT OF RECORDS (EDUCATIONAL RIGHTS)

The first objective of the FERPA is to provide access to the student's records for parents and students who are either eighteen years of age or who are enrolled in a postsecondary school (eligible students). If an eligible student or that student's parents make a request to inspect the student's records, the school must respond within a reasonable period of time but not later than forty-five days. The school authorities must also explain or interpret the records upon request and provide copies if an explanation is necessary to a review of the information.[131]

Student records may be destroyed either on a systematic or periodic basis. Records cannot be destroyed, however, after an eligible student or parent has made a request to review the record. So long as the student records are maintained by the educational institution, records of access and explanations placed in them must also be maintained.[132]

After inspecting a student record, an eligible student or that student's parent can request that the information be amended if the student or parent believes the record to be inaccurate, mislead-

130. Ibid.

131. Ibid., Sections 99.11, 99.8.

132. Ibid., Section 99.13.

ing, or in violation of the privacy rights of the student. Within a reasonable time, the responsible school authorities must decide whether the records are to be amended and advise the parties accordingly. If the school authorities decide not to amend the records as requested, the eligible student or parent must be advised of the right to a hearing.[133] Should the parties choose to request a hearing, it must be held within a reasonable period of time with advance notice of the time and place being given to the parent or eligible student. Although the hearing officer may be an employee of the school, that person cannot have a direct interest in the outcome of the hearing. The parties are entitled to present evidence through an attorney of their choice and at their expense. Within a reasonable period of time, the hearing officer must then make a written decision summarizing the evidence and the reasons for the decision. This decision must be based solely upon evidence presented at the hearing.[134]

A decision to amend the record as requested ends the matter. However, should the hearing officer determine that the record should not be amended, the parent or eligible student must be advised of their right to place a statement in the file disagreeing with the school official's decision. These explanations must be preserved as a part of the student's file so long as the record it explains is maintained. If the explained record is disclosed to any party, the explanation must also be disclosed.[135]

DISCLOSURE OF PERSONALLY IDENTIFIABLE INFORMATION (PRIVACY)

As a general rule, the written consent of a parent or student over eighteen years of age (eligible student) is required before a student record can be disclosed to others. Depending upon the laws of a state regarding the capacity of a minor to give consent, students under the age of eighteen may be able to give consent to the release of student records. For consent to be effective, it must be signed and dated by a parent or eligible student, and the specific records to be released must be identified. The release must identify

133. Ibid., Sections 99.20, 99.21.

134. Ibid., Section 99.22.

135. Ibid., Section 99.21.

the purpose of the disclosure, and the party or class of party to whom the information is to be given must be stated.[186]

Written consent of a parent or the eligible student is not required if (a) the record is released to a parent or the eligible student or (b) if the information is directory. Other school officials within the school who have a legitimate educational interest in a record are not required to secure consent before reviewing the record.[187] In several instances, school officials may transfer the records of students to other school districts where a student seeks to enroll without the consent of a parent or the eligible student. One such situation occurs when a school district includes a notice in its policies that it forwards school records to other schools upon request when a student seeks, or indicates an intention, to enroll. A second situation where no consent or notice of transfer is required is when a parent or an eligible student initiates the transfer of the records to the other school. If a school receives a request for records from another school and not from the parents or the student, and there is no provision in the school's policy for the transfer of records, the procedure is somewhat more complicated. That school must (a) make a reasonable attempt to notify a parent or eligible student at the last known address that the request for records has been made by the other school, (b) provide the parent or eligible student with a copy of the records transferred to the other school if the parent or eligible student requests them, and (c) provide an opportunity for a hearing should a parent or the eligible student ask to amend the records.[138]

Directory information such as a student's name, address, school and student activities may be given to the public if the school follows a few simple procedures. The FERPA and HEW Rules and Regulations give examples of personally identifiable information that is considered directory. Public notice of the school's categories of directory information must be given to the parents and eligible student who then have the right to advise the school that any or all of the categories of directory information concerning the stu-

136. Ibid., Section 99.30.

137. Ibid., Section 99.31.

138. Ibid., Sections 99.31, 99.34.

dent shall not be released to the public. In giving this notice, the school must specify the time limits within which a parent or an eligible student must advise the school in writing that all or any categories of directory information are not to be released.[139]

When student records are released to a parent or an eligible student, or to others with their consent, no record of the requests for the records are required to be kept. Similarly, no records of the disclosure need be maintained. The same is also true of the release of directory information or the disclosure of a student's records to school employees who have a legitimate educational interest in the records or to other school districts where the student intends to enroll. The same is not true when the release of the records is to the other agencies and individuals who are provided limited access under the FERPA.[140] Although certain federal and state officials, school accrediting agencies, and research organizations have specific rights of access to some student records,[141] the school must maintain not only a record of each request made for student records but also a record of which information was disclosed. These records of request and disclosure must identify the person making the request and the legitimate interest the person had in the information. The record of disclosures may be inspected by the parents or the student together with the school's custodian of the records and the custodian's assistants. The disclosure records may also be inspected during certain audits.[142] These same disclosure records must be maintained when a parent of a dependent student seeks access to the records,[143] when the records are provided in compliance with a court order or subpoena,[144] or when the records are released to meet a health or safety emergency.[145]

139. Ibid., Sections 99.3, 99.32 (b), 99.37.

140. Ibid., Sections 99.32, 99.33.

141. Ibid., Section 99.31 (a) (3) (5) (6) (7). Students' records may also be released without prior consent for determining financial aid. Ibid., Section 99.31 (a) (4).

142. Ibid., Section 99.32.

143. Ibid., Sections 99.31 (a) (8), 99.32.

144. Ibid., Sections 99.31 (a) (9), 99.32.

145. Ibid., Sections 99.31 (a) (10), 99.32, 99.36.

Historically, school officials have released student records to law enforcement officers, the courts, and officials of other governmental agencies without question. The FERPA severely limits access by these heretofore unquestioned authorities, and these records can now be released only in specific circumstances. A school official must supply student records pursuant to a court order or subpoena, but in advance of compliance with the court's directive the official must first make a reasonable effort (for example, a telephone call or letter) to notify a parent or the eligible student.[146] This advance notice is to provide the parent or the eligible student an opportunity to contest the issuance of the order or subpoena if desired. Student records may be released to health and safety officials if the knowledge of the contents is necessary to protect the health and safety of the student or others. The seriousness of the threat to health and safety together with the need for the information in meeting the emergency must be considered. Time must be of the essence in dealing with the emergency, and the official to whom the record is released must have the ability to deal with the emergency.[147]

When student records are disclosed to others under the provisions of the FERPA, there are restrictions on those individuals redisclosing the information to other parties. Personally identifiable information concerning a student is released under the FERPA with the condition that it is not to be disclosed to another party without the prior written consent of a parent or the eligible student. The exception is that officers, employees, and agents of an institution may use the records for the purposes for which the information was supplied. A third party who is not required to have the consent of the parents or student to secure the records may disclose the records to others under the provisions of the FERPA if the recordkeeping requirements of the FERPA are met. In other words, a school that receives a student's records from another school may use and disclose those records in the same manner as it does the records of other students.[148]

146. Ibid., Section 99.31 (a) (9).

147. Ibid., Sections 99.31 (a) (10), 99.36.

148. Ibid., Sections 99.33, 99.34.

IMPLEMENTATION PROVISIONS

The FERPA requires educational institutions that receive federal funds for programs administered by the Commissioner of Education to follow certain procedures in implementing the act. An entire section of the HEW Rules and Regulations provides for the enforcement of the FERPA.[149] This enforcement section requires, among other things, that certain records be kept and reports be made. A complaint procedure is provided, and the termination of funding process for the failure to comply is described.

In order to comply with the FERPA, a school must have written policies that must be made available to parents and students upon request.[150] These policies must provide notification to the parents or students of their rights under the act. Procedures for access to records are to be stated, and parents and eligible students must be permitted to inspect and review records. The school must state what constitutes a legitimate reason for denying a copy of a record and set forth a schedule of fees for securing copies.[151] A list of the types and locations of the student records maintained together with the titles and addresses of those who maintain the records must be kept. Directory information is to be defined, and a statement of whether the school will disclose information to third parties where the prior written consent of a parent or the eligible student is not required must be included. If this information is to be released, specific criteria must be established for determining who "school officials" are and what is considered a "legitimate educational interest." As reviewed above, a school must maintain a record of requests for access to and for the disclosure of student records when required to do so. The policy must also provide a parent and the eligible student an opportunity to seek an amendment of the records through a hearing if necessary. A parent or eligible student must be allowed to place a statement in the file as prescribed by the FERPA.[152]

Each year the school must notify the parents and the eligible

149. Ibid., Subpart E, Sections 99.60 ff.

150. Ibid., Section 99.5.

151. Ibid., Sections 99.5, 99.8.

152. Ibid., Section 99.5.

students of their rights under the FERPA. The notice must inform all parents and eligible students of the school's policies concerning student records and advise them of the location where a copy of the policy can be secured. The notice must also include a statement advising them of their right to file complaints alleging failures by the school to comply with the FERPA.[153] The annual notice requirement provides an opportunity to comply with the requirements and to advise the parents and eligible students of the policies of the school with regard to directory information.

The notice must be made in a manner which is "reasonably likely" to inform the parents and eligible students of the policies. The method of notice may vary from individual letters to newspaper notices or announcements, depending upon the circumstances; however, elementary and secondary schools must make special provision to notify parents whose primary or home language is other than English.[154]

## Conclusion

An individual's zones of privacy are created, expanded, and constricted by balancing the right of privacy against the public's right to know. Privacy is not a stagnant concept; it fluctuates with the mores and climate of the times. Additionally, one may be a public figure for one phase of one's life yet be strictly a private individual for another phase. What may be deemed an invasion of one individual's privacy may be considered public information when dealing with another person. Legislation, whether enacted to safeguard privacy or to expand the permissible scope of inquiry by the public, will doubtlessly be enacted. The balance struck by legislation can, of course, be changed by subsequent legislatures to conform to the needs of the times.

Due to this interdependence between the public and private sectors of a person's life, no sweeping generalization or predictions can be made concerning privacy rights and the law. There is no strict prescription with which educators can protect their own privacy or avoid infringing the privacy of another. Even the courts

153. Ibid., Section 99.6.
154. Ibid.

are not in accord; some state and federal courts view the right of privacy restrictively while others construe these rights liberally. Each instance of an alleged abridgment of privacy must be considered independently and in light of all the underlying and surrounding circumstances. Each situation involving individual privacy is unique unto itself.

# CHAPTER XII

# The Legal Protection of Academic Freedom

VIRGINIA DAVIS NORDIN

## Introduction

While freedom of thought has been a subject of importance for scholars at least since the time of Socrates, its existence and legal protection is especially important at the present time because the concept of academic freedom, laboriously rooted and nurtured in this country by the dedicated work of the American Association of University Professors (AAUP) and others, is now being challenged by a number of new forces. Among these forces are (a) the civil rights movements for minorities and women, including affirmative action; (b) the extension of increased governmental regulation to all educational institutions, particularly colleges and universities; (c) the student protest movement; (d) the changing role of professional associations, such as the AAUP, with the advent of collective bargaining in education; (d) the increasing tendency to view education as a business enterprise subject to management principles; and (e) the no-growth educational market, including the possible oversupply of teachers and professors. With all these forces at work, it seems possible that despite the heroic efforts of the AAUP the present fragile structure of academic freedom may crumble from within or be nibbled to death from without. Strong legal protection against the varied and subtle pressures presently at work seems paramount, given the number of counterbalancing legal interests that are themselves increasingly strong and complex.

A realistic review of the law indicates that very little legal protection actually exists for academic freedom. It is the thesis of this chapter that the educational community ought not to wait for the possible evolution of the right of academic freedom in Supreme

Court case law,[1] but ought instead to advocate a constitutional amendment that establishes a distinct legal protection for that right. Such an amendment would protect a necessary and fundamental aspect of our democratic society and would be of at least as much value as some other amendments currently being considered.

## Defining Academic Freedom

As numerous authorities have asserted, academic freedom as we presently know it comes from the development of *Lehrfreiheit* and *Lernfreiheit*, the freedom to teach and the freedom to learn.[2] The German ideal, developed by Baron von Humboldt in the early seventeenth century,[3] concerned the freedom of teacher-professors to speak without fear of reprisal and the right of students to visit other institutions of higher learning, to choose their courses, their mode of study, and their curriculum in any manner they thought fit as long as they could pass the final examinations for a degree. It has been argued that neither of these concepts translated well into American society. The professor's right to speak freely was originally granted in a context in which the average citizen did not have that right, and free academic inquiry was considered deserving of special protection. Since the First Amendment to the U.S. Constitution gives all citizens the rights to freedom of speech, of the press, of assembly, and of religion, it is argued that there is no need for a separate "right" of academic freedom.[4] Indeed, in one sense the right of academic freedom exists for and extends to the whole citizenry because of the extreme importance of free inquiry in a system of self-government. The question to be considered here is whether there is a definable legal right to academic freedom that relates specifically to educational institutions and to the members of academic communities as opposed to the gen-

1. See Thomas I. Emerson, *The System of Freedom of Expression* (New York: Vintage Books, 1970), pp. 611-16, for an exposition of this view.

2. Most authorities refer to Richard Hofstadter and Walter P. Metzger, *The Development of Academic Freedom in the United States* (New York: Columbia University Press, 1955).

3. See Fritz K. Ringer, *The Decline of the German Mandarins* (Cambridge, Mass.: Harvard University Press, 1969), pp. 23-24, 111-12.

4. Mr. Justice Douglas stated in *Griswold v. Connecticut*, 382 U.S. 478, 483 (1965), that academic freedom is protected by the "penumbra" of the First Amendment.

eral rights accorded all citizens by the Bill of Rights, and, if there
is no such clearly defined right, whether one ought to be established.

Although many commentators conclude that the primary development of the American doctrine has been in the area of the
freedom to teach, I intend to discuss both the right of freedom to
teach and the right of freedom to learn as the two sides of the
coin of academic freedom. There has been a development in
American jurisprudence regarding the freedom to learn, although
American higher education has always been comparatively highly
structured in content and in control of student life, carrying the
common law concept of *in loco parentis* even to the college level.[5]
The right of a university student to structure his own curriculum
has never been recognized here as a legal right, although recent
assertions of student rights may lead in that direction.[6]

Although many articles on academic freedom provide a specific definition of the term, none of them contains a clear legal
definition.[7] If it is true that there is no real protection in case
law for academic freedom as an independent, unique concept, then
it must follow that no legal definition has as yet clearly emerged.
An enunciated definition, of course, is not in itself a requirement
for legal protection. There is no clear definition of religion, yet

5. Whether this concept still survives in American higher education is
problematic and outside the scope of this paper. Certainly for those students
above the age of majority the doctrine no longer applies.

6. For an argument that assertion of student rights demanding internal
academic due process (which could be interpreted as being in the *Lernfreiheit*
tradition) is an infringement on the professor's academic freedom, see James
L. Grace, Jr., "Academic Freedom versus Student Rights," *NOLPE School
Law Journal* 5, no. 2 (1975): 110.

7. In 1955, Machlup defined "academic freedom" as follows:
Academic freedom consists in the absence of, or protection from, such re-
straints or pressures—chiefly in the form of sanctions threatened by state or
church authorities or by the authorities, faculties, or students of colleges and
universities, but occasionally also by other power groups in society—as are
designed to create in the minds of academic scholars (teachers, research workers, and students in colleges and universities) fears and anxieties that may inhibit them from freely studying and investigating whatever they are interested
in, and from freely discussing, teaching, or publishing whatever opinions they
have reached.
See Fritz Machlup, "On Some Misconceptions concerning Academic Freedom," in *Academic Freedom and Tenure*, ed. George L. Joughin (Madison,
Wis.: University of Wisconsin Press, 1969), p. 178.

religious freedom is protected by the Constitution. In this chapter I shall attempt to determine whether the courts have defined academic freedom by creating a protectable interest. Neither careless, expansive usage of the term nor careful disquisitions on meanings that *ought* to exist are of help in this endeavor.

Beginning with the drive in 1930 for tenure for academics and aided certainly by a note in the *Harvard Law Review* in 1968,[8] the concept of academic freedom has grown until the very idea is in danger of death by overexpansion.[9] Perhaps the most useful way to approach the problem of defining academic freedom as a legal right, as both Van Alstyne and Goldstein have noted,[10] is to indicate the areas to which the term has *not* been applied in court decisions.

First, the courts have not extended the term to include personal rights, such as the right to wear long hair or other aspects of personal freedom that should not be confused with the freedom to think, to inquire, and to disseminate the results of inquiry.

Second, the courts have not held that the concept of academic freedom should be used to protect public employees in colleges and universities from improper activities of the government in its role as employer or to protect the evolving rights of all public employees to be free from coercion in areas unrelated to their work, unless these rights directly affect free inquiry and the dissemination of its results.

Third, citizenship rights, such as those affirmed by the Supreme Court in *Pickering* v. *Board of Education*,[11] and which are held in

8. "Note: Developments in the Law—Academic Freedom," *Harvard Law Review* 81 (March 1968): 1045-1159.

9. For a case in which the court denied relief in part because of the plaintiff's overbroad definition of the term, see *Jones v. Board of Control*, 131 So. 2d 713, 716-17 (Fla. S.C. 1961). The court ruled that a law professor has no constitutional right to run for a judgeship.

10. William van Alstyne, "The Constitutional Rights of Teachers and Professors," *Duke Law Journal* 1970 (October 1970): 841-879; Stephen Goldstein, "The Asserted Constitutional Right of Public School Teachers to Determine What They Teach," *University of Pennsylvania Law Review* 124 (June 1976): 1293.

11. *Pickering v. Board of Education*, 391 U.S. 563 (1968). In this case the Supreme Court affirmed the right of a school teacher to criticize the school board when he was speaking as a citizen living in that school district.

common by all citizens whether in academic employ or not, have not been included by the courts under the concept of academic freedom.

Fourth, the concept of academic freedom has been largely limited by the courts to higher education. Scholarly and judicial analysts have pointed out that it is important to the progress of society and to the protection of self-government that there be untrammeled inquiry into truth and that the results of that inquiry be freely disseminated. Dissemination includes the right to teach and publish as well as the right to learn. Obviously, the right to learn extends to professors as well as to students, since professors are, in a sense, the original lifelong learners. According to this view, true academic freedom exists primarily at the postsecondary level, since it is in those institutions that the duty to inquire arises. It is argued that mandatory universal secondary schooling includes a socializing mission that cannot be harmonized with free inquiry and dissemination. Although a number of issues have been raised in elementary and secondary schools dealing with the use of controversial teaching methods,[12] or with controversial teaching materials,[13] or with library books,[14] these cases have almost uniformly been decided in favor of the authority of school boards to regulate public education. Decisions in favor of individual teachers are generally based on failure to give adequate notice of the applicable rules and standards, the reasonableness of the teacher's approach within the appropriate rules, or other aspects of due process and procedure rather than substantive rights. This conclusion has recently been exhaustively documented by Goldstein.[15] According to Goldstein, the attitude of the courts is undoubtedly based on the view that many policy decisions in elementary and secondary education are ultimately political and therefore ought not to be left solely to teachers.[16] Since there is little duty to make original in-

12. *Raney v. Board of Trustees*, 48 Cal. Rptr. 555 (Calif. Ct., App. 1966).

13. *Parducci v. Rutland*, 316 F. Supp. 352 (M.D. Ala. 1970).

14. *Presidents Council, District 25 v. Community School Board No. 25*, 457 F. 2d 289 (2d Cir. 1972).

15. Goldstein, "The Asserted Constitutional Right of Public School Teachers to Determine What They Teach."

16. Ibid., p. 1356. Although Goldstein objects to constitutional protection of

quiry at the secondary level, there is little need for the protection accorded by academic freedom. In *Cary* v. *Board of Education of Adams-Arapahoe*, however, a district court in Colorado recently took a very strong stand for academic freedom for secondary-school teachers.[17]

Thus, with the possible exception of the students' right to learn, education below the college level is not covered by the concept of academic freedom unless there is a substantial extension of the term for reasons independent of those now justifying such as extension. As for secondary students, their position is in some ways more similar to the situation of the German students, which led to the development of *Lernfreiheit*, than is the position of American college students, since there is less direct governmental control of higher education than of elementary and secondary education. Some of the "library" cases are consistent with the idea of an evolving student right to learn on the secondary level, although the cases, still at the lower court level, are by no means uniform in conclusion as to whether school boards or other authorities may remove books from school library shelves.[18] Generally, however, the core right of academic freedom has been applied only on the postsecondary level, where it is assumed that there is no necessity to serve the melting pot theory of American social development or to inculcate patriotic and democratic values. Those purposes have presumably been accomplished in early education or at the secondary level.

Fifth, if academic freedom is to be limited to higher education, it is also necessary to make a distinction between academic freedom and tenure. Important as the latter is to the development and protection of the former, the two are not identical. The use of the term "tenure" has become increasingly generalized and its mean-

---

teachers' curricular control (p. 1357), that objection evidently does not extend to higher education. See generally, "Academic Freedom, Its Meaning and Underlying Premises as Seen through the American Experience," *Israel Law Review*, 2, no. 1 (1976): 52.

17. *Cary v. Board of Education of Adams-Arapahoe*, 427 F. Supp. 945, (D. Colo. 1977).

18. For an extensive review of library cases and an argument for more freedom of expression there, see Robert M. O'Neil, "Libraries and the First Amendment," *University of Cincinnati Law Review* 42, no. 2 (1973): 209.

ing therefore confused. There is more similarity between the reason for the nature of professorial tenure and judicial tenure than
there is between professorial tenure and teacher tenure, but there
is more tendency to combine the definitions of the latter two because they fall generally within the same profession. It is unfortunate that much of the voluminous writing on the subject fails
to note the difference between statutory tenure for teachers in
elementary and secondary schools and tenure for university professors. Tenure for the latter is closely tied to research and publication. The difference is crucial in defining the relationship of
tenure to academic freedom.[19]

A seminal article, which no doubt began the equating of tenure
with academic freedom, appeared in the *Yale Law Journal* in 1937.[20]
At that time it was illegal in many states to commit the public purse
to a contract for more than a year with an instructor in a public
institution. Tenure was seen as an all-important practical step to
protect the instructor from being fired or not renewed for holding
and expounding unpopular views. At that time, the explosive
growth of educational institutions had not begun, and tenure was
viewed as a way to allow professors free comment without fearing
for their jobs. Even tenure, however, cannot overcome "financial
exigency"[21] and, of course, it leaves probationary professors with
no protection whatsoever unless a clear violation of existing constitutional rights can be found under the standards established in
*Perry* v. *Sindermann*[22] and in *Board of Regents of State Colleges*
v. *Roth*.[23] It is this aspect of tenure that relates to academic freedom, even as tenure for judges relates to a fair and unbiased rendering of opinion from the bench. If a professor can be summarily

19. For an interesting history of the development of tenure of public school
teachers in one state, see James R. Maloney, "A History of Tenure Law in
Illinois" (Ph.D. diss., University of Illinois, 1976).

20. Bruce Wasserstein, "Academic Freedom and the Law," *Yale Law Journal*
46 (March 1973): 670-86.

21. See *Johnson v. Board of Regents*, 377 F. Supp. 227 (W.D. Wis. 1974),
aff'd. 510 F. 2d 975 (7th Cir. 1975) and *Bignall v. North Idaho College*, 358 F.
2d 243 (9th Cir. 1976) and authorities cited therein.

22. *Perry v. Sindermann*, 408 U.S. 593 (1972).

23. *Board of Regents of State Colleges v. Roth*, 408 U.S. 564 (1972).

dismissed for any kind of professional statement not in accord with the current political drift of the state legislature or campus administration, the free development of thought and ideas is indeed inhibited. However, the guarantee of the right of freedom of expression by restraining institutional or governmental intimidation through employment practices is not the same as a guarantee of lifelong job security for a privileged professional class and the two concepts should remain distinct. Professors have no more guaranteed right to a lifetime income than any other class of citizens except as that right relates to the freedom of academic inquiry and dissemination.

### Academic Freedom as a Legal Concept

Although distinguished scholars such as Fellman[24] and Van Alstyne,[25] as well as various Supreme Court justices, have argued for the existence of a First Amendment right of academic freedom, the development of the concept has come more through the writings of scholars, and especially through the efforts of the AAUP, than through the actual development of case law under the First Amendment. While there are a number of opinions, concurrences, and dissents filled with ringing rhetoric, most of the decisions actually are based on rather narrow procedural grounds and never reach the underlying question of whether and how academic freedom might be practically protected by the law. The value of the academic freedom cases, like the AAUP code, lies in their moral suasion on society during a period of great need. The innate feeling that academic freedom *ought* to be protected under the law has led to a number of different theories as to the ways in which it is protected, including the creation of a new tort action,[26] but actually academic freedom is not adequately protected by the law at the present time.

The majority and dissenting opinions in the *Keyishian* case (to

24. David Fellman, "Academic Freedom in American Law," *Wisconsin Law Review* 1961 (January 1961): 3-46.

25. Van Alstyne, "The Constitutional Rights of Teachers and Professors."

26. Thomas A. Cowan, "Interference with Academic Freedom": The Prenatal History of a Tort," *Wayne Law Review* 4 (Summer 1958): 205-27.

be considered later) seem to indicate that in the academic anti-communist cases the Supreme Court was wrestling with the proper balance between the necessity for the self-preservation of the republic and the importance of academic freedom. It would seem that while a shifting majority of the Court recognized the value of academic freedom it was reluctant to establish a new right of that nature at the time when the very roots of the democratic system seemed threatened by communist revolution. It might seem regrettable that the question of academic freedom had to come to the Court counterpoised with communist revolution, but it was a fair test. As Mr. Justice Holmes said, the principle of free thought means not free thought for those who agree with us but freedom for the thought that we hate.[27] Even though the courts became the bulwark for protection of beleaguered academics in the McCarthy era, they did so by standing very carefully on technical and procedural grounds, not by establishing a new right. That it is now important to incorporate such a right into our law through constitutional amendment is indicated by the variety and subtlety of the undermining forces. As the complexity of society inexorably forces us toward "group think," stronger protection of the freedom of thought, inquiry, and dissemination becomes imperative.

A final but extremely important factor arguing for strengthening the legal protection for academic freedom is that its major defender in the community of scholars now finds itself in what many regard as, at best, a compromising position. The AAUP first published a "Declaration of Principles" on academic freedom and tenure in 1915, and then became active in the drive to establish tenure.[28] In 1940, the widely respected "Statement of Principles on Academic Freedom and Tenure" was issued. During this time the AAUP, through its "Committee A," formed many smaller committees to investigate complaints in the area of academic freedom. By countless hours of selfless effort in courts and on campuses this organization and its leaders succeeded in righting many wrongs. It is particularly impressive that much change was effected solely through procedures based on moral suasion, although there has

27. *U.S. v. Schwimmer*, 279 U.S. 644 (1929).

28. Wasserstein, "Academic Freedom and the Law."

been an occasional institution that seemed unperturbed by its continued presence on the list of censured institutions. The AAUP has also filed a number of *amicus curiae* briefs arguing for the protection of academic freedom.[29] More recently, however, the AAUP has decided to serve at least a limited role as a collective bargaining agent in higher education and thus, in the minds of many, has put itself clearly into the role of adversary with respect to those administrations it had formerly judged. Many assert that this is a difficult moral position from which to argue for academic freedom, since the suspicion may arise that other more political issues of faculty organization are behind any such arguments. An advocate cannot be an impartial authority, even aside from the legal considerations where a contract actually exists. The *Starsky* case, to be discussed later, is perhaps an indication of a weakening of the Association's position. In that case the Arizona Board of Regents chose to disregard the findings of the AAUP Committee, as well as the recommendations of the university president, and terminated Starsky on extremely questionable grounds, possibly feeling that a faculty committee would simply be a faculty apologist. Of course, the growing tendency of governing boards to want to plan an increasing role in campus administration and to exercise their power more independently also played a role in this decision.[30]

### THE MC CARTHY ERA CASES

Some discussions[31] of the case law of academic freedom begin with an analysis of *Meyer* v. *Nebraska*,[32] the case in which the Court found it beyond the competence of the state to forbid the teaching of the German language (and the use of the German language in the teaching of other subjects), and with *Pierce* v. *The Society of Sisters*,[33] which denied the power of states to com-

29. For a general summary of AAUP activities, see Joughin, *Academic Freedom and Tenure.*

30. The AAUP report on the *Starsky* case is in the *AAUP Bulletin* 62 (Spring 1976): 55-69.

31. See, for example, Emerson, *The System of Freedom of Expression.*

32. *Meyer v. Nebraska*, 262 U.S. 390 (1923).

33. *Pierce v. The Society of Sisters*, 268 U.S. 510 (1925).

pel attendance at public schools. The first case in which the concept
was really discussed, however, was *Adler* v. *Board of Education*,[34]
in which New York's Feinberg law (a pre-loyalty oath attack on
subversive organizations) was upheld. In his dissent to *Adler*, Mr.
Justice Douglas gave the first of his many stirring comments on
academic freedom:

What happens under this law is typical of what happens in a police
state. . . . A pall is cast over the classrooms. There can be no real
academic freedom in that environment. . . . Supineness and dogmatism
take the place of inquiry, . . . fear stalks the classroom. . . . A deadening
dogma takes the place of free inquiry. Instruction tends to become
sterile; pursuit of knowledge is discouraged; discussion often leaves off
where it should begin.[35]

The Feinberg Act was originally passed in 1949 to implement
statutes passed in 1917 and 1939, and was amended in 1953 to extend its provisions to the personnel of public colleges. A case under
the new law reached the Supreme Court in 1967 and the result was
the landmark decision in *Keyishian*.

In the meantime, between *Adler* and *Keyishian*, the Court had
had occasion to discuss the issue of academic freedom in several
"red scare" cases, including *Wieman* v. *Updegraff*,[36] in which it
upheld a challenge by faculty members of the Oklahoma A & M
College to a state loyalty oath. This is the case in which Mr. Justice
Frankfurter, joined by Mr. Justice Douglas, referred to teachers
as the "priests of our democracy," a status that he accorded to all
teachers, including primary teachers. This special status was to enable teachers to "foster those habits of openmindedness and critical
inquiry which alone make for responsible citizens who in turn,
make possible an enlightened and effective public opinion."[37] This
is one of the best court statements as to why society, as opposed to
the individual teacher, has an interest in academic freedom. Frankfurter went on to argue that teachers must have freedom of inquiry
in order to teach by example:

34. *Adler v. Board of Education*, 342 U.S. 485 (1952).

35. Ibid., p. 510.

36. *Wieman v. Updegraff*, 344 U.S. 183 (1952).

37. Ibid., p. 196.

They must be free to sift evanescent doctrine, qualified by time and circumstance, from that restless, enduring process of extending the bounds of understanding and wisdom to assure which the freedoms of thought, of speech, of inquiry, of worship are guaranteed by the Constitution of the United States against infraction by national or state government.[38]

Unfortunately for the development of a case law of academic freedom, this statement is in a concurring opinion. The majority, concerned with the distinction between "innocent" and "knowing" membership in a communist organization, drew no particular conclusions from the fact that the case had come from an institution of higher learning.

Probably the strongest case for academic freedom decided during this period was *Sweezy* v. *New Hampshire*.[39] In that case the Court refused to uphold Sweezy's conviction for contempt for his refusal to answer questions about a lecture on socialism at the University of New Hampshire, although he did agree to state that he was not a member of the Communist Party. Although once again the Court's opinion includes strong words on the essential nature of free thought in a democratic society, the words are *dictum*, the Court deciding simply that the authority of the Attorney General of New Hampshire to propound the questions that resulted in the conviction had not been sufficiently established. Some may argue that the Court would not have said the same of a nonacademic public employee, but the fact remains that the actual holding is extremely limited.

Thus, by the time *Keyishian* came before the Court in 1967, in the cases directly touching higher education, there had been one decision upholding the Feinberg law, one decision holding that an overbroad oath is invalid, and one decision defining the authority of a state attorney general. In 1959, the Court upheld a conviction of a college instructor for contempt of the House Committee on Un-American activities. Unlike Sweezy, the defendant, Barenblatt, had not been questioned about his teaching or other academic activities, but rather about his membership in the Communist Party.

38. Ibid., p. 197. Thought and inquiry are not, of course, specifically mentioned in the Constitution, as are speech and worship.

39. *Sweezy v. New Hampshire*, 354 U.S. 234 (1957).

A strong argument for the establishment of academic freedom as a legal right was made in that case, but the Court found that the issue was not one of academic freedom. This conclusion comports with a narrow definition of that freedom that does not extend it to the nonprofessional aspects of a professor's life and is thus correct, even though the pressures brought against Barenblatt are clearly examples of those brought against faculty members during this period. Thus, while the Court acknowledged a role of protector of colleges from congressional intrusion, it also added that the investigatory power of Congress was not to be denied "solely because the field of education is involved."[40] Evidently agreeing, Justices Black, Warren, Douglas, and Brennan confined their arguments in dissent to the First Amendment rights, strictly enumerated.

Meanwhile, in another line of cases, which involved academic personnel, the Court continued to consider the constitutional propriety of loyalty oaths. By considering these cases chronologically we may give some idea of the prior progression of issues before the Court when it came to decide *Keyishian*. In 1956, the Court decided another landmark case for academic freedom,[41] ruling that a college instructor could not, by statutory authority, be summarily and automatically dismissed for pleading the Fifth Amendment before a congressional investigative committee. The Court specifically stopped short of creating a constitutional right to teach, or invalidating dismissal under the circumstances, as long as due process was complied with. In 1958, the Court upheld the dismissal of a public school teacher who pleaded the Fifth Amendment and was dismissed for "incompetency."[42] In 1960, the Court decided that an Arkansas statute requiring every teacher and professor in a public institution to file a yearly list of organizational affiliations (aimed at uncovering membership in the National Association for the Advancement of Colored People) was unconstitutionally overbroad, stating that the "unlimited and indiscriminate sweep of the statute . . . goes far beyond what might be justified in the exercise of the state's legitimate inquiry into the fitness and competency

40. *Barenblatt v. U.S.*, 360 U.S. 109, 130 (1959).

41. *Slochower v. Board of Education of New York City*, 350 U.S. 551 (1956).

42. *Beilan v. Board of Public Education*, 357 U.S. 399 (1958).

of its teachers."[43] In 1961, it found a Florida loyalty oath statute unconstitutionally vague,[44] and in 1964 the Court invalidated a Washington loyalty oath statute, as well as a law requiring all teachers "to promote respect for the flag and the institutions of the United States of America and the State of Washington, reverence for law and order, and undivided allegiance to the government of the United States," on the basis that the laws were unduly vague, uncertain, and broad.[45]

Thus in 1967, when the Feinberg law, then applicable to colleges, was again under consideration in *Keyishian*, Mr. Justice Douglas finally wrote a majority opinion, this time invalidating the Feinberg law, its administrative regulations, and the two earlier laws on which it was based, stating:

Our nation is deeply committed to safeguarding academic freedom, which is of transcendent value to all of us and not merely to the teachers concerned. That freedom is therefore a special concern of the First Amendment which does not tolerate laws that cast a pall of orthodoxy over the classroom.[46]

The actual grounds for the decision, however, did not rest on the primacy of academic freedom over government regulation, but rather on "vagueness of wording . . . aggravated by prolixity and profusion of statutes, regulations, and administrative machinery, and . . . manifold cross-references to interrelated enactment and rules,"[47] and on the earlier established standard that public employment, including but not limited to academic employment, may not be conditioned upon the surrender of constitutional rights which could not be abridged by such government action as the proscription of membership without the showing of specific intent to further the unlawful aims of the Communist Party.

The dissent, while recognizing the genius of our public education system, nevertheless did not see free speech, thought, press, assembly, or association as the issue, but rather the right of self-

43. *Shelton v. Tucker*, 364 U.S. 479 (1960).

44. *Cramp v. Board of Public Instruction*, 368 U.S. 278 (1961).

45. *Baggett v. Bullitt*, 377 U.S. 360 (1964).

46. *Keyishian v. Board of Regents*, 385 U.S. 589, 603 (1967).

47. Ibid., p. 605.

preservation. Regarding the basis for the majority opinion, the dissent stated: "No court has ever reached out so far to destroy so much with so little." The view of *Keyishian* as a keystone of academic freedom would seem to have been diminished further during the Court's next term, when it affirmed a district court decision validating a loyalty oath.[48] The case was brought by faculty members at Adelphi University. The oath involved read as follows:

I do solemnly swear (or affirm) that I will support the Constitution of the United States of America and the Constitution of the State of New York, and that I will faithfully discharge, according to the best of my ability, the duties of the position of _____, to which I am now assigned.

In reaching its conclusion the three-man district court specifically rejected any special standard of free speech which might be applied to teachers:

A state does not interfere with its teachers by requiring them to support the governmental systems which shelter and nourish the institutions in which they teach. . . . Indeed it is plain that a state has a clear interest in assuring . . . careful and discriminating selection of teachers by its publicly supported educational institutions.

Thus, in sum, the Court validated the interest of the government in self-preservation over the inchoate concept of academic freedom in the First Amendment, stating only that the quest for self-preservation and its manifestations must not be overly broad, vague, or lacking in due process or clear legislative mandate.

The excellent descriptions of the nature and importance of academic freedom contained in these opinions are not, unfortunately, holdings of law. The cases are extreme in the sense that the interest balancing academic freedom appears to be the very survival of the republic when threatened by advocacy of violent overthrow of the government. While the courts often seemed to be the only institutions defending individual freedoms during the McCarthy era, they did not go very far toward establishing an independent right to academic freedom under the Constitution and

48. *Knight v. Board of Regents of the University of the State of New York*, 269 F. Supp. 339, aff'd, without opinion, 390 U.S. 36 (1968).

the Bill of Rights. Subsequent cases bear out the essential non-existence of this freedom as a legal right and the continued dim view taken by the Supreme Court of its importance.

### THE NONEXISTENCE OF THE RIGHT TO LEARN

*The Mandel Case.* In 1972, the Court decided a case in which rights of academic freedom were strenuously argued.[49] The case is distinctive in that it concerns the *right to learn* aspect of academic freedom. While the Court did find precedent for a freedom to hear (or learn) in the First Amendment guarantee of freedom of speech, the rest of the opinion was totally negative as to the existence of any academic freedom. Ernest Mandel was a Belgian Marxist journalist-intellectual, but it was not his rights that were tested in this case; rather, it was the rights of the university faculty members and students who had invited him to their campuses to speak and who were unable to hear him because his entry was prohibited by the Immigration and Naturalization Service.[50] Mandel, who described himself as a "revolutionary Marxist" but not a member of the Communist Party, was editor of a journal and author of a two-volume work on Marxist economic theory. He was invited to Stanford to respond to a speech by John Kenneth Galbraith. Once his acceptance became known he was also invited to Princeton, Amherst, Columbia, and Vassar and to speak to several other academic groups. The refusal of the Immigration and Naturalization Service to grant him a visa was supposedly based on his failure to observe the restrictions placed on his entry permit on a prior visit, although it ultimately became clear that these restrictions had never been communicated to Mandel, and his unknowing infractions were without great significance. A three-judge district court found that citizens in this country had a First Amendment right to have Mandel enter and to hear him. The question posed on appeal to the Supreme Court was: "Does ap-

---

49. *Kleindienst v. Mandel*, 408 U.S. 753 (1972).

50. This peculiar juxtaposition of interests is reminiscent of the case in which Bertrand Russell was denied a chair at City College of New York because he was not a citizen and because "academic freedom cannot teach that . . . adultery is attractive and good for the community." *Kay v. Board of Higher Education of the City of New York*, 18 N.Y.S. 2d 821, 829 (1940).

pellants' action in refusing to allow an alien scholar to enter the country to attend academic meetings violate the First Amendment rights of American scholars and students who had invited him?" The Supreme Court agreed that the right to free speech, as it has evolved, includes the right to hear, and that this right is nowhere more vital than in our schools and universities; that it is the essence of self-government. Nor did they quibble with the need to speak face-to-face in academic discourse in order to have a full and free flow of ideas. Having found *for* the right of academic freedom up to this point, however, they simply "balanced" it out of existence. The real issue, the Court said, was the long-established plenary congressional power to make policies and rules for exclusion of aliens. Here, the right to free speech must yield to the historical right of the executive to decide issues relating to the expulsion of aliens. The overbalancing precedents upon which the Court relied included the *Chinese Exclusion Case*[51] and *Fong Yue Ting v. U.S.*,[52] heretofore largely unnoticed milestones of the law of academic freedom, as the dissent by Mr. Justice Marshall rather pointedly noted.[53] Dissenting Justices Marshall and Brennan saw the issue as whether the Bill of Rights reaches the government in all its phases, including the war power, national security, and foreign affairs, and concluded that it does. They would have allowed the plaintiff professors to compel the Attorney General to allow Mandel's admission.

Mr. Justice Douglas, dissenting separately, saw the issue somewhat more colorfully:

The Attorney General stands astride our international terminals that bring people here to bar those whose ideas are not acceptable to him. Even assuming, *arguendo*, that those on the outside seeking admission have no standing to complain, those who hope to benefit from the traveler's lectures do.

Thought control is not within the competence of any branch of government. Those who live here may need exposure to the ideas of people of many faiths and many creeds to further their education. We

51. *Chinese Exclusion Case*, 130 U.S. 581 (1889).

52. *Fong Yue Ting v. U.S.*, 149 U.S. 698 (1893).

53. *Kleindienst v. Mandel*, pp. 781-2.

should construe the Act generously by that First Amendment standard, saying that once the State Department has concluded that our foreign relations permit or require the admission of a foreign traveler, the Attorney General is left only problems of national security, importation of heroin, or other like matters within his competence.

We should assume that where propagation of ideas is permissible as being within our constitutional framework, the Congress did not undertake to make the Attorney General a censor. . . . "The very purpose of the First Amendment is to foreclose public authority from assuming a guardianship of the public mind through regulating the press, speech, and religion. In this field every person must be his own watchman for truth, because the forefathers did not trust any government to separate the true from the false for us. (*Thomas v. Collins*, 323 U.S. 516, 545 [1945])."[54]

Nor did Justice Douglas find any great threat to national security from the visit of a Belgian journalist.

The majority opinion, however, effectively minimizes the question of academic freedom by finding no reason to distinguish Mandel from any other alien to whom any American citizen might want to "talk." Thus, by again failing to find any distinct academic freedom to learn within the larger First Amendment freedom to hear, the Court was able to state that allowing the right to hear to prevail over the executive's power to exclude would either render that power meaningless or force the Court to weigh the importance of the right to hear in each case, a task the Court declined to undertake. The Court failed to take the obvious step of distinguishing the right to learn and weighing it more heavily in the balance with executive authority, which would have avoided both problems posed by the Court. The more serious question is why the Court failed to make this distinction in order to protect the freedom to learn in a free society.

*Disruption of campus lectures.* The problems raised in *Mandel* have been considered by several lower courts in a different context: the presence of controversial speakers on campus, which may create a riot. Both administrators and students have sought to prevent this type of campus address in a variety of ways. In *Brooks v. Auburn University* the court invoked the doctrine of prior restraint to invalidate the ability of the administration to keep a

54. Ibid., pp. 772-73.

controversial speaker (the Rev. Sloan Coffin) off campus, since no threat of immediate and present danger had been shown.[55]

One intricate and involved problem directly related to the academic freedom to learn is the student disruption of unpopular speakers, and the affirmative duties, if any, of the university administrative officials under such circumstances. A recent report by a Yale faculty committee discusses the problems caused by visits to their campus by Governor George C. Wallace, General William Westmoreland, Secretary of State William Rogers, and Professor William Shockley, none of whom was able to speak as requested, and concludes that "failure or equivocation in defense of free speech was fairly attributable to the University in some degree."[56] The Yale committee looked to the reeducation of the university community on the value of free expression as well as the setting of clear limits for dissent and better administrative arrangements and firmer actions by the administration to better preserve free expression. A minority report by a graduate student member of the committee takes the position, essentially, that the niceties of academic freedom or freedom of expression must yield to the all-out fight to overcome racism in American society.

At least two cases have reached the courts challenging the power of universities to discipline students for disruptive behavior, including the disruption of teaching. In *Furumoto* v. *Lyman*, Stanford University suspended certain students for disrupting a quiz in an electrical engineering class being taught by Professor William Shockley, the proponent of certain controversial ideas on genetics and intelligence.[57] After being indefinitely suspended, the students sought an injunction for reinstatement, and damages, based on the Civil Rights Act of 1871, the Bill of Rights, and the Fourteenth

55. *Brooks v. Auburn University*, 412 F. 2d 1171 (5th Cir. 1969). See also, *Pickings v. Bruce*, 430 F. 2d 595 (8th Cir. 1970); *Dunkel v. Elkins*, 325 F. Supp. 1235 (D. Md. 1971); *Hammond v. South Carolina State College*, 272 F. Supp. 947 (D.S.C. 1967); Charles A. Wright, "The Constitution on the Campus," *Vanderbilt Law Review* 22 (October 1969): 1027-88; William van Alstyne, "Political Speakers at State Universities: Some Constitutional Considerations," *University of Pennsylvania Law Review* 111 (January 1963): 328-42.

56. "Report of Committee on Freedom of Expression at Yale," *AAUP Bulletin* 62 (April 1976): 28, 30.

57. *Furumoto v. Lyman*, 362 F. Supp. 1267 (N.D. Calif. 1973).

Amendment. The plaintiff students claimed that Shockley's writings were racist, highly offensive to those opposing racism, creating "antagonism and anger," and were in violation of Section 1983 of the Civil Rights Act. They also alleged violation of their own First Amendment right of free speech since they were punished for their public opposition to racism. The court, in granting a summary dismissal for the university, found that the disruptive tactics employed by the students validated the exercise of authority by the university administration to maintain the order which would protect free expression by all. The court cited the Report of the President's Commission on Campus Unrest.[58] Interestingly, the court gave serious consideration to the plaintiff's claim that in academic life a professor must debate his views publicly if challenged, which Shockley had refused to do. No such duty exists, said the court. "Such a requirement, if widely adopted, could drive otherwise qualified and valuable scholars from academic life," since many individuals do not have the talent or personality for oral debating. "Such a requirement would in itself be a potential inhibitor of academic freedom."[59] And in an earlier case, in which a student challenged the constitutional right of a university to expel him for making a speech that caused a riot, the same court also upheld the university, finding no infringement of constitutional rights or lack of due process.[60] These lower court cases are a meager but heartening addition to the common law of academic freedom in the protection of actions upholding the freedom to learn, even though once again there is little in the language of the opinions upon which to base a right of academic freedom distinct from other First Amendment rights.

*The nonexistence of the freedom to teach: Starsky.* While the Supreme Court has most recently considered the freedom to learn, a current case still pending in the courts illustrates that the old issues are not dead, but are more than ever in need of definitive

58. *Report of the President's Commission on Campus Unrest* (Washington, D.C.: Government Printing Office, 1970).

59. *Furumoto v. Lyman,* p. 1282.

60. *Siegel v. Regents of the University of California,* 308 F. Supp. 832 (N.D. Calif. 1970).

resolution. The *Starsky* case is interesting because it is a continuation of the classic line of communist cases (Starsky is actually a Marxist socialist), because it includes an assessment or evaluation of the AAUP and campus faculty proceedings, and because it includes an analysis by the district judge which differentiates at some length the free speech rights of a professor as a citizen from his rights of free speech on campus.[61] On the other side, *Starsky* seems to take the "education as business" approach. The conclusion of the opinion seems to be that the rights of a professor as a citizen are greater than his rights as a professor to free speech, thus again pointing to the necessity for a clear constitutional protection of academic freedom which *would* reach the professor's rights on campus. There is also a circuit court opinion in *Starsky* confirming the constitutional findings of the district court, but it is not a clear finding for Starsky due to certain technical questions as to whether Starsky gave up his right to pursue his case by accepting a terminal sabbatical year.

The *Starsky* case would also seem to be a classic case of an administration "making book" on a professor it wanted off campus for political reasons that are related to community views of his campus activities and his criticism of the university administration. "Making book" is a public school term referring to the administrative practice of getting rid of undesirable employees by keeping a cumulative record of minor infractions, rather than attempting to terminate on the basis of the actual problem (for example, homosexuality, civil rights activism, irritating personality). The district judge referred to the case of the Earl of Strafford "of whom Rushworth wrote in his 'Historical Collections' that being forced to find a way to dispose of him, Charles I, by bill of attainder, piled blunders and misdemeanors into a package called 'treason by accumulation,' then sent the Earl to his death in 1641."[62] The incident that precipitated the efforts to terminate Professor Starsky, who had achieved "employment stability" (the Arizona State University semantic equivalent for tenure), was the dismissal

61. *Starsky v. Williams*, 353 F. Supp. 900 (D. Ariz. 1972), aff'd and modified 512 F. 2d 109 (9th Cir. 1975).

62. Ibid., p. 926, footnote 9.

of a class by Starsky so that he might attend a rally in front of the administration building and make a speech protesting the arrest of certain students at the University of Arizona. There were "lengthy hearings, voluminous evidence and formal charges, findings, resolutions, and examination and cross-examination by attorneys during administrative hearings."[63] So there appears to be no due process issue. There was a "summary charge" that Starsky had "failed to act responsibly as a member of the teaching profession, had willfully violated Regents' policies and University regulations, and had not exercised appropriate restraint as becomes a university professor in his public activities." "General charges" and "subcharges" followed, the latter referring to specific factual incidents. The Committee on Academic Freedom and Tenure, consisting of six Arizona State University professors who conducted the hearings, found substance in only three of the subcharges. The Board of Regents found substance in all charges, and, against the recommendation of the University president, dismissed Starsky. Under the circumstances, the court found it necessary to make detailed factual findings of its own.[64] After an extremely detailed analysis of the allegations and the facts supporting them, the court concluded that the evidence was not sufficient to support the basic charges of the Regents or to warrant termination.[65] The finding of facts was not sufficient for the court to hold for Starsky, however, because the courts "do not normally review matters within the Board of Regent's discretion."[66] The only way the Regent's decision could be attacked in court would be that the "primary or substantial cause of the discipline is an impermissible restrain on plaintiff's constitutional rights."[67] Since the activities causing the dismissal included both constitutionally protected actions and others not constitution-

63. Ibid., p. 904.

64. Ibid., p. 907 states the rationale for this conclusion.

65. For a similar case where different facts tipped a court the other way, see *Rozman v. Elliott*, 335 F. Supp. 1086 (D. Neb. 1971). There "the competing interests . . . are that of freedom of expression, assembly, and petition on the one hand and freedom to employ or not to employ on the other." (p. 1088).

66. *Starsky v. Williams*, 353 F. Supp. 921.

67. Ibid.

ally protected, the court went on to analyze whether the actual reason for discharge was constitutionally impermissible.

The primary-cause test used by the court would appear to refer to something more than the mere existence of some constitutionally protected activity in a mixed situation. It is there that the court's analysis becomes especially interesting, and significant for future cases. The court balanced the *Keyishian* interest in academic freedom against the administrator's right from *Tinker* to forbid conduct which would "materially and substantially interfere with the requirements of appropriate discipline in the operation of the school."[68] (Here again, the court made no distinction between public school and university standards, which is unfortunate). The court found that free speech as construed in *Keyishian* did not give Professor Starsky the right to call a minor administrator a bastard in the hearing of students, but that his speech making and leaflet distribution were constitutionally protected even though the administration protested that the latter was "out of keeping with . . . the austere surroundings of a faculty assembly meeting."

It is in regard to Starsky's off-campus activities (denouncing the Board on television) that the court made an interesting comparison between the rights of professors on campus and off, concluding that it may be easier to show an overbalancing administrative interest where speech is closely connected with on-campus duties.

Thus, there may be circumstances in which school discipline requires that a professor acting within his capacity as a teacher, or in his personal relationship on campus, may be held to professional standards of appropriate restraint or greater personal courtesy than that which may be demanded of other citizens, and when a teacher speaks within his own expertise, the school may have a substantial interest in holding him to higher standards of accuracy than if he were an ordinary citizen. However, these narrower standards may not be applied to a faculty member when he speaks publicly as a citizen, in the absence of a showing of an employer's interest sufficient to counterbalance the citizen's interest in his constitutional rights.[69]

68. *Keyishian v. Board of Regents*, 385 U.S. 589, 603; *Tinker v. Des Moines Independent Community School District*, 393 U.S. 503, 509 (1969).

69. *Starsky v. Williams*, 353 F. Supp. 921.

The Board improperly found, said the court, that Starsky had not exercised appropriate restraint as becomes a university professor in his public activities because this finding applied a narrow professional standard to Professor Starsky's speech as a citizen.

Thus, the right of academic freedom, which started out in Germany to give professors a greater right to speak out freely, has been translated into this country to give them a *lesser* right than the ordinary citizen now possesses, at least as against the interests of government as public university employer.[70] Where political repression has failed, administration and management seem to have succeeded, although in this particular case it is heartening to find that the court concluded that the primary reason for the discipline of Professor Starsky was impermissibly grounded on his exercise of his First Amendment rights in expressing unpopular views. At the same time it is only fair to observe that Starsky's activities were on the periphery of those intended to be protected by academic freedom.[71]

*Departmental autonomy: the freedom to act on ideas held.* The threat to academic freedom from institutional management was defined differently in the more unusual *Peacock* case, also from Arizona.[72] The circumstances described as an academic power struggle were not so unusual.[73] It was unusual, however, that the losing party sought to enforce his rights in the federal courts, thereby further testing whether our present constitutional provisions do indeed protect academic freedom in some of its nether reaches. Yet the legal definition of the protection afforded against political-governmental regulation, both external and internal, is important to those considering the potential for death by nibbling, particularly in view of what would appear to be the inevitable

70. For a corroborative holding, see *Roseman v. Indiana University of Pennsylvania at Indiana*, 520 F. 2d 1364 (3d Cir. 1975), in which it was found that a faculty member's communications at a faculty meeting were not protected by the First Amendment and might form the basis for discharge.

71. Compare, for example, the Kent State faculty activities reported in *Hammond v. Brown*, 323 F. Supp. 326 (N.D. Ohio 1971).

72. *Peacock v. Board of Regents of the University and State Colleges of Arizona*, 510 F. 2d 1324 (9th Cir. 1975).

73. Ibid., p. 1325.

decline in the influence of the AAUP and other professional organizations.

In this case, a department chairman was summarily dismissed from his administrative duties as department head by the University of Arizona. During the subsequent strife he was further summarily dismissed from his tenured faculty position, without a prior hearing, although he was offered a postsuspension hearing. He brought suit for damages and equitable relief to redress the denial of his due process right to a hearing prior to his dismissal. It was essentially an internal due process case, testing what procedures, if any, the (public) university must grant an academic before relieving him of administrative duties. It is a case important to academic freedom because it has to do with departmental autonomy, the theoretical power base of faculty freedom.

It is interesting to note that the court recognized that the university never questioned Professor Peacock's professional competence but sought to remove him solely because of his lack of cooperation stemming from *differences of opinion about how to run a medical school*[74] and did not intimate that Peacock refused to perform tasks assigned by the administration or that his lack of cooperation ever damaged the medical school or the hospital.[75] Nevertheless, the court never raised or discussed the concept of academic freedom but instead took a *Roth-Sindermann-Arnett* approach,[76] which analyzed Peacock's personal liberty and property interests in the department chairmanship. Perhaps there is no legally recognized interest other than one personal to Peacock, and perhaps his personal interest does not encompass departmental autonomy, a term not synonymous with, but related to, academic freedom. Nonetheless, the court did see fit to cite "the common law of the campus"[77] to establish that heads of departments are appointed by and serve at the sufferance of the university president, that they can attain no tenure in the position, that they are subject to the unfettered discretion of the president who can dismiss them

74. Ibid., p. 1329 (emphasis mine).

75. Ibid., footnote 5.

76. *Board of Regents of State Colleges v. Roth*, 408 U.S. 564 (1972); *Perry v. Sindermann*, 408 U.S. 593 (1972); *Arnett v. Kennedy*, 416 U.S. 134 (1974).

77. *Peacock v. Board of Regents*, p. 1326.

at any time for any reason, and, above all, that the position of department chairman is "quasi-administrative." The court found that this "common law" overcomes a written contract with clear provisions. The court might also have ventured into the murky waters of the importance of departmental autonomy to academic freedom in a public university, at least to the extent of granting a predismissal hearing in this case.

Thus we come to the question of whether academic freedom, like religious freedom, includes the freedom to act on ideas held. A finding that the concept of academic freedom includes not only the right to research and to disseminate conclusions through publications or speaking, but also the right to organize curriculum and take *academic* action based on those conclusions, does not necessarily mean automatic anarchy any more than the constitutional protection of the free exercise of religion has allowed any and all religious practices to prevail in our society (for example, polygamy or snake-handling). In this case, for example, the plaintiff, on appeal, was asking only for a right to a predismissal hearing—a hearing which might have brought out whether or not a serious deprivation of constitutional freedom was the basis for the action. The Ninth Circuit Court of Appeals, using a strictly employment approach, found that postsuspension hearing satisfied the requirements of due process, since loyalty and cooperation are imperative. "We conclude that the potential threat to the administration of the medical school, and the incidental threat of disruption at the University Hospital outweighs his interest in a presuspension hearing."[78]

## Summary and Conclusion:
## A Constitutional Amendment is Necessary

While one hesitates to fault the court for standing on this comparatively sound ground, it is disappointing to see the management-administrative analysis of academic rights furthered in this manner.[79]

78. Ibid., 1329.

79. See *Rozman v. Elliot*, 335 F. Supp. 1086 (D Neb. 1971). But see also *Vallejo v. Jamestown College*, 244 N.W. 2d 753 (N.D.S.C. 1976), where the dismissed chairman received $15,000 for breach of contract. The statement in the faculty manual on academic freedom was considered to be part of the contract.

Taxpáyer irritability, evidenced in legislative and bureaucratic demands for accountability, has already begun to cast higher education in a business mold with "consumers" and "products." The growth of this concept is both unfortunate and dangerous for the social concepts of mental freedom embodied in academic freedom. While there is nothing wrong with business concepts for *business entities*, a wholesale translation fails to recognize and protect the unique functions, qualities, and social contributions of educational institutions. It would seem that a stronger delineation of academic freedom is needed to preserve that idea in the ongoing application of business standards, a process which seems to be increasing for a number of reasons, including collective bargaining.

The increasing appearance of collective bargaining units on campus is another reason for more strongly defining and protecting academic freedom in our legal system. While the development of academic freedom under constitutional case law has been largely rhetorical, the 1915 and 1940 codifications by the AAUP have been quite precise.[80] The enforcement of these standards by persuasion and moral sanction and by pressure from the academic community has been quite effective, despite the fact that a few institutions have remained on the censure list for years. The citation of the AAUP standards by the court in *Starsky* indicates the authority and integrity of these standards. Nevertheless, the role of the AAUP is changing, along with that of other professional organizations. It is becoming a collective bargaining agent, which substantially changes its relationships with campus administrations and governing boards, even on those campuses that are not organized to bargain collectively, since the possibility for collective bargaining, with its legal and organizational ramifications, always exists. This evolving status will inevitably cause a shift in stance from impartial professional arbiter to faculty advocate. The organization's position may become even more anomalous if different procedural standards are found in Association statements and in individual contracts or proposals. If all campuses were to be covered by collective bargaining contracts, which seems unlikely at this juncture, academic freedom might be protected to some extent

80. Joughin, ed., *Academic Freedom and Tenure.*

through contract provisions, but this would be uneven at best.[81] Worse, it does not take into account the social interest in academic freedom that may not necessarily be reflected by a compilation of individual protections. Finally, at least one case indicates that collective bargaining agreements have the potential for *weakening* academic freedom. In *Cary v. Board of Education of Adams-Arapahoe* the court held that high school teachers *did* have some measure of constitutionally protected academic freedom in assigning outside reading, but that they had forfeited their constitutional rights by entering into a collective bargaining agreement which gave the final decision on questions of academic freedom to the school board.[82]

The protection which ought to be afforded academic freedom could be found in a constitutional amendment similar to the provision in the Prussian Constitution of 1850, which stated that "Science and its teaching shall be free."[83] The Prussian provision is classic in its simplicity and could be used as it is with the substitution of the more contemporary term "learning" for "science." The amendment would thus read, "Learning and its teaching shall be free." Even though the statement is absolute in tone, it is no more so than the present related clauses on the free exercise of religion and free speech and would no doubt be subject to the same balancing tests that the Supreme Court has applied to those

81. For a case in which a union was dismissed as a party plaintiff in a termination case alleging violation of academic freedom, see *Cook County College Teachers Union, Local 1600, A.F.T. v. Byrd*, 456 F. 2d 882 (7th Cir. 1972).

82. *Cary v. Board of Education of Adams-Arapahoe*, 427 F. Supp. 945. The contract provision read as follows:

Academic Freedom—the parties seek to educate young people in the democratic tradition, to foster a recognition of individual freedom and responsibility, to inspire meaningful awareness of and respect for the Constitution and the Bill of Rights.
Freedom of individual conscience, association, and expression will be encouraged and fairness in procedures will be observed both to safeguard the legitimate interests of the schools and to exihibt by appropriate examples the basic objectives of a democratic society as set forth in the Constitution of the United States and the State of Colorado. The final responsibility in the determination of the above rests with the Board.

83. Noted in Machlup, "On Some Misconceptions concerning Academic Freedom," p. 179, footnote 3.

concepts.[84] A constitutional amendment might also reach the idea of institutional academic freedom (related to but distinct from institutional autonomy). This idea has been talked about increasingly with the growing government regulation of universities through affirmative action plans, regulations on scientific research, and in other areas. As President Kingman Brewster has so colorfully expressed this view, the government seems to feel that because it has bought the button it can design the coat.[85] Although there is a present strong protection of free speech in our society, the problems enumerated above are not really reached through a free speech analysis. The coming years should include an increasing study of the real meaning and extent of the term "academic freedom" and a stronger legal protection for that concept, whatever it may be, in order to protect free thought in a free society.

84. Emerson suggests that our original Constitution might have contained the provision "academic freedom, being essential to the welfare and progress of the nation, shall be respected," which would not have been any more difficult to construe than the First Amendment, but he is generally not in favor of a current amendment. Emerson, *The System of Freedom of Expression*, p. 612. See also William P. Murphy, "Academic Freedom—An Emerging Constitutional Right," *Law and Contemporary Problems* 28 (Summer 1963): 447.

85. Kingman Brewster, "Coercive Power of the Federal Purse," *Science* 188 (April 11, 1975): 105. See also Dallin Oaks, "A Private University Looks at Government Regulations," address to the National Association of College and University Attorneys, June 18, 1976; Derek C. Bok, "The President's Report: 1974-1975," report to the members of the Board of Overseers of Harvard University; and Earl F. Cheit, "What Price Accountability?" *Change* 7 (November 1975): 30-34, 60.

# CHAPTER XIII

# Frontiers of the Law

LARRY W. HUGHES
and
WILLIAM M. GORDON

## Introduction

In this chapter we shall highlight the nature of current legal struggles involving schools and universities, place these struggles in historical perspective, and suggest likely outcomes. Specificity will at times give way to conjecture as we attempt to extrapolate the implications for the future from current legal activity.

Shannon puts the issue in a positive perspective:

Controversy over . . . issues of public school governance and administration is actually symptomatic of the robust health of our system of government. Education has assumed an importance in our society that it did not have just a few decades ago. Today, we are in a time of profound change in society. It is natural that public education would be the subject of spirited community discussion and debate, as competing values and philosophies of our polyglot society are filtered into courses of action on educational policy matters. Instead of weakness, community involvement, although sometimes rancorous and bitter, is in reality a strength of the public school system and augers for continuing improvement in educational offerings to meet the changing demands of our changing world. As frustrating and difficult as controversy may be at times, it is a hallmark of our open and free society. Instead of rejecting it, we must learn to live with it—even in educational matters—which, in the final analysis, is clearly an area of life where reasonable opinions may differ.[1]

Educational institutions are affected by enactments from several sources and levels of government: laws passed by federal, state,

1. Thomas A. Shannon, *Current Trends in School Law* (Topeka, Kansas: National Organization on Legal Problems of Education, 1974) p. 5.

and local legislative bodies; court decisions; constitutional provisions; and rules and policies promulgated by regulatory agencies
such as state departments of education, health departments, and
so forth. All these serve as sources of legal control. State legislatures and Congress have often directly affected practices and procedures in matters of curriculum, testing, and the nature of student
bodies by using "purse string power" as well as legislative fiat.
Federal and state courts have also increasingly engaged in determining educational policy and practice. This latter was not always
so and has changed dramatically over the years.

Three historical phases may be discerned with respect to court
interest in matters of educational import. Some of the current legal
activity is sufficient to suggest that the United States may be
entering a fourth phase, with the *Rodriguez* case perhaps bannering
a shift in the nature of federal court activity.[2] To this point we
shall return.

Phase one occurred from the inception of the republic until
about the mid-1800s and evidenced a general disassociation of the
federal courts from educational matters. Moreover, there was little
state court action with respect to school issues; these issues were
considered largely of local concern, with state courts only infrequently called in to adjudicate.

The years from the mid-1800s until about three decades ago
comprised phase two. During this period the common legal posture
was that education was exclusively of state and local concern. Few
cases reached the Supreme Court,[3] and a body of state case law
developed that often actually permitted educational practices and
policies not in accord with the standards of the federal Constitution. The end of this era might be dated as occurring in 1943 in
the *West Virginia* v. *Barnette* decision, which reads in part:

The Fourteenth Amendment . . . is now applied to the State itself and
all of its creatures—boards of education not excepted. These (that is,
boards of education) have, of course, important, delicate, and highly

2. *San Antonio Independent School District* v. *Rodriguez,* 411 U.S. 1
(1973).

3. In *Plessy* v. *Ferguson,* for example, the court held that a "separate but
equal" policy for schools that provided racial segregation was constitutional.
*Plessy* v. *Ferguson,* 163 U.S. 537, 41 L.Ed. 256, 16 S.Ct. 1138 (La. 1896).

discretionary functions, but none that they may perform except within the limits of the Bill of Rights.[4]

Thus, phase three began, a period of considerable federal court activity concerned with social reform, often specifically involving the schools. With the recognition that state case law and legislative enactments frequently failed to conform to the federal standards, the federal courts began to apply basic constitutional requirements to public schools.

Direct supervision of schools by the courts is a more recent phenomenon. The current tendency of both federal and state courts to expand their scope of authority to include direct intervention in the administration, organization, and program reform of schools is unparalleled in judicial history in this country. Jurisdiction is maintained in such instances until the orders of the court have been met and until there is evidence that the orders will remain in effect.[5] *Hobson* v. *Hansen* serves as a clear initial example of this kind of court activity. In this case the court insisted that the Washington, D.C. public schools desist with "curricular tracks" because of the apparent negative effect on minority children and the discriminatory nature of the practice.[6] A more recent example is the court assumption of administrative control of the schools in Boston after the failure of school officials to implement a desegregation plan effectively.

Despite the activities of the court in the Boston situation, there is evidence to suggest that a fourth legal phase may have been entered—a phase Hogan labels "the stage of strict construction."[7] Whether this will develop fully—either to exist concurrently with phase three or replace the vigorous social activity of previous courts—is a matter for conjecture only. One might date the be-

---

4. *West Virginia v. Barnette*, 319 U.S. 64 (1943).

5. *Hobson v. Hansen*, 269 F. Supp. 401 (1967).

6. *Education, U.S.A.*, "News Fronts," 15 December 1975.

7. John C. Hogan, *The Schools, the Courts, and the Public Interest* (Lexington, Mass.: D. C. Heath, 1974), p. 6. Hogan identified five historical "stages," choosing to keep separate the actions of the court that result in direct supervision of the schools. This would seem to be simply a logical extension of the intense federal interest, rather than a distinct phase.

ginning of the strict constructionist phase at the time of the Supreme Court decision in the *Rodriguez* case, where the Court said:

Education, of course, is not among the rights afforded explicit protection under our Federal Constitution. Nor do we find any basis for saying it is implicitly so protected.[8]

This was in response to plaintiff's claim that the right to an equal educational opportunity was a fundamental right. Just such a principle had been affirmed in a similar school finance case tried in 1971 in the California state courts. In the *Serrano* case the California Supreme Court stated:

We are convinced that the distinctive and priceless function of education in our society warrants, indeed, compels our treatment of it as a "fundamental interest."[9]

Yet according to the U.S. Supreme Court decision in *Rodriguez* the interest of the public is not served by federal court intervention in educational issues unless these issues contain infringements of basic rights.[10] This would seem to portend important departures from the posture of federal courts of the past two decades. The high court did remark on the inequities of the system of financing the schools and challenged the state legislature to correct the situation, while holding that the Texas system was not in violation of the U.S. Constitution. A further example of a

8. *San Antonio Independent School District v. Rodriguez*, 411 U.S. 1 (1973). This changing position will of course be reflected in the lower courts as well. In a Dayton, Ohio desegregation hearing, in which the authors of this chapter were recently involved, the presiding district judge said, in his charge to participants: "This court will not engage in an examination of social issues, but will hear the case solely on the basis of whether or not there is compliance with the desegregation order." In so stating the judge ruled from consideration any arguments about the educational merits of one desegregation plan over another and any consideration of such future negative effects of one plan over another with respect to "white flight" and subsequent resegregation. The issue of "white flight" was addressed recently by the Supreme Court when it held that a local school district was not obligated to restructure its attendance boundaries in instances where mobility patterns had caused resegregation. *Pasadena City Board of Education v. Nancy A. Spangler et al.*, 44 U.S.L.W. 5117. It appears that the courts will not hold school officials responsible for retarding resegregation.

9. *Serrano v. Priest*, 96 Cal. Rptr. 618 (1971).

10. Hogan provides a good review of this kind of court activity. Hogan, *The Schools, the Courts, and the Public Interest*, pp. 9-11.

general shift might be seen in the decision in the *Milliken* case. In this case the Detroit Public Schools had proposed, for the purpose of desegregation, to bus black students across city lines into the metropolitan suburbs. The Court decided (5-4) against the plan. Mr. Justice Douglas's comment in dissent is thought-provoking:

Desegregation is not, and was never expected to be an easy task. Racial attitudes ingrained in our Nation's childhood and adolescence are not quickly thrown aside in its middle years. But just as the inconvenience of some cannot be allowed to stand in the way of the rights of others, so public opposition, no matter how strident, cannot be permitted to divert this Court from the enforcement of the constitutional principles that issue in this case. Today's holding, I fear, is more a reflection of a public mood that we have gone far enough in enforcing the Constitution's guarantee of equal justice than it is the product of neutral principles of law. In the short run, it may seem to be the easier course to allow our great metropolitan areas to be divided up each into cities—one white, the other black—but it is a course, I predict, our people will ultimately regret. I dissent.[11]

One may expect a general decline of interest by the federal courts in matters of social and/or educational concern unless constitutional rights have been abrogated; even in this instance the courts apparently will decide on narrow constitutional principles. Thus, social and educational reform shifts back to state courts and state legislatures.

Prescience is an uncommon intellectual commodity; nevertheless, a chapter concerned with legal frontiers must, if it is to meet its true obligation, deal in futures. We live in an increasingly legalistic environment—a not unpredictable by-product of a secularized society characterized by massive cultural and subcultural pluralism. In such a society, the "rules to live by" become codified into laws that protect against the infringement of one group on another. As cultures and subcultures interface, ways of believing and ways of behaving become subject to challenge and the source of much litigious conflict. Legal controversy affecting the operation of the school will continue and probably increase in intensity. The use of the school as an instrument of social reform is well established and this, if for no other reason, will give rise to continued litigation.

11. *Milliken v. Bradley*, 418 U.S. 717 (1974).

## The King Can Do Wrong

Issuing out of English common law, sovereign immunity has existed for centuries as a legal principle. The doctrine of sovereign immunity rests with the concept that the King, as a sovereign entity, cannot involuntarily be held to account in the courts of the kingdom. This applies, however, solely to governmental rather than proprietary activities.[12] The application of sovereign immunity to governmental bodies in this nation has historically kept school districts free from tort liability and free from the financial encumbrance of liability insurance. Recent years, however, have seen a considerable trend away from the doctrine of sovereign immunity. For example, until about a decade and a half ago, school districts were generally immune from litigation involving pupil injury.[13] Within this period of time about half of the states have eliminated or very sharply restricted such immunity.

A continuing trend of some magnitude is the replacement of sovereign immunity with the doctrine of *respondeat superior*, a doctrine holding that the employer is liable for the acts of the employee. The degree to which liability is imposed does, of course, vary among those states operating under *respondeat superior*, depending on the specific legislative enactments and court decisions in these states. In some states legislation has been enacted that not only requires a school district to provide for the legal defense of an employee who is sued as a result of actions taken in a contractual course of employment, but also to pay judgment made against the employee.[14] Where such legislative enactments exist the individual employee alleged to be the transgressor is often not even specifically named as the defendant.[15]

12. Whether a specific activity, such as an athletic contest for which admission is charged, is "proprietary" rather than "governmental" varies from state to state.

13. The individual school employees were not immune from responsibility for their own negligent acts, but the school district as a governmental body was.

14. For example, Section 995 of the *California Government Code* contains such a provision. In the future, provisions such as these may make it unnecessary for the various education associations and unions to provide liability insurance for their membership.

15. Often, however, the school district and the individual employee will be named as codefendants and be required to share the cost of the judgment.

The trend is to view the school system in the same light as any corporate entity. While this may result in some psychological comfort for school employees, it may also cause some monumental headaches for school boards and school attorneys. A successful plaintiff might well expect to receive a substantially higher judgment from a school district than from an individual school employee because of an assumed greater ability to pay. This could affect the school budget because it may require the purchase of liability insurance heretofore unnecessary because of the doctrine of sovereign immunity.[16]

## Fundamental Rights of Students

The laws of the land establish an ethical framework because these laws reflect the morals of the majority culture. The spirit of the law is pervasive. Moreover, the spirit and intent of the law applies equally to young people as well as to adults; a person is not denied certain fundamental rights just because of being young.

Essentially, people have no more rights today than they ever had, but the according of these rights is under increasing review of the courts. Historically, school administrators and teachers have placed themselves in the position of acting simultaneously as judge, jury, and prosecuting attorney, overstepping the bounds of good sense, if not legal authority, in zealous attempts to maintain order or in misguided efforts to anticipate disorder. The principle followed was often *in loco deo* rather than *in loco parentis*. But of one thing we are certain: students may not always *be* right, but they always *have* rights.[17]

The courts have been making it increasingly clear that constitutional protections apply to students both in and out of school.

16. Some particularly agonizing moments may be in store for those districts in states that still employ the concept of sovereign immunity, especially in those instances where the concept is overturned by the courts and the state law enjoins the district from spending public funds for the purchase of liability insurance.

17. In Dayton, Ohio, the Center for the Study of Student Citizenship publishes the *Student Rights Handbook* for young people in the area. The booklet informs students of their rights. Inquiries should be directed to 1145 Germantown St., Dayton, Ohio 45009. See also *Student Rights Litigation Packet* (Cambridge, Mass.: Center for Law and Education, 1972).

Basic human rights such as freedom of expression, for example, if not always well defined in the school, are well established in the law. Further, it is now well established in law that a specific process (procedural due process) be followed in order that those basic human rights be protected against the abuse of institutional authority. Procedural due process provisions were recently re-clarified by the Supreme Court in *Goss* v. *Lopez*.[18]

The Court ruled in the *Goss* case that school officials must accord students their constitutional right of due process, even in routine disciplinary actions. It was ruled that a junior high school student, suspended for as much as a single day was entitled to the elements of procedural process.[19] In another 1975 case the Supreme Court ruled that school board members and school officials can be personally liable for pecuniary damages when students are denied constitutional rights, even by accidental omission.[20] At issue, then, are the rights of individual students, balanced against the duty of the school board and administrators (a) to protect the rights of all students to obtain an education and (b) to protect the school system.[21]

Educators may argue that the courts have become unnecessarily restrictive and that their hands are being tied by court actions that make it difficult to meet the school officials' other legal charge to promote the well-being of all children within the school. This argument is unpersuasive because it misunderstands the nature of

18. *Goss v. Lopez*, 419 U.S. 565 (1975).

19. Ibid. Only a rudimentary process may be required in minor offenses, however. The Court said: "There need be no delay between the time 'notice' is given and the time of the hearing. In a great majority of the cases the disciplinarian may informally discuss the alleged misconduct with the student minutes after it has occurred. We hold only that, in being given an opportunity to explain his version, . . . the student first be told what he is accused of doing and what the basis of the accusation is."

20. *Wood v. Strickland*, 240 U.S. 308 (1975).

21. It is important to note that while procedural due process does take on some of the vestments of a court of law, it is not a court of law. It is simply the provision for fair and impartial treatment. After the process is complete the individual still has the right to "take the case to court," if the student feels that the act for which the punishment was given was not a punishable one, or that the punishment was inappropriate. Following the steps of procedural due process will be influential with the courts, for it does mitigate any charge of capricious action.

a secular society and avoids the reality of perceived or real inequity in treatment. Established, well-understood mechanisms to insure positive corrective action, when such actions are needed to insure rights are vital. As the Court pointed out in *Tinker*, "Students do not surrender their rights at the schoolhouse door."[22] Moreover, in a much earlier case the Court revealed great pedagogical insight when it stated:

That they are educating the young for citizenship is reason for scrupulous protection of constitutional freedom of the individual *if we are not to strangle the free mind at its source and teach youth to discount important principles of our government as mere platitudes.*[23] (emphasis added)

Much is available in the literature about procedural due process. Procedural due process is an orderly established process for arriving at an impartial and just settlement of a conflict between parties. It is well to remember that there must also be substantive due process and this is equally subject to court review. The aspects of substantive due process are (a) the legality of a specific legislative enactment of the school board or a rule invoked by an administrator and (b) sufficient evidence of violation to warrant action by school officials or sufficient reason to believe that if the rule were not invoked current or subsequent acts by the perpetrating persons would result in disruption. (The burden of proof for the latter rests with school officials, not the alleged transgressor.)

Applying the elements of substantive due process, a person punished or denied a right has legal recourse to make a rule or policy invalid if the rule is contrary to existing statutes or constitutional law. In fact, according to the decision in *Wood*, the person may even seek pecuniary damages.[24] Moreover, the presumption that disruption will follow if a rule is not invoked may violate substantive due process unless there is clear evidence of the validity of the presumption. In the instance of presumed disruption, a school administrator or teacher says in effect, "If this rule is not

22. *Tinker v. Des Moines Independent School District*, 393 U.S. 503; 89 S. Ct. 733 (1969).

23. *West Virginia v. Barnette*, 319 U.S. 64 (1943).

24. *Wood v. Strickland*, 240 U.S. 308 (1975).

enforced and obeyed, the process of education in this school will be impeded." [25] The courts insist there be evidence to support the presumption.

Guidelines have been developed which help clarify the meaning of substantive due process:

1. *Legality.* Is there a basis in state and federal constitutional and legislative law for the policy, rule, or regulation? Are the constitutional rights of those for whom it was written protected?

2. *Sufficient specificity.* Are the conditions under which the policy, rule, or regulation will be invoked detailed? Are definitive terms and phraseology used? Vague and unclear statements are sufficient to cause the courts to abrogate.

3. *Reason and sensibleness.* Does the rule or regulation really enhance the educational climate; that is, is it really necessary? Is there sufficient reason to believe that without the rule, the rights of others will be unprotected or that the school will be disrupted? A rule may be declared unreasonable in and of itself *or* in its particular application.

4. *Adequate dissemination.* Has information about the rule been distributed and in such a way that persons affected can be expected to know about it, to understand what it means, and to realize what the penalties are?

5. *Appropriate penalties.* Are the punishments appropriate to the nature of the infraction? Severe penalties for minor transgressions need to be avoided.[26]

25. *Tinker* serves as a good illustration of the dimensions of substantive due process. In the *Tinker* case students were suspended for wearing black arm bands to school to protest continued American involvement in Viet Nam and to serve as a symbol of mourning for those military personnel who had died there. The school had established a rule prohibiting this kind of protest behavior, subsequent to which some students wore the arm bands in open defiance. The Supreme Court applied the aspects of substantive due process and found for the students, holding that (a) there was no disruption; therefore the presumption of disruption was false and the students had a right to defy the rule; and (b) the wearing of arm bands was analogous to free speech (First Amendment guarantee); therefore the students had the right to express themselves.

26. Larry W. Hughes and Gerald C. Ubben, *The Elementary Principal in Action* (Boston: Allyn and Bacon, forthcoming).

## School Records and the Right to Privacy

Laws and court decisions seldom move on a single front. Renewed efforts to protect individual rights have characterized litigation and legislation in recent years in both the private and public sector, including, of course, the schools. This has been especially true about matters of individual privacy.

Ultimately highlighted by some of the excesses revealed by the Watergate scandal, there has been an increasing concern over the past decade about the protection of individual rights of privacy. Such concerns can be expected to intensify and at times to conflict with another issue—that of the presumed or actual "need to know" by other individuals and agencies. The issue has become one of developing a necessary balance between an individual's right to privacy and government's need to know in order to protect the public. The 1970s have become a time in which many new regulations have been developed. Directly affecting the schools has been the Family Educational Rights and Privacy Act (FERPA), which became law in August, 1974.[27]

Government and private industry have been found to be making improper use of information about people in diverse instances—including such practices as the systematic interception of mail by the Central Intelligence Agency; illegal wire tapping by the executive branch of the government; careless credit reports in the private sector; and indiscriminate release of pupil records by school officials. Infringement upon individual rights and prerogatives has been extensive. The issue, however, is not clear cut. Westin has written:

Free societies have never treated privacy as an absolute right. They have had to balance three competing social values—the individual's need to be left alone, the government's need for personal information in order to act intelligently and fairly, and the government's duty to monitor antisocial activity to protect lives, property, and public order. Bal-

27. FERPA (Public Law 93-380) is popularly called the Buckley Amendment. Senator James Buckley of New York sponsored the amendment to the 1974 Elementary and Secondary Education Act. In effect, the amendment denied federal funds to any school or college that failed to allow parents to inspect, to challenge, and to refute the public use of the school records of their children.

ancing privacy, disclosure, and surveillance has been a major concern of law and politics in democratic societies for centuries.[28]

The United States Constitution is specifically silent on individual rights to privacy although the courts protected those rights during the 1800s and the first half of the 1900s under the Fourth and Fifth Amendments.[29] Within the past quarter of a century, rights to privacy have more frequently been defended on the basis of the First Amendment, which guarantees freedom of expression, including free speech, religion, press, assembly, and association. The legal issue has been that unless one has the right to decide when and to whom one will disclose personal information, thus preventing forced disclosure without consent, the First Amendment is inoperative. Concurrent with this has been the extension of the due process clause in federal and state constitutions to insist that individuals have the right of access to information that others (individuals or agencies) may have about them. In the latter issue, individuals in legal proceedings whose welfare and rights are being adjudicated have been guaranteed the right to inspect and challenge the evidence to be used.[30]

Historically, the United States has collected and stored a minimum of information about its citizens. Even statistical censuses were kept in strict confidence and anonymity was protected. In 1881, for example, a Supreme Court decision prohibited investigations by the Congress into "the private affairs of citizens." Clearly

28. Allen F. Westin, "Protecting Privacy in the Computer Age," in *World Book Yearbook* (Chicago: Field Enterprises Educational Corporation, 1976), p. 131. Westin, a Columbia University legal scholar, provides an exceedingly good treatment of the privacy issue.

29. The Fourth Amendment guarantees freedom from unreasonable searches. The Fifth Amendment guarantees the right to remain silent and not incriminate oneself.

30. What makes the issue so complex and difficult to administer is the technological sophistication that exists, whereby information about individuals may be collected, stored, and manipulated. It is interesting to note that permanent records for students kept in every school in the nation often bulge with data including academic grades, personality profiles, disciplinary reports, family relations information, I.Q. scores, and so forth. Much of the information may be subjective and unsubstantiated. Previously, potential employers, secretaries, credit bureaus, insurance salesmen, police, and others had access to the records. Everyone but the child and the parents could examine them.

evident by mid-century were many changes generated by the increasing complexities of American society, advances in technology, and the implications of a highly mobile society. The increased mobility of workers resulted in employers keeping detailed personnel records; a host of social welfare programs required the collection and monitoring of individual records; and a mass educational system resulted in permanent files that followed students from school to school, containing both relevant and unfortunately oftentimes irrelevant information that was sometimes negatively persuasive. Frequently an individual about whom information was kept was unaware of its nature.

The computerization of school records will become virtually universal by the 1980s. Administrators and teachers will have at their immediate disposal a myriad of facts about any given learner who may have only recently enrolled in the system. While such a technological advance can immeasurably improve the ability of educators to respond to learner needs, it carries with it the real danger that previous transgressions and shortcomings—real, alleged, or imagined—will be indelibly recorded and affect the individual for the rest of his or her life on a much wider scale than was heretofore possible. *Pygmalion in the Classroom* revisited on a national scale is thus a stark reality and the plaintive cry of Private Slovik may be destined to repetition.[31]

It is as a protection against misuse and possible inequity that the Family Educational Rights and Privacy Act assumes its importance. Placed in social and legal perspective, this act is a natural outgrowth of the more generalized concern for the protection of individual privacy in an increasingly complex age and is a product of an educational concern that began to manifest itself specifically a decade or so ago in the activities and publications of such agencies as the American Civil Liberties Union and the Russell Sage Foun-

---

31. In their *Pygmalion in the Classroom* (New York: Holt, Rinehart and Winston, 1968) Robert Rosenthal and Lenore Jacobson report on their research on the self-fulfilling prophecy. In *The Execution of Private Slovik*, a biography of the only military person executed for desertion in World War II, Slovik, crying out against the inequity of it all, says, "And all I ever did was steal an apple!" This was the precipitative act in his childhood as he saw it, each subsequent act of social disobedience being dutifully recorded by authorities because of the previous transgressions. William B. Huie, *The Execution of Private Slovik* (New York: Delacorte Press, 1970).

dation. Basically, FERPA requires that schools and other educational agencies permit an individual (or, if the individual is a minor, the parents) to (a) determine what records pertaining to him or her are maintained in the systems of records; (b) gain access to those records and have copies made; and (c) correct or amend any record pertaining to him or her. Further, disclosure of the record to outsiders may not occur except by the consent of the individual whose records are sought. The consent must be in writing and must specifically state to whom the records may be disclosed and the time frame within which the disclosure may be made.[32] FERPA simply makes legal and mandatory practices that should have been routine procedures in any school—the right of access, and even more important, the right to correct erroneous information or to modify subjective judgments of a possibly prejudicial nature. Such practices would seem to be ethically inviolate; the fact that they were lacking in many schools gave rise to the act.[33]

The rights to privacy and one's right to access to one's files have implications as to the nature of materials located in staff personnel files. This, too, may well be for the general good. The right of individual staff members to review material, including evaluations and recommendations contained in their own file may have a salutary effect on the accuracy of such files, the objectivity of the evaluations, and the improvement of practices in personnel evaluation.

It appears that the rights of agencies, governmental and other-

---

32. There are some exceptions. Disclosures may be made without consent of pupils or parents in some instances. These exceptions are: (a) within the school, to teachers and guidance counselors and other professional personnel who have a "need to know"; (b) under a court order; (c) where there is required disclosure under the Freedom of Information Act; and (d) for "routine usage" such as publications of honor rolls, award winners, members of athletic teams, or school brochures that might contain such information as names, addresses, sex, age, birthplace, and so forth. Even in this latter instance, however, it would be prudent for the school to obtain permission by some routine process.

33. The privacy regulations in FERPA, however, were delayed in coming to the schools. The Department of Health, Education, and Welfare, which was charged with the responsibility for developing guidelines for school officials following the passage of the act, was slow. The first part of the complete guidelines finally appeared in the *Federal Register* in March, 1976; part two followed in a subsequent edition.

wise, may be becoming more constrained while the rights of individuals in their interaction with these agencies more specifically established.

## Staff Personnel Issues

### BASIC RIGHTS AND RESPONSIBILITIES

Many of the current staff personnel issues are developing from questions of both due process and fundamental individual rights and freedoms. *Pickering* v. *Board of Education* is one of the landmark cases in establishing parameters in freedom of speech, out-of-school associations, and the rights of teachers to criticize both administrative and school board actions.[34] This decision protects teachers' rights of speech and opinion, treating teachers as private citizens rather than as a special group of public servants subject to a special set of codes. Even though certain individual freedoms have reasonably clear definitions, there are still some important gray areas in which further litigation can be expected.

Challenges to arbitrary retirement age policies constitute such an issue. The right to work as long as one is physically able is not established. In *Weiss* v. *Walsh* the issue of forced retirement at age sixty-five was addressed by the court.[35] The court held that the retirement requirement was valid and that the teacher was "not the victim of an invidious and impermissable discrimination."[36] But the court also stated that "vindication of the exceptional individual . . . may have to attend the wise discretion of the administration."[37] Further, a U.S. district court recently held that a teacher could not be forced by the local board to retire at age sixty-five if that retirement age was different from the state requirement. The court reasoned that because the board policy of mandatory retirement at age sixty-five was more restrictive than the state law of mandatory retirement at age seventy, the board policy was invalid.[38]

34. *Pickering v. Board of Education*, 391 U.S. 563 (1968).
35. *Weiss v. Walsh*, 324 F. Supp. 75, 77 (S.D. N.Y., 1971).
36. Ibid.
37. Ibid.
38. *Davis v. Griffin, Spaulding County Board of Education*, U.S. District

The fact that people now live longer and many enjoy good physical health and mental acuity into later years raises questions of substantive due process and of arbitrary and capricious action by policy-making bodies. But, there must also be safeguards for the schools in order to protect them from teachers who, because of aging, have lost their abilities to function in a satisfactory manner. There appears to be ample evidence that there will be modifications in the mandatory retirement laws but these modifications will be couched in language that will provide for due process. Similar concerns about unfair employment practices with respect to sex and racial or ethnic minorities have achieved legal clarification within the past fifteen years.[39]

Current or soon-to-surface situations comparable to those mentioned in the last paragraph are those where teachers and administrators are denied employment, promotion, or tenure because they are physically handicapped, homosexual, ex-convicts, former mental or psychiatric patients, and so forth. These several groups of people in many instances find themselves denied rights because of some deviation that may not bear on their abilities to instruct. The vague umbrellas of "morals" or the "ability to maintain a safe learning climate" will be replaced by a court's concern for the denial of rights through discriminatory and arbitrary denial of employment.

That special group, labeled as "handicapped," now suffers significant discrimination throughout the profession extending from the denial of placement for student teaching to denial of teaching positions within a "normal" classroom setting. These policies on the part of schools are clearly discriminatory and probably will not stand the scrutiny of the courts.

The rights of homosexuals, transvestites, ex-convicts, and other

---

Court, Northern District Georgia Newman District, Civil Action, C-75-6-7-n, Dec. 2, 1975, April 15, 1976. The federal government has developed regulations to prohibit discriminatory employment practices with respect to age. See *United States Code*, Supplement V, vol. 2 (Washington, D.C.: U.S. Government Printing Office, 1970) or Public Law 90-202 (1967), pp. 2390-94. A good source with respect to this issue, as well as other teacher "rights" issues, is David Rubin, *The Rights of Teachers* (New York: American Civil Liberties Union, 1972).

39. Title IX of Public Law 92-318 (1972) addressed the issue of sex discrimination and Title IV of the Civil Rights Act (1974) addresses racial discrimination. Other "titles" will undoubtedly follow.

groups who deviate markedly from accepted societal norms of conduct, appearance, or expectations are not clearly defined.[40] State and local laws do allow school systems to discontinue contracts for those who pose unacceptable moral and ethical influences. The vagueness of these statutes, coupled with the inconsistency in their application, appears to present fertile ground for litigation. It must be assumed that universal laws or rules applying to *all* homosexuals, *all* criminals, *all* transvestites, or *all* of any identified subgroup will be found unacceptable, but the rules will be allowed to stand where the individual is granted a right of hearing and the outcome is not predetermined—provided, of course, that the presumed shortcoming can be further shown to have a negative influence on performance on the job.

These questions are part of a larger set of issues now being addressed by the courts. The rights of teachers and administrators to procedural due process in questions of evaluation, promotion, and tenure are currently being established.

FACULTY TENURE

There is some evidence to suggest that within the next decade tenure as it is conceived today will cease to exist—almost certainly in higher education, and with substantial revision at lower levels of education. Two current events, one legal and the other demographic, suggest this conclusion. First, it would seem that activity in the legal arena may ultimately accord certain rights of due process to all employees. Irrespective of whether or not a teacher has tenure, courts may begin to insist that appropriate procedural due process be followed in dismissal or nonrenewal of contracts. This will tend to reduce the necessity for tenure because the guarantee in tenure is against capricious and arbitrary action by the

40. *Morrison v. State Board of Education*, 1 Cal. 3d 214-34, 82 Cal. Rptr. 175-91, 461 P. 2d 375-91 (1969). See also *Morton v. Macy* 417 F. 2d 1161-67 (D.C. cir. 1969), 1 Cal. 3d 239, 82 Cal. Rptr. 194, 461 P. 2d 394, which stated that "no person can be denied government employment because of actions unconnected with the responsibilities of that employment," and concluded that "the power of the state to regulate professions and conditions of government employment must not arbitrarily impair the right of the individual to live his private life, apart from his job, as he deems fit." Finally, the court observed that "unqualified proscription against immoral conduct would raise serious constitutional problems."

employing board. In essence, this is what due process provisions accomplish.

Second, with relatively fewer younger people to be educated, institutions of learning are faced with certain reductions in programs and staff. This has especially been true in higher education. It is a fact that tenured faculty in some instances have been released not for reasons of gross incompetence or moral turpitude—the two commonly stated conditions for termination—but simply because their part of the "shop" was closed down, or its program sharply curtailed.

Frequent changes in the status of heretofore tenured professors are occurring throughout the nation. The most common change is the provision for limited tenure only—tenure provisions that place the recipients in a time frame (often five years), at the end of which a formal review process occurs to determine whether employment will continue. The context within which tenure will operate in the future will undoubtedly not include a lifetime job guarantee; rather, tenure will be granted for fixed periods only.

## RIGHTS OF NONTENURED TEACHERS

One of the most interesting cases involving the rights of nontenured instructors, and perhaps a benchmark, occurred in 1972.[41] Robert Sindermann had been employed in a Texas junior college for four successive years under a series of one-year contracts. In May, 1969, his one-year contract was not renewed and he was terminated. The College Board of Regents further issued a press release setting forth allegations of insubordination. The board provided no official statements to Sindermann delineating the reasons for his termination and provided him no opportunity for a hearing.

Upon appeal the U.S. Supreme Court upheld the Fifth Circuit Court of Appeals judgment that Sindermann's lack of tenure did not defeat his claim. Among other claims, the plaintiff had alleged that the college has a de facto tenure policy and he had tenure under that program. While "subjective expectancy of tenure" is not protected by procedural due process, the alleged de facto tenure policy did entitle Sindermann to an opportunity to prove the legit-

41. *Perry v. Sindermann*, 430 F. 2d 939, aff'd, 408 U.S. 593 (1972).

imacy of his claim to job tenure. He claimed that he had relied on the Teacher Tenure paragraph of the Faculty Code, which stated:

Odessa College has no tenure system. The administration of the college wishes the faculty member to feel that he has permanent tenure as long as his teaching services are satisfactory.

Thus, the court held that Sindermann should have been given a hearing to challenge the reasons for his nonretention in the light of his "proprietary interests" in his position.

Mills points out that *Perry* v. *Sindermann* establishes a new kind of property right, that of expectancy of employment. The court did indicate that mere subjective expectancy on the part of a teacher is insufficient *unless* it can be proven to exist in the light of the policies and practices of the institution, including the unwritten common law of the institution.[42] It was also held that a teacher's lack of contractual or tenure right to employment by itself does not bar the teacher from claiming that nonrenewal of a contract violates First Amendment rights.[43]

## RIGHT TO STRIKE

State legislatures and courts continue to address the rights of teachers to negotiate, to bargain collectively, and to strike. These issues are in many instances being resolved because states are enacting collective bargaining agreements. But, the rights of public employees, including teachers, to strike legally is still unclear. The right of a school board to terminate a teacher who does strike

42. Joseph L. Mills (ed.), *The School Law Newsletter* 4 (July-August, 1973): 11. However, in *Board of Regents v. Roth*, the Supreme Court reversed a Court of Appeals judgment and held that nontenured teachers did not enjoy the protection of the Fourteenth Amendment in a dismissal. Roth's rights to due process had been upheld by two lower courts but the Supreme Court held, among other things, that where the term of appointment was specific and there was no indication that reemployment was assured and where there was no statute or university policy that secured an interest in reemployment, or created a legitimate claim to it, then there was no Fourteenth Amendment property interest sufficient to require university officials to grant a hearing when the contract was not renewed. 310 F. Supp. 972; aff'd 446 F. 2d 806; rev'd 40 U.S.L.W. 5079 (June 29, 1972).

43. The First Amendment reference developed as the result of one of Sindermann's other claims, namely, that he was being denied contract renewal because of his public criticism of college policy.

illegally is established, however.[44] These definitions are built upon the principles of procedural due process and in those states where termination for striking is sanctioned by statute, the issue of lack of substantive due process appears inevitable. Such statutes probably will be eliminated. The elimination will come as the courts establish more clearly that individual rights will take precedence over the needs of the public or the state.

### RESIDENCY REQUIREMENTS

There is a growing trend to require public employees to live within the geographic limits of the governmental unit that employs them. The residency requirement is common among firemen, policemen, hospital employees, and city workers. School boards have also begun to employ this same policy with respect to the teaching and administrative staffs of a district. Litigation about such requirements continues. Recently, for example, the Supreme Court of New Hampshire voided a city ordinance that required all classified employees of the city, including school teachers, to become residents of the city. The court ruled that "the right of every citizen to live where he chooses and to travel freely not only within the state but across its borders is a fundamental right which is guaranteed by the federal Constitution."[45]

Interestingly, however, the required residency rule has been imposed by the Chicago City College upon all its employees. The rule as adopted "requires all future employees to live within Chicago city limits and gives present employees until July 1, 1980 to move into the city or face summary dismissal."[46] On the surface such rules appear to be a violation of individual rights and will in all probability be declared invalid once they are tested in court. Required residence rules appear to be a type of regulation that will not survive when questioned in courts of law and may be expected to disappear within the next decade.

44. See, for example, *Hortonville Education Association v. Hortonville Joint School District No. 1*, 66 Wis. 2d 469, 225 N.W. 2d 658 (1975), 49 L. Ed. 2d 1.

45. *Donnelly v. City of Manchester*, 274 A. 2d 789, 791 (NH 1971).

46. Residency rule imposed by the Board of Trustees of the Chicago City College, July, 1976.

EDUCATIONAL MALPRACTICE

A new kind of litigious issue that appears likely to become a major concern for educators is that of educational malpractice. The most common malpractice complaints that have come under litigation have dealt with students who graduate from high school without being functional in certain basic skills, primarily reading. Plaintiffs have claimed that instead of being provided the individual attention needed for learning basic skills, they are simply being passed from grade to grade in programs that are little more than holding actions. Students and parents are claiming that if the attendance at school is compulsory then the schools have an obligation to "cause" learning to occur.

The arguments in these cases have not yet had much impact on the educational community. Perhaps the most celebrated case to date has been *Peter Doe* v. *San Francisco Unified School District*.[47] In this case, the plaintiff failed to establish his claim. He had been graduated from high school but was functionally illiterate and unable to secure employment. He charged that the school district, board members, and superintendent were guilty of educational malpractice and subject to a claim for pecuniary damages. The court found, however, that the school had made a reasonable effort to provide an education for the plaintiff. This decision was appealed, but a hearing was denied.

In a quite different kind of educational malpractice suit, Ms. Ianniello, a college student at the University of Bridgeport, sued to recover her tuition expenses because she said she had gained nothing from a required course in education except credit. The class had received a "blanket" grade of "A." She claimed that the organization, instruction, and content of the course was inadequate.[48]

These two examples, though widely separated and different in their points of litigation, appear to represent only the tips of a

47. *Peter Doe* v. *San Francisco Unified School District*, No. 653-312 (Cal. Super. Ct., September 1974). For a good review of previous cases impinging on this issue see David Abel, "Can a Student Sue the Schools for Educational Malpractice?" *Harvard Educational Review* 44 (November 1974): 416-36. For a full discussion of the *Peter Doe* case, see chapter 10 in this volume.

48. "Suing for Not Learning," *Time*, 3 March 1975, p. 73.

much larger malpractice iceberg. Legal questions about teaching methodologies, learning environments, and the degree to which an individual learner has acquired certain basic skills will increasingly be raised. These are not clearly defined areas for litigation, however, because for one student who does not become functional, there are thousands who do become functional by the same methodologies and within the same learning environments.

Another possible litigious issue is the usual practice of placing students in various instructional settings as a result of standardized testing. Placement by testing is especially common for students who are assigned to special education or educable mentally retarded classes. Generally, placement in a class for the educable mentally retarded occurs because a student has a tested I.Q. of 50 to 80. These practices are sanctioned by state laws and policies within school districts.[49] The question of malpractice arises in instances where it can be established that the student was, in fact, not of inferior intelligence and was arbitrarily placed in a learning climate that not only was detrimental to the acquisition of appropriate knowledge and skills but was also stigmatizing. The process by which a student is identified as mentally retarded or as having a learning disability labels that student both inside the learning setting and in the community. This labeling and eventual stigmatizing could limit a student's opportunities within the society and could result in denial of access to additional education, to the professions, or to other productive employment. A companion to labeling is the practice of retaining students at a specified grade level. This may also be viewed as a labeling and branding practice that carries over into the society at large.

The issue of malpractice may be raised when the criteria employed to determine pupil replacement or retention are examined. Standardized tests are imperfect instruments even when administered under optimum conditions by specially trained persons. Moreover, ideal conditions seldom exist when testing large groups

49. *Cuyahoga County Association for Retarded Children and Adults, et al. v. Martin Essex et al.*, #c 74-587, U.S. District Court, Northern District of Ohio, Eastern Division, April 5, 1976.

of students within a school setting. Judgments are made in many instances by people who are not skilled in testing, test interpretation, or behavioral analysis. Additionally, judgments are often quite subjective, even when test data are available. Students who deviate from behavioral, economic, or social norms, or who are from minority groups stand the greatest chance of being "labeled" or of being held back.[50]

There are still other areas where charges of educational malpractice appear to be a possibility. The use of paraprofessionals in the classroom is a case in point. It would appear that even though the paraprofessional may have special certification and status on a teaching team, the classroom teacher is still responsible for the learning climate and is accountable to any charges of nonperformance or misperformance of students.

It is becoming increasingly common for hyperactive children to have medical prescriptions for drugs that will cause them to assume a more passive role in the classroom. In accordance with a regimen prescribed by the child's physician, a school nurse or a teacher may be asked to give the child the required medication. The student is in effect tranquilized so as not to disturb the learning climate. There is little evidence to support the position that the child's learning is improved. In fact, the opposite appears to be true. Further concerns relate to when and how a student stops using the drugs and what chemical alterations are made within the body. When and if the use of drugs is found to injure the education or the physical growth of the students, then both educator and medical practitioner will become codefendants in malpractice litigation.

Teacher organizations also appear to be likely defendants in some kinds of malpractice litigation, especially where specific curricula or program procedures have been negotiated as a part of a master contract. In such instances there is the possibility that the organization may be held liable or at least become codefendants with a school board for injuries suffered by students as a result of the implementation of the negotiated agreement.

---

50. The saving grace may be the Family Educational Rights of Privacy Act, which denies access to these records. See *Federal Register*, 41 (March 1976).

CERTIFICATION AND PROFESSIONAL RENEWAL

Judicial definitions affecting the professional renewal activities of educators may be forthcoming. Recently, for example, the school board of the city of Cincinnati refused to recognize, for salary and promotion purposes, external degrees that were granted by Nova University, an accredited Florida university.[51] Other school boards and some universities have refused from time to time to recognize credits earned through television instruction when the instruction is from certain universities or colleges. There appears to be ample room for litigation here because of the inconsistency with which the standards of acceptability are applied. For example, a well-known child psychologist can make a set of video tapes for purposes of instruction. These tapes when played on television by a well-known university may be defined as acceptable for students to view for the purpose of earning transfer credit, while similar students viewing the same tapes under the same conditions at another university could find that the credit is unacceptable to the school district or to other universities. The litigation will probably be based upon the inconsistencies of policies and alleged arbitrary decisions of a given university or a school system about the value of an individually developed professional renewal program. It would seem that school district and university policies about individual renewal programs will need to be developed in such a way that prior approval of deviations from normally accepted patterns would be required. "Normally accepted patterns" will have to be defined and designed in such a policy.

A related aspect to the professional renewal issue that would be a subject of possible litigation has to do with "approved" college credit. The traditional route to credit has been through the college or university classroom, with quarter or semester units as the accepted standard. Teachers and administrators have historically returned to the college campus to take advanced courses. This migration to the college campuses appears to be ebbing with the upward spiral of costs of education and with questions about the

51. *Cincinnati Enquirer*, 1, 2, 3 July 1976. See also *Phi Delta Kappan* 55 (November 1973) for articles that examine the various facets of external degree programs.

efficacy of the experience. Currently, graduate credit in a public institution averages approximately $55 per semester hour and in a private institution, $75 per semester hour.[52] To accommodate the renewal needs of professional educators, some local systems and professional organizations have begun awarding their own in-service renewal credit. In many instances, the experiences offered are provided by graduate level professorial faculty employed as consultants and the circumstances of the instruction frequently are quite similar to those found in university classrooms.

Litigious questions may rise when universities attempt to establish themselves as the sole sources of credit and when accrediting agencies and state departments of education refuse to recognize credits earned in a nonsanctioned setting. The problem will be compounded when teachers and administrators attempt to transfer credits as a result of professional relocation in the same state or in another state.

The picture is further complicated when one considers state certification. Differences between local certification requirements and the state requirements comprise one issue. The nontransferability of certification between states, even for an experienced teacher, is another issue. Finally, special state certification requirements tied to local state universities, as in Michigan,[53] which are designed to exclude or at least inhibit teachers trained in other states from qualifying for certification, may well become a source of litigation. It is difficult to predict the direction that the courts will take in matters of certification, but it is likely that the courts will not hamper a teacher's mobility within the profession and the courts will not uphold university monopolies on renewal credit, unless sufficient evidence can be provided that the specific requirements of the certification agency can be shown to make a substantial difference in the performance of professional duties. The responsibility for such a determination will rest with the certification agency.

52. *Chronicle of Higher Education*, 3 April 1976.

53. The Michigan requirements for elementary certification are a bachelor's degree from an approved or accredited teacher training institution plus three minors of twenty semester hours each, or a major of thirty semester hours with one minor of twenty semester hours.

## Curriculum Issues

The essence of the educational enterprise consists of the learning activities that are provided for the students. The effort is to provide a minimum number of opportunities for each student to allow the development of lifetime skills. Because of the enormity of client needs and demands, educators have always looked for ways to improve the instructional programs.

Although the intent underlying many of the new programs is commendable, there are instances where the individual's rights and needs are sacrificed to larger program goals. One such example is found in *Hobson* v. *Hansen*.[54] At issue was the fact that, while students were placed in one of several "curricular tracks" in order to facilitate instruction, the practice resulted in racial segregation. Further, the charge was made that those in the lower tracks suffered learning damage because of an inferior program of instruction in those tracks. In order to group the children standardized intelligence test scores were used. The court found that such tests did not measure innate intelligence; rather they measured intellect gained through cultural experience. *Hobson* v. *Hansen* has been a precedent in law since 1968, but it seems to have had minimal impact upon the practice of ability grouping or tracking. It can be established that some students do become trapped in tracks that do not fit their changing interests and/or needs. The entrapment occurs because of educational labeling and decreased teacher expectations, which results in a self-fulfilling prophecy. Studies of behavior modification and self-fulfilling prophecies tend to show that persons in charge of the learning environment will experience the behavior in others that they expect to find.[55] A lack of mobility, especially upward, between tracks can result in damage to the student's development as well as a loss of social, business, professional, or educational opportunities. It therefore appears that, with

54. *Hobson* v. *Hansen*, 269 F. Supp. 401 (1967). Also see *Hart* v. *Community School Board of Brooklyn, N.Y. School District No. 2*, 383 F. Supp. 699 (1974), which was another "anti-tracking" decision and further provided for the appointment of a court "Master" to oversee the remedy.

55. Rosenthal and Jacobson, *Pygmalion in the Classroom*; Huie, *The Execution of Private Slovik*.

increased litigation in desegregation and increased malpractice litigation, tracking and/or ability grouping will be found to be unacceptable. Even in those instances, however, where a student who is classified as "special" is mainstreamed,[56] care will still need to be exercised to avoid an attitude of presumed inferiority that might affect the nature of teacher expectation and quality of instruction.

Within specific educational programs there appear to be some practices that will be altered by litigation. The conflict between religious dogma and scientific theory is still an active issue even though fifty-three years have elapsed since the Scopes trial in Dayton, Tennessee. The courts have held that religious beliefs, even though not advocated by the schools, may also not be destroyed by the schools.[57] The doctrine of the separation of church and state is established in the courts but seems to undergo regular updating. The grounds for litigation arise when books are banned for religious reasons, as in Kanawha County, West Virginia,[58] or when materials advocating a religious dogma are introduced into the curriculum.

The right of the public to make curricular decisions is yet another issue for which the courts can be expected to help establish some clearer definitions. There have been numerous instances where community groups have tried to change school curricula materially. These efforts have extended from that of book censorship, to requiring a school to offer environmental education, to disallowing the teaching of sex education. The range of demands reduces to the right of the public versus the right of the profession to have

56. Mainstreaming is the practice of integrating special children into the regular program of the school for a portion of their instruction.

57. Joe Whittman, "The Amish and the Supreme Court," *Phi Delta Kappan* 54 (September 1972): 5052. The Supreme Court held that the Amish could not be forced, through compulsory education laws, to attend school past eighth grade. The Court indicated that compulsory education beyond eighth grade would greatly endanger, if not destroy, free exercise of the Amish religious beliefs. *Wisconsin v. Yoder*, 406 U.S. 205 (1972).

58. An excellent report of the Kanawha controversy may be found in John Egerton, "Battle of the Books," *Progressive* 39 (June 1975): 13-17. The issue was far more complex than religious differences, of course, and revealed some social, economic, and political cleavages.

the final say in curriculum decision making. As litigation develops, and if the courts continue on their current course, the decisions that restrict individual freedoms, or deny equal opportunity, will be found to be indefensible. Moreover, curriculum decisions that select materials to be used, determine learning activities, determine course offerings, or determine how controversial issues will be treated will in all probability be found to be within the decision-making powers of the professional educators who operate the schools.

## Trends in the Reorganization and Control of Schools

New demands on schools issuing from societal changes and differing expectations have resulted in new ways of structuring aspects of the school organization. Many forces—social and legal—have provided impetus for examining fundamental changes in the organization and control of schools. The issue has been how to best structure a socially responsive educational system to help insure quality education in a mass, technologically oriented, culturally diverse society.

The problem is complex and fraught with anomalies. For example, the multiplicity of public and private agencies in urban areas suggests the need for new and larger structures for the coordination and governance of a mass welfare delivery system, including education as a subsystem. There is great pressure and need for specific agency accountability, decentralization, and direct community control of various subsystems. Despite presumed economies of scale, the sad fact is that bigger has not been better. Basic services are too frequently lost in a bureaucratic maze and inequities abound; coordination of the various welfare delivery subsystems in urban areas is often an accidental happening. On the other hand, rural and small town America have been continually faced with declining population, inadequate financial bases, and pressures to remain independent and to preserve uniqueness. The people with the "best of all worlds" seem to be the almost exponentially increasing breed of suburbanites and exurbanites. That the cities are faced with a diminishing financial base and spiraling costs and are increasingly composed of racial and ethnic minorities who themselves are often in financial despair is not news. Neither is it news that there are vast areas of rural poverty—often forgotten because the population is relatively few and dispersed—where people are struggling against economic inequity and insufficient welfare delivery systems.

There are several possibly synchronistic events that have implications for the conditions just described, some of which are mitigating in nature, while others may exacerbate the situation. In this section we shall focus on certain issues in school administration that are in a state of flux and would seem to have many legal implications. These may be identified as financial issues; trends towards metropolitanism; and formalized cooperation among school districts and, at times, other public and private agencies.

FINANCIAL ISSUES

There are two different legal aspects that relate to the question of school finance: (a) the question of how to achieve equity in the distribution of support monies; and (b) the question of what the basic source of support monies shall be. These questions are clearly interrelated. Historically, there have been wide variations between communities in both the ability and the willingness to support educational programs. Most of the money to support public education has been collected locally by means of a tax on the property of residents. Great inequities have thus occurred because of the unequal distribution of taxable wealth.

*The property tax.* Over the past few years, there has been an effort, largely as a result of federal legislation, to address the question of equity. The result has been a variety of compensatory education programs. These sorts of programs undoubtedly will continue—with changes only in areas of emphasis.[59] As great as the

59. It is not only in education that the federal government attempts to redistribute wealth on a national scale. As a result of this spending and its taxing policies the federal government taxes wealth from some geographic areas or states that are "better off" and transfers it to less prosperous parts of the country. *Time* magazine reported: "In fiscal 1975 the Great Lakes states gave the federal government $62.2 billion in taxes and got back only $43.3 billion. The mid-Atlantic states of New York, New Jersey, and Pennsylvania lost $10 billion in the exchange." *Time*, 6 September 1976, p. 8. Where did this money go? According to the same *Time* article, southern states received $11.5 billion more than they paid in taxes; California and other west coast states, $7 billion; the mountain states, $3.6 billion. The items making the difference were in the massive federal spending for military bases and defense contracts. Thus, the general principle of redistribution of wealth is well

federal interest is, it represents but a small portion of the sources of money for a typical school; state and local sources remain primary.

Two trends seem apparent, both occurring at the state level. As a result of *Serrano* v. *Priest* and other cases (for example, *Robinson* v. *Cahill* in Michigan and *Milliken* v. *Green* in New Jersey)[60] and despite *Rodriguez*,[61] increasing efforts can be expected in the various states to redistribute wealth between separate school districts so that a more equitable financial basis for supporting local schools will be provided.[62] There have been a host of law suits in the past few years filed in both federal and state courts challenging the constitutionality of sources for public school financing. Because of *Rodriguez*, however, those cases that are successful will rest on state constitutional grounds alone. The legal principle will be that of identifying education as a "fundamental right,"[63] a principle that the U.S. Supreme Court denied in *Rodriguez*.

Problems are caused by the use of property taxes as the primary, and sometimes sole, source of funding for school financing formulae. For example, in the previously cited *Serrano* case, Serrano had argued that poor school districts (that is, those lacking taxable wealth) were discriminated against because of their inability to raise sufficient monies to support adequately the schools of the

established on the national level but less so on the state level, although even here states have maintained minimum foundation programs that have provided some redistribution.

60. *Serrano v. Priest*, 96 Cal. Rptr. 618 (1971). See also *Robinson v. Cahill*, 287 A. 2d 214 (1972) and *Milliken v. Green*, 283 N.W. 2d 457 (1972). To make the issue even clearer and to establish obtaining an education as a basic right in California and thus subject to a California constitutional guarantee of equity, state assemblyman Alex Garcia introduced a constitutional amendment into the California legislature: "All people are by nature free and independent and have certain inalienable rights among which are . . . pursuing and obtaining an education." (Assembly Constitution amendment no. 37, April 2, 1973).

61. *San Antonio Independent School System v. Rodriguez*, 411 U.S. 1 (1973).

62. Hawaii is the only state that would be unaffected by this because it maintains a single statewide school system.

63. Between 1968 and 1972 alone there had been over forty suits filed. In its issue of March 8, 1972 *Education Daily* provided a summary of the court cases to that date.

district even with tax rates that far exceeded wealthier districts. It is interesting to note, however, that in the great number of cases introduced since *Serrano*, none has challenged the constitutionality of the property tax per se. The challenges have been directed to the way the property tax has been allocated.

The property tax, as the largest single source of revenues, will possibly be substantially augmented by other taxes and sources. A portion of revenues collected by sales tax and personal income tax is in some states allocated to the state educational fund. This trend will continue and it can be expected that state distribution formulae will provide more equitable allocation of funds from state coffers given increasing legal and social pressure. Interesting developments in many states are those of legalizing gambling and holding state lotteries in an effort to find new sources of revenue. (The "jury" is still out on state lotteries as a good source. Administrative costs have been quite high; and the percentage allocation to welfare services has been considerably lower than anticipated and advertised.)

Stauffer sees reform taking place on three fronts in response to financial pressures: (a) reform of formulas for distribution of revenues to schools; (b) property tax relief; and (c) reform of property tax administration.[64] He cites several specific actions on all three fronts in several states.

*Public aid to private schools.* One other, and somewhat different, school finance issue receiving continued legal interest is that of using public monies to support educational programs in private schools, including those that are church-supported. While a considerable degree of clarity has been achieved, this issue will probably continue to be a matter for litigation from time to time. Public financial aid that meets the test of three legal criteria will be adjudicated as appropriate, and in accord with the establishment and the free exercise clauses of the First Amendment. The "test" specifies that such aid must (a) result from a secular purpose or intent; (b) be neutral to the point of neither advancing nor inhibiting religion and (c) must not lead to excessive governmental

64. Allan C. Stauffer, "The Schools and Property Tax," in *Handbook on Contemporary Education*, ed. Steven E. Goodman (New York: R.R. Bowker Co., 1976), p. 30.

entanglement with religion. Key considerations in determining compliance with the criteria are the availability of aid to sectarian and nonsectarian public and nonpublic schools, the degree of religious permeation in the schools, and adequate stipulation restricting the aid to secular purposes.

Most recently the criteria were applied by the U.S. Supreme Court in testing a Maryland law under which direct operating support was given to three Roman Catholic-related institutions of higher education.[65] The five justices deciding in favor of the Maryland law found no First Amendment violation because "the act specifies the aid cannot be used for sectarian purposes and cannot be given to institutions that award 'only seminarian or theological degrees.' "[66]

### METROPOLITANISM

Metropolitanism, as a form of local governance, was the subject of a previous yearbook of the National Society for the Study of Education and has been increasingly studied not so much because of presumed efficiencies but because of desegregation efforts.[67] With cities more and more described as racially, ethnically, and economically identifiable civil units surrounded by more prosperous and largely white enclaves, recent desegregation cases have featured proposals to create metropolitan school districts. Court decisions have been mixed. In *Milliken* v. *Bradley* with respect to Detroit and in *Bradley* v. *School Board of City of Richmond* in Richmond, Virginia, the U.S. Supreme Court decided against cross-busing and

---

65. *Roemer v. Board of Public Works*, civil action no. 72-307-4 (D. Md. October 1974), appealed to U.S. Supreme Court, which handed down its decision in June, 1976. See 426 U.S. 736.

66. *Roemer v. Board of Public Works*, 426 U.S. 736. See also *Everson v. Board of Education*, 330 U.S. 1 (1974); *Abington School District v. Schempp*, 374 U.S. 203 (1948); *Board of Education v. Allen*, 392 U.S. 236 (1968); *Walz v. Tax Commission of the City of New York*, 197 U.S. 664 (1970); *Tilton v. Richardson*, 403 U.S. 672 (1971); *Lemon v. Kurtzman*, 403 U.S. 602 (1971); *Livitt v. Committee for Public Education*, 93 S. Ct. 2814 (1973); *Committee for Public Education v. Nyquist*, 93 S. Ct. 2955, (1973); *American United v. Dunn*, Civil action no. 6940 (D. Tennessee, November 1974).

67. *Metropolitanism: Its Challenge to Education*, Sixty-seventh Yearbook of the National Society for the Study of Education, Part I, ed. Robert J. Havighurst (Chicago: University of Chicago Press, 1968).

interchange of students on constitutional grounds.[68] In the case involving the Wilmington, Delaware schools, however, the Supreme Court upheld (5-3) a federal court order for city-suburban desegregation.[69] The metro plan will result in a merger of the 83 percent black Wilmington schools with the 94 percent white suburban student population.[70]

The key legal point is whether or not desegregation has resulted from a state action, deliberate or not. In Detroit, even though it was determined that segregation had resulted from past action, it was also determined that these actions had occurred solely within the boundaries of the city and therefore the remedy had to be sought within those boundaries. In Wilmington, the federal court ruled that by specifically eliminating the city from a state reorganization plan the state had involved other districts in an action that did in fact result in the segregation of blacks. This being true, the other districts must be involved in desegregation efforts. Further, since bus transportation of whites to private schools had been subsidized and because publicly-assisted housing has been established in the city but not the suburbs, the judges held that officials had helped perpetuate racial imbalance in the schools.

Court action with respect to the desegregation issue has been at least partially responsible for school system mergers in other parts of the nation.[71] Moreover, some states already have enabling legislative enactments that facilitate the development of metropolitan civil units—not just for school reorganization, but also for general local governance.[72] Other states lack such enactments and although no state could be found that specifically prohibits metropolitan forms of government, the laws with respect to governance,

68. *Milliken v. Bradley*, 418 U.S. 717 (1974); *Bradley v. School Board of City of Richmond*, 412 U.S. 92 (1972).

69. *Education, U.S.A.*, 1 September 1975 and 31 May 1976.

70. For a discussion of a similar case in Indianapolis, see chapter 4 in this volume.

71. In 1975, for example, Louisville, Kentucky was merged with surrounding Jefferson County.

72. Tennessee, for example, has had such enabling legislation since 1958. To date, however, only two such civil units have formed—Nashville-Davidson and Clarksville-Montgomery.

shared services, tax structures, and so forth, are often such as to greatly impede such a move.

EDUCATIONAL COOPERATIVES AND CONSORTIA

Not directly related to the question of metropolitan forms of government nor to the desegregation questions but a possible influencing force is the recent trend to formal cooperation between school districts. This trend may be progenerative.

Hughes and Achilles define an educational cooperative as follows: "[It] . . . entails a joint effort of two or more educational organizations to enlarge the scope, quality, and accessibility of educational programs and service." [73] It is important to the concept that the relationship be formal and require some sort of official governing body including representatives of the participating institutions.[74] The mandate and legal constitution of such jointures varies but generally fall under one of four headings:

1. *Voluntary cooperative.* These are nonstate mandated associations existing under permissive legislation. The primary function is to share costs and personnel generally for specific educational programs.

2. *Industry/Education cooperatives.* These cooperatives usually operate on a regional basis, are voluntary, and their functions are administered by a joint school-industry council of some type.

3. *School Study Councils.* These associations usually function with the sponsorship of a university, or at least collaboration between a university and public school system, and focus on individual problems of member institutions.

4. *Intermediate Education Service Services.* These are more formalized than voluntary cooperatives and membership is frequently mandated by state law. The Board of Cooperative Educational Services of New York State and the Texas Education Agency

73. Larry W. Hughes and Charles M. Achilles, "Educational Cooperatives and Regional Education Service," in *Handbook on Contemporary Education,* ed. Goodman, p. 89.

74. There are many different modes or organizations, and educational cooperatives go under many different names including, for example, Board of Cooperative Educational Services (mandatory in the state of New York), Educational Services Agency, Intermediate District, Regional Service Agency, Educational Cooperative, and so forth.

would be two examples. Stephens and Ellena described this as a two-fold trend:

> In state school systems historically having a three-echelon structure—state education agency, county system, and local school district . . . establishment of a new middle echelon, multi-county regional service unit.
> In state school systems having a two-echelon structure—state education agency and local school district— . . . establishment and promotion of cooperative arrangements between and among local school districts.[75]

*University consortia.* Born on the one hand from desperate financial straits and on the other from a desire to provide creative educational programs while achieving some economies, many colleges and universities have turned to consortia arrangements. Survival, economy, better delivery of educational services, and innovative programming are all intended outcomes. It is a hopeful trend, but in the instance of public institutions of higher education, one which is largely unfacilitated by enabling legislation.[76]

## Concluding Statement

What has been attempted here is an examination of the structure of education and the current trends in the courts, and then to attempt to discern probable future actions. No attempt has been made to project a redefinition of school or schooling; such an effort would be well outside the purpose of this yearbook. When changes of structure and underlying philosophies do occur, however, new areas of litigation will naturally follow. Moreover, the influences of population changes, scarcity of resources, and changing political climates, will undoubtedly alter the educational enterprise. The legal implications of these and other sociopolitical changes will be many, indeed, and will require a watchful eye and a responsive profession.

75. Robert E. Stephens and William J. Ellena, "Regionalism of Education," *School Administrator* 30 (June 1973): 19.

76. One important piece of federal legislation exists, however. It is Title III of the Higher Education Act, which provides funds for consortia developed to provide help from established universities to "developing institutions" in matters of program development.

# List of Cases Cited

Each of the cases listed on the following pages has been mentioned by name in the text of this volume, or quotations from decisions in the case have been given in the text, or there has been some discussion in the text of the circumstances involved in the case. Cases cited only in footnotes are not included in the list.

# Index

# INFORMATION CONCERNING
## THE NATIONAL SOCIETY FOR THE STUDY OF EDUCATION

1. *Purpose.* The purpose of the National Society is to promote the investigation and discussion of educational questions. To this end it holds an annual meeting and publishes a series of yearbooks and a series of paperbacks on Contemporary Educational Issues.

2. *Membership.* Any person interested in the purpose of the Society and in receiving its publications may become a member by sending in name, title, address, and a check covering dues and the entrance fee (see items 4 and 5). Graduate students may become members, upon recommendation of a faculty member, at a reduced rate for the first year of membership. Dues for all subsequent years are the same as for other members.

*Membership is not transferable. It is limited to individuals and may not be held by libraries, schools, or other institutions, either directly or indirectly.*

3. *Period of Membership.* Membership is for the calendar year and terminates automatically on December 31, unless dues for the ensuing year are paid as indicated in item 6. Applicants for membership may not date their entrance back of the current calendar year.

4. *Categories of Membership.* The following categories of membership have been established:

> *Regular.* Annual dues are $13.00. The member receives a clothbound copy of each part of the current yearbook.
>
> *Comprehensive.* Annual dues are $27.00. The member receives a clothbound copy of the current yearbook *and* all volumes in the current year's paperback series on Contemporary Educational Issues.
>
> *Special Memberships for Retired Members and Graduate Students.*
>> *Retired members.* Persons who are retired or who are sixty-five years of age *and* who have been members of the Society continuously for at least ten years may retain their Regular Membership upon payment of annual dues of $10.00 or their Comprehensive Membership upon payment of annual dues of $20.00.
>>
>> *Graduate Students.* Graduate students may pay annual dues of $10.00 for Regular Membership or $20.00 for Comprehensive Membership for their first year of membership, plus the $1.00 entrance fee in either case.
>
> *Life Memberships.* Persons sixty years of age or above may become life members on payment of a fee based on the average life expectancy of their age group. Regular life members may take out a Comprehensive Membership for any year upon payment of an additional fee of $10.00. For further information apply to the Secretary-Treasurer.

5. *Privileges of Membership.* Members receive the publications of the Society as described above. All members are entitled to vote, to participate in meetings of the Society, and (under certain conditions) to hold office.

6. *Entrance Fee.* New members are required to pay an entrance fee of one dollar, in addition to the dues, for the first year of membership.

7. *Payment of Dues.* Statements of dues are rendered in October for the following calendar year. Any member so notified whose dues remain unpaid on January 1 thereby loses membership and can be reinstated only by paying the dues plus a reinstatement fee of fifty cents ($.50).

School warrants and vouchers from institutions must be accompanied by definite information concerning the name and address of the person for whom the membership fee is being paid. Statements of dues are rendered on our own form only. The Secretary's office cannot undertake to fill out special invoice forms of any kind or to affix a notary's affidavit to statements or receipts.

Cancelled checks serve as receipts. Members desiring an additional receipt must enclose a stamped and addressed envelope therefor.

8. *Distribution of Yearbooks to Members.* The yearbooks, normally ready prior to the February meeting of the Society, will be mailed from the office of the distributor only to members whose dues for that year have been paid.

9. *Commercial Sales.* The distribution of all yearbooks prior to the current year, and also of those of the current year not regularly mailed to members in exchange for their dues, is in the hands of the distributor, not of the Secretary. Orders may be placed with the University of Chicago Press, Chicago, Illinois 60637, which distributes the yearbooks of the Society. Orders for paperbacks in the series on Contemporary Educational Issues should be placed with the designated publisher of that series. The list of the Society's publications is printed in each yearbook.

10. *Yearbooks.* The yearbooks are issued about one month before the February meeting. Published in two volumes, each of which contains 300 to 400 pages, the yearbooks are planned to be of immediate practical value as well as representative of sound scholarship and scientific investigation.

11. *Series on Contemporary Educational Issues.* This series, in paperback format, is designed to supplement the yearbooks by timely publications on topics of current interest. There will usually be three of these volumes each year.

12. *Meetings.* The annual meeting, at which the yearbooks are presented and critiqued, is held as a rule in February at the same time and place as the meeting of the American Association of School Administrators. Members will be notified of other meetings.

Applications for membership will be handled promptly at any time. New members will receive the yearbook scheduled for publication during the calendar year in which application for Regular Membership is made. New members who elect to take out the Comprehensive membership will receive both the yearbook and the paperbacks scheduled for publication during the year in which application is made.

KENNETH J. REHAGE, Secretary-Treasurer

5835 Kimbark Avenue
Chicago, Illinois 60637

# PUBLICATIONS OF THE NATIONAL SOCIETY FOR THE STUDY OF EDUCATION

## 1. The Yearbooks

**NOTICE:** Many of the early yearbooks of this series are now out of print. In the following list, those titles to which an asterisk is prefixed are not available for purchase.

*First Yearbook, 1902, Part I—*Some Principles in the Teaching of History.* Lucy M. Salmon.

*First Yearbook, 1902, Part II—*The Progress of Geography in the Schools.* W. M. Davis and H. M. Wilson.

*Second Yearbook, 1903, Part I—*The Course of Study in History in the Common School.* Isabel Lawrence, C. A. McMurray, Frank McMurry, E. C. Page, and E. J. Rice.

*Second Yearbook, 1903, Part II—*The Relation of Theory to Pratice in Education.* M. J. Holmes, J. A. Keith, and Levi Seeley.

*Third Yearbook, 1904, Part I—*The Relation of Theory to Practice in the Education of Teachers.* John Dewey, Sarah C. Brooks, F. M. McMurry, et al.

*Third Yearbook, 1904, Part II—*Nature Study.* W. S. Jackman.

*Fourth Yearbook, 1905, Part I—*The Education and Training of Secondary Teachers.* E. C. Elliott, E. G. Dexter, M. J. Holmes, et al.

*Fourth Yearbook, 1905, Part II—*The Place of Vocational Subjects in the High-School Curriculum.* J. S. Brown, G. B. Morrison, and Ellen Richards.

*Fifth Yearbook, 1906, Part I—*On the Teaching of English in Elementary and High Schools.* G. P. Brown and Emerson Davis.

*Fifth Yearbook, 1906, Part II—*The Certification of Teachers.* E. P. Cubberley.

*Sixth Yearbook, 1907, Part I—*Vocational Studies for College Entrance.* C. A. Herrick, H. W. Holmes, T. deLaguna, V. Prettyman, and W. J. S. Bryan.

*Sixth Yearbook, 1907, Part II—*The Kindergarten and Its Relation to Elementary Education.* Ada Van Stone Harris, E. A. Kirkpatrick, Marie Kraus-Boelté, Patty S. Hill, Harriette M. Mills, and Nina Vandewalker.

*Seventh Yearbook, 1908, Part I—*The Relation of Superintendents and Principals to the Training and Professional Improvement of Their Teachers.* Charles D. Lowry.

*Seventh Yearbook, 1908, Part II—*The Co-ordination of the Kindergarten and the Elementary School.* B. J. Gregory, Jennie B. Merrill, Bertha Payne, and Margaret Giddings.

*Eighth Yearbook, 1909, Part I—*Education with Reference to Sex: Pathological, Economic, and Social Aspects.* C. R. Henderson.

*Eighth Yearbook, 1909, Part II—*Education with Reference to Sex: Agencies and Methods.* C. R. Henderson and Helen C. Putnam.

*Ninth Yearbook, 1910, Part I—*Health and Education.* T. D. Wood.

*Ninth Yearbook, 1910, Part II—*The Nurses in Education.* T. D. Wood, et al.

*Tenth Yearbook, 1911, Part I—*The City School as a Community Center.* H. C. Leipziger, Sarah E. Hyre, R. D. Warden, C. Ward Crampton, E. W. Stitt, E. J. Ward, Mrs. T. C. Grice, and C. A. Perry.

*Tenth Yearbook, 1911, Part II—*The Rural School as a Community Center.* B. H. Crocheron, Jessie Field, F. W. Howe, E. C. Bishop, A. B. Graham, O. J. Kern, M. T. Scudder, and B. M. Davis.

*Eleventh Yearbook, 1912, Part I—*Industrial Education: Typical Experiments Described and Interpreted.* J. F. Barker, M. Bloomfield, B. W. Johnson, P. Johnson, L. M. Leavitt, G. A. Mirick, M. W. Murray, C. F. Perry, A. L. Stafford, and H. B. Wilson.

*Eleventh Yearbook, 1912, Part II—*Agricultural Education in Secondary Schools.* A. C. Monahan, R. W. Stimson, D. J. Crosby, W. H. French, H. F. Button, F. R. Crane, W. R. Hart, and G. F. Warren.

*Twelfth Yearbook, 1913, Part I—*The Supervision of City Schools.* Franklin Bobbitt, J. W. Hall, and J. D. Wolcott.

*Twelfth Yearbook, 1913, Part II—*The Supervision of Rural Schools.* A. C. Monahan, L. J. Hanifan, J. E. Warren, Wallace Lund, U. J. Hoffman, A. S. Cook, E. M. Rapp, Jackson Davis, J. D. Wolcott.

*Thirteenth Yearbook, 1914, Part I—*Some Aspects of High-School Instruction and Administration.* H. C. Morrison, E. R. Breslich, W. A. Jessup, and L. D. Coffman.

*Thirteenth Yearbook, 1914, Part II—*Plans for Organizing School Surveys, with a Summary of Typical School Surveys.* Charles H. Judd and Henry L. Smith.

*Fourteenth Yearbook, 1915, Part I—*Minimum Essentials in Elementary School Subjects—Standards and Current Practices.* H. B. Wilson, H. W. Holmes, F. E. Thompson, R. G. Jones, S. A. Courtis, W. S. Gray, F. N. Freeman, H. C. Pryor, J. F. Hosic, W. A. Jessup, and W. C. Bagley.

*Fourteenth Yearbook, 1915, Part II—*Methods for Measuring Teachers' Efficiency.* Arthur C. Boyce.

*Fifteenth Yearbook, 1916, Part I—*Standards and Tests for the Measurement of the Efficiency of Schools and School Systems.* G. D. Strayer, Bird T. Baldwin, B. R. Buckingham, F. W. Ballou, D. C. Bliss, H. G. Childs, S. A. Courtis, E. P. Cubberley, C. H. Judd, George Melcher, E. E. Oberholtzer, J. B. Sears, Daniel Starch, M. R. Trabue, and G. M. Whipple.

*Fifteenth Yearbook, 1916, Part II—*The Relationship between Persistence in School and Home Conditions.* Charles E. Holley.

*Fifteenth Yearbook, 1916, Part III—*The Junior High School.* Aubrey A. Douglas.

*Sixteenth Yearbook, 1917, Part I—*Second Report of the Committee on Minimum Essentials in Elementary-School Subjects.* W. C. Bagley, W. W. Charters, F. N. Freeman, W. S. Gray, Ernest Horn, J. H. Hoskinson, W. S. Monroe, C. F. Munson, H. C. Pryor, L. W. Rapeer, G. M. Wilson, and H. B. Wilson.

*Sixteenth Yearbook, 1917, Part II—*The Efficiency of College Students as Conditioned by Age at Entrance and Size of High School.* B. F. Pittenger.

*Seventeenth Yearbook, 1918, Part I—*Third Report of the Committee on Economy of Time in Education.* W. C. Bagley, B. B. Bassett, M. E. Branom, Alice Camerer, J. E. Dealey, C. A. Ellwood, E. B. Greene, A. B. Hart, J. F. Hosic, E. T. Housh, W. H. Mace, L. R. Marston, H. C. McKown, H. E. Mitchell, W. V. Reavis, D. Snedden, and H. B. Wilson.

*Seventeenth Yearbook, 1918, Part II—*The Measurement of Educational Products.* E. J. Ashbaugh, W. A. Averill, L. P. Ayers, F. W. Ballou, Edna Bryner, B. R. Buckingham, S. A. Courtis, M. E. Haggerty, C. H. Judd, George Melcher, W. S. Monroe, E. A. Nifenecker, and E. L. Thorndike.

*Eighteenth Yearbook, 1919, Part I—*The Professional Preparation of High-School Teachers.* G. N. Cade, S. S. Colvin, Charles Fordyce, H. H. Foster, T. S. Gosling, W. S. Gray, L. V. Koos, A. R. Mead, H. L. Miller, F. C. Whitcomb, and Clifford Woody.

*Eighteenth Yearbook, 1919, Part II—*Fourth Report of Committee on Economy of Time in Education.* F. C. Ayer, F. N. Freeman, W. S. Gray, Ernest Horn, W. S. Monroe, and C. E. Seashore.

*Nineteenth Yearbook, 1920, Part I—*New Materials of Instruction.* Prepared by the Society's Committee on Materials of Instruction.

*Nineteenth Yearbook, 1920, Part II—*Classroom Problems in the Education of Gifted Children.* T. S. Henry.

*Twentieth Yearbook, 1921, Part I—*New Materials of Instruction.* Second Report by Society's Committee.

*Twentieth Yearbook, 1921, Part II—*Report of the Society's Committee on Silent Reading.* M. A. Burgess, S. A. Courtis, C. E. Germane, W. S. Gray, H. A. Greene, Regina R. Heller, J. H. Hoover, J. A. O'Brien, J. L. Packer, Daniel Starch, W. W. Theisen, G. A. Yoakam, and representatives of other school systems.

*Twenty-first Yearbook, 1922, Parts I and II—*Intelligence Tests and Their Use,* Part I—*The Nature, History, and General Principles of Intelligence Testing.* E. L. Thorndike, S. S. Colvin, Harold Rugg, G. M. Whipple, Part II—*The Administrative Use of Intelligence Tests.* H. W. Holmes, W. K. Layton, Helen Davis, Agnes L. Rogers, Rudolf Pintner, M. R. Trabue, W. S. Miller, Bessie L. Gambrill, and others. The two parts are bound together.

*Twenty-second Yearbook, 1923, Part I—*English Composition: Its Aims, Methods and Measurements.* Earl Hudelson.

*Twenty-second Yearbook, 1923, Part II—*The Social Studies in the Elementary and Secondary School.* A. S. Barr, J. J. Coss, Henry Harap, R. W. Hatch, H. C. Hill, Ernest Horn, C. H. Judd, L. C. Marshall, F. M. McMurry, Earle Rugg, H. O. Rugg, Emma Schweppe, Mabel Snedaker, and C. W. Washburne.

*Twenty-third Yearbook, 1924, Part I—*The Education of Gifted Children.* Report of the Society's Committee. Guy M. Whipple, Chairman.

*Twenty-third Yearbook, 1924, Part II—*Vocational Guidance and Vocational Education for Industries.* A. H. Edgerton and others.

*Twenty-fourth Yearbook, 1925, Part I—*Report of the National Committee on Reading.* W. S. Gray, Chairman, F. W. Ballou, Rose L. Hardy, Ernest Horn, Francis Jenkins, S. A. Leonard, Estaline Wilson, and Laura Zirbes.

*Twenty-fourth Yearbook, 1925, Part II—*Adapting the Schools to Individual Differences.* Report of the Society's Committee. Carleton W. Washburne, Chairman.

*Twenty-fifth Yearbook, 1926, Part I—*The Present Status of Safety Education.* Report of the Society's Committee. Guy M. Whipple, Chairman.

*Twenty-fifth Yearbook, 1926, Part II—*Extra-Curricular Activities.* Report of the Society's Committee. Leonard V. Koos, Chairman.

*Twenty-sixth Yearbook, 1927, Part I—*Curriculum-making: Past and Present.* Report of the Society's Committee. Harold O. Rugg, Chairman.

*Twenty-sixth Yearbook, 1927, Part II—*The Foundations of Curriculum-making.* Prepared by individual members of the Society's Committee. Harold O. Rugg, Chairman.

*Twenty-seventh Yearbook, 1928, Part I—*Nature and Nurture: Their Influence upon Intelligence.* Prepared by the Society's Committee. Lewis M. Terman, Chairman.

*Twenty-seventh Yearbook, 1928, Part II—*Nature and Nurture: Their Influence upon Achievement.* Prepared by the Society's Committee. Lewis M. Terman, Chairman.

Twenty-eighth Yearbook, 1929, Parts I and II—*Preschool and Parental Education.* Part I—*Organization and Development.* Part II—*Research and Method.* Prepared by the Society's Committee. Lois H. Meek, Chairman. Bound in one volume. Cloth.

*Twenty-ninth Yearbook, 1930, Parts I and II—*Report of the Society's Committee on Arithmetic.* Part I—*Some Aspects of Modern Thought on Arithmetic.* Part II—*Research in Arithmetic.* Prepared by the Society's Committee. F. B. Knight, Chairman. Bound in one volume.

*Thirtieth Yearbook, 1931, Part I—*The Status of Rural Education.* First Report of the Society's Committee on Rural Education. Orville G. Brim, Chairman.

Thirtieth Yearbook, 1931, Part II—*The Textbook in American Education.* Report of the Society's Committee on the Textbook, J. B. Edmonson, Chairman. Cloth, Paper.

*Thirty-first Yearbook, 1932, Part I—*A Program for Teaching Science*. Prepared by the Society's Committee on the Teaching of Science. S. Ralph Powers, Chairman.
*Thirty-first Yearbook, 1932, Part II—*Changes and Experiments in Liberal-Arts Education*. Prepared by Kathryn McHale, with numerous collaborators.
*Thirty-second Yearbook, 1933—*The Teaching of Geography*. Prepared by the Society's Committee on the Teaching of Geography. A. E. Parkins, Chairman.
*Thirty-third Yearbook, 1934, Part I—*The Planning and Construction of School Buildings*. Prepared by the Society's Committee on School Buildings. N. L. Engelhardt, Chairman.
*Thirty-third Yearbook, 1934, Part II—*The Activity Movement*. Prepared by the Society's Committee on the Activity Movement. Lois Coffey Mossman, Chairman.
Thirty-fourth Yearbook, 1935—*Educational Diagnosis*. Prepared by the Society's Committee on Educational Diagnosis. L. J. Brueckner, Chairman. Paper.
*Thirty-fifth Yearbook, 1936, Part I—*The Grouping of Pupils*. Prepared by the Society's Committee. W. W. Coxe, Chairman.
*Thirty-fifth Yearbook, 1936, Part II—*Music Education*. Prepared by the Society's Committee. W. L. Uhl, Chairman.
*Thirty-sixth Yearbook, 1937, Part I—*The Teaching of Reading*. Prepared by the Society's Committee. W. S. Gray, Chairman.
*Thirty-sixth Yearbook, 1937, Part II—*International Understanding through the Public-School Curriculum*. Prepared by the Society's Committee. I. L. Kandel, Chairman.
*Thirty-seventh Yearbook, 1938, Part I—*Guidance in Educational Institutions*. Prepared by the Society's Committee. G. N. Kefauver, Chairman.
*Thirty-seventh Yearbook, 1938, Part II—*The Scientific Movement in Education*. Prepared by the Society's Committee. F. N. Freeman, Chairman.
*Thirty-eighth Yearbook, 1939, Part I—*Child Development and the Curriculum*. Prepared by the Society's Committee. Carleton Washburne, Chairman.
*Thirty-eighth Yearbook, 1939, Part II—*General Education in the American College*. Prepared by the Society's Committee. Alvin Eurich, Chairman. Cloth.
*Thirty-ninth Yearbook, 1940, Part I—*Intelligence: Its Nature and Nurture. Comparative and Critical Exposition*. Prepared by the Society's Committee. G. D. Stoddard, Chairman.
*Thirty-ninth Yearbook, 1940, Part II—*Intelligence: Its Nature and Nurture. Original Studies and Experiments*. Prepared by the Society's Committee. G. D. Stoddard, Chairman.
*Fortieth Yearbook, 1941—*Art in American Life and Education*. Prepared by the Society's Committee. Thomas Munro, Chairman.
Forty-first Yearbook, 1942, Part I—*Philosophies of Education*. Prepared by the Society's Committee. John S. Brubacher, Chairman. Cloth, Paper.
Forty-first Yearbook, 1942, Part II—*The Psychology of Learning*. Prepared by the Society's Committee. T. R. McConnell, Chairman. Cloth.
*Forty-second Yearbook, 1943, Part I—*Vocational Education*. Prepared by the Society's Committee. F. J. Keller, Chairman.
*Forty-second Yearbook, 1943, Part II—*The Library in General Education*. Prepared by the Society's Committee. L. R. Wilson, Chairman.
Forty-third Yearbook, 1944, Part I—*Adolescence*. Prepared by the Society's Committee. Harold E. Jones, Chairman. Paper.
*Forty-third Yearbook, 1944, Part II—*Teaching Language in the Elementary School*. Prepared by the Society's Committee. M. R. Trabue, Chairman.
*Forty-fourth Yearbook, 1945, Part I—*American Education in the Postwar Period: Curriculum Reconstruction*. Prepared by the Society's Committee. Ralph W. Tyler, Chairman.
Forty-fourth Yearbook, 1945, Part II—*American Education in the Postwar Period: Structural Reorganization*. Prepared by the Society's Committee. Bess Goodykoontz, Chairman. Paper.
*Forty-fifth Yearbook, 1946, Part I—*The Measurement of Understanding*. Prepared by the Society's Committee. William A. Brownell, Chairman.
*Forty-fifth Yearbook, 1946, Part II—*Changing Conceptions in Educational Administration*. Prepared by the Society's Committee. Alonzo G. Grace, Chairman.
*Forty-sixth Yearbook, 1947, Part I—*Science Education in American Schools*. Prepared by the Society's Committee. Victor H. Noll, Chairman.
Forty-sixth Yearbook, 1947, Part II—*Early Childhood Education*. Prepared by the Society's Committee. N. Searle Light, Chairman. Paper.
Forty-seventh Yearbook, 1948, Part I—*Juvenile Delinquency and the Schools*. Prepared by the Society's Committee. Ruth Strang, Chairman. Cloth.
Forty-seventh Yearbook, 1948, Part II—*Reading in the High School and College*. Prepared by the Society's Committee. William S. Gray, Chairman. Cloth, Paper.
Forty-eighth Yearbook, 1949, Part I—*Audio-visual Materials of Instruction*. Prepared by the Society's Committee. Stephen M. Corey, Chairman. Cloth.
*Forty-eighth Yearbook, 1949, Part II—*Reading in the Elementary School*. Prepared by the Society's Committee. Arthur I. Gates, Chairman.
*Forty-ninth Yearbook, 1950, Part I—*Learning and Instruction*. Prepared by the Society's Committee. G. Lester Anderson, Chairman.
Forty-ninth Yearbook, 1950, Part II—*The Education of Exceptional Children*. Prepared by the Society's Committee. Samuel A. Kirk, Chairman. Paper.
Fiftieth Yearbook, 1951, Part I—*Graduate Study in Education*. Prepared by the Society's Board of Directors. Ralph W. Tyler, Chairman. Paper.
Fiftieth Yearbook, 1951, Part II—*The Teaching of Arithmetic*. Prepared by the Society's Committee. G. T. Buswell, Chairman. Cloth, Paper.

Fifty-first Yearbook, 1952, Part I—*General Education*. Prepared by the Society's Committee. T. R. McConnell, Chairman. Cloth, Paper.

Fifty-first Yearbook, 1952, Part II—*Education in Rural Communities*. Prepared by the Society's Committee. Ruth Strang, Chairman. Cloth, Paper.

*Fifty-second Yearbook, 1953, Part I—*Adapting the Secondary-School Program to the Needs of Youth*. Prepared by the Society's Committee: William G. Brink, Chairman.

Fifty-second Yearbook, 1953, Part II—*The Community School*. Prepared by the Society's Committee. Maurice F. Seay, Chairman. Cloth.

Fifty-third Yearbook, 1954, Part I—*Citizen Co-operation for Better Public Schools*. Prepared by the Society's Committee. Edgar L. Morphet, Chairman. Cloth, Paper.

Fifty-third Yearbook, 1954, Part II—*Mass Media and Education*. Prepared by the Society's Committee. Edgar Dale, Chairman. Paper.

*Fifty-fourth Yearbook, 1955, Part I—*Modern Philosophies and Education*. Prepared by the Society's Committee. John S. Brubacher, Chairman.

Fifty-fourth Yearbook, 1955, Part II—*Mental Health in Modern Education*. Prepared by the Society's Committee. Paul A. Witty, Chairman. Paper.

*Fifty-fifth Yearbook, 1956, Part I—*The Public Junior College*. Prepared by the Society's Committee. B. Lamar Johnson, Chairman.

Fifty-fifth Yearbook, 1956, Part II—*Adult Reading*. Prepared by the Society's Committee. David H. Clift, Chairman. Paper.

Fifty-sixth Yearbook, 1957, Part I—*In-service Education of Teachers, Supervisors, and Administrators*. Prepared by the Society's Committee. Stephen M. Corey, Chairman. Cloth, Paper.

Fifty-sixth Yearbook, 1957, Part II—*Social Studies in the Elementary School*. Prepared by the Society's Committee. Ralph C. Preston, Chairman. Cloth, Paper.

Fifty-seventh Yearbook, 1958, Part I—*Basic Concepts in Music Education*. Prepared by the Society's Committee. Thurber H. Madison, Chairman. Cloth.

Fifty-seventh Yearbook, 1958, Part II—*Education for the Gifted*. Prepared by the Society's Committee. Robert J. Havighurst, Chairman. Cloth, Paper.

Fifty-seventh Yearbook, 1958, Part III—*The Integration of Educational Experiences*. Prepared by the Society's Committee. Paul L. Dressel, Chairman. Cloth.

Fifty-eighth Yearbook, 1959, Part I—*Community Education: Principles and Practices from World-wide Experience*. Prepared by the Society's Committee. C. O. Arndt, Chairman. Cloth, Paper.

Fifty-eighth Yearbook, 1959, Part II—*Personnel Services in Education*. Prepared by the Society's Committee. Melvene D. Hardee, Chairman. Paper.

*Fifty-ninth Yearbook, 1960, Part I—*Rethinking Science Education*. Prepared by the Society's Committee. J. Darrell Barnard, Chairman.

Fifty-ninth Yearbook, 1960, Part II—*The Dynamics of Instructional Groups*. Prepared by the Society's Committee. Gale E. Jensen, Chairman. Cloth.

Sixtieth Yearbook, 1961, Part I—*Development in and through Reading*. Prepared by the Society's Committee. Paul A. Witty, Chairman. Cloth, Paper.

Sixtieth Yearbook, 1961, Part II—*Social Forces Influencing American Education*. Prepared by the Society's Committee. Ralph W. Tyler, Chairman. Cloth.

Sixty-first Yearbook, 1962, Part I—*Individualizing Instruction*. Prepared by the Society's Committee. Fred T. Tyler, Chairman. Cloth.

Sixty-first Yearbook, 1962, Part II—*Education for the Professions*. Prepared by the Society's Committee. G. Lester Anderson, Chairman. Cloth.

Sixty-second Yearbook, 1963, Part I—*Child Psychology*. Prepared by the Society's Committee. Harold W. Stevenson, Editor. Cloth.

Sixty-second Yearbook, 1963, Part II—*The Impact and Improvement of School Testing Programs*. Prepared by the Society's Committee. Warren G. Findley, Editor. Cloth.

Sixty-third Yearbook, 1964, Part I—*Theories of Learning and Instruction*. Prepared by the Society's Committee. Ernest R. Hilgard, Editor. Paper.

Sixty-third Yearbook, 1964, Part II—*Behavioral Science and Educational Administration*. Prepared by the Society' Committee. Daniel E. Griffiths, Editor. Paper.

Sixty-fourth Yearbook, 1965, Part I—*Vocational Education*. Prepared by the Society's Committee. Melvin L. Barlow, Editor. Cloth.

Sixty-fourth Yearbook, 1965, Part II—*Art Education*. Prepared by the Society's Committee. W. Reid Hastie, Editor. Cloth.

Sixty-fifth Yearbook, 1966, Part I—*Social Deviancy among Youth*. Prepared by the Society's Committee. William W. Wattenberg, Editor. Cloth.

Sixty-fifth Yearbook, 1966, Part II—*The Changing American School*. Prepared by the Society's Committee. John I. Goodlad, Editor. Cloth.

Sixty-sixth Yearbook, 1967, Part I—*The Educationally Retarded and Disadvantaged*. Prepared by the Society's Committee. Paul A. Witty, Editor. Cloth.

Sixty-sixth Yearbook, 1967, Part II—*Programed Instruction*. Prepared by the Society's Committee. Phil C. Lange, Editor. Cloth.

Sixty-seventh Yearbook, 1968, Part I—*Metropolitanism: Its Challenge to Education*. Prepared by the Society's Committee. Robert J. Havighurst, Editor. Cloth.

Sixty-seventh Yearbook, 1968, Part II—*Innovation and Change in Reading Instruction*. Prepared by the Society's Committee. Helen M. Robinson, Editor. Cloth.

Sixty-eighth Yearbook, 1969, Part I—*The United States and International Education*. Prepared by the Society's Committee. Harold G. Shane, Editor. Cloth.

Sixty-eighth Yearbook, 1969, Part II—*Educational Evaluation: New Roles, New Means*. Prepared by the Society's Committee. Ralph W. Tyler, Editor. Paper.

Sixty-ninth Yearbook, 1970, Part I—*Mathematics Education*. Prepared by the Society's Committee. Edward G. Begle, Editor. Cloth.

Sixty-ninth Yearbook, 1970, Part II—*Linguistics in School Programs*. Prepared by the Society's Committee. Albert H. Marckwardt, Editor. Cloth.

Seventieth Yearbook, 1971, Part I—*The Curriculum: Retrospect and Prospect.* Prepared by the Society's Committee. Robert M. McClure, Editor. Paper.
Seventieth Yearbook, 1971, Part II—*Leaders in American Education.* Prepared by the Society's Committee. Robert J. Havighurst, Editor. Cloth.
Seventy-first Yearbook, 1972, Part I—*Philosophical Redirection of Educational Research.* Prepared by the Society's Committee. Lawrence G. Thomas, Editor. Cloth.
Seventy-first Yearbook, 1972, Part II—*Early Childhood Education.* Prepared by the Society's Committee. Ira J. Gordon, Editor. Cloth, Paper.
Seventy-second Yearbook, 1973, Part I—*Behavior Modification in Education.* Prepared by the Society's Committee. Carl E. Thoresen, Editor. Cloth.
Seventy-second Yearbook, 1973, Part II—*The Elementary School in the United States.* Prepared by the Society's Committee. John I. Goodlad and Harold G. Shane, Editors. Cloth.
Seventy-third Yearbook, 1974, Part I—*Media and Symbols: The Forms of Expression, Communication, and Education.* Prepared by the Society's Committee. David R. Olson, Editor. Cloth.
Seventy-third Yearbook, 1974, Part II—*Uses of the Sociology of Education.* Prepared by the Society's Committee. C. Wayne Gordon, Editor. Cloth.
Seventy-fourth Yearbook, 1975, Part I—*Youth.* Prepared by the Society's Committee. Robert J. Havighurst and Philip H. Dreyer, Editors. Cloth.
Seventy-fourth Yearbook, 1975, Part II—*Teacher Education.* Prepared by the Society's Committee. Kevin Ryan, Editor. Cloth.
Seventy-fifth Yearbook, 1976, Part I—*Psychology of Teaching Methods.* Prepared by the Society's Committee. N. L. Gage, Editor. Cloth.
Seventy-fifth Yearbook, 1976, Part II—*Issues in Secondary Education.* Prepared by the Society's Committee. William Van Til, Editor. Cloth.
Seventy-sixth Yearbook, 1977, Part I—*The Teaching of English.* Prepared by the Society's Committee. James R. Squire, Editor. Cloth.
Seventy-sixth Yearbook, 1977, Part II—*The Politics of Education.* Prepared by the Society's Committee. Jay D. Scribner, Editor. Cloth.
Seventy-seventh Yearbook, 1978, Part I—*The Courts and Education,* Clifford P. Hooker, Editor. Cloth.
Seventy-seventh Yearbook, 1978, Part II—*Education and the Brain,* Jeanne Chall and Allan F. Mirsky, Editors. Cloth.

*Yearbooks of the National Society are distributed by*

THE UNIVERSITY OF CHICAGO PRESS, CHICAGO, ILLINOIS 60637

Please direct inquiries regarding prices of volumes still available to the University of Chicago Press. Orders for these volumes should be sent to the University of Chicago Press, not to the offices of the National Society.

## 2. The Series on Contemporary Educational Issues

In addition to its Yearbooks the Society now publishes volumes in a series on Contemporary Educational Issues. These volumes are prepared under the supervision of the Society's Commission on an Expanded Publication Program.

The 1978 Titles

*Aspects of Reading Education* (Susanna Pflaum-Connor, ed.)

*History, Education, and Public Policy: Recovering the American Educational Past* (Donald R. Warren, ed.)

*From Youth to Constructive Adult Life: The Role of the School* (Ralph W. Tyler, ed.)

The 1977 Titles

*Early Childhood Education: Perspectives and Issues* (Bernard Spodek and Herbert J. Walberg, eds.)

*The Future of Big City Schools: Desegregation Policies and Magnet Alternatives* (Daniel U. Levine and Robert J. Havighurst, eds.)

*Educational Administration: The Developing Decades* (Luvern L. Cunningham, Walter G. Hack, and Raphael O. Nystrand, eds.)

The 1976 Titles

*Prospects for Research and Development in Education* (Ralph W. Tyler, ed.)

*Public Testimony on Public Schools* (Commission on Educational Governance)

*Counseling Children and Adolescents* (William M. Walsh, ed.)

The 1975 Titles

*Schooling and the Rights of Children* (Vernon Haubrich and Michael Apple, eds.)

*Systems of Individualized Education* (Harriet Talmage, ed.)

*Educational Policy and International Assessment: Implications of the IEA Assessment of Achievement* (Alan Purves and Daniel U. Levine, eds.)

The 1974 Titles

*Crucial Issues in Testing* (Ralph W. Tyler and Richard M. Wolf, eds.)

*Conflicting Conceptions of Curriculum* (Elliott Eisner and Elizabeth Vallance, eds.)

*Cultural Pluralism* (Edgar G. Epps, ed.)

*Rethinking Educational Equality* (Andrew T. Kopan and Herbert J. Walberg, eds.)

All of the above volumes may be ordered from

McCutchan Publishing Corporation
2526 Grove Street
Berkeley, California 94704

## The 1972 Titles

*Black Students in White Schools* (Edgar G. Epps, ed.)

*Flexibility in School Programs* (W. J. Congreve and G. L. Rinehart, eds.)

*Performance Contracting—1969-1971* (J. A. Mecklenburger)

*The Potential of Educational Futures* (Michael Marien and W. L. Ziegler, eds.)

*Sex Differences and Discrimination in Education* (Scarvia Anderson, ed.)

## The 1971 Titles

*Accountability in Education* (Leon M. Lessinger and Ralph W. Tyler, eds.)

*Farewell to Schools???* (D. U. Levine and R. J. Havighurst, eds.)

*Models for Integrated Education* (D. U. Levine, ed.)

PYGMALION *Reconsidered* (J. D. Elashoff and R. E. Snow)

*Reactions to Silberman's* CRISIS IN THE CLASSROOM (A. Harry Passow, ed.)

A limited number of copies of the above titles (except PYGMALION *Reconsidered*) are still available from the Office of the Secretary, NSSE, 5835 Kimbark Avenue, Chicago, Ill. 60637.